MERGER
TAKEOVER
CONSPIRACY

MERGER
TAKEOVER
CONSPIRACY

A Business Story

By *DAVID J. THOMSEN*

BeardBooks
Washington, D.C.

FOREWORD

Mergers are said to be our modern substitute for war. The language of the subject....."takeover"....."raid"....."hostile tender"....."poison pill"......"strategic plan"......"white knight"....."greenmail"..... surely reflects this. Others claim mergers mirror the ancient and cruel form of advancing one's cause at the expense of others. For as with war, there are winners and losers. While mass killings may not occur, suffering, ruined lives and destruction do. And as with war, there are always many losers among those who fight the battles.

Mergers are most often described in the press with the vocabulary of the modern business school. Their effects are illustrated with numbers, theories and concepts. The reality is that mergers are human stories, hundreds and thousands of them. This work, *Merger*, is an attempt to tell such a story.

Although a work of fiction, I have attempted to partially describe the underlying framework of corporate mergers. The reader must understand that these "facts" are what create the pressures and motivations that explain why people act as they do. I apologize for any complexity.

I would wish to thank those who have read and commented on drafts of this novel. I have appreciated, often used, and always respected your advice. Any shortcomings in this work are mine alone.

March 22, 1985

David J. Thomsen

Newport Beach
California

For all those who fight merger battles,
and for their spouses and their children.

"VANITY, VANITY, ALL IS VANITY!"
(Ecclesiastes 1:2)

CAST OF CHARACTERS

Arrow Corporation
    A Delaware corporation, headquarters now at 20222 Wilshire Boulevard, Los Angeles, California 90999. Formed 1951 with Phillip Arrow as major stockholder, member of the New York Stock Exchange.

Phillip Arrow
    Chairman, Chief Executive Officer, and founder of Arrow Corporation. Age 67, WW II 6th Army Tank Officer, two years Indiana State, three children.

Aaron Goldstein
    Attorney with New York firm of Shaffer, Schwab & Meyers. 42 years of age, divorced, Harvard undergraduate and Columbia University Law School.

Dane Hughes
    Corporate pilot with lead responsibility for CEO's Lear, 39 years of age, Vanderbilt B.S., U.S. Naval Air Reserve, Viet Nam veteran, widower.

John Jamison
    Vice President of Administration and later new Rail Division President, age 51, U. of Alberta, Stanford MBA, naturalized U.S. citizen, married to:

Meg Jamison
    Housewife, resident of Santa Barbara, former model in Toronto, age 46,

Canadian citizen, McGill University (two years), two daughters-ages 19 & 22.

Everett Lacey   Director of Planning, Black, only minority on the executive staff, MBA with graduate work at Univ of Loyola and Notre Dame, single, age 35.

Lawrence Massendale   Chief Legal Counsel of Arrow Corporation, 42 years of age, California Berkeley, USC Law School, J.D. but never passed the Bar Exam, married to:

Mary Sue Massendale   Housewife, resident of San Marino, California, 38 years of age, U. of Oregon, B.S. in mathematics, Arrow's only daughter, with four school age sons.

Caroline O'Brian   Assistant to the Chairman and new Executive Vice President, Rail Division, 34 years of age, Vassar and University of Michigan, MBA.

John Smedt   Investment Banker with New York firm of Arlington, Bothell & Hyde, 41 years of age, married, Yale BS and a Wharton MBA.

Frank Turner   Executive Vice President, second in command of Arrow Corporation, age 54, 22 years with the Company, married, Duke University, Harvard MBA.

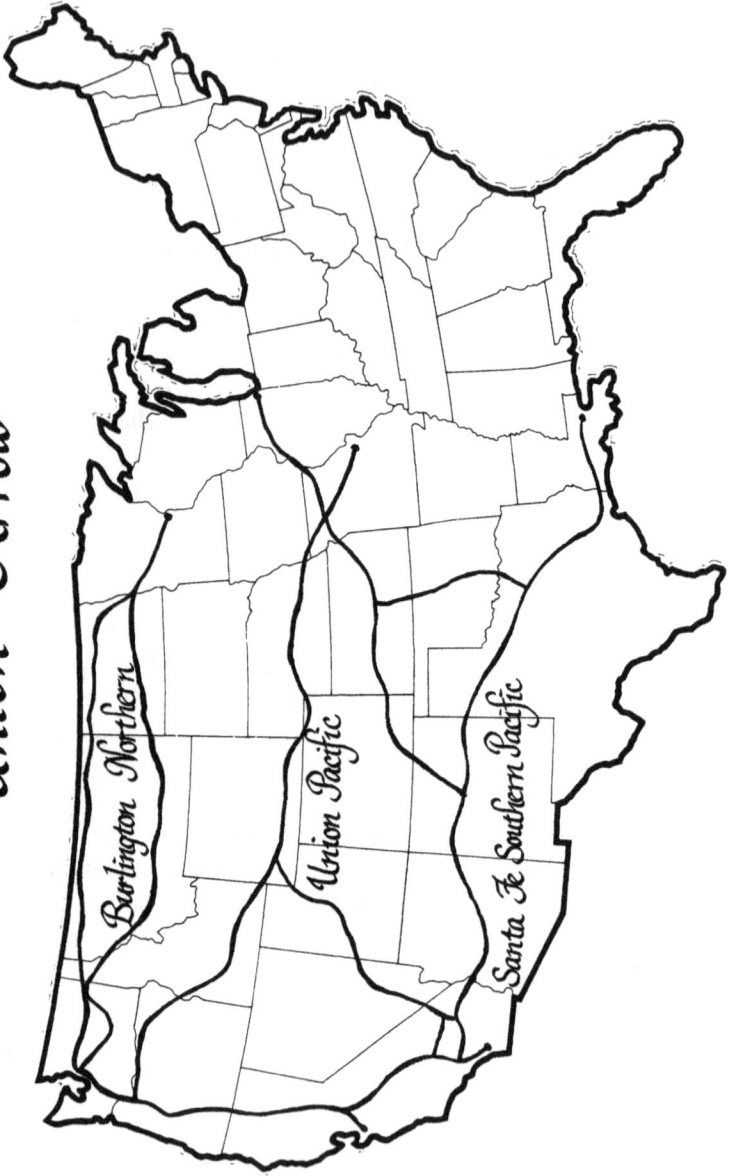

Union Arrow

Burlington Northern

Union Pacific

Santa Fe Southern Pacific

PROPOSED
FINANCIAL PROFILE
AS OF SEPTEMBER 1985
(shown in *millions* of dollars)

	Arrow Corporation	Burlington Northern	Santa Fe SouPacific	Union Pacific	Proposed New Company
ASSETS					
Current	3,500	2,200	2,700	2,600	3,500 (1
Property	7,100	8,700	8,600	7,600	21,700 (2
Goodwill	0	0	0	0	2,900 (3
Total Assets	10,600	10,900	11,300	10,200	28,100
LIABILITIES					
Cur/Long Term	3,600	6,400	5,600	5,800	3,600
Acquis Debt	0	0	0	0	8,600 (1
EQUITY	7,000	4,500	5,700	4,400	15,900 (4
Total Lia & E	10,600	10,900	11,300	10,200	28,100
REVENUE					
Rail Lines	0	4,100	4,800	3,800	12,900 (5
Air/Truck/Ret	3,000	0	0	0	3,500 (6
Natural Resour	2,000	600	1,400	4,900	8,900
Total	5,000	4,700	6,200	8,700	25,300
EXPENSES					
Administrative	3,000	3,200	4,800	7,000	17,000 (7
Interest	0	150	150	250	1,850 (8
Depreciation	400	500	500	650	2,350 (9
Profit					
Before Tax	1,600	850	750	800	4,100
Taxes	600	350	250	300	1,300(10
After Tax Profit	1,000	500	500	500	2,800
# SHARES (in millions)	112.8	74.0	190.0	115.0	161.0(11
Earnings per share	$ 8.87	$ 6.76	$ 2.63	$ 4.35	$ 17.39
Market Price	$ 186	$ 40	$ 21	$ 35	$ 261
Price Earnings Ratio	21	6	8	8	15(12
TOTAL VALUE OF COMMON STOCK OUTSTANDING	21 Billion	3 Billion	4 Billion	4 Billion	42 Billion (13

NOTES TO THE PROPOSED FINANCIAL STATEMENT

*The following notes are provided for the accountant
(and interested non-accountant):*

1) Sufficient current assets exist among the three targets and Arrow Corporation to pay 50% of the necessary cash required without further debt. Debt is incurred to maintain cash for operations.
2) Property valued at Arrow's original value plus purchase price of 17.5 billion dollars for the three targets. This price is a 60% premium over the targets' 11 billion dollars present market value.
3) Goodwill shown as the difference in the purchase price of 17.5 billion and the proposed targets' book value (assets less liabilities) of 14.6 billion dollars.
4) Equity adjusted to simplify more complex accounting adjustments with purchase of assets above book value.
5) A slight increase in revenue is projected via the combination of the targets, deriving from an increase in rail fees. Only 200 million is anticipated because of formal Government monitoring of rates.
6) A far greater increase in revenues is projected for the substitute freight alternatives now controlled by Arrow Corporation. Raising these rates over those of rail would now be economically sound. If customers shift to rail, no profits would have been lost.
7) Significant decreases in administrative costs are anticipated with the combination of the competing rail companies. Cost savings would be derived from closedown of facilities, administrative staff cuts, elimination of duplicated services, and other economies of scale.
8) The increase in interest costs is caused by the 8.6 billion dollars in debt assumed by Arrow Corporation to purchase the three companies. Interest rates are projected to be at 15%.
9) The increase in depreciation cost is derived from a modest write up in value of the acquired companies' assets and the amortization of goodwill.

10) A lower tax rate (30%) is caused because depreciation for tax purposes is greater than for accounting reporting purposes. The ability to write off higher depreciation in tax reporting in the U.S. allows for lower taxable income and lower taxes. Hence, present Tax Codes allow most mergers and acquisitions to be paid, in part, by the U.S. Treasury.

11) The greater number of Arrow Corporation shares, 48.2 million, are the shares required at the present market price, $186, to pay for the "back half," 51%, of the purchase. These shares would be traded for (and hence retiring) the outstanding shares of the targets.

12) The price earnings ratio (the premium that the stock market places on a company's stock expressed as a multiple of earnings per share) is forecasted to drop because of the addition of rail lines and their historically low PE's of 6 to 8 (as compared to Arrow's high of 21 at the start). A mid range PE of 15 was expected.

13) The product of the PE taken times the expected earnings taken times the number of shares outstanding. The difference between this amount and Arrow's original market value is the mergers' value. Arrow expects to double its original market value with the mergers making its stockholders an immediate $10 billion in stock market appreciation.

Prologue

Wednesday
April 10, 1985
8:30 AM

Richard Smith looked at the notes written in longhand on the margin of the discarded *Wall Street Journal*. Someone had outlined the key points of a negative corporate investor relations campaign. Scrawled across the top of the page was a graph line that showed the Corporation's stock's price decreasing by 90 %. Smith knew that he had found that for which he had been blindly searching. His peers would die to have such a discovery, some would kill. As Manager of Corporate Security of Arrow Corporation, he now knew that his future was forever assured with the Company. This work would not be forgotten.

He looked again at the open trash chute. The building had a special hollowed column that led to a "materials' shredder," what the employees jokingly called "Henry." Henry was a diamond tipped, enhanced paper shredder that would take typewriters, file cabinets, tape spools - anything that could be pushed through the special three foot by two foot trash chute openings found far above on the executive floors. Like most corporations, his employer, Arrow Corporation, had spared no funds to protect its confidentiality. Any search warrant could be quickly circumvented by Henry's ability to diamond cut, compress, and disintegrate, all to be automatically packed in small, heavy duty bags and then sealed unseen by human eyes.

It was in this second floor basement room where a special catch slide existed known only to the top executive office. Along with a review of each executive's wastebasket at the day's end, Smith's job description included a review of all light materials sent down Henry's throat. Any papers would slide out for inspection, heavy items would tip the levered catch slide and fall on through to Henry's teeth.

Quickly going through the rest of the material, Smith stuffed the paper and scraps back into Henry's mouth. The room's green paint and flickering neon light cast a depressing pallor over his success. He hated this stuffy little room which had originally been a janitor's closet. He stopped for a moment to catch his breath and admitted what he had known for days. He was suffering from a gradually growing sense of paranoia.

In the silence of his pause, he saw the room's doorknob silently and slowly turn. Sweat immediately broke out on his forehead and his heartbeat jumped. Only top level executives had a key to open the door. He shook his head to control himself. Hadn't he just called the executive floor with the phone on the wall to his right to ask someone to see this discovery as he had found it? He needed collaboration.

He knew that he had to still his suddenly discovered panic. Why this sudden feeling of terror?

Smith relaxed, "Oh, it's you. I am glad to see you....uh, I also mean it's good to see you. The reason I called is right here. Look what I found."

Richard Smith turned toward Henry's mouth in a motion to close the trash chute's door. He never felt the hard hammering blow that severely damaged his skull. He did not feel the struggle to lift his six foot-four inch, two hundred and twenty pound body onto the trash slide. He did not feel the gradual tilting of the axis of the slide as his body weight shifted into the yawning corridor, nor did he feel the short fall to Henry's waiting teeth. He did not feel the light weight of the papers that followed as someone cleaned up the litter left on the small room's floor. Nor did he hear the shutting of the door as that person hurried off to prepare for a top level morning meeting.

Richard Smith was no more.

1

Wednesday
April 10, 1985
11:00 AM

"It has to be one of you sitting here."

With a soft, quiet voice, Phillip Arrow, Chairman of the Board, Chief Executive Officer, and founder of Arrow Corporation, accused one of his top corporate staff of treason. In a two minute speech he had voiced violations of SEC regulations, the secret purchases of stock of Arrow Corporation's acquisition targets, and most important to Phillip Arrow, the violation of his personal trust.

Tall and confident, Phillip Arrow stretched his 67-year old frame to a full standing position. He had chosen to use the Directors' Room this morning for just this moment. The dark walnut walls, golden framed windows that overlooked the skyline of Los Angeles, a fifty foot table, and expensive crystal added to his intimidating presence. Arrow wanted them to feel unease, to sense the potential for power which was not yet theirs, a power that they might easily lose because of some momentary error of judgment or single misspoken word.

Arrow began to slowly survey the faces. The conference room was silent as death.

Years of working with people had taught Arrow to work by instinct, what he called "A Twinge of Experience." He carefully viewed the seven executives spread in isolation around the Boardroom's table. "Don't anyone speak up. One of you is a millionaire a hundred times over.

"One of you just stole from our stockholders and the public. The Brinks' Robbery was for only ten million. You have made them look like pikers, amateurs."

Arrow looked for a change in roles, the honest man who suddenly looked too honest, a reaction which Arrow had learned as derived only from planned or practiced thought. He looked for the liar, who suddenly looked uncertain, as if he were the honest man struggling with a dishonest act that would be admittedly considered, but never acted upon. It was the change in roles that triggered Arrow's deep gut feel. He had fired many managers because of it. He knew that he had hurt some good, honest men, but the price was always too high to do otherwise.

Arrow sensed that he was close to seeing the human reaction that would tell him who it was. Slowly, he mentally phrased the discovery of the nearby investment firm's accumulation of Union Pacific, Burlington Northern, and Santa Fe Southern stock. Who in the group would flinch, show a trace of color, cough, or look up or down? Or perhaps, he would see the honest man's reaction, a look to the right and left for a subconscious selection ..... unless that looking were too obvious......

As Arrow's eyes scanned those seated with their backs toward the conference room's side door......the door opened. Framed in its opening was one of the Company pilots, Dane Hughes. The opened door let in the sounds of a typing secretary and a ringing telephone, sounds that cut through the sullen silence of the conference room like a cannon on a foggy morning. In such a moment, Arrow had lost the initiative and like a hunter stocking a kill, he knew it. Phillip Arrow bowed his silver white head.

Oblivious, Dane Hughes strode purposely across the room and placed a packet by John Jamison, the Vice President of Administration. Among the thousand dollar suits, Hughes' overalls and tennis shoes were decidedly out of place. The pilot's five foot eleven, football guard stature somehow made him look smaller than he was. No one, however, commented; no one noticed. The silence of the room obviously now had an effect on the pilot.

Arrow's eyes flashed with anger. Hughes was a non conformist. A fine pilot, but too old even at thirty-nine to learn corporate habits. No one over thirty can be taught corporate mores, thought Arrow. He would have to try again to replace Dane Hughes, but that he thought would be a most difficult task. Arrow knew he had no better all-around pilot than Hughes in his twenty pilot Corporate Air Department.

Long ago, Arrow had found the secret to building an organization... expect people to come and go, but when they do - never, never replace them until you have found someone better than the person who had left. Hughes was just too good a pilot. Phillip Arrow took pride in his careful selection of men who flew him around the world. Arrow had never flown with a more calm, cautious or capable Lear Captain.

Like water, Arrow adjusted his mood around this obstacle. One never has a chance to go back in life. He would go from here and see what he could salvage. Dane, what timing! He would now have to wait to see who took over the meeting's conversation.

Slowly, deliberately, Hughes turned from Jamison at the conference table. Dane Hughes' mind was racing. He felt as though he had just walked into a mortuary. Yet, he would be damned if this group made him hurry his actions! If he was only a Company pilot to these large egos, he was far more than an errand boy like this stuffed shirt dummy Jamison assumed. Sixty-five F4H missions in Nam, a body that still showed evidence of being a Conference all-star, and a mind that was just as good as these forty and fifty year old MBAs - degrees which haunted Hughes, degrees they received while he was defending their Country - all combined to create actions too quick and too filled with pride in a situation such as this.

He quickly surveyed the room. His friend Ev Lacey sat stoically silent next to a flip chart with a wooden pointer in his hand. Lacey was a slim, studious looking man whose glasses and habit of wearing clothes a size too large, hid a powerful young frame. To his left sat a black haired, handsome Eastern financial type and close to this unknown, too close, sat Caroline O'Brian, Danes's sometime dinner companion on various Arrow trips and newly appointed Assistant to the Chairman of the Board. Caroline was Dane's unreachable dream, everything that a woman should be. Dane's unreturned affection for her was growing daily. Lord! He worshiped the ground she walked on. But why in a room when one could sit ten feet apart, did she need to sit right next to whomever he was?

3

"Sorry, Captain, truly sorry." Arrow smiled broadly across the table. "If Jamison and I would have our act together, we'd have anticipated that we would need that material............ whatever it is. Ah - hope that that plane will be ready in Burbank for Dallas at 7:00."

Arrow had one of his frequent lightning thoughts. Had he favored Hughes because he too was a widower? He was smiling at himself as much as the pilot as he awaited the answer.

"Yes Sir." Hughes looked and nodded with a grin. Damn Arrow! He'd surmised the Jamison rush, demand, and sensed the slight. He could probably even recount the words and tone of voice that Jamison had used to make Dane feel like an errand boy. His look showed understanding. Most great leaders are like that, thought Hughes, they have a sense of the important to whomever, whether it's their barber, janitor, driver, top lawyer. It was a rare talent, something that one did not teach. But even more important at this particular moment, it gave him a chance to escape this cold chill with honor.

With a quick turn and a flash of a smile, Hughes walked back through the door. He then forced himself to be disciplined under pressure. In the quick, brief conversation with Arrow, he had recognized that he had stopped looking at the room's occupants once his eyes had caught Caroline's posture.

He traced back through his quick glance that had captured the audience. He had first seen his friend, Everett Lacey, one of the few friendly corporate staff people, even though Hughes' Virginia background sometimes grated across Lacey's young tense Black sensitivity. Hughes constantly tried to guard his accent. Then Caroline, whom Hughes would hope to see either tonight or when he returned. Ah, Caroline, you who were so desperately on the upward corporate track! Arrow, who had first glared pure heat and then turned salesman. Frank Turner, the Executive Vice President, Arrow's foil - mean, tricky, angry, and a corporate killer. A smooth ladies' man with a Harvard MBA and financial connections, he seemingly had the ability to satisfy what Arrow was looking for in a first lieutenant. Sitting to Turner's left was the nervous Lawrence Massendale, III. Arrow's only daughter, Mary Sue, saw to the fact that Massey had a place of closely guarded and secure employment as the Company's Chief Legal Counsel. Hopefully, that was another lawyer, probably also from New York, who was sitting next to Massendale. What had Mary Sue Arrow ever seen in Lawrence Massendale?

4

Dane chided himself again as he walked into the elevator for its rapid twelve story descent. He had let another woman capture his thoughts, one that he did not even know. She was just a picture of a passenger on his plane, a lively, laughing pretty lady always busy watching over four very active boys. He made himself dive back into his review of those in the room.

Let's see, the other Manhattan type sitting next to Caroline, a type whose tailored dark pinstripe suit and school tie surely spoke of a financial institution. And who else, ... ah, Jamison, the Corporate V.P. of Administration. Dane wondered what such a type was doing at this meeting, it looked and sounded high level with its mix of talent. Jamison? How could Jamison's mind keep pace with the others at the meeting? What possibly could he offer and what was the meeting about?

Dane had been interrupted in Burbank at 8:30 by John Jamison who had left his confidential papers at home, papers that he believed necessary at an unexpectedly called meeting at 11:00. "Could Dane fly over to his residence in Santa Barbara and pick up the bundle?" What a stuffed shirt! What a dull, risk avoiding, overweight, naive, overeducated trained talking seal. Dane had met many of these types, WASPs turned out of the same mold with a desperate fear that someday they might have to use their minds. Perhaps it would have been an acceptable request if Jamison's bothersome western Canadian cowboy English accent had been accompanied by proper grammar. Sure, Dane "could," the question was "would" he and what, the Hell, was a "bundle?"

If it hadn't been for being greeted by Jamison's wife, Meg, Dane would have felt the quick flight over to the Santa Barbara Airport a total waste. He had heard others talk of Meg Jamison, the beautiful 46 year old former Canadian model that Jamison hid away in Monticedo. He had been awed at her beauty. Tall at 5' 10", her slender height had matched the football, bulldog height of Hughes. She had invited Dane into a beautiful rustic California ranch home while she "bundled" the papers. Brown hair piled high on her head, a peaceful quiet laugh, she flustered Dane who felt totally out of place. In his casual flying clothes he had met a fashion model who was obviously going morning shopping in Santa Barbara. At 39, Dane was reaching the point of bachelorhood where he was totally bored with the young - a state that was either a defense mechanism or an enlightenment, a

5

point of which he was not sure. Yet, he had not been ready to be overwhelmed by Meg Jamison's chiseled features, her Toronto English accent, and the grace in which he was received. He had been totally entranced.

The Jamison home was situated high above a southern part of Santa Barbara, 80 miles to the northwest of Arrow Corporation's Los Angeles headquarters and a three hour drive, not allowing for commuter traffic. Dane's taxi had slowly wound its way down the hill with a fantasy view of the coastal islands and a jewel of a bay. Fresh air and an ocean view, what a place to live! But what a price to pay! To live here must mean at least six hours each day in an automobile in Jamison's daily commute, thought Dane. And he wondered why Jamison's mind had a reputation of cold mush among the corporate staff!

What Dane Hughes did not know was that Meg Jamison had almost fainted of fear for her husband when she heard his voice that morning telling her of the pickup of the material. Meg had carried her husband both morally and lovingly through their twenty-four years of marriage. John was no mental giant, this she knew, but he was a fine honest family man who had given her two wonderful daughters, both now away in private church universities. John's voice had a nervous terror in it. As the V.P. of Administration, he knew that the phones were monitored and hence his message was brief. He had been called to Arrow's office "on a matter that would decide his career with the Arrow Corporation. Would Meg please bundle together his papers left on the den desk?"

Meg's instinctive reaction toward survival would have been a subject that Dane would have long discussed with her, if he had known her plight that morning. Meg was totally sensitive to her husband's world and viewed it with an ironic idealism that would have doubly saddened Dane. As an outsider with a rare view of the internal workings of a company, Dane had seen the price Arrow extracted of his people. All lived in fear, all lived by instinctively cutting down opponents and peers as quickly as possible...with the exception of Lacey, who did not have to play the game. Jamison was a master of the craft, Caroline, bless her, was the worst of them all. No, that honor had to go to Turner, but Lacey did not even rate. Lacey measured zero on that competitive scale, he did not need to compete. So, thought Dane ironically, as he stepped into his sports car to leave the Corporate

6

Headquarters, one's race does sometimes pay off......at least for one manager per corporation.

Sitting in the Boardroom, Lacey envisioned the sight of Dane getting into his Porsche. Lucky basatrd, thought Lacey, as he made his mind turn back to Frank Turner and his five-minute monologue that had said nothing beyond the point that all should respect his bloodily earned spot as second to Arrow. Arrow was strange. He often talked of throwing his executives into the same room and waiting for the survivor to walk out. Great for survival of the fittest, but tough on team building. Turner was the worst evidence of the corporate evolutionary process. Why did Arrow love this guy so much? What an ass! For some reason after Dane's interruption, Arrow had let Turner talk without returning to the topic of stock trading. Finally, Lacey could not stand the overtalk, "Aren't you really trying to ask a simple question... Do these acquisitions make sense?"

He knew he had to quickly continue or Turner would crucify him, "I know that two weeks ago, some of this came as a surprise. I suppose what I should do is quickly summarize the key points. Four months ago, Mr. Arrow gave me a confidential research project. It was to assess the feasibility of acquiring all or any of three major U. S. railroad lines, Union Pacific, Burlington Northern, and/or the Santa Fe Southern Pacific. These three companies, with their real estate, natural resources and rail lines will be a perfect match for our transportation, financial, oil, and processing/manufacturing subsidiaries. As you now have heard, there appear to be no or little antitrust problems. Burlington Northern is a northern and western line, Santa Fe Southern Pacific is midwestern, western, and southern and Union Pacific is a central and midwestern company. The present Republican administration appears to allow such noncompeting competitors to join or be acquired.

"More important, these companies make sense from a financial perspective. Each has stock selling at about 7 times earnings while our stock sells at 21 times. It appears that approximately three billion dollars will purchase 50% of either the Union Pacific or the Santa Fe Pacific's stock, while less will control Burlington Northern's stock. This combination of these companies with ours will double our present earnings per share simply because of their heavy cash flow, increased earnings and low price earning ratio. For example, Burlington earned $6.76 per share with $850,000,000 in before tax earnings on 74,00,000 shares and now has a total market value of approximately $3 billion. We are assuming that we will have to pay a 40% premium with borrowed funds that would cost 15% per year in interest. That will mean $450 million in interest charges, leaving us $400,000,000 a year in before tax earnings to pay off the debt and add to our earnings which last year were twice Burlington Northern's. That means the Burlington Northern acquisition will add 25% to our earnings per share alone. And as you all know, this effect would be more pronounced if we used common stock rather than borrowed funds. Since our stock sells at a price earnings ratio of 21, that is a $7 billion addition to our stock's market value for a purchase that costs half that and that we can basically pay for from the acquired company's earnings. Additionally, we believe that a combination of these companies will allow us to significantly decrease administrative costs, as much as again doubling our total earnings per share.

"From a financial point of view, any individual acquisition would be pure genius for our stockholders, a combined acquisition would be unbelievable. We are all talking about the largest corporate acquisition in terms of people affected and the third largest in terms of dollars, third only to the purchases of Gulf and Getty. We are all to be part of business history."

That should get him some points, thought Turner, who riled at this dumb Black cutting him off. Damn Arrow and his love for the bleeding hearts of America! If he had his way, both Lacey and O'Brian, the corporate bitch, would be long gone. Turner couldn't stand it any longer, "Don't you think you are being a little naive? A corporate takeover is not a matter of numbers. It is a matter of death and blood. People are going to get hurt. They are going to fight. Their families are going to fight. You are talking of putting two thousand white shirt executives out of jobs. Shit, Lacey, grow up! This is war, that's how you have to present it." In his typical manner, Frank Turner banged the table with his fist.

Lacey looked at the handsome flushed face of Frank Turner. Blond, with a hairline that showed no trace of receding at age 54, Turner was the cold killer whom no one crossed. He was known to have an insatiable appetite to control, to dominate. Lacey thought he must tread carefully with his reply, so he limited it, "Yes Sir!"

"Yes Sir" what? What the Hell had been the question? This dumb Black was laughing at him! He would have his ass on a petard! This

God Damn Coon was dead meat, thought Lt. Turner!

"And if I might add, Mr. Lacey," it was Aaron Goldstein, the New York lawyer whom Hughes had seen sitting next to Massendale who jumped in to join in the scorn and earn points with Turner and hopefully, Phillip Arrow. "As you know, since the start, each of you has been asked to speak of the targets through only the use of code names, Cardinal, Oriole, and Blue Jays, if you remember correctly. Even if we are close to tendering the offers, I must insist that all spoken and written words use only these titles and not those that you, Mr. Lacey, so freely mention."

Silence again enveloped the room. Lacey chose not to respond to the whining voiced, young potbellied Manhattan lawyer. Faddish, foppish, Lacey could give Goldstein credit only in that he was less repulsive than his companion Smedt from the investment banking firm of Arlington, Bothell & Hyde. At least Goldstein's firm used the real Jewish names of its founding fathers, not names picked at random out of the New York phone directory. Lacey knew that the tradition continued in Smedt's firm and wondered what Smedt's last name really was.

"Still sounds like it's for the birds to me," hesitantly voiced Lawrence Massendale. Silence. The feebly spoken joke drew no smiles or laughs. Sweat broke out on the forehead of John Jamison. He'd been about to mention playing baseball.

The room was silent. Then Arrow picked up the pieces. "Thank you, Gentlemen, but if I may be blunt - all this misses the point. I wanted all of you here, especially Smedt and Goldstein since they were in L.A. today, to discuss the run up in the price of stock of these three companies." Again Arrow surveyed the room, but he knew that he had lost the chance of a surprise. They had been forewarned by his earlier statements.

"For the four and one-half months Lacey looked at these companies and from the time I lined up the funds, no public stock market interest had been shown in any of these companies. Two weeks ago, just the eight of us met to review our progress, although each of you had been introduced to the concept at various times during this four and one-half month period. You, Mr. Goldstein, were told four months ago when I asked your law firm to allow you, alone, to prepare a formal anti-trust study and another on the targets' By-Laws and Corporate Charters. You, Smedt, were told 98 days ago as I initiated the search and arrangement for the necessary cash and secondary funds. Caroline, you heard at about the same time as Lacey. Turner and Massendale both heard 84 days ago, while Jamison, you should have heard only 22 days ago, although your internal information system is fairly good.

"Since our meeting two weeks ago when we decided to go forward, the following has occurred. First, all of these potential acquisition's common stock has increased its trading volume by an average 10 fold. On the same average basis, each of these company's stock has risen in price by 20%. Meanwhile, Arrow Corporation's stock has fallen 30% on trading that has increased two fold. Obviously, someone during the past two weeks has either told someone or become an active trader and we've been lucky that the Securities and Exchange Commission hasn't as yet started inquiries."

"Couldn't all this be a coincidence," asked Jamison.

Typical comment thought Turner. Jamison should have been a consultant. He was always talking when he should be silent and usually silent when he should be talking. He must die a thousand deaths whenever he reviews his day on his commute home. I wonder what his wife says when he recounts his contributions to meetings such as these? Didn't he recognize that Arrow's addressing him wasn't an invitation to speak, that it had been a putdown, that mention of his internal corporate gossip system was a corporate joke?

The comment had made Turner's thoughts turn to the striking wife of Jamison. He thought she must truly be naive and sheltered to put up with a lifetime of Jamison's dumb statements. Could she be innocent enough for him to put a move on her? He had only talked to her once, she seemed bright.......had a beautiful body.....maybe a little too tall, but great legs, a fantastic waist, and firm...... Would she spread for a corporate promotion if the terms were right?

All the others had turned their attention to Jamison. Tall at six foot four, Jamison matched all the other executives in their height. It was as though one had to ·pass a "tall" test to be successful in the corporate world. With his height, however, Jamison carried a gentle peace that was a sharp contrast to the avarice and predatory nature of a Turner or the competitiveness of Phillip Arrow.

Seemingly to let him off this hook, Lawrence Massendale, Arrow's opinionated and nervous son-in-law, agreed, "Absolutely, Old Man, it sounds far too much like cloak and daggers." To whom Massendale addressed the "Old Man" was open to interpretation. At 67 years, Arrow was by far the oldest in the room. On the other hand, all doubted that even Arrow's daughter could save Massey from the forthcoming wrath. Arrow had turned a dark shade of red under his silver white hair.

"No, I don't believe in coincidences," said Arrow. "In this case, we have several, and hence my belief is even more faint. Obviously, I had to find out what I could during the last several days. We are set to discuss our offers publicly in New York in five days, next Monday, with the initial tender offers to be placed the day after tomorrow. I must admit that I trust none of you. But I did need some help and it appeared to me that the least likely of you to do this was Caroline, simply because she neither had the resources nor the time to set up such a complicated purchase transaction. Caroline, would you please tell the group what you have discovered?"

At least he did not say the real reason, thought Caroline as she adjusted her papers. What he really should have said was that he would doubt that a young woman from average means could have set up a $400 million investment. No, forget the "average means" part. Arrow just did not think that business was a place for a human being who wore panty hose.

Caroline was wearing her Scot's business suit, blue and white shoes, pleated skirt, high white collar and navy blue blazer. It was her 10th day of the month outfit. In her apartment she kept a working closet with exactly 31 outfits, 31 pairs of matching shoes, 31 sets of hosiery and accessories. No change in clothing parts was allowed. Each outfit had been carefully selected with professional assistance. Caroline's first businessman boyfriend, a very successful IBM sales representative mentor, had taught her the role of style and dress. This, and her other work habits, reflected Caroline's careful attention to detail, her avoidance of mistakes at all costs, her ability to use the judgments of others to assist her in her daily decisions, and most of all, her determination to never fail. But today, she was in trouble and she knew it.

This morning she knew she had to be extremely careful. All corporate meetings worked alike. Everyone would have to have at least two minutes to talk every ten minutes or lose his spot in the pecking order. With seven men in the room, she knew their critiques and criticisms would be fast and furious. In cases such as this she needed to be sure of her material and she would spend weeks in preparation and always be sure that she was correct in her recommendations. This morning she felt rushed, totally unsure of her material, and without the slightest idea of who could be manipulating the stock. She would have to do her best to put "each" and everyone on an equal footing.

"During the past week, I have visited 'each of you' and know that 'each of you' has been following the targets' stocks in their trading. I have asked 'each of you' whether you know 1) who is buying the targets' stock and 2) where they might have gotten the information. As 'each of you' know, the targets' stock was selling at an average price of $40 per share, with the exception of Santa Fe's which has twice as many shares outstanding and hence was selling at $20 per share. As 'each of you' know, our plans are to purchase at a 40% premium over this price. Hence any outsider's purchase at this time of any of the targets' stock would be assured of a 40% return just over this coming weekend."

"Hump, hump, my dear," interrupted Massendale, "I hope that 'each of us' are acutely aware of the implications of SEC violations, the statutory requirements for reporting, the 'insider rules' that apply. The Insider Trading Sanction Act of 1984 requires a repayment of three times any amount made by an individual on material, non public information." Taking his pipe from his mouth and eyeing it suspiciously, Lawrence T. Massendale, III took a breath to begin what was surely to be a college lecture on the subject. His eyes squinted as he also framed the words to chastise this repetitious, but beautiful, young lady for again mentioning the target companies' names. Perhaps he would go easy on her, he had always appreciated a good bust line and after all, he had been partly responsible for her employment ten years ago.

"Oh cut the crap, both of you! Caroline, do you know who it is and where they are getting their information or don't you? If you don't, I suggest that we ask our friends from New York." As the Executive Vice President of Arrow Corporation, Frank Turner was noted for both his hard brashness and ability to concentrate on the jugular.

"Wait, one minute, Mr. Turner. I resent your implication! Before anything more is said," demanded Goldstein, "my partners have asked me to specifically tell you, to assure you, that Shaffer, Schwab & Meyers have had absolutely nothing to do with the increase in these stocks' value. We have been aware of the increase in trading and it is

12

very embarrassing to us. We are totally mystified. The purchases have been checked as only we can check them. They are all small, no more than 120,000 shares have traded at any one time, and the purchases are from all over the Country, indeed, the world. Speaking for myself, and I am sure, Mr. Smedt, who is the only other outside individual for whom your remarks may have been intended, we adamantly dispute, and are insulted by, allegations that we could be involved in something this illegal."

"Thank you, Mr. Goldstein, well said," added John Smedt, "but I might add that for my Firm and yours, that we are long established New York acquisition and merger firms. Our reputation is built on our confidentiality and honesty. To insinuate that we would be so involved is unthinkable!"

Oh, I am very sorry to have had the thought, thought Lacey, and "Bullshit" to both of you. Arlington, Bothell, & Hyde's fee for the acquisition will be 1% of the value of the acquisitions, which might be as high as 200 million dollars for five weeks of work, while Shaffer, Schwab and Meyers will be looking at half of that amount. What you should have said was that you could make more money from commissions should the deals go through. Why would you do something to foul up the deal when you have learned to steal honestly?

"I am quite certain that that was not the point that Mr. Turner was making, Aaron & John." It was Massendale speaking again and Caroline smiled. The meeting was going exactly as she had wished. She would let them talk and perhaps she could escape without showing her ignorance or uncertainty.

But Phillip Arrow would not let her off that easily. He bruskly interrupted Massendale with a contempt of a suffering father-in-law. "Caroline, you have had the assignment, do you have any idea of who might be behind purchasing this stock?"

Caroline flushed. Damn! Arrow knew that she did not know. She would never come to such a meeting without first briefing him. Why was he putting her on the spot like this? As she took a breath to speak, Lacey broke in, "I think I can help."

Ev Lacey had watched Caroline's discomfort with some amusement. Even though Arrow had had him do the acquisition and merger analyses, he had not asked Lacey to investigate the buying. Obviously, Arrow had not trusted him. Thus, he must have been most surprised to receive Lacey's unsolicited one-half page report that detailed the potential insider dealings. And contrary to Ms. O'Brian's opening remarks, she had not visited Lacey to discuss her investigation. Lacey knew that Caroline looked upon him as one of her competitors and her actions toward him spoke of corporate hostility.

Lacey continued, "Let me begin by saying that I believe we have been asking the wrong questions. We have asked 'who' it is and 'where' they heard their information. We could just as easily be asking 'why' someone would be giving out such information. The question's not 'who' or 'where,' but 'why'?

"Let's review the facts. The Monday before last, these three targets' stock began trading at a rate 10 times higher than normal. Trades of 100,000 shares became common rather than 10,000 shares. That's coincidence # 1. Coincidence # 2 is that in the first day of increased trading, almost 1% exactly of each of the three target's stock sold. It appeared that some large, financially sound entity with a set plan is involved. Coincidence # 3 is that this trading began on the Monday immediately following our Friday meeting where we decided to go forward. I don't believe in coincidences either, especially three in concert. Moreover, I don't like the feel of it. It could be that there is an entity out there who bought the first day, either because it is going to compete with us or because it is a potential partner of these companies. But I also admit that both these reasons are highly speculative."

I finally have him, thought Caroline. I have been waiting for him to come up with that one idea that is too creative, too crazy. Look at the time he has taken to express it! Arrow must be bored and I have to shut him up before he completely steals the spotlight. (Experience had taught her that if you let someone talk long enough, people would forget what had been said.) "That's exactly what I did not wish to do at this session, Mr. Lacey. I think it's best if we stick to facts. I might note, Everett, that these gentlemen's time is valuable, so if we don't talk about a 'feel' or 'speculate' on what it might be, but rather focus on what we know, we might make some progress."

"Caroline, I intend that we do make progress. You see, there is another alternative. What sounds most reasonable to me is that someone has already taken a position. Let's suppose that it's 5% in each of these companies. Then all this makes sense. It makes sense to leak the word and drive up the stocks' value, it makes sense to start the trading strong on Monday, it makes sense to do everything one can to encourage the acquisitions .... it makes sense if you already hold a position and are very, very careful. All you would want is to have the stock appreciate in value. You wouldn't then care if the acquisitions occurred or not. You could ride the stock up in its speculative appreciation and get off the train before Arrow Corporation tendered."

"Oh, come on my dear fellow," interrupted Massendale again, "We all know that positions of over 5% have to be reported to the Securities and Exchange Commission. I specifically read in your first report on these targets that no new position had been created. That work was carefully checked by both Mr. Smedts and Mr. Goldstein's firms. We just don't have any way of checking if the amount is under 5%, but if it is someone and they are operating on inside information, we will not deal with them again."

"Why would they want to work with us again, Massey?" It was Arrow and Lacey, indeed, had his attention. Arrow sensed that Lacey knew that his career was on the line by taking over this meeting. He also knew how hard Lacey had worked to get where he was and how much he valued his job. "If someone has a position, it has cost him or his sponsor $400,000,000 of which he may just get a percentage of the 20 to 30% premium. Say his percentage is 25%. That's a four week cut of the profits equaling $25,000,000. I'd say that whoever it is will not have to work again, so I would not worry about 'dealing' with him again, Mr. Massendale. That will be his choice, not ours. Go on Mr. Lacey."

"Each February 15th, any individual holding more than 5% of a company's stock must report with the SEC on a Schedule 13-G. I rechecked my research of two months ago just to be sure and found that a new report had been filed six weeks ago. I might add that this brings up another coincidence. Mr. Massendale's Legal Department and Mr. Turner's financial people .... and especially the firms represented by Mr. Goldstein and Mr. Smedt should have been doing this. Monitoring new filings with the SEC of potential targets is a common task, one that I was told was specifically being done by all four of you."

With those words Lacey pulled a three page copy of a SEC Schedule 13-G filing from his folder and read, "Just over six weeks ago, an investment firm of Blarnef & Blarnef reported that its

15

purchases had exceeded 5.8% of the Blue Jays. In checking, I have found that they hold slightly lesser percentages of each of the other two targets. They state that these holdings are 'for investment purposes only' which is no doubt the truth. But the largest coincidence of them all, Ladies and Gentlemen, is the fact that we know Blarnef & Blarnef. They are investment advisers for certain of the union pension retirement trusts to which we contribute, are one of the largest 25 such firms in the Country, and have their principal office but three blocks away from where I am now speaking. Mr. Turner and Mr. Jamison, I know that you work with them constantly."

"Let me see that report," barked Turner. The room again fell silent as he read it. The only change was the noticeable growing redness to Turner's complexion. Without a word, he handed it across to Phillip Arrow. With a wave of the hand he motioned for Lacey to resume speaking. Caroline interrupted, "If I might speak....." Arrow's hand was held out to silence her. He, too, motioned for Lacey to continue.

"I think it would be best if I voiced all the possibilities as to what may have happened. My reasoning is that if we get it all out on the table, we will be healthier as a Company for it. It will also, perhaps, save us all time in coming up with a resolution. I am assuming that you will all agree that it now appears that an entity would be greatly enriched by our going forward with the acquisitions. It also appears that they are the ones responsible for the recent running up of the stocks' price.

"I see three possibilities in light of the position taken by someone during the past few months. First, it could be one of our outside assisting firms, either Mr. Smedts or Mr. Goldstein's, or perhaps they themselves have arranged this action. Second, it could be someone who has heard of the proposed tender offers, perhaps only by accident. Perhaps, they have decided to act upon only a 'tip.' Third, it could be one of us here on the corporate staff."

Lacey paused to look around the room. He had described all those present, excepting Phillip Arrow, as suspects. The criticisms from the floor had ceased. All were silent, even Caroline looked down in defeat.

"Let me review these possibilities in order. The magnitude of the funds spent to take this position exceeds 400 million dollars. This should exceed either Mr. Smedts or Mr. Goldstein's personal assets, or any of our own for that matter. I sincerely doubt that either of their two firms would have taken this type of position. We know that they

16

have done so in the past, but only very carefully through foreign investment brokers and Swiss bank accounts and not through a highly visible firm such as Blarnef and Blarnef. I would also rule out the possibility that a stray comment or a confidential tip would trigger such an investment. It would be difficult to imagine an expenditure of this magnitude just on hearsay."

Lacey again paused, "So that leaves just the corporate staff and the coincidence that the money was invested three blocks from here. I would speculate that one of us knows an individual or a group of individuals here in Los Angeles who have such funds. Whoever it is might have gone to them two months ago and told them of these plans and assured them that at least one of the three targets would be acquired.

"To conclude, if they bet on all three, they would at least score on one and the other two stocks would hold at least stable. These investors, in turn, might have told him that how, where, with whom, and by whom the funds would be invested would be solely up to the investors. Hence, the resulting embarrassment of a local investment manager."

"Following that reasoning, should not you also say that either Mr. Smedt or Goldstein could have similar close New York friends with contacts in Los Angeles," interrupted Turner.

"Please, Sir, I beg of you........," began Smedt.

"Yes," continued Lacey. "But that also brings up another subtle possibility. Perhaps the use of a Los Angeles investment firm is only intended to throw us off the scent. We were soon going to find out about these positions anyway. The percentage ownership above 5% would have to be included in the targets' proxies that are soon due to be published. Perhaps the Los Angeles investment is intentionally taken, knowing that when we find out about it, we will be deluged in acquisition activity. Since we all don't trust one another now anyway, it could be intended to play on our mutual paranoia."

Caroline, sat angry and frustrated. Damn Lacey! Why hadn't she thought of checking the 13-Gs? Obviously, she had thought Massendale would check, but what had Massey ever followed up on in his life anyway? Smedt and Goldstein looked very nervous, but then looking at her hands, so did she. All of those present are suspects. There just were no other possibilities. Arrow had kept the number of individuals knowledgeable regarding his interest in the targets to a minimum.

Both Lacey and she had typed their own material. No secretary knew. Lacey was right, it had to be one of them. Would Turner do it? The answer was 'Yes,' but of all the executives, he had the most to lose. He was the heir apparent, and besides, Turner is turned on by power, not by money, thought Caroline. Could it be Jamison? What a joke, besides he only knew about it two or three weeks ago, long after the shares were purchased. Would Massendale attempt it? Who would give him 400 million dollars or base such an investment on his credibility?

Arrow stared at the table, deep in thought. Finally, he replied, "Well, this may change our plans a bit. We had planned to make the tender offers in two days with filings with the U.S. Securities and Exchange Commission and full page announcements of the tenders in all editions of the *Wall Street Journal*. Caroline, this was to be your meeting, what do you suggest?"

He is laughing at me, thought Caroline, but then this may be the chance to salvage something. Damn Lacey! It was a sure thing that he had briefed Arrow before the meeting. "I would think we might wish to delay the tender offers and wait several weeks to see who this entity might be. Mr. Lacey is correct regarding the disclosure of his initial findings in the soon to be published proxy material, but he has one hundred other guesses that may be totally incorrect. I would think caution would be in order."

"I agree exactly," voiced Massendale. "And I also suggest that we go to Blarnef and Blarnef and threaten a suit. This is a clear case of potentially manipulating the market. They should give us the information as to whom it is .... otherwise, we will get it through the Courts."

"Just another thought, Massey," interjected Aaron Goldstein who could not believe this suggestion from what had to be a lay counsel, "we have found investment firms to be loath to disclose such information and they have clear legal statutes to protect them. Also, we would have to openly suggest that a potential Securities and Exchange Commission violation is in process. We might be placing Arrow Corporation at some liability should we continue with any acquisition. I too agree, however, that caution is in order. What do you say Mr. Smedt?"

"I would reluctantly agree with delaying the tender offers. Arlington, Bothell & Hyde would counsel for caution."

All turned to Frank Turner who had sat looking at Arrow. "Ah,

18

Hell, Phillip, let's find out who this bastard is! The targets will sit still until we burn this bird, whoever he or," turning to Caroline, "she is."

There was silence. None could catch Phillip Arrow's thoughts. Whoever it was, had left a trail. First, he would look for someone who tried to exclude people like Lacey on his staff who might have discovered this during their previous work. Second, he would look to see who had been filtering him information on this. He couldn't believe that only Lacey knew of the Schedule 13-Gs. Finally, he would look for those who had really encouraged him to go forward.

The silence continued. Phillip Arrow added another thought. He supposed that there would be one other clue as to whom of them in this room might be making a few hundred million on this. He would be the first one of them to quit after all this was over. If not the first, he would be a close second. Whoever it was, would no longer have to work.

"John?" Arrow then turned to face John Jamison who was one of the two executives seated at the table who had not yet voiced an opinion.

"Yes Sir." Jamison had appeared stricken when Lacey mentioned his working with Blarnef and Blarnef. Surely Arrow did not suspect him! Jamison had prided himself all his life on the fact that he did not steal, lie, or cheat. He had been raised that way.

"Do you have an opinion?"

"Well Sir, as you know, all this is new to me. I would agree with everyone. I certainly would not want the Corporation to look bad. I think caution is in order."

"Mr. Lacey, that leaves you."

"It is your decision, Mr. Arrow."

"Yes, I agree. Ladies and Gentlemen, my reaction to all this, and I especially thank you, Mr. Lacey, is that this is just the price of doing business. All it means is that our purchase price will be higher than it would have been. Even if we have to pay a 50% premium, the acquisitions will be sound. Consequently, nothing has changed.

"I will ask you all to keep the contents of this session confidential, but also to keep your eyes open. We will find out who it is in time. I will fly to Dallas tomorrow to finalize the finances and make the announcement to the corporate staff the next day at Frank's evening party. The tender offers will be made public earlier that day.

"I would appreciate a detailed review of the three acquisition plans on Saturday morning at 8:00 AM, although Jamison, I don't think that you have to be involved in the planning on Thursday and Friday, but I would want you there on Saturday. I might ask that all of you pay special attention to the targets' possible defensive strategies. Each of them has had approximately 5% of their stock purchased at the direction of one of us here, whoever he or she is. Since those purchases were made by investment people housed but three blocks from here, I would suspect that our targets have had ample warning. I would think that their battle flags are up and that Arrow Corporation is their suspected opponent.

"All of the targets have been forewarned and have probably guessed our intentions for the past three months. We might very well feel like we are revisiting the Little Big Horn on Monday, but as I stated, it's part of doing business at this level.

"So I thank you for your opinions, but we are going ahead as planned.

"I also thank you for all dropping by this morning. Now I suggest that we all get back to work." With those words, Phillip Arrow rose from his chair and deep in thought, walked out of the room.

2
Thursday

Dane Hughes leveled the Lear Jet off at 41,000 feet heading east to Dallas. His untalkative copilot, Hank Labear and he settled into what was now a long routine of introspection. Dane preferred this type of silent arrangement, a working style that he had adopted in the Navy. He loved flying, especially on a morning such as this. The San Bernardino Mountains had raised their peaks above a white cotton cloud cover. The flight path to Dallas was set on the southern route, Tucson, El Paso, Midland, and then up in a gentle curve to Love Field. At 440 knots it would take them 3 hours, all to turn around and fly back tomorrow.

If it hadn't been for a disastrous evening with Caroline, he would have felt even better. He had been only too pleased to have Caroline give him a call and he quickly agreed to dinner. By the evening's end, he had been totally destroyed - the French forces facing the German in WW II. "Where was Dane's ambition? How could he have been so stupid as to just walk into Arrow's Boardroom? When was he going to give up driving a glorified bus and become serious? What was he going to be when he grew up? Why didn't he want to go back to school to pursue an MBA and better himself? How could he look himself in the mirror? Why did he continue (unsuccessfully) to establish a physical relation? He knew that if their relationship was to become long lasting that they would have to be sure of what he called 'love'."

Distracted, Dane reached below the left panel and moved a thin computer switch in a one long, two short, and a quick double short sequence. This accessed a system that he had installed shortly after coming to work with Arrow. On his first day of employment, the Chief Mechanic and Richard Smith had met with him and a surprised new employee had been introduced to the tape recording system that monitored all passenger conversations. He was then told that both his job and an annual bonus of $10,000 depended upon his both retrieving the tapes and keeping that task totally confidential. These tapes were to be packaged and sent to Richard Smith's office. It appeared that only twelve head pilots, the chief mechanic and Richard Smith....... and Phillip Arrow, Dane assumed, knew of the system. It had been a simple moral decision. Conversations of employees or personnel riding Arrow aircraft were the private property of the Corporation. Did or did not Dane Hughes want the job?

Dane had been tremendously bothered by this question during his first few months of employment. At the time, it didn't seem fair that his job was not fully described to him before it was offered. Strange, how that as time passed, the importance of the matter lessened.

Dane had always been interested in electronics and it had been an easy job to tap into these microphone feeds via the power cord. Using a technology developed by the Navy to tap an enemy's computer system, he had hooked this bypass up to his earphones with the volume on low. Perhaps it was Dane's Naval experience and introduction to intelligence or perhaps it was an ill father, who after nineteen years of tenure with a company, had been fired the day before he vested in a pension, Dane shared the belief that his future depended upon him and himself alone. Arrow, who enjoyed riding copilot on his long trips, had once told Dane that he trusted no one. It was at that moment that Dane decided to take Arrow at his word. Passengers constantly talk about their pilots during a flight, especially right after takeoff and before any landing. He wanted to make sure of what they were saying. If his job was on the line, he wanted to be the first to know, not the last.

Moreover, it gave him an opportunity to listen to corporate conversations and hear some occasional corporate gossip. From this information, Dane could draw unique forecasts. Secretly, Dane totally believed that his sage advice given to Caroline had greatly assisted her in her rise to the position as sole Assistant to the Chairman. He also sensed that Caroline knew this too and sought him out when she was most upset or unsure of herself. Unfortunately, last night she had not told him what was bothering her, nor could Dane have helped her.

Perhaps today he would be allowed to again wile away the time and learn something. Dane concentrated on the voices of the two passengers. He had not seen the second gentleman get on the plane. Arrow had asked that the pilots be forward and had, himself, secured the door. There was nothing unusual in this, it had been done before. But the meeting that Dane had invaded yesterday and the tension packed evening with Caroline suggested that something was stirring. Dane admitted to himself that this morning was one morning that he had no intention of missing any of the conversation.

He heard Arrow's voice first, "........then you don't think it could be someone from your end. They handle one of your funds."

"No, absolutely not! Phillip, none of the people working for me know. This idea is independent of them. It's my show now, my idea."

"I don't know why I ever let you coerce me into this?"

"Oh, come on Phillip, you know 'why'. If you don't cooperate, my tiny, little union funds will eat up your big bad company. Thank Goodness that this is a democracy. No monarchy would have ever had Congressmen that we could buy. Just remember, blame Congress and the system, our Founding Fathers if you like, but don't blame me."

There was a pause before Arrow's reply.

"The Multiemployer Pension Plan Act of 1980 has to be one of our greatest National disasters. You and other union pension funds basically waste away billions of dollars of assets and discover that you can not pay your members the benefits that you had promised them and which I had been funding for years. So you hire several consulting firms to create some way to escape and they get the Congress to pass a bill for you, you get lucky and have an outgoing President who is dazed enough to sign it, and all of a sudden I find that three unions each have the right to 30% of my corporation's assets based upon nothing more than the amount of the debt of their pension trusts. You are rewarded for the depth of your squandering! Even more hilarious is the fact that most companies continue to employ these consulting firms as their actuaries. To think that organizations hire actuaries to watch over their pension plans! It's like having the fox guard the chicken house. No, even more hilarious is the fact that no one, especially the press, is talking about this nationally historic ripoff. No one is willing to alienate either you or the great American public who is to be rewarded with the dead body of my Company and others. American business is becoming as crippled as Canada's. I believe that God must think that criminal."

"God has a sense of humor, Phillip. Look at it from my perspective. I control two of those three unions' funds. For everyone's bad day in business, there is a good day for someone. Feel happy for me."

Again there was silence. Dane had thought that he had heard a snarl, but perhaps it was only Arrow coughing.

"Two wrongs don't make a right. These proposed acquisitions are insane. The Government will never allow them. If, and that's a big 'if,' if we are successful, it could drive Arrow Corporation into bankruptcy. Note that I said 'successful.' We are also broke if they are unsuccessful. Furthermore, the Railroad Retirement Fund is in the worst shape of any plan except for the Civil Service's, the military's, and Social Security's."

"Come, come Phillip Arrow. So many incorrect statements for a man known to speak with the best mind in the business. One, the Multiemployer Pension Plan Amendments Act was not written to apply to Civil Service or the railways. Congress would have to pay the bill. Two, Arrow Corporation is already bankrupt under the Act. Three, no plans are as bad off as multiemployer plans. Four, the Government will allow it and you know it. None of these companies compete anymore. They used to, but since the '40s they've been forced to shrink down to regional markets. They just don't overlap anymore. The Government has no case to say that you are limiting competition after the Santa Fe acquisition."

"What about how I got into this mess in the first place, with the purchase of a large trucking company? We compete with the railroads with substitute services, both highway and air. Indeed, we piggyback more truck trailers these days than ever in our history. We will be greatly assisted by owning the freight alternatives for the shipment of our energy and manufactured products."

"Phillip, we live in a unique time. Who would have thought that a Gulf Oil and other major oil companies could be purchased by their U.S. competitors without Federal interference? Who would have thought that a Republic and a LTV would be allowed to combine their steel operations? Blatant horizontal mergers, let alone vertical and substitute horizontal mergers, as you mentioned, are permissible today. Let's face it. America will someday be a nation with only ten or twenty major companies. It's your choice if you wish Arrow Corporation to be one of them."

"I don't know. Maybe I am getting too old. I just don't have the fire necessary anymore. It's not the type of legacy that I wished to leave my grandchildren."

"Hell, you're not leaving a legacy, not with that damn idea of a Foundation that you set up! How you can leave most of your wealth to a damn non profit corporation's board of directors is beyond me. Look at what happened to Howard Hughes! His idea of a medical foundation to take all his corporation's profits as non taxable dividends and to apply them to medical research was outstanding. What he didn't calculate was the avarice of his corporate managers."

"I don't follow."

"Have you ever visited their work facilities? There are no finer furnishings in the world, no better computer equipment, no finer staffed engineering departments, no higher paid staffs. The damn corporation is damn sure to spend all its money so that it doesn't have any profits. Hughes' medical facility is getting only a fraction of what it deserves. It was a good idea, but like most good ideas, when it comes to execution, it fails. No wonder their Trustees are selling them."

"I suspect, though, that there is more to a legacy than profits."

"Now I don't follow......but speaking of a legacy. Perhaps you should fire up a search for a new corporate name. I don't think that I would mind if you kept Arrow in it, but I would like Pacific's first name to be included. It would be rather fitting, don't you think?"

"Fine, I will have Massendale work on it. That's something he would enjoy. He might even be able to do it without messing it up. He is especially good when there is no right answer. I think, though, that we should turn our attention to finances. I don't think Smedt's firm can deliver the funds in Dallas today. I think it's auspicious that he isn't going to be present when we meet with his New York management this afternoon."

"Don't worry about it. Smedt is just a minor player in New York. I agree, let's get down to business and discuss the finances. Here's what's going to happen when you meet with Arlington, Bothell & Hyde to finalize the financing. City American National Bank's consortium will guarantee a credit line of twelve billion. Not known to your finance folks, we will have supplied a supplementary guarantee, which should be easy as we own the lead bank in the group, lock, stock and vault. If you need more than twelve billion, we could go as high as twenty."

"It pains me to think that we will be paying Smedt's firm a $ 200 million fee for arranging those funds and that they will have to perform no real service. You are handing it to them on a platter."

"Just as long as they don't know that, we are all fine. You may not know this, but we also control Security Financial Express which recently purchased Arlington, Bothell & Hyde. In effect, we ....I mean you, will be paying us for the service. Everything works out in the end. There is justice in the world after all, Phillip."

"I still don't understand why you say that the Government will provide no opposition to these acquisitions."

"Phillip, I represent thousands, hundreds of thousands of union members, all of whom vote if you remember. Washington D.C. is my home, that's where we have our offices. What do you think we do there? Have you ever visited my marble palace? The lobby is a museum and no one has a prayer of seeing anyone in my offices. We have just three tasks: count our money, line up votes, and buy off agencies. Rest assured, Phillip, the Government is the least of your worries."

"I guess I must be getting old. It does not seem fair that I work all my life to build Arrow Corporation to see this happening at this time. How was I to know that the trucking and air companies that we purchased in the late 1960s would have a union membership that would come back to haunt me? Who would have suspected that Congress would have pledged my Firm's assets to your pension trusts in September 1980?"

"Oh, cut the crap! You are doing business as usual. Your only role at this time, indeed, your fiduciary responsibility to your stockholders is to maximize their position. If you play the game with us, Arrow Corporation will continue to flourish and your present stockholders will continue to make their dividends and appreciation. Indeed, they could make a bundle on this deal if the acquisitions pay off as we expect. Your alternative is to say 'No' and we will pull the plug on your pension liabilities. You will note that I have made this little speech without once referring to your 8 % ownership of Arrow

Corporation. You could be personally worth close to three billion dollars or nothing. It is strictly your choice."

"Oh, I have made my choice. I sometimes wish that you had more class, however, and most of all that you did not smoke those cigars. No, I take that back, I most regret putting up with Frank Turner, though I know I must. He is a necessity. He also violates all sensitivities."

"He does? Well that must mean he is doing his job. Wonder what old Frank is up to or into at this moment? He is such a mean bastard."

At that moment, Frank Turner was starting an early Thursday morning meeting to finalize the plans for the acquisition. He too had chosen the Boardroom with its view across a smoggy downtown Los Angeles. Less than a half mile away, one could barely see the shape of thousands of cars streaming into the City. With his back to those present, he stood staring out one of the large windows. He thought it a fitting view. One could not see the horizon because of human waste.

With a heavy burst of adrenaline, he turned, "Let's see, who do we have here this morning? I know that Arrow invited you all here this morning with the exception of John Jamison. As you know, we may have operational plans for Jamison, but he has had no role planning the tender offers. Without a reason to know, I didn't think that he should be here and Arrow agreed. Unfortunately, I didn't have time to discuss all the key players with Arrow so we will do some rearranging now, if you all don't mind. Massey, as Corporate Counsel, you have to stay, along with Mr. Goldstein and Smedt, but I will be darn't if I know why either you, Caroline or you, Lacey should be here. Give me a good reason, Lacey, and I will let you stay. Otherwise, you must leave."

The conference room was stone silent. Both Smedt and Goldstein smiled across the table at one another. Caroline looked first at them and then at Turner. Finally she turned her head to see Everett Lacey. How many times has he been so excluded, she wondered? She could see his pride, yet there was a sudden slump of the shoulders. His tall six foot two frame looked shrunken, his glasses too diminishing. What could he possibly say in reply to Turner? Caroline waited for him to answer. She could see that he was obviously beaten.

Lacey did not reply. Instead, he gathered his papers, stood up, and without a nod or any facial expression, walked to the door and left the room. Caroline O'Brian sat unmoved in her chair, looking at Turner.

"Caroline, your turn, give me one good reason why you should stay?"

"That is easy, Mr. Turner, I simply refuse to leave." Caroline sat straight in her chair with a gracious smile that was intended to infuriate Frank Turner. And of course, Caroline did more. Shapely at five foot six and dark brunette hair, Caroline knew her bust line was better than average. In times such as these, she made certain that she sat tall, with her tan jacket buttoned snugly against her body. If having a woman in the room bothered Turner, the more she looked like a woman, the more she would bother the man.

"Caroline, that is not good enough. I will have to ask you to leave." Frank Turner smiled. He loved combat like this. How dare she challenge him in front of these men from New York? At least Lacey knew his place. He'd humble this cold bitch good before he was through. Thank God these types did not breed.

"With all due respect, Frank, Go to Hell! Mr. Arrow personally asked me to attend. Indeed, I have specific questions that he wishes us to address this morning. Again, Frank, Get Fucked!"

Anger clouded Turner's face. Seconds passed as the two combatants stared at one another. God Damn women and their use of profanity in the Boardroom! They were like sixth grade boys, they thought that the use of swear words made them sound like a man. Get an operation O'Brian or get the Hell out of my life! Finally, Frank Turner gave in, "Alright, Ms. O'Brian, you may stay. We just might have need of a secretary."

Frank Turner carefully looked at his papers to let the knife sink. In one way, it was appropriate that she stayed. Lacey could easily be shown as the source of the leak. Caroline hated Lacey with a passion, he was a competitor for Arrow's favor. Perhaps he, Turner, could use her zeal to force the Black out onto the street.

Turner turned to the task at hand, "O.K., Smedt, let's get on with a review of the steps. I would like to be out of here by Noon. There is no reason why we have to spend two days on this. We have been over the three plans before and you heard the Old Man say yesterday that 'nothing has changed'."

As John Smedt rose from his chair and walked to the front of the room, two hundred feet away in the same building, Ev Lacey, with a "What the Hell" decision and with his own surge of adrenaline, took a sharp U-turn and walked back to Phillip Arrow's computer room. A woman guard sat at the window. Lacey knew that he was about to risk his career. "I believe that there are eight of us with access to the confidential computer terminals and system this weekend."

"That's right, Mr. Lacey. Mr. Smedt and Goldstein are the outside people and you, Mr. Turner, Jamison, Massendale and Ms. O'Brian have access - along with Mr. Arrow. Smedt and Goldstein have the use of the terminals in the Boardroom."

"Thank you. If you don't mind, I will work on the terminal in the room here rather than at my desk. There are too many distractions and I don't think I want anyone looking over my shoulder this morning."

Uncertain, the guard let Lacey into an unmanned computer room with two terminals set to both control and guard the Executive Information System at Arrow Corporation. Lacey knew that the term "computer room" was in fact a misnomer. What Phillip Arrow had assembled was a combination of computers from all his different subsidiaries, a network that allowed him to compile information on an ad hoc basis via powerful new software. In addition, Arrow had access to numerous other computer systems, some accessed on a rental basis and some accessed on a basis unknown to their owners. This computer room contained a small, powerful operator free IBM minicomputer that served basically as a "feed" for these one thousand or so computer systems based all over the world.

Like many modern corporate executives, Arrow had spared no expense on his computer facilities. He had then forced all his executives to become totally proficient in the use of computers, including himself. Arrow recognized that the world was rapidly dividing into two, those who had access to information for decision making and those without that information. Information and computers were becoming synonymous.

Of all the Arrow executives, Ev Lacey was the most proficient user. Other executives still felt uncomfortable, even with their training. Caroline O'Brian refused to have a terminal in her office. She fully believed that a rising female star could not look like a secretary. Ev Lacey often teased about this opinion, it was a strategy of the sixties, not the eighties where computer terminals demanded typing skills.

Everett Lacey had taken computer programming as a doctoral language instead of the traditional German or French. Although he had been unable to stay in school to complete his dissertation, Lacey had often thought that his inadvertent computer training had been the most important single skill he had ever learned. Typing was second. Today, he was determined to use both.

Lacey had two initial goals. He had learned from his research that these system control terminals were the only ones set up to access all the data bases to which Phillip Arrow had access. Today he needed this type of unlimited access and the system override capabilities found only with a control terminal. Otherwise, he would have to know the passwords and combinations of keystrokes and entry that are impossible to guess, if at all, in any short period of time. For today, he wished to develop a test of all the data bases for any combination of interests with the acquisition targets, Smedts and Goldstein's firms, Blarnef & Blarnef, and the individuals connected with the acquisitions to this date.

Lacey relaxed in the hard chair in front of terminal. He loved this bright room with its beautiful, new equipment.

Lacey first called the Supermaster series of commands that he had noted from his research of IBM manuals. He then accessed his data sets through the interlinking systems and recalled a program that he had worked on over the past two weeks. Although complex in its data base access protocols, it was a simple program. Lacey could enter a series of up to eighty variables, such as the suspected acquirers of the targets' stock. The program then accessed a mathematical review of the relationship of these variables' profiles and associated data to the data that was being read. For data that showed a high similarity, the source and mathematical measurement of this relationship were stored. After a review of the data bases, the program then returned to review the discovered relationships, one against another. Finally, a summary analysis informed Lacey of the total relationships. Relationships lead to actions and Lacey believed they most often explained causes.

Lacey quickly set the program to work. He knew that the program worked at the speed of light and that any visual review on his part would only slow the process. The problem was that he could not leave the room. If a technician were to enter, Lacey would have to cancel his program and return the system to its stable position. Since Arrow was not in the building today, his only danger was in someone visiting this room. Hence, he would have to wile away the time while staying awake. Lacey walked over to the second terminal. Arrow had said that he wanted a thorough review of possible defensive strategies. Perhaps, he could find out what each of the targets was actually doing. If he could, he had a built in excuse for his unauthorized access to all the data bases. Arrow would know of his work once the weekend summaries were printed. Quickly, Lacey typed in the commands to access Burlington Northern's computer system and sat down to review their files.

Dane Hughes was also punching in commands. Like all survivors, he was operating at half attention with his senses spread about the cockpit. There was no warning.

The left front flight pane simply shattered into a caked web of snow.

With the fear that the cockpit air was just starting to leak through the window into the no pressure, frozen world of 41 thousand feet, Dane had the Lear on its side in a quick turn with air brakes out and landing gear down. Thrice trained in the Lear Simulator, hundreds of times trained in an F4H, Dane increased pressure in the Lear in a falling arrow to earth.

Then, still forced back in their seats in a spinning dive, LaBear and he began the slow task of donning the oxygen masks. Careful of the passengers, the 45 degree angled spin was designed to keep them in the vicinity of their seats and not forced against the ceiling of the Lear. Dane struggled with the air speed and the mask. At 440 knots and then a dive, it was no trick to reach the sound barrier, the build up of air turbulence, and the flame out of jet engines. Dane hoped that the passengers were coping. The seconds drained away like hours. Dane and his copilot went through their steps like clockwork. Five hundred fifty knots still meant three minutes until they leveled out.

Finally, Dane slowly edged the nose of the Lear up. The ground rushed at them and the pressure mounted in the seats of the pilots. For some reason Dane thought of his Naval flight training. Next to eyesight, hemorrhoids were the most frequent cause of failure to pass a flight physical. He smiled as he thought of the two passengers. He hoped that neither was the one in three Americans who could not pass this test.

Brown, brown land with scattered green continued to rush up at them. A road streamed off to the North. What a desolate land! There was so much land! The United States would never be overpopulated. It would be a thousand years before anyone found the meteor hole that the Lear could have dug for itself.

They were nine hundred feet above the ground and two hundred forty knots before Dane gave over the controls. "No," he could not explain his fast reactions, "Yes," he was about to again check on the passengers.

"Mr. Arrow, permission to come back and check on you and the condition of the plane."

"No thank you Captain. I think I am perfectly capable of checking the craft. I believe my passenger friend is quite alright. What the Hell happened?"

Dane smiled. Nine out of ten passengers in a plane that did a half roll preliminary to a spinning dive, would have said, "Why did you do that?" Phillip Arrow did not think that way.

"The front left pane shattered and I thought we might lose pressure. Both are impossible if you have read the manual." Dane wondered at the children's game that they were playing. So Arrow was riding with a union hood. What else was new? It sounded to Dane that the deal was good for Arrow too.

If the Government was the one who was to foot the pension bill for the railroads, they would never let another union bankrupt Arrow Corporation if it were the parent company of the rail lines. Dane had had little business training, but at least he could think that through. Why did Arrow protest so much? For that matter, the union chief probably understood it too. If so, why was he insisting on the mergers?

"I have. Can you fly it like it is?"

"No Sir, we would do better to land in Albuquerque. I suspect that before I get this repaired, you could be picked up and flown on by another of our planes. I'll call now and have them fly in. They should be here in a couple of hours."

"No. You patch me in to Burbank. I want that second plane there in one hour. We should have someone close when we have a fleet of twelve corporate planes. I will just commandeer one. Being Chairman of the Board has to mean something."

An hour and one-half later, a sweating Dane Hughes was watching a second Arrow Lear take off toward the East. The switch of passengers had been made sight unseen to the pilots. Dane had a sick feeling that he had not experienced since Viet Nam. He could easily trace the laser drilled cuts on the pane's edges. Once Dane had flown with wooden blocks inserted in his flap cables. Once before, he had seen a laser bore. Navy pilots were too often downed by their own men.

Someone had wanted to take either Phillip Arrow or his passenger out. Arrow had told Dane to put a temporary in the Lear and take it back to Burbank. There, Arrow Corporation's security men were to go over the plane in detail. Dane set to work to dismantle the recording system and while he was at it, he planned to also take out his masterpiece. What a disaster!

Everett Lacey's masterpiece was also a disaster.

Lacey had just taken a first look at his program's results. The printer listing surprised him, or as he thought, should not have surprised him. Arrow had access to data bases that were shared by all the targets. No major expenditure or revenue item appeared to be confidential among the targets. These shared data bases created perfect correlations or relationships among the variables that he had entered. The targets had almost unlimited data on which they were perfectly matched. He would have to drop the names of the targets because they were messing up any results. What happened to competition in America, thought Lacey as he looked at the shared personnel data bases? It appeared that the targets rarely hired from another. Whenever one found an employee of another applying for a job, that application went into the data base which confidentially informed the employee's company of the individual's search. With all compensation data known, there was no way for the dissatisfied employee to test the market place, let alone find a job with one of the competitors. Take that back, thought Lacey, as he discovered a section on "Employee Trades." They did, after all, allow for some movement of human talent.

Lacey sighed with exhaustion. He would have to repeat the process on those data bases already reviewed. He quickly looked at the count of data covered and his eye caught on the data base names.

Program names, program command names and data base names are chosen randomly by humans. Often, one can learn much about the programmers or users by their name selection. Lacey had often seen the use of swear words in program addresses and had followed the history of the users or programmers who placed them there. It was most often a measure of their dissatisfaction with their work and a forecast of their tenure. This was not the case here. Someone was now using the names of private men's colleges in Arrow Corporation's confidential internal Executive Information System.

Lacey scanned the access codes next to these names. A singular code

33

stood out. Could it be Phillip Arrow, himself? No, Lacey looked to other data bases and saw the Phillip Arrow code. It was singular to the control terminal and the only one, besides Arrow's that he could identify. Lacey frowned. One question led to another. Arrow's code should be associated with all the data bases. Who would have a data base on Arrow's own system that would be restricted from even Arrow himself?

Lacey called up his program. He quickly deleted the names of the three targets from the variable list. The project was going to take longer than he had anticipated. He would review relationships among the players without regard to the acquisitions. And in doing so, he would pay special attention to the hidden data bases. Going to the Tolerance paragraphs, he increased the sensitivity to any data bases with this unknown code identifier. He started the program again and returned to the manual and visual review of Santa Fe Southern Pacific's computer system. What a mess! They obviously had not yet coordinated their computer systems from the merger of the Santa Fe and the Southern Pacific several years ago. If John Jamison was going to blend together three companies, he had some real problems ahead. Just these two companies showed problems that could not be solved.

Lacey wondered about the Jamison selection. It would take a tough son-of-a-bitch like Frank Turner, not a John Jamison, to make these mergers work.

John Jamison relaxed in his patio that looked west over both a pool and a view of the coast of Santa Barbara and further out over the ocean to the outlines of the brown cliffed coastal islands. The afternoon was delightfully warm, tulips and daffodils brightened the poolside. Jamison and his wife, Meg, had just sat down for an afternoon cocktail. He had waited until this time of day to tell her of his excitement and the promised fulfillment of all his working dreams. But Meg had been called away to the telephone and had motioned that it was one of the girls, probably just checking in for the week. They would soon both be home for the Easter Vacation and Meg was aglow to see them again.

John never took a day off during the week, but he had been in Los Angeles until late last night, his presence Friday night was required, as was Saturday, and Sunday was the trip to New York. A man deserves to spend one of his vacation days freely once in awhile, he thought, and besides, he needed the time to sort out his thoughts.

34

It had been a shock three weeks ago when he learned of Arrow's plans. Arrow was truly taking his company to a place of eminence alongside Exxon, General Motors, Ford and IBM. Arrow Corporation was becoming the working man's company and Jamison was proud to be a part of Arrow's ego trip, if that was what it was. But it was a small shock compared to that that had occurred late yesterday when Frank Turner indicated that he was his, Turner's, choice to become President of the new Rail Division and that Phillip Arrow had given his approval. What a surprise!

Frank Turner's description of his reasoning had been straight forward. As the Company's highest ranking personnel man, Jamison was best suited to handle the major task of the new rail division in that it would basically be a role of combining personnel, systems, and peoples' efforts with an eye to non-duplication of functions and the wasting of administrative resources. Arrow was convinced that economies of scale and great efficiencies could be derived from this combination of rail companies. Since Jamison knew the people of Arrow Corporation, understood the systems, and all the "ins and outs," he was the perfect man for the job. Arrow never fooled around when he acquired a company. The rail lines would have to conform to Arrow Corporation systems and not vice versa. Frank Turner had been succinct, the job was his; that is, he was the perfect man for the job, if he wanted it.

Want the job! This, thought Jamison, is what he had been waiting for for twenty-five years.

"Hello! A kiss for your thoughts. That was you number two daughter and all is well."

John Jamison jumped out of his thoughts. "Meg, dear, don't scare me like that. You know that my heart skips whenever I am surprised."

Meg had brought a new martini for her husband and she carefully poured it, neat, and added a twist of lemon. "Oh posh, you are over your heart palpitations. The Doctor said it was from stress. If you would/could only get some exercise rather than ride around in that company car of yours. We worry about you so."

"Well, don't. I have never felt better, ever."

Meg Jamison looked thoughtfully at her husband. While she kept to a regimen of exercise that kept her body young, her husband possessed no such habits. Hours in automobiles and accompanied snacks had left his body with a decided midriff bulge. While Meg could stand before a mirror and still see a flat stomach and shapely curves, her husband's body had shifted positions "Alright, I give up. John, you have been a basketcase all day. I know that you have wished to wait until now to discuss it. What is going on?"

"Honey, it is a dream come true. You know that administrative men never become presidents of companies. It is an unreasonable aspiration. Just one out of five hundred of the Fortune 500 Companies' presidents came out of general administration."

"What happened to Frank Turner? You don't mean that Arrow is going to make you Arrow Corporation's new President. Oh, John, I am so happy for you. But surely Frank Turner ...."

"No, no, no, Meg, that's not what I mean. Now you have got to keep this confidential. Only eight other people know of his total plans. Phillip Arrow is going to buy the three largest railroad companies in the West and combine them as Arrow Rail."

Meg was silent. Her smile had turned to a look of total incomprehension. "Why would Phillip Arrow want to do that?"

"Meg, there are many sound reasons. All these companies have huge corporate staffs. If they were combined, we could cut these total costs by two-thirds. These companies have much to share and they all have strengths. If one could use the best of each and discard the worst, there is the potential for huge cost savings. They also offer Arrow Corporation subsidiaries a break over the competition. We will, in effect, capture the western market in transportation. Our products should cost less because of our economies of scale. From a financial perspective which they emphasize Downtown, there are all sorts of advantages. Our stockholders will be enormously benefited. People-wise, we will be greatly helped. As you know, Phillip Arrow has cut all our training programs to the bone during the past five years. We are very short of middle management talent. Two of these companies have an excess. We can use their good young people in our other subsidiaries.

"No, John, that is not what I meant. I asked why Phillip Arrow would want to do this. What is it that could possibly motivate him? Does not he have enough money and wealth now? How could he have more recognition? He can not be searching for self-satisfaction. Does he have to do this to have the Company survive?"

"Meg, sometimes you surprise me. That sounds like a college lecture on a hierarchy of needs. I think Arrow wants power. Why

36

would he have made the acquisitions that he did in the early 1970s and late 1960s? He is just getting a second wind in his late sixties. I look for him to be going strong until he is eighty-six like Hammer at Occidental. By that time he will have Arrow Corporation right up there with General Motors."

"I guess I just don't understand the reason why an individual wishes to have an organization that large. Even they must know that that much power is corrupting. If competition is good for America, they must know that they are the opposite of 'good.' Are the Hammers of the world really happy?"

"Who cares? It is the system that we care about. America has no limits to the man who wishes to build an empire. That is what makes our economy tick."

"John, how can Phillip Arrow be doing all this by himself? Is not he employed by a Board of Directors who are in turn selected by the stockholders of a public corporation? I would think that they would have to approve these acquisitions."

"Well, 'Yes' and 'No.' 'Yes,' to the fact that the stockholders elect a Board of Directors who in turn employ the Chief Executive Officer. What has happened, though, is that the Arrow Board of Directors has shrunken in numbers of members over the past years, I believe, in anticipation of such a merger. We now have just six members. More will be added when the mergers are completed by accepting some of those now serving on the Boards of the acquired companies.

"It is 'No' to the fact that the members are really the choice of the stockholders. They vote for just those who are nominated. Of the six on the Board, one is Turner, another Massendale, and the third is Arrow himself. These are called 'inside' members since they also work as employees for the Company. Then there are two seventy-five year old gentlemen who fought with Arrow in World War II. They are both nursing home cases and are wheeled in to supplement their pensions with Director's fees. They are called 'outside members' and serve on the independent committees regarding audit and compensation. Even if they ever disagreed with Phillip, which they wouldn't, they could not outvote the inside members. As to the stockholders, those are the only names that they will ever see on a proxy ballot and the process to offer another slate of candidates is so complex that it is impossible to imagine anyone ever trying to do it.

"Phillip Arrow's personally selected management now controls the future of Arrow Corporation. The Board is nothing more than a rubber stamp."

"You said that there were six members, but you only named five."

John Jamison grinned his biggest grin. "That is right, there are now just five. There will be six when your husband goes back to work tomorrow and accepts the presidency of the new rail division."

Meg wanted to congratulate her husband, but if she did she knew that she too would be accepting the opportunity. She changed the subject, "Won't you be adding a tremendous amount of employees to Arrow Corporation's rolls?"

"You bet, we will grow by at least 150,000 people. Think of that, Mrs. Jamison, your husband is going to be President of a division with almost half the number of people in the State of Alaska and with corporate resources that stretch across all of western America!"

John Jamison closely watched his wife. He had to keep the conversation going, he could sense her hesitancy, her natural wariness. It was this damn house and community. Meg would resist any move. She had designed the house herself. He often felt that she loved her nest more than she loved him. "You might have asked what was going to happen when Phillip Arrow adds six new people to his Board, two from each acquired companies' Boards, all of which will be outside directors."

"What will happen?"

"This is just my guess, but the count as of tomorrow will be 4 inside with 2 outside and really 6 to 0 in favor of Phillip Arrow. As of a few months it will be 6 to 6. Our Board can be expanded to 15 so I expect the 3 children of Phillip Arrow to be added making the count 4 insiders, 3 children, 2 old friends, and 6 new outsiders. That will be enough to control the Board......."

Jamison was interrupted by his wife, "Why would you want the job?"

"Why would I want the job? You have got to be kidding! First, I will earn at least three times the salary and have a host of stock options. Second, I have been preparing for this all my life. Indeed, it is my life, it is my work, it is what people will recognize me for after I am gone. It is security forever for you and the girls. Please, Meg, don't be negative."

"I am not negative John. It is just that we have security. We have our girls, they are what we will be known for after we are gone. Who

38

ever remembers the name of any past president of any company after he is gone? We don't need the money."

"Look, Meg, all my life I have striven to be somebody. I will be honest with you. I can not help but think of my next high school and college reunions. I want to say, look, I made something of myself!"

"John, I can't believe you said that! Those people mean little to us. As adults we have to grow, not stagnate in personalities known thirty years ago. Why would you care what they felt?"

"I don't know. Perhaps it is just being a male. As a young man you are taught to be competitive, to win. Corporate life takes so long to play the game. It's frustrating, there is no way to prove your worth quickly."

"John, one never proves his worth by accomplishment. In life, you are what you are. I am sure God measures you day by day, not just at the end of some race, nor the end of some year. Your worth is not judged as a static measure. Your life is a span, not a spot in time."

"Meg, it is just not that. You take this competitive nature with you into a corporation. For people doing staff work, there is no outlet. Or the only outlet there is is to be competitive with the people with whom you work. That is destructive. Carried to an extreme, one finds corporations destroying themselves internally. So the only healthy thing one can do is to stay young, to relive high school and college life, to compete with imaginary devils such as those peers who have clearly changed from the competitive image that one carries."

Meg Jamison took her husband's hand. Did other men also think this way? Were all men this flawed? "Alright, John, I am with you. When haven't I ever supported you? I am sorry to sound negative. It's just that I guess I don't know all the facts. Honey, I am proud of you! We will be fine no matter what happens." Meg looked into her husband's eyes. She was admittedly confused by the conversation, yet her husband's eyes also showed confusion. Could he be as confused as she?

It had been a confusing day. Dane Hughes guided a low altitude return to Los Angeles. Who could have wished his Lear crashed? Everett Lacey stared at meaningless numbers on a computer screen. The more he worked and the more computer time he used, the further he seemed from any solid answers. Phillip Arrow sat in Dallas looking at credit of over twelve billion dollars for Arrow Corporation's acquisition binge. Who could have really guessed the ability to borrow such funds, what was the real reason behind the unions' greed? Caroline O'Brian sat in her office tracing the course of both yesterdays and today's meetings. Who could it be that had taken the position in the stock? She only knew that she could exclude herself. Lawrence Massendale was also confused. Where in the Hell had his golf ball gone? He had seen it slice over near the next fairway. Thank God for Frank Turner and his half day meetings! Finally, Frank Turner was also confused. Where in God's world did Everett Lacey go? Turner had walked down to Lacey's office at the day's end to mend a fence or two so he would be in the clear tomorrow.

Everett Lacey's non future at Arrow Corporation was assured. Turner had worked the scenario out in his mind. Lacey was Dead Meat! Caroline would see to that. Damn, where was he! Lacey had not returned after leaving for the morning meeting. Could he have been so mad that he went home? It did not sound like Lacey. What in the Hell could he be up to? Did Arrow have him on some other project? Turner made a note to make sure that he checked on that possibility before the group confronted Phillip tomorrow about Lacey's future with the Company. Right now he had to drive home to calm a wife worrying about tomorrow's corporate evening party.

3

Friday Evening

Phillip Arrow sat back and watched the side of the road as his limousine slowly wound its way up the Bel Air hill to Frank Turner's home. Arrow was tired. Too many matters to attend to in too short a time. Tonight he would have to turn his attention to shaping the management of the new Rail Division. He knew that he had been putting it off. John Jamison was going to be a problem.

Arrow sighed. What an afternoon! With acquisition targets' headquarters in New York, Chicago, and Seattle, he had been able to follow the developing reactions much like an old fashion time sequence movie. All the companies were calling in their favors, all were reacting almost as he had expected. His marching orders were simple. He would meet with any of their Chief Executives Officers next Monday. All other communication was to be directed to the law firm. No one from Arrow Corporation was to talk to the press. Indeed, none of the corporate staff was to take any telephone calls during the next week.

In a way, Arrow was surprised. He had forecast that at least one of the three companies would have been savvy enough to refuse to meet with his representatives when they announced their presence Thursday. Perhaps they were just curious. Arrow knew that he would darn well tell anyone showing up on a late afternoon to forewarn of a tender offer that absolutely no one was available. Smedts and Goldstein's people had probably lied to get their way in, or perhaps, they had set up the sessions long ago. Arrow searched back in his mind to think of who had suggested the Thursday tender offer forewarnings with invitations to visit in New York on Monday. Damn, was his memory failing him too?

Arrow was still seething. Los Angeles' major newspaper had published a morning review of his confidential plans. The *Journal* had done an even better job, although that was easily expected knowing the competition. Somewhere, somehow there was a leak from one of his staff. The information was too complete, too accurate. There were but eight people who knew those facts: himself, Massendale, Turner, O'Brian, Lacey, Jamison, Smedt, and Goldstein. The union didn't know the particulars of what had been published. It was a direct recounting of his plans.

Arrow could think of but one reason for the leak. It was intended to drive up the price of the targets' stock and the profit that Blarnef & Blarnef would receive. Damn them!

Phillip Arrow shook his tired head. The anger and fatigue were making his thoughts jump. The mental stimulation was like a drug. Without it, he went through a withdrawal. The constant, ever building, doses were just as destructive. He knew his life had no counterbalance.

Arrow missed his wife in times like these. Mary had died last year due to cancer. She had often helped him in the tough times. At least his three children were secure and happy. That was more than most company leaders could claim and perhaps, he could pull this off. Arrow thought of his two adopted sons, adopted by his wife and him years after their marriage. Shortly after the boys arrived, his wife had become pregnant. The doctor had told them that this was a commonplace occurrence. Mary Sue had been the result.

Phillip Arrow had often guiltily felt cheated that she had not been a son. No true Arrow blood was to survive with the Arrow name. All that was to have his name and blood in it was to be his Company. Strange how often he felt of the Company and its people as if it were his family of children.

Arrow again tried to concentrate. What bothered him the most at the moment? Could he set his priorities and deal with the most important matters first? He found that he could not.

He was still greatly bothered by the meeting demanded by his executive staff that afternoon. All had been present: Jamison, Turner, Massendale, O'Brian and their guests, Smedt and Goldstein. All had concurred. Everett Lacey was both the source of the leak and an inside trader. Lacey had to be fired.

Phillip Arrow had resisted. Their thinking was fuzzy. He could not remember such poor thinking from an executive staff. Who had tried to force his hand? Who was it who was pushing this slander, who had convinced the others that Lacey was the man behind the 400 million dollar position?

His staff's position was clear. Everett Lacey was the newest member of the staff, a relative newcomer when one looked at the tenure of the others. All agreed that neither of the New York firms would have taken such an amateurish position. They would have been far more subtle. Most damning to all present was that Lacey was not from their culture. Who could trust a Black who lived in a Black community in West Los Angeles? Lacey could have no loyalty to them or to Arrow Corporation.

Arrow had sat and listened. When all agreed, he chose not to disagree. He was silent and had waited. The suspense of who it might be to suggest that Lacey be terminated had built as each member spoke.

John Smedt had talked at length regarding Everett Lacey's friends. Several were in his business of investment banking. Smedt alluded to these men's poor reputations, their previous shoddy work, and the fact that none were connected with firms of Arlington, Bothell & Hyde's size and would thereby be far more likely to engage in illegal efforts.

Aaron Goldstein had dwelled at length on Lacey's background in Chicago. Since one of the targets was headquartered there, it made great sense that Lacey's college contacts were in play.

Lawrence Massendale had traced Lacey's early history, his start in life on a Louisiana sharecropper's farm. Massey never trusted a farmboy. It was his contention that they had a different set of ethics, that their standards were not the same as his.

Frank Turner had strayed to Lacey's Jesuit training with much the same argument that Arrow had heard a hundred times before. It saddened Arrow that Turner had such a blind spot. He had cut him short.

Caroline O'Brian had joined in the hunt. She traced the fact that Lacey was the one Arrow Corporation executive who had worked full time on the proposed acquisitions, that he was the most likely to have developed a scenario to take a position. Obviously, it had taken some time to acquire the targets' stock. The purchases must have started early. The stock trading volumes were not substantially above average for the past four months. Yes, she was certain that whoever was the culprit, the buying had started almost immediately. It had to be traced to Everett Lacey.

Only Jamison had been quiet. Arrow had waited. It was finally Lawrence Massendale who had suggested that the damage be minimized. Since a complaint filing with the Justice Department would be impolitical, they would best be rid of him. He suggested that Lacey be told immediately.

Frank Turner had leapt in to assist Massendale. If Massey would see that the legal aspects were attended to, Jamison could file the papers in the Personnel Department immediately. He, Turner, would be glad to deliver the word. He had stated that he looked forward to firing Lacey for his incompetence and treachery.

Phillip Arrow had resisted. He noted that Lacey was still working on a project or two. He asked them to wait until after the final briefing now scheduled for early tomorrow morning. It was a minor sacrifice and one that he could cover. Arrow knew that he had missed the clue to tell him who it was. Perhaps it was tied to Lacey's employment. Who had given him a job at Arrow Corporation when he first joined the Company? Who had given Caroline her first trial? He knew of Turner and, of course, Massendale's entries. Perhaps their actions in removing Lacey would still tell him the story. Unsaid, this reason had led to his acquiescence.

Arrow had often seen the pecking order at work in the corporate setting. Always, always, one person was selected by the group to be eliminated, "pecked" to death. It was now Lacey's turn. But within this blind aggression, didn't they know that once Lacey disappeared, one of them would have to take his place? And of course there was more. The best defense against discovery of one's part in a crime is to shift suspicion elsewhere. Who was the subtle supporter, instigator of the Lacey hunt?

It was indicative of the pressure that existed that a Black was taking the heat of the pecking order. At this corporate level, minorities were most often protected......or better put, still excluded from this part of the power struggle.

44

The car stopped and Arrow shook his head. So many related thoughts, yet so diverse. He had heard that when tired, the brain's organization of long neurons would let electrical impulses jump among adjacent brain cells. Nights like this told him how his brain was organized. He slowly climbed from the car. Frank Turner's home was far more grand than Arrow's. Sitting on the brow of the hill, it looked over the Los Angeles basin. A band's music drifted out among the trees from the back yard. It was a clear night, a night that oldtimers talked about when one could see for six miles across the Los Angeles basin. Arrow paused to let the evening's softness sink into his tired body.

Looking to his right he saw the Jamisons drive up behind his car. What a burden! Massey and his daughter were walking out the path to meet him. Obviously, his daughter, Mary Sue, had been looking for him. They had paused to say greetings to Dane Hughes and Caroline. What a job of flying he did yesterday! The word was that the asshole Arrow was riding with would recover, but only barely. Too bad! Turner and his wife were at the top of the steps. All the players were present. As Phillip Arrow was reaching to embrace his daughter, he was wondering who it was who had the right to expect the New York Stock Exchange to produce 250 million dollars in profit next week once the targets' stocks were allowed to trade.

"Dad, Oh Dad! Is it true? It can't be true. Massey told me all about it. I can't believe that someone could be doing it! I told Massey that I knew it was Caroline...."

"It's alright, Honey, it is alright. Let me look at you. You look great! Let's go attack this party, I am ready to enjoy myself." With a loving swing of his thirty eight year old daughter who had given him four grandsons and a nod to her husband, he started up the path. It was always a marvel to Arrow how this one daughter and he thought alike, and often thought of the same thing at the same time. Someday, though, he would throttle this son-in-law of his. 'Absolute confidentiality' was of unknown meaning to the dumb idiot. Arrow's anger boiled and he breathed slowly to control himself......Massey, Massey, Massey, we all agreed not to discuss the acquisitions with anyone.

Meg Jamison gasped and flushed with quick embarrassment. Phillip Arrow had swung about right in their faces as her husband started to introduce her to the Massendales and Phillip Arrow.

John Jamison was obviously flustered, "Meg, let's look at the roses before we go up. It will be awhile before the Turners have finished greeting those folks."

Meg smiled. "No, John, let's just go up to the door and introduce ourselves. It would look most strange to see people inspecting roses at this time of day and most conspicuous." As Meg led the way and reached back to pull her husband along, she thought of how conspicuous she felt. John had wanted her to wear something daring. She pulled her thin shawl about her as she felt her dress cut a little too low, her heels a little too high. Yet, this was to be John's night. She was proud of him and if he wished to be proud of her, it was a fair trade.

Meg felt totally satisfied and secure. She had driven down earlier in the day and checked in at the Bel Air Sands in a suite that John had reserved. With his having to be at the office at 8:00 tomorrow morning, it made no sense to drive home to Santa Barbara after the Turner get-together. It felt good to be out and independent and happy. She had laughed at the tall ladies in heels and the short men she had seen frequenting the halls of the hotel that Friday afternoon. When John had driven in from work for a quick shower before driving the short distance to the Turners, she had been ready. If a man strived all his life to "make it," then she was going to try to enjoy his success with him.

There was a crowd in the front hall when they reached the top of the stairs. The pilot she had met the other day and a very pretty date were standing talking to the Massendales, Turners and Phillip Arrow. It was Frank Turner who took the lead.

"John, here you are! Thanks for coming. This must be your beautiful wife, Meg. We met once before if you remember. Meg, do you know these people? Caroline? This is Caroline O'Brian and our chief pilot, Dane Hughes."

"Hello Mr. Hughes. It is good to see you again."

"My pleasure Mrs. Jamison."

As they shook hands and exchanged greetings, Phillip Arrow unexpectedly broke into the conversation. "If you don't mind. I don't want to spoil the party, but I have about an hour of business to cover with Ms. O'Brian and John here. It's about the coordination and control of the targets in the future and I find that my schedule allows no time for such a discussion during the next two days, and after that......well the die will have been cast. Now we can do it either later

46

this evening, or we can get it over right now and then party the night away. What do you say?"

Caroline spoke first as John Jamison looked to his wife, "Let's do it now. Dane, you don't mind, do you? Perhaps you can look after Mrs. Jamison."

"Oh, No, that won't be necessary." It was Frank Turner who stepped between Dane and Meg. "I have greeted about everyone who is to come. If they haven't made it by now, they can find their own way in. Besides, John will be answering to me now and I find it useful to get to know a man's wife. Come, let me show you around. Phillip, you can use the den down the hall." Turning to his wife, he said, "Dear, why don't you show them the way."

Phillip Arrow walked ahead and turned into the den. His thoughts were on his many acquisitions with such good people over the past twenty years. Where had they gone? Yet, he knew. Phillip Arrow had always liked more senior men to work for him. At sixty-seven he had to face the fact that his good subordinates had all retired or died. Now when he faced the greatest acquisition challenge of his life, or any man's life, what did he have ...... an untried aggressive youngster and a corporate bureaucrat. He closed the door behind them.

"Caroline, John, let me first apologize and then get down to business. It appears that the acquisitions could go much faster than I had ever expected. I find that the finances for our venture are unlimited and all available at a rate better than prime."

"The other day Frank Turner said that an acquisition is a 'bloody fight' and he will undoubtedly be proven correct. To handle such a situation one needs information and quick decisions. Caroline, the former will be your main role. John, yours will be in carrying out the decisions. Now, I plan for a threesome management team. John, you will head it up in name only. Frank Turner will have any final say, when he is on the site. Caroline, you are the spy."

"Sir, what do you mean, I will be a 'spy'?"

"It is a ruse I have often used in a takeover, Caroline. John will be given the title and the targets' people will look to him for decisions. You will have unlimited access to the companies and wander around a great bit. Both of you will have the goals of coordination and consolidation. I am more interested in people and organization structure than I am in their accounting. We will flood them with auditors and accountants and concentrate on trapping what any business is all about - either the making or selling of a product or service. Remember that all the rest is superfluous. Don't get confused or waste your time with the bean counters of the world.

"That's not to mean that you won't have clout. John, if she says something or someone should change or go, I will expect that they will be changed or gone. No arguing or questioning, understood?"

"Yes Sir!"

"Now I want to carefully go over the probable course of action of the next two weeks, but first, let's discuss a few personal items. Caroline, I just raised your salary to $80,000 and Frank Turner suggests that we hold you there and give any extra reward for a job well done in the form of a special bonus when the acquisitions are organizationally integrated. It will, however, be a promotion with a title change to Executive Vice President of Special Projects. Is that acceptable?"

"The period of time sounds rather fuzzy and what type of bonus, cash or stock and will any of the payment be deferred?"

"Cash, say anything up to 100% of your salary. It would be paid by this time next year."

"Agreed." Caroline accepted the offer with a slow nod of the head. She had been hoping for a better title and a much higher salary along with stock options. She struggled with her keen disappointment. It was no time to negotiate. Phillip Arrow would never forgive her for asking for a pay increase in front of an audience. At least she would have some consolation in the fact that he would probably take the chance to hold Jamison down too. She saw him turn to John and smiled. She was not going to be disappointed.

"John, you are more of a problem. Let me see, I think you make $170,000 plus a bonus. That's just not enough for the structure. The position of Rail Division President with three subsidiary Presidents reporting to it has to earn at least 25% more than the highest of those three men. As you know, we will have to raise several of those salaries to keep those people on after the acquisition. Both Frank Turner and I see your slot as worth a $650,000 salary and a bonus equal to 60% of that amount, along with the usual stock options, limousine, clubs, etc. Is that acceptable?"

"Yes Sir." Jamison sank into a fog. He had to run to the bathroom, he had to tell his wife. Surely, Arrow could not mean to keep him here for an hour. What could he possibly talk about? Caroline handed him a thick, bound report, one of three that she had taken from her stylish briefcase that Dane Hughes had teased her about as she walked up the path. Obviously, this time she was well prepared for her hour with Phillip Arrow. He watched her cross her beautiful legs. Embarrassingly, he also had to cross his. It was going to be a long, long hour.

Dane Hughes was already on his second Plymouth gin, straight, on the rocks with a twist of lemon. It was a corporate staff party with the top outside people, lawyers, bankers, accountants, suppliers and other big shots with whom Arrow Corporation dealt. Dane had yet to see another pilot with whom he could talk. Obviously, Caroline was his ticket. Dane was sorry that Turner had imposed himself on Meg Jamison. At least Dane would have had someone with whom to talk.

"You are certainly looking sorry for yourself." It was Everett Lacey.

"Lord Lacey, you look terrible! What's wrong with your eyes? They are bloodshot. Hell, I can even see black under your eyes."

Lacey put an arm around Dane and gave him a hug. "You have the damnest ways with words. What I need to do is sit down. Do you want to shoot the bull for awhile? Come on, I have found the place where we can get away from this throng."

Lacey turned and walked out of the room and down a long hall, turned and then down another. He stopped at a french door, opened it, and led Dane to a small patio that overlooked a hedge and a walkway from the backyard to a side pool. This second pool was an exercise, lap pool, no more than six feet wide that stretched from the right of the patio up to a bath or guest house behind the wide garage. Obviously, this was where Turner stayed so fit. Lacey slumped into a patio chair.

"O.K., Ev, what have you been up to?"

"My man, I have been married to a computer for 30 hours and I know less than when I started. I worked all night and quit around 2:00 this afternoon to go home and get some sleep. I hear Turner is looking for me and is fighting mad. He wasn't at the door when I came over tonight. I had been dreading that."

"That doesn't sound like an answer to my question."

"It doesn't? Sorry...the question...well, you see once upon a time a farmer was going to buy three special little pigs, but one of his children purchased the pigs before he got there and then had the pigs sold to his Dad at a higher price. What created value was the son knowing that his Dad was going to buy three little porkies that day."

"You are talking about the tender offers. Don't tell me that one of Arrow's sons has taken a position in the companies that I heard about this morning and what I understand this party is all about.

"No, I don't think it was one of the children. I don't think they had the information. It is screwy. The whole acquisitions are screwy. Nothing makes sense. I know one thing for sure. Ev Lacey is through with this Corporation. My secretary told me that her friend in Personnel had to type a termination appraisal this morning. My name was on it."

"Who would fire you? Arrow likes you."

"It is not that type of termination. As I understand it, I have resigned and been given three years salary. It will be their first offer. They sure as Hell don't want a suit from the only minority on their management staff."

"Only minority? What about Caroline?"

"Dane, that's not what I meant. Women don't really count on the affirmative action scale. I am done, kaput! It is Frank Turner. I did something that really offended him. He must have seen my access code all over his files this morning. That will teach him to have hidden files in Arrow's confidential system."

"Why would Turner get rid of you?"

"He is the child who is buying piggies. It all makes sense except none of the facts fit. He is obviously in line to be Arrow's replacement. There is absolutely no personal connection between him and the investment firm, or none that I can find. I can't even confirm that the hidden files are Turner's. It's a mess! I get the feeling that I am getting an image, but not even close to seeing the picture. There is something a Hell of a lot bigger than what I can see going on out there. Anyway, I think I am going to tough it out for a while. I have no place to go, even if there is a severance pay package. I think that I am going to make them fire me. One might as well go out in style.

"Ev, maybe I can help you out. Look, I trust you like a brother. Let me tell you of what happened yesterday on the flight to Dallas, but first I have got to tell you how I heard the information. My livelihood is at stake, just like yours on this. Will you pledge not to tell anyone of the source?"

"Dane, if you have to ask that question, you can't be sure of even yourself."

Dane admitted the fact and then quickly told Lacey of his bugging the Lear's recording system. Lacey sat in cold silence. He was more astounded at the recording system than at Dane's liberty with the equipment. Then came the story of the flight, the discussion of the pension liabilities and potential union claim of Arrow Corporation assets, the mysterious guest, the arrangement of financing for the acquisitions, and the sabotage and near crash on the New Mexico desert.

"That's a good story. Let me think a bit on it. Get me another drink and let me look at the view."

Lacey was silently staring at the Santa Monica mountains as Dane returned. "Well, you are right about the potential importance of those liabilities. You see, it's even more complicated than what you heard. Two years ago, the Nation's accounting gurus decided that they should be reporting such liabilities on corporate balance sheets. That means companies like International Harvester and others would have a negative net worth just because of single employer pension plans' underfunding, let alone multiemployer. Arrow Corporation won't fare much better if the Financial Accounting Standards Board's proposed opinion is expanded to include multiemployer plans. This proposed new ruling could ruin the Company, even if the unions never make a claim. Just the exposure will ruin Arrow's stock price. And although not yet accepted as an accounting rule, it will someday be accepted. You can be sure of that.

"You see, all any company will have to report is an underfunding number given to them by the unions. Under ERISA, a contributing company has no right to request the underlying information, let alone review an actuary's work papers. ERISA allows only employee participants to request a summary and a plan document. Hell, I have seen actuaries come up with any number that is needed or requested! The Central States Teamsters' Plan has increased by as much as three billion dollars in underfunding from one year to the next. Think of that, three billion dollars! What we are seeing is a set-up where union pension funds will be able to either ruin or enhance a company's earnings per share and hence control the company's stock price. One doesn't need much more control than that to control any corporation."

"What solution is there?"

"None right now. It is a bad law that hurts business and helps the general population. I expect that in the future we will see it take our stock to rock bottom. Still, that doesn't answer the question of the

51

night, that is 'What the Hell is happening?' I am rambling a bit, let's quietly sip on our drinks and think about it for a bit longer........if you have the time and don't mind."

"No, I don't mind. It will be 30 minutes or so until Caroline is out of her meeting."

Sitting silently on the raised patio behind the shrubbery row, they looked west into the night only to be disturbed by two voices of individuals whom they could not see. The couple stopped immediately below them as they looked at the lap pool and the western view. The voices were those of Meg Jamison and Frank Turner.

"Here's the spot I wanted to show you Meg. Thanks for agreeing to let me call you Meg. It will make what I have to say easier. You don't mind if I am forward with you, do you?"

"No. Do you exercise here often?" Why was it that she wanted to run away from this man? Meg now felt the light breeze across her exposed skin, her senses were tensed.

"Every chance I get. Meg, I wanted to show you this spot for another reason. It allows me a chance to get you aside and talk to you of your husband's new assignment without anyone interrupting us. You know, I find you most delightful to talk to. Any man would be proud to have someone as intelligent and beautiful as you for whom to work. I see why John wants to provide you only with the best."

Meg's stomach churned. What was he about to say? How she wished she could tell him that John was not the man for the job. Yet she knew her husband. Not to get this assignment now would kill him. This was the culmination of his professional life. Perhaps even if he failed, it would be a success. He could still this hunger in himself. She restrained herself. Oh John, how could you want any job so badly?

Above her, Dane Hughes was restrained. As he started to rise, Ev Lacey had put his hand on his arm. Dane looked at his Black friend in the dark. How often had his people silently gone their own way?

"Do you know what you husband will make, beginning tonight?"

There was no answer. Meg Jamison looked out across the mountains. Did not this man who exuded aggressive charm know that an increased salary meant little to her?

"I believe we settled on $650,000 a year as a salary. John should make more than a million dollars this year with his bonus. Of course, there are also stock options and other benefits. In short, your financial security for your and John's and perhaps the lifetime of your children will be assured. It's a once in a lifetime chance. The only open question is where his corporate office is to be. I suspect that it will be back East. But what I am most interested in is whether you, Meg, are willing to pay the price that your husband is."

"Oh, I don't know. John had not talked about moving back East. Our girls are both back there, but......."

"No, that's not what I meant when I said 'paying the price.' You see, John reports to me. I make the decision whether he is through or continues. Tonight when we announce his promotion, we will announce the promotion of the replacement for his present position. You see, there is no place for John back at Arrow Corporation should he fail in the Rail Division. I and I alone control your husband's corporate destiny. What I was asking was whether you understood that."

Meg Jamison fought for her breath. She had never expected to be attacked like this. Frank Turner's voice had turned hard as steel. Meg felt weak in the knees and leaned forward on the path's guard rail. Why had she allowed him to fix her a second drink? She knew that she had been nervous and too chatty. It was the party and Turner's sure presence. A chill of goosebumps covered her body on this warm night as she suddenly felt Frank Turner's hand. She froze in her fear as she felt his hand move across and up her dress. Why did she wear a dress cut so low, heels so high? Had she invited this? Why did she not react or resist. Was she frozen in her fear? Could she offend him?

"You see, Meg, after years of leading people, I find that corporate wives either make or break their husbands' careers. They either understand or do not understand the sacrifices. Now you are as beautiful a wife as I have ever seen, but I sense that you have always been sheltered. I ask myself if you have any idea of the mental suffering that your husband will pay to hold his present position. I question whether you have the experience and whether you really want your husband to be successful."

Frank Turner moved close along the rail and forced Meg to twist her body around. "On the other hand, you do have great style. This dress is most attractive, especially right here."

Meg reached for Turner's hand and was greeted with pain. She gasped.

Turner's voice had turned to a low series of clipped commands. His body was pressed hard against hers.

"Now listen and listen closely. You have two choices. Be a meek, mild lady and walk back across the lawn to the party to your soon to be unemployed husband or be a vivacious, happy woman and meet me in the guest room down at the end of the pool. Your choice is like your husband's. Either you do everything and anything I say, or you get out of Arrow Corporation. If you stay, you stay of your own free will. I don't care to put up with recriminations, sorrows, or demands. I expect efficient, pleasing, and talkative associates who do everything and anything I ask of them. I will wait for you there for only five minutes. It is totally your choice."

Ev Lacey released his grip on Dane's arm. Dane's mind was in a roll. The situation was no different than yesterday over New Mexico. Danger had to be met by action, there was no other way. Lacey shook his head. Dane caught the thought. If Meg Jamison walked across the lawn to the left there was no problem. Relax Dane, relax, he told himself, yet he knew he should move. So what if it was 'Good-by Job,' there would be another, but would there be another Caroline? What about Lacey's job? Wasn't Meg Jamison a grown woman? She should be able to make her own decisions. It was obvious to Dane by Turner's tone that he was playing a bluff.

The seconds on Dane's illuminated watch slowly ticked away, then the minutes. There was no sound from below the patio. Almost three minutes thought Dane, perhaps she had silently crept away across the lawn.

Somehow Dane felt that time was suspended. The blackness of the mountains, the glow of the City to his left and right, and the sound of the soft band music combined in a timeless way. Dane looked at the faint stars, the bright pin points of planes circling for LAX, and smelled the soft perfume of magnolia and honeysuckle. Dane Hughes felt his body relax. Nothing could go wrong on a night like this. Evil could not exist in a heaven.

Dane first heard the sound and then felt the first chill of the night, yet he sat still. Time and youth appeared to slip away together in the soft night.

The quick, then hesitant, then quick "click, click, click, click" of Meg Jamison's high heels on the concrete to their right was heard and then .... silence. They had both heard the open, waiting door close.

Dane felt suffocated, he willed himself to breath. Lacey whispered, "Somehow, I feel sick. I am going to go make my presence known in front of Mrs. Turner so she can report me present and accounted for and then I am going to go home and get some sleep. Why don't you do the same? See you."

Dane rose after the departed Lacey and slowly walked back into the house. Caroline was still in her meeting. He walked to the front door to leave word with the Doorman to tell Caroline that he would be in the backyard. As Dane approached, he saw the back of Lawrence Massendale as he talked to a sobbing woman.

"Mrs. Smith, get hold of yourself. You are not being lucid. I asked that I be called when you arrived if you looked at all upset. This is an important party for Arrow Corporation. All our friends and our associates are here. We just can't stand to have anyone here as distraught as you are at this moment."

The answer was almost a whisper. Dane had to strain to catch her words. ".....but I was invited. My husband was invited. I brought the invitation."

"But Mrs. Smith, you were not invited to tell the Los Angeles Police Department to call at our offices this afternoon. That was most outrageous of you. We know that your husband is missing. We also know that there is no reason to be upset. We know that he enjoyed other ladies."

"That is not true!" The woman, who Dane quickly guessed was Richard Smith's wife, screamed at Massendale. She then fought the two security men who grabbed her from either side and began leading her down the steps. Dane noted her dress. She had obviously been invited and had dressed for the occasion. What had he missed in the early conversation? Perhaps he could assist this plain, sobbing woman.

"Mr. Massendale, may I help?"

"Yes, get the Hell out of here and mind your own business!"

Dane looked first at the glowering Lawrence Massendale and then at the departing Mrs. Richard Smith. At 6' 4", Massendale's nervous slender frame was well conditioned from his daily running. Dane shared no such love of pounding his body. He did, however, use his daily exercise time to work on quickness and strength. Massendale would be no match for the quick sure blow Dane now resisted throwing at his groin. It would be months before Massendale recovered.

Instead of releasing his blind fury, he turned again to the Doorman and mentioned his destination. Massendale would have his day if there was justice in this world. As he walked away, he remembered the words of his father. "Don't expect justice in your lifetime. Justice occurs, but only over a span of history. Defend yourself, take a shot when you can, but ignore most harm done to you. To do otherwise is to spend one's precious life chasing shadows." Massendale would probably go to his grave unrepaid, thought Dane, as he tried to wipe the man from his mind.

Dane's anger clouded an unspoken question. It had all been so unlike Massendale. When had he developed a command presence like that?

It was a half hour later, as Dane made his twentieth turn around the huge yard, reminding himself of a crazed dog, that he was caught off guard by Caroline storming into him.

"That God Damned Frank Turner! That mean, woman hating, chauvinistic son-of-a-bitch! I will have his balls before I am through!" With those words, Caroline pulled Dane behind a nearby evergreen. "Here, that's what I think of him."

Dane felt his sturdy solid frame pummeled by angry fists battering away at his chest. Strange, that it felt so good. He let Caroline storm away. He looked into her eyes. She was not crying. Dane thought he saw his reflection in her determined madness. As long as he could stand, he would take her energy. Suddenly she stopped. She stepped back and looked at him closely. "What's the matter?" Gasping for air, Caroline had finally noticed that Dane welcomed her blows.

"Nothing. I suppose that I have the right to ask the same question." Dane smiled. How this beautiful woman excited him!

"Yes, you do and I will tell you. That damn Turner convinced Arrow that I shouldn't have a raise. Do you know what they are going to give John Jamison, well do you?"

"Probably around $650,000."

Caroline looked at the smiling Dane Hughes. What a strange man. She'd have to break down one of these days and give him a night or two in Las Vegas. What a lucky guesser! For a dumb uneducated non-MBA, he did alright at times. "That's close enough. Hell, it will be a million dollars before they are through! And you know what they are paying me. $80,000 for having what is truly a more important job! I know that's a lot of money to you, what, about twice what you make, but it is nowhere near enough for what I do. Shit, I bet Lacey even made more!"

"I wouldn't think so." Dane noted her use of the past tense. She knew of Everett's fate, but she had not shared it with him. Didn't she trust him?

Dane looked closely at the flushed lady. What attracted him so to her? With her dress's high neckline, it accentuated her figure. Hair piled high on her head, she looked the picture of the modern corporate princess. It must be pure chemistry, he thought, nothing more than the attraction of senses.

Caroline leaned her head to the side. Her adrenaline was up and the night was soft. She looked around her. Behind the tree she made out the outline of a hedge and as she dragged Dane behind her she found a reclining lounge chair. "Come here you great big brute." Caroline prided her self control. She liked Dane's ardor, it tested her skill and self-determination and she knew she was building her strength to control all types of situations. She also knew it was tough on Dane's blood pressure, but that's why she had chosen him. He was strong, he could take it and perhaps the way she felt tonight, she would ......

"Announcements, announcements," it was Frank Turner on the band stand with Phillip Arrow standing beside him. "Could you ask all those in the house to come out and hear the news? Please, everyone gather around. Let me first tell you that any rumors you have heard are probably incorrect. We want you to be the first to know what is really happening, hence this party with your wives and our other friends."

Caroline brushed by Dane as she hurried to hear and see the speech. She did not notice his pulling back, his hesitancy, his total unwillingness, nor could she sense his revulsion. While she watched with anticipation, Dane visited the bar for straight shots that would hopefully wash away his physical and mental sadness.

Phillip Arrow stepped to the microphone. He waited a bit until people quit streaming out of the Turner house. In all, he guessed that there must be three hundred people in Frank's large back yard.

"As you may have heard, late yesterday afternoon Arrow Corporation representatives personally delivered invitations to discuss the tender offers in New York next week to three U.S. rail companies, the Union Pacific, the Burlington Northern, and the Santa Fe Southern Pacific. In our planning, we have worked for weeks using the code names of Cardinals, Blue Jays, and Orioles so perhaps if you have overheard those names, we can now assure you that we were not planning an

57

aviary or a zoo." Laughter and applause interrupted his speech.

"Thank you. As you probably know, any tender offer is subject to great chances of falling through. We suspect that several of these may in fact not occur. However, we would assume that at least one will be successful and within the scope of the unique effort to bring together three systems, we believe the daring exists for a total success. We are thus planning for total success and not for failure of any type." Again applause and cheers met these remarks.

"We expect to proceed quickly with these offers. Our price is substantially higher than we had first planned. The verbal offers secretly delivered yesterday were a changed offer from the publicly announced tenders and will give all present stockholders of these rail companies a 60% premium. We see no way that present management of these lines, if they are truly representing the best for their stockholders, can now oppose our offers." Again there were cheers. Only Frank Turner and Caroline looked at all upset. Phillip Arrow had never talked to them about changing the tender offer prices. Had he gone mad? The prices were far too high. Interest would eat up most of the targets' earnings.

"What we are envisioning is a new railroad company of the West. It will be called U.S. Union Arrow, unless we think of a better name in the meantime." Again there was laughter.

"Like any new company, it should have new leadership. Bringing together three diverse companies will be a great adventure. From experience, I know that the greatest challenge will be in getting the 150,000 employees of these companies, along with our 100,000 employees to work together. I believe we have the man to do that job on our staff. Over the past years he has served in many 'people positions' and has handled each with great skill. He will need to draw on that skill like never before and I ask that you all cooperate with him. May I introduce to you, the new President of U.S. Union Arrow's Rail Division, Mr. John Jamison!"

John Jamison walked with pride to the microphone to a sustained applause. He was smiling his largest smile. He had just caught sight of his wife standing at the back of the crowd and he waved to her.

"Thank you Mr. Arrow and for all of us here tonight, thank you Mr. Turner for your gracious hospitality. Ladies and Gentlemen, I have but two things to say. First, I will do my best. Second, I owe all I have done and will do to my wife, Meg, who stands behind you ....."

that's right, over there in light grey .... wave Meg. She's bashful! Well, again, I will do my best in what are certain to be most exciting times. Thank you."

Phillip Arrow again returned to the microphone. "During the next week we will be having serious negotiations with each of the potential new partners of Arrow Corporation. For those of you here, please follow these guides. In effect, we are acquiring the firms, conquering them if you will. That has a bad sound and is poor for those companies' morale. Hence, I ask you that from this time forward, we term this acquisition a 'merger.' Agreed? It is to be a merger, although we will all know differently. Now these acquisitions.....er, I mean, merger partners....." Arrow's speech was broken by cheers and laughter.

"To continue, these merger talks will be most sensitive during the next weeks. May I ask you all to refrain from making any comment of any type to anyone about the tender offers? Usually, whatever is said is misconstrued by the press. Let's keep this all to ourselves until it is over. That will mean a few weeks of not answering our phones. Thank you and 'Yes,' as John Jamison so ably stated, Frank, we thank you for your hospitality."

Frank Turner took the microphone. "Thank you Phillip and for all of you, my wife and I accept your thanks and in turn give you ours. You know, it is a great honor to work for a company guided by a hand that dares greatness. For those of us who choose to be a part of such an experience, we trade security for the unknown. We learn, we share in ways that we never expected, and surprisingly, we are immensely rewarded by the newness and excitement. Please stay as long as you wish, but if I am not at the door to bid you 'Good Night,' may I thank you all now for accepting our hospitality. Tonight was truly my pleasure."

Ev Lacey sat on the side bench and watched Phillip Arrow walk down from the stand. Ev had not gone home, he couldn't. Some sense had told him that the announcements tonight would hold a clue. As he got up and headed for his automobile he shook his troubled head. Perhaps he did not understand what the game was or any of its rules. Who would ask 300 people to keep something secret? Who would offer a 60% premium for those companies stock? Whoever it was who had taken the early position would now be making 250 million dollars rather than 160. Who was it? Where did the unions really fit in? Who was the mysterious Dallas Lear passenger? Why John Jamison, why not Lawrence Massendale or Turner as the new Rail Division President? Who would wish Arrow or his mysterious passenger dead? Why did they use a method that had a good chance of failing? Why use Blarnef & Blarnef when other investment firms were available? How had Frank Turner found out about his snooping so soon? Was that code his? If so, where was the evidence? Why couldn't he find any telling relationships? Nothing, just nothing, made sense.

And most of all, Everett Lacey was wondering why he was being terminated from employment at Arrow Corporation. He had been ready to give his life to the Company.

4

Saturday

Meg Jamison drove into the Los Angeles parking garage and took a ticket from the automatic gate. The clock showed 10:30 AM and she had an hour and one-half to wait for John. The hotel room had been oppressive, she had to escape. Perhaps there would be a magazine or two to read in her husband's office.

She thought back on the evening. John had been ecstatic. He couldn't keep from talking. She had looked at her husband in the returning light of passing automobiles and had seen the flush of excitement, the thrill, the enthusiasm. How could she break that spell? Her choice had been her own. She remembered patting his arm in the car as he repeated every word Phillip Arrow had said to him. Perhaps all things work out for the best. Sitting back, she had vowed to forget her part of the evening and stay as far away as possible from her husband's new boss.

Meg was on the third level of the garage before she started concentrating on an available place for her car. The month before John had splurged on her in buying their only family automobile. Meg loved the yellow little German SL Mercedes. Next to her husband's huge company automobile which she just passed, it looked so small. She looked at the names on the garage wall, all were reserved although it was doubtful that these corporate holders of the parking spaces would be using them on a Saturday morning. Orderly to a fault, Meg had decided to park only in an unmarked slot. She finally found one next to an old battered, black truck on the fourth level.

She hadn't noticed the following automobile that pulled in on the other side of the truck. Meg spent a minute adjusting her hair in the mirror. There was plenty of time. Opening the door and standing, she straightened her skirt and adjusted the tie on her blouse. She closed the door and turned. It was then she saw the knife.

A long shining silver knife held by a black bearded Latin dressed in dirty blue denims. Meg backed a step and reached for the door. She felt pressure on her back. Catching a breath to scream, her thoughts were tumbled. Two of them. Oh please, just be after my purse.

A hand gripped her hair and pulled her head back just a fraction. The message was clear, the knife pointed at her neck. She was pushed forward by the unseen tormentor. The knife wielding boy, he was just a teenager, threw back the flap of the cloth curtain on the truck. Everything was happening so fast! A hand reached down between her legs to take a firm grip and lift. She saw the dirty mattress. No! She breathed to start a scream, the tip of the knife was at her throat......

"Boys, boys, what are you up to?"

It was a tall Black in a sportscoat, red tie, and light pants. He carefully took off his glasses and stored them in his left inside coat pocket, then he smiled. Standing 20 feet away, he slowly circled Meg and her attackers.

"This could get a bit messy, couldn't it?" The Black's right hand had not left the inside of his coat. "As they say in the movies, which one of you two is going to make this....... a 'memorable morning'?"

The two youths looked at one another and then back at the surprise player who wanted to ruin what was going to be an unbelievable morning prize.

There was no answer. Ev Lacey knew that he couldn't let a silence occur. It would be a demand on these two young hoods' part to take some action.

Everett Lacey had been late. Somehow his alarm had been turned off and he had failed to get up for the 8:00 AM meeting. The previous 30 hour stint at the computer and the brief nap, combined with several hours of wakefulness last night when he did get to bed after the party, all caused his oversleeping. Suddenly, as he slowly dressed, he felt it did not matter. They would listen to him when he got to the meeting, he would confront Turner, and life would go on. The best advice that Everett Lacey had ever received was from Phillip Arrow. Arrow had told him that if he ever had a coming event that was causing him stress, that he should try to deal with it immediately. Tough phone calls should be made in the early morning, not delayed until after lunch. Confrontations should be immediate, not postponed.

He had parked his car and closed the door when he saw Meg Jamison drive by in her conspicuous and expensive automobile. A battered green Chevrolet followed and Lacey quickly caught the intensity of the two occupants, the avarice on their faces. In a quick bound, he had been to the stairwell and raced up to the fifth level. If Mrs. Jamison drove by, he would stop her. Otherwise, he should be able to escort her from her car to the office. As he ran, he thought of how strange life was. He would not have recognized her, if it had not been for last night. He had sp cifically searched her out during the speeches after the Turner rush and had seen her poise during her husband's dumb remarks.

"Boys, don't just stand there. Let the lady go. Walk over to your car, get in, and drive away. I don't want to spend the morning explaining to people why you were wasted away. I don't need the hassle. Just bug off. Get out of here!" Lacey's voice carried with it the command presence that he had unwilling learned in the Army.

Indecision. One of the men looked at the other. The one with the knife motioned toward the car. Suddenly, Meg found herself standing free. She ran to her savior. He walked behind her and with his left hand pushed her up the ramp.

"Back out around by here and head down the ramp. Once you get in that car, all I want to see is the back of your heads."

The two Latins jumped into the car. Lacey had Meg almost to the top of the ramp before it turned to the fifth level. Should those two get smart, he had a chance to reach the stairwell. Damn women in high heels! She couldn't run down stairs, just up. Wearing high heels in a downtown Los Angeles parking garage must be something like going into a battlefield with your right arm tied behind you and a bull's eye on your shirt. He watched their car back up, stop, and drive down the ramp. Only then, did he breath a sigh of relief.

"May I thank you, oh may I thank you? Thank you so much. Why didn't you arrest them? Why did you let them go? I wouldn't expect you to shoot them, but surely they will try again. What about their next victim?"

"Mrs. Jamison, I know that you don't know who I am. I work with your husband at Arrow Corporation and saw you last night when your husband pointed you out to all of us. Congratulations by the way, you should be most proud. But first, I am not a policeman, second, I have no gun or weapon of any type and third, we would have been in big trouble if they had called my bluff."

"Oh my! Why didn't they?" Meg was feeling faint again. She grasped the man's arm as he walked her back down to her car.

"Oh, I expect that one of them had taken a course in Risk Analysis Statistics."

"What?"

"The study of probabilities of success and the attributed rewards associated. They have such easy pickings in Los Angeles that they did not need to try a crime where they could have been shot. Say the percentage of my having a gun was just 10%. They threw in the fact that I was Black and that if I were White, they would most assuredly not be fired on. But since I was Black - that is if they were me - there would be a 50-50 chance of my using a gun if I had it. 50% times 10% is a neat 5%. They faced a 5% chance of being dead.

"Whatever they were looking for from you wasn't worth the price."

Meg Jamison did not answer. Rather, she looked closely at this tall thin man who was now returning his glasses to his face to study the parked truck. He slowly walked around the truck and looked in the back. She caught his attention, "I don't believe I know your name."

"It's Everett Lacey, originally of New Orleans with stops at Loyola of Chicago and Notre Dame. I am also blind as a bat without my glasses, but I don't look half mean enough with them on. You know, it was strange that they were going to use this truck. Tell you what we will do, you get in the passenger side of your car and I will drive it to a place where they won't bother it again this morning. In the meantime, I might leave them some work."

Meg Jamison was sitting in her car when Lacey slumped in. She had watched him slash each of the truck's tires in her view and assumed that from the settling of the truck, he had done so on the far side. Lacey fumbled with the keys. "Haven't done that in a long time. That should give them something to do and attract some attention. Sure hope it was their truck." Lacey was smiling. "Will they try to

"Will they try to get back at you?" How could he joke at a time like this?

64

"No, I doubt it. But they will take it out on someone else who's Black. You see, Mrs. Jamison, what I don't think you realize - or I am assuming that you don't realize it because you do things like park on the fourth floor on an almost vacant Los Angeles parking garage on a Saturday when not one other car will drive by in an hour - you don't realize that Los Angeles is in a state of armed conflict."

Meg held back her reply. She was not used to either his tone or the rebuke. She immediately believed that she had found another of those minorities who had found success and turned his back on his brethren. As a Canadian Liberal, Meg believed that progress could only be achieved when all sectors of the society strived for the same goals. She listened intently as Lacey continued.

"L.A. is the new Ellis Island. We have over two million un-registered citizens of Mexico living within the City limits right now and we are adding over 5000 a day. Television has come to Mexico and their daring poor are saying 'why not?' California, after all, should be part of Mexico. The City of the Angels is a Hispanic city in origin. The U.S. sent an army to steal the land in 1846 or so. Bet you didn't know that it is Mexico's second largest city in terms of native population. Anyway, these new people have only one thing in common." Lacey paused.

"I give, what's that?"

"Oh, sorry, my mind wandered back to a computer program. Maybe I have been asking the wrong question. It should have been what they should have in common but do not. I have been looking for relationships among variables that exist. What is really important is whether they exist at all. Perhaps I don't have all the players identified."

"I'm sorry."

"What Hispanics have in common? They all hate the Blacks. Oh, I know that that is a generality and untrue, but the dislike exists. Look, the Hispanics really don't challenge the Whites. They don't take semi-skilled or professional positions, they don't live in suburbia. What they do is work for less than the minimum wage wherever possible and take the jobs traditionally held in this city by Blacks. Maybe you have seen some of the statistics. If violations of the minimum wage continue, there won't be a job left for the Blacks. Moreover, many White employers believe that the Hispanics work longer, harder, are smarter and more punctual, and are far more easy to control. Los Angeles has a major problem on its hands.

"You could soon find a million unemployed Blacks on your hands. There is no way out, there are just so many City jobs that can be filled. The market for the Black worker is disappearing."

"What you just said is that the Blacks hate the Hispanics."

"Well, Yes and No. I suppose that the word 'hate' is incorrect. It is more natural survival. The Blacks in this City are first cheated on education, so they really don't know how to deal with situations such as these. You see, the School Board has forgotten that education is really a self-discipline, possible only in an environment of discipline. Their campuses are battlegrounds of intimidation. Blacks don't have the opportunity to pursue the thrill of learning, a thrill possible only in a non threatening environment. There is a difference in the definition of 'dumb' and 'ignorant.' Whatever the system is, it sure is successful in keeping minorities ignorant. Native Mexicans have an excuse for being uneducated, my people have none."

"But aren't there other ways to become educated. What of television, community colleges, libraries......"

"Sure, libraries, there is a good example. Thirty years ago, the City of Los Angeles kept its libraries filled with books and open seven days a week for up to twelve hours a day. Now it is four days a week and some libraries are open only four hours a day. And more important, the Mayor is closing libraries, never to open them again. He started slowly and the rate of closings has accelerated of late. The reason for the closings is that the savings on books, facilities, and salaries for college educated folks can then be freed for funds for innercity jobs. Hell, L.A. City's management brags of receiving money from developers from the sale of closed library facilities. Our schools are doing the same. During this same period, they have doubled their downtown workforce. Hell, the City's schools have just as many twelve month non teacher employees as they do teachers."

Meg thought that he was rambling. Could he have been as scared as she? "I suppose that it is a matter of setting priorities."

"Sure," answered Lacey, "but think about it a minute. We live in a community where libraries are closed so people can eat. Soon we will be burning books so that they can stay warm. That is not my idea of civilization. That is not the type of help that my people need. Now how did we ever get on this subject?"

"I don't know but I like it. Who has an answer to problems of people? I suppose that like all cultures, time will favor those groups who have the most children. I think that you are a little to harsh on your City." The auto's driver turned slowly to look at Meg and study her face. Had she insulted him?

"You could be right. You know my most fervent wish? It would be that all the suburban housewives of this area would admit to the fact that they are afraid of the minorities. When you talk to them, they are liberal as Hell. When you look at the place where they demand that their husbands live, they are phony as Hell! Hopefully, in a hundred years peoples' fears will make no difference, no difference at all."

Meg could not let that go unanswered. "What you have been saying is that you have yours, you will let the rest eat cake."

Ev Lacey had pulled Meg's car into a slot marked for Phillip Arrow in front of the Arrow Corporation building. He walked Meg over to the guard and introduced her as the wife of the new Rail Division President. Arrow wouldn't be needing the space this morning as he had used his limousine. At the door, Lacey shook her hand and asked the receptionist to direct her to Mr. Jamison's office. Meg mumbled a word of thanks, but Lacey had already turned and was bounding to the elevator. Quickly to the top floor, he paused at the door of the Boardroom and then ran on down the hall. Eat cake, he thought. A typical comment from a housewife.

The Boardroom was stuffy and the conference table was littered with coffeecake and empty coffee cups. For some reason the air conditioning was not working well this morning and Frank Turners, Aaron Goldsteins and John Smedt's cigars were hazing the room to a point where the inside air looked like the outside air. It had been an excruciating three hours. Phillip Arrow had forced them to go over, for what seemed the hundredth time, all the planned steps of the acquisition. He had asked questions that he had asked before. The three scenarios were repeated again in summary.

Frank Turner looked at his wristwatch. If he weren't feeling so fit this morning, he would have been cutting up the conversation. But as it was, if this were how Phillip Arrow wanted to spend his Saturday, he would oblige. Throughout, he too had been interjecting questions. The conversation had been at two levels. Arrows, Goldsteins, and his mind had raced through alternatives with Smedt and O'Brian playing catchup. Massendale had grown quiet as he had finally recognized the pace and a careful, smiling John Jamison remained silent. Turner grinned, to Jamison the pace meant nothing.

"Good," said Phillip Arrow, "That covers the plans as I desired. Let's see, it is 11:30. What say that we all go grab an early bite to eat and return at 12:30 to cover the targets' possible defenses. In the meantime, I want someone to see if they can find Everett Lacey. Call him on the tennis court or wherever. I thought that I had indicated that he was specifically to be here this morning." Arrow had turned to address these remarks to Frank Turner. "By the way, has anyone learned anything about the newspaper leaks?"

Frank Turner appeared not to have heard Arrow's last question. "No Sir, that was John Jamison that you mentioned regarding the Thursday and Friday meetings, but I too thought Lacey would be here. Just so you understand, it was Lacey who was suppose to develop the list of tentative defenses. If you remember, his original proposal had such a section. Caroline, will you be able to fill in?"

"Not completely on such short notice. To be quite candid, Sir, Lacey stormed out of our first meeting on Thursday and did not return. I personally thought he was totally unprepared for the questions that were asked of him. I am sure that he hasn't heard of your decision."

Arrow's stare made her continue, "It looked suspiciously like he just got mad and perhaps Frank doesn't have to worry about terminating him. On the other hand, he may have heard of the upcoming dismissal."

"I totally agree with Caroline, Phillip." It was Frank Turner. "What do we really know of him anyway? He is one of those tough Jesuit trained types. I have found Jesuits to be well trained, disciplined, and excellent businessmen. Their problem is that there is nothing wrong with them lying to you if you ask them a question as a Gentile which you have no business asking. If that is the case, they are free to tell you anything. I just have never trusted him. Good riddance, I say!"

"Since you are all picking on poor Lacey," added Lawrence Massendale, "I suppose that I too would say that he hasn't earned our trust and perhaps never will. I have never met a Black who didn't really hate Whiteys. Think of what he must tell his Black friends. No, I don't think that we would have ever be able to trust him.

"And to answer your other question, no one has reported to me, anything new about the newspaper leaks. We are paying to see if we can buy the Los Angeles reporter who broke the story. No one here seems to have heard of him, he is new from the Chicago area. I might note for the record that this morning's paper had nothing new. It is as if whoever was the leak, did not make the Friday meeting. That leaves just one possible suspect," concluded Massendale, "Everett Lacey!"

"Blarney," replied Phillip Arrow as he looked to see if they sensed his anger. "Alright, let's just try to find him. I suspect that with the talent here this morning, we should be able to cover all the alternatives. I suppose that in retrospect, Mr. Goldstein, we should have kept at least one copy of his original report when we denuded this building of all material in any way connected to, or which referred to, either the Cardinals, Orioles, or Blue Jays." Arrow caught the quick flinch of Aaron Goldstein who he had suddenly included in the conversation. If his observation was correct, Aaron had been spending the last thirty minutes mentally undressing Caroline O'Brian. Arrow had to get away from this miserable group of youngsters for an hour.

Arrow slowly walked down the hall toward his office. It was strange how such an effort affected him these days. To think of having to use energy to walk! Suddenly, he stopped. Perhaps he could find a reference on takeover defenses in his Information System, in fact he knew he could. Walking quickly, he entered his office and switched on his desk terminal. The screen showed 'IN USE - SYSTEM MASTER TERMINAL OVERRIDE.' What was going on?

Phillip Arrow purposely strode out of his office to walk down the hall to the Executive Computer Room door. A guard stood at the window. "Is anyone in there?"

"Yes Sir, Mr. Arrow, Mr. Lacey is working in there."

"How long has he been there?"

"Since just awhile ago. Here's the log."

Arrow bent over the log's record which also showed the activity of the past week. Hell! Lacey had been living in there. Arrow smiled. Everett Lacey was a damn fine man, probably the only one on the present staff with the true potential of successfully running his Arrow Corporation. If he were only fifteen years older! Phillip Arrow did not worry about Lacey's seeing his personally protected files - no, Lacey must be after something else. Arrow smiled in anticipation. Lacey's mind could run as fast or faster than his. He'd have to keep Lacey off guard and motivated to use it.

"Let me in."

"Yes Sir."

Ev did not hear the door open. He looked up into the stern face of Phillip Arrow amid the clatter of the printer and the glow of computer screens. "Good Morning Sir. How are you?"

"Fine, Everett. Hope you are the same. What are you doing?"

"Sir, I have been trying to figure this all out and I am especially interested, as you know, in who is accumulating the targets' stock. I might add, Sir, that I know the penalty for my unauthorized access and the fact that I was terminated yesterday. I have even checked my records to confirm it. It was surprising that Mr. Turner did not have my access code cancelled this morning, so I took advantage of that fact to see what I could while the equipment was available."

"Maybe he won't terminate you, I will. But you did not answer my question, or perhaps it was badly stated. How are you doing and have you found anything yet?"

"Sir? Uh, Yes Sir, I have found bits and pieces, but nothing that makes sense. Let me be disciplined about this. One, there appear to be hidden files existing not accessible to you. Second, I find that all the targets' share everything, I mean everything. The reason I came in here this morning was because a lady gave me a clue. You see, not one of the targets has a file on Arrow Corporation, yet they have known of the possibility that we could be acquiring their stock for two months. My conclusion is that they have some hidden files also."

"Or no files at all. What I would do is never put that type of information on the computer."

"Yes Sir, but I think I have found what they have done. Somehow they have learned that we have access to their systems. The critical information is disk protected, that is a hard disk that is only accessed at certain times when they probably pull every power plug except the main power in their buildings. It is a technique developed at Rand whenever they work on energy related problems."

"That should not bother us as long as we know that access time. We should be able to drain their entire information in seconds."

"That's right. Uh, third, I find that the Cardinals have historically retained Shaffer, Schwab & Meyers as their legal counsel on merger and acquisition defenses. I accessed Shaffer, Schwab & Meyers' computer accounts receivable system and pulled up this printout of an example Cardinal billing. They have been very active during the past two months, in fact billing over $200,000, for 'Provision of Takeover Defenses.' Obviously, Shaffer, Schwab & Meyers have been playing

70

both sides against the middle. What do you make of it, Sir?"

"It's probably the Cardinals' major defense. At the last moment Aaron Goldstein will pull a disappearing act claiming conflict of interest. Any chance of our getting a copy of their preliminary and final report submitted to their client? It has to be in there somewhere."

"Yes Sir, it is coded to their billing and I have already pulled it electronically from their word processing hook-up. I routed it downstairs to the high speed printer. It should be ready now if you wanted to pick it up. My job name was 'Tiger' and the number was EX211." I also pulled up and printed any correspondence from them to the Cardinals. That's also part of that job number."

"Anything else? Any idea of what the other two might be doing for defensive purposes?"

"Sir, I don't have a clue regarding the Orioles. They are a complete mystery to me. It does appear, however, that the Blue Jays have looked to a White Knight. As you know, we keep a listing of all the chief executive officers' unlisted phone numbers of the major U.S. and foreign corporations. Look at the use of the phone from the Blue Jays' front office. That matches perfectly with, let's see, that one, your friends out of St. Louis. I suspect that they have that Company ready to step in and offer a higher bid or perhaps they are doing what Carter, Hawley, Hale did and selling off, on an option basis, the best parts of their organization. I think that's it."

"Interesting, but not conclusive. That's not evidence like a law firm's billing invoice or copies of their reports."

"No Sir, but I do have one other bit of information. Here are the records of the St. Louis travel agency that handles all their business and all those who have taken a trip to the Blue Jays' home city. I have selected their top two people, see ... you know them?" Arrow nodded his head. "I accessed their charge card records. See? One uses this type and the other this. They are staying at the hotel near the Blue Jays' corporate headquarters. Finally, here's a records of reverse billings on telephone calls. You can see that they made them from the private men's luncheon club next to the Blue Jays' headquarters to what appears to be the subsidiary they would be placing under option."

"All right. I believe, I believe! Have you made any progress on finding which one of us here are getting rich on all this?"

71

"No Sir. All that I have shown you I have done by hand while waiting for my program to sort out who might be controlling the investment. Here are my variables and their profiles including a code for a hidden set of files that won't come up when you call for all the files. As I mentioned, that is a real surprise. I just can't seem to make any sense of it or anything else for that matter."

Arrow closely reviewed the listing. It was using some type of mathematics that he couldn't even begin to understand. But he did have a suggestion, "Tell you what I'd propose. You drop John Jamison as a suspect and add my two boy children. No, I have no suspicions, maybe its just a Biblical response. As for Jamison, he's honest, that's why I chose him for the Rail Presidency."

"You chose Mr. Jamison? I thought Mr. Turner had that power to hire and fire."

"Who gave you that idea? Jamison will be around here longer than Turner. Ev, let me give you a piece of advice. You are so smart, so good, that sometimes you let your initial findings or impressions make decisions for you when what has happened is that you don't have all the information. Your conclusion is erroneous because you have the bad habit of trying to anticipate the mind and thoughts of your employer. A good example would be your future with Arrow Corporation."

"Sir, I truly would like to continue working for the Company."

"No, I don't think that best. Here is my proposition and why I allowed Jamison's office to prepare your termination papers. Beginning today, I want you to start your own consulting firm. Your first client will be Arrow Corporation under a five year contract at $100,000 per year plus all, and I mean all, expenses that you incur. In addition to this you will continue to get your severance pay. Arrow Corporation will give you free access to all its data, people, and equipment — such as this. If you need help, which I am sure you will, hire them and bill them as an expense. What I want from you is a simple monthly billing with two entries: fees for services and reimbursement required for all costs. Your task is simple, to find who purchased that stock. During that time if I discover who's buying some other way, you can come back to work for Arrow Corporation. If you discover who it is, it will mean a project termination bonus that will be double the total of any fees that you have received and the same offer to return. All this will be contractual, the letter is in my office written in my handwriting.

My secretary will notarize it whenever you wish to sign it. It is just between you and me and must be totally confidential. For the rumor mill around here, you have resigned and are just finishing up some work. Agreed?"

"Yes Sir. But I don't understand. Why do you have to fire me, have me terminated? Couldn't I do this as an employee?"

"Yes and No. If you stayed on as an employee, it would hinder your freedom. There would be executives who would demand to know what you are doing. Anything that you do wrong, such as an invasion of privacy, which I am sure will have to occur would place the Company at some jeopardy. No, I think it best that you be on your own."

Arrow shook a stunned Ev Lacey's hand and walked out of the room. He hoped that Lacey would survive. Heading a search for people behind an illegal 250 million dollar scam with an initial 400 million dollars invested could be unhealthy. He looked at his watch. Time had disappeared again as he made his way back to the Boardroom. The Tiger report would have to wait a moment or two.

Caroline O'Brian was standing at a flip chart with a list of acquisition defenses. "Sir, if I might begin."

"No, I don't believe that that will be necessary. Let's just skip the discussion of defensive strategies and go home and get some rest. Frank, I want you to spend some time with John Jamison and review what I went over with him last night. Otherwise, I suspect we have done what can be done. The planes leave LAX beginning at 9:00 AM. What I have here in this packet are commercial airline tickets for various flights on Sunday morning. After Thursday, I intend to fly our Corporate planes back only as a ruse. We will all go coach as is our standard Corporate policy, unless that is, you wish to upgrade at your own expense. Pick up your tickets as you leave. See you in New York tomorrow night. Sorry Caroline."

Sorry Caroline! Sorry Caroline! The thoughts were echoing in her mind as she rushed out of the room. Was Dane there? She could not remember ... that's right, he was going to meet her at two in the lobby and then spend the afternoon at a Dodger baseball game. To Hell with the sun and beer, they would have to find a bar!

Two drinks later in a dark cocktail lounge, Caroline felt slightly better. She had taken Dane to her favorite business and most relaxing luncheon/drinking place, something she had not done before. Looking at him, he just did not look right without a beer in his hands.

Caroline wished that she could get a membership in one of the two prestigious downtown clubs. Unfortunately, "she" was a she and shared the same fate as Blacks, Jews, Armenians, and the handicapped. Today though, she did not have to seriously worry about being seen by anyone important in the business community. Even if she did, Dane looked a bit like a stud in his casual wear and he was usually up to what she wished to discuss. And after all, it was Saturday afternoon and who knows, he might do her image some good.

"I guess I shouldn't be so upset. At least I am included in the group going to New York."

"Caroline, I think you make too much of the little things. That's a great insight! Keep your eyes on the important matters. You're right, you're included, that's what counts .... although in the history of the world, I don't think it will record Arrow's trip."

"Now why do you say that? First you say something meaningful and then you degrade the situation. Sometimes, I think even you should be aware of how your insecurities show through."

"That is not what I meant. What I wished to say is that we are but flashes of light that sparkle and disappear. Some are brighter than others, but in the end they dissolve. What counts in the end are the genes you leave behind, nothing more. Our children will be our only records through their children's children. The only exception might be those teachers who have an impression on those children's lives and change or affect their or our course as they or we fall through the sky so that it might then affect our children's children."

"That's the most anti-feminist Bullshit I have ever heard! You God Damned men are all the same! The woman's place is in the maternity ward. Shit! With an attitude like that, it's just spread your legs and make your mark. Bullshit! Bullshit, Dane Hughes! I don't buy that crap! There is more to life than having children. Look at you, there is such a thing as enrichment. Why, why don't you go back to school and get an MBA? Then you will have a chance to really go someplace."

"That may be so, but it looks to me like education is a false god to this Country's bright people."

"A false god? Education is what sets you free! Education is what allows you to really enjoy life. Education allows you to develop your abilities, reach for the stars, realize your potential. It is the greatest good ever created."

74

"Ah, but Caroline, look at it from this perspective. For millions of years, evolution has governed our development as God's Plan. We have reproduced the strong, the smart, those able to best survive by brute and brain, with brain being much the more important. Suddenly within the last fifty years, this Country has changed the selection process. People go to school until they are 22 and then they go on to graduate school until they are 24 or 27. Then they apprentice or join the competitive world where every minute counts. Also there is the common struggle to purchase a home and the need for two incomes. Women such as you find yourselves at age 34 with your first thoughts of having a family and when you do, it's only a child or two."

"What's wrong with that? People shouldn't have more than two. It's their replacement ratio. The world has an overpopulation problem."

"Maybe so, but the tide swings quickly on the human gene mix. What the modern U.S. educational system does is create a negative evolutionary scale. The bright genes are weeded out. How many children will you have? One ...... none? You should be the one to have ten children."

"Thank you for the compliment, but No Thank You! Kids bug me, it's a task for the mentally incompetent. What females need in America is the freedom to do whatever they wish. If you selfishly wish to have kids that's fine Fly Boy. If women wish to have careers, they should be encouraged. Think of it this way. Our populace is our greatest resource. As a country when we confine one-half our talent to limited roles, we are squandering a national resource. Think of the advances that have not been made because women have been limited in their horizons. That's the natural tragedy, Dane, not your phony gene dilution argument and ten kids."

"Kids are young goats, Caroline. I am talking about children, the future of mankind."

Caroline held her jaw tightly, what her uncle had called "torqued jaws," Hughes was really torquing her now. Damn, men made her mad! "Bullshit, you are talking about any excuse to screw!"

Dane looked at the beautifully dressed lady. He very much liked the dark blue outfit she was wearing. Sitting tall with an angrily thrusted jaw, she exuded male aggressiveness. Did she realize it? What could she really accomplish in Dane's rough physical world? He knew that she couldn't begin to carry through with her aggression unless protected by an artificial world.

The silence grew. It seemed as if the entire bar matched their mood. Dark and secret, gloomy and sad, all full of gutter phrases. Dane then wondered if that was really what bothered him about the conversation. Caroline was always suggesting that he continue with his education. Like so many "educated" young people, she could not correctly speak the English language. He wondered when she had last taken an English class of any type. He doubted if her business training had even a single class in communications. Somehow, he had to break the ice. "Men can't carry children in a womb, Caroline."

"God Damn You! When will you ever get your mind off sex? Don't you know that it's no different than going to the bathroom? Why can't you listen to me? I don't think we speak the same language you ignorant boob! God, I get so mad at you! Why are you so dumb?" Caroline knew that she had won her point. Dane Hughes was smiling his dumb smile again. He had only been twisting her tail.

Dane traced a figure on the table with a wet stirring stick. At that same moment, John Jamison was doing the same with a pencil on the now empty Boardroom's huge conference table. With his wife, Meg, sitting down the hall in his office, he was desperately hoping that the room's soundproofing was adequate to contain Frank Turner's screaming. The man had absolutely no class.

"You Dumb Shit! Haven't you figured out what this is all about yet? Your job is simple. You are the one to fire every damn man and woman in these three corporations other than a skeleton crew. You are the 'Fall Guy,' Jamison, the 'Lightning Rod.' Why do you think we will pay like we will? You are to be the Genghis Khan of railroad history!

"So let's get all this straight, buddy. You are to fire, terminate, retire anybody and anyone at anytime. You are to cut all advertising, sales promotion, research and development, marketing, legal and other discretionary activities. We will operate by spending money on only those things that are absolutely necessary to keep the companies running in the short term. Short term, got that?"

"Yes, Sir."

"When I tell you to jump, you jump! When that bitch O'Brian tells you to do something tough, you do it! If she tells you to keep something, retain some program, or any of that Midwest graduate school mumbo jumbo, you check with me. Most of all, I don't want to hear any crap about ethics or moral obligations. Now you tell me what you expect."

"I expect a tough job and a lot of tears from the way you describe it."

"Not just tears, Jamison. You better damn well expect good men to jump off roofs, to cause divorces, family suicides. Denuding those corporations of their staffs will ruin men and their families. Hell, you might even wipe a town or two off the map when you shut down their subsidiary headquarter locations. Are you really listening Jamison? I am telling you that from day one you will have grown men pleading with you for mercy, you will have fine performers fired, ruined by your actions. Nine out of ten men you will let go will be better than you, and that's conservative. You have just never, ever faced a task such as this."

"I can be toughened."

"Sure you can, we have all been toughened. But that is not the question. Don't you realize that to survive you have to be 'coldened.' Hell, that not the word! Jamison, I think you a soft son-of-a-bitch. You have got to turn to marble. I wish to God that there was something that I could do to get to you before you flame out playing Railroad King."

"Mr. Turner, I thought you said I was your choice for the job, that you had convinced Mr. Arrow. You don't sound like you want me to take the job."

"That may be true, but is probably only an admission of my mistake. Take my word for it Jamison, this is a life and death struggle that we started yesterday. Now get the Hell out of here! I have to steel myself to wasting a day flying East tomorrow, coach class."

As Jamison walked out of the room, Turner shook his head. any corporate executive was only as good as his wife. Indeed, corporate selection processes at this level were more often decided by matrimonial stability and the person standing behind the man, than the man himself. At least he had a start. Maybe these two could be toughened to steel and last a bit. What did he guess? Maybe ten to twelve months at the best. By that time, the worst should be over and a new man without blood on his hands could step in and take control. The Rail Division would need a "good guy" to replace the "bad guy" by that time. It would be somebody from one of the target companies. He'd be bought off, but fully accepted by the target companies' employees, that is, those that would be left on the payroll. Yes, he supposed Phillip Arrow was right in insisting on Jamison, even though Turner didn't think John Jamison would last more than three months.

Thank God that taking over a corporation wasn't that complex a job. There were only three important tasks. One, find an organization chart and make certain that the right people are in the right slots and that the slots are designed to achieve the Company's goals which in times such as these was always to make money. Two, put in incentive and compensation plans that would reward a management for its operating performance and getting the job done. Three, grasp hold of the control over the capital expenditure program. If these three things could be done, and done well, the acquired company would run by itself. Perhaps, just perhaps, Jamison would survive. In a way, though, it made no difference. Turner knew he would make his money either way.

Turner rose and walked out of the Boardroom and turned toward Phillip Arrow's office. That Damn Lacey hadn't shown. That did it! Turner was determined to terminate Lacey before he left for New York. Image Phillip actually once considered allowing him to participate in their talks! Who the Hell could picture a Black sitting there with you while you negotiate with potential takeover targets? It would be a slap in their faces. With any luck, he'd find the bastard somewhere here in the building today. Imagine the turkey dropping out of sight when things got serious? With any luck, he would have the pleasure of delivering the news himself. Perhaps he could make a lasting impression on the arrogant son-of-a-bitch that would ruin him psychologically for life. "When the going gets tough, the tough get going," thought Turner.

Perhaps then he could turn attention to doing the same with the bitchy broad. She would be one tough proposition. If either of the Jamisons were half as tough as O'Brian, he thought as he walked down the hall, the next months would be more than twice as easy. At least he had screwed up her compensation. He knew that that move must be eating Caroline from the inside like sulfuric acid. Perhaps she would self destruct. He chuckled at the thought. He didn't think that there was a woman alive in business that he couldn't destroy.

5

Sunday

As the Arrow executives sped across the Midwest sky, Meg Jamison looked across a beach patio table at the square framed Mary Sue Massendale. Meg was older than Mary Sue by perhaps as many as ten years, yet she knew that passersby would guess the opposite. Meg felt most relaxed sitting in the sun, while Mary Sue sat in the shade, seemingly always alert for four sons scattered among surfboards, volleyball nets, ocean breakers and the Club hamburger stand. Meg could not quite get used to the noise at the Bel Air Beach Club. Twenty years ago, the luncheon crowd she remembered had been nowhere as boisterous. She supposed it was the same reason why she no longer liked to visit West Los Angeles to attend the theater. The crowds were always talking, totally oblivious to others' attention. It was a strange trait.

She looked closely at Mary Sue. It was hard to believe that a daughter of Phillip Arrow could look so ordinary. Meg knew that she was overdressed for the Los Angeles beach, but Mary Sue's plain cotton dress was no more appropriate. It neither fit the Club nor the body. Red hair, cut straight and short, and a round freckled smiling face looked at her over the remains of a cheeseburger piled high with lettuce and tomatoes.

"I suppose you wish to know the real reason why I invited you here today. And also, Mrs. Jamison....I know, Meg.... why I am so happy we could meet at a neutral site. I know that it was a long drive, but with the four boys....."

"Mary Sue, please, I had to drop John off at LAX anyway and I enjoyed the trip. With my girls away in school, it gave me an outlet for a continued adventure. With John gone, it was a pleasure to find something to do this afternoon and the Club is on the way....."

Meg had ended her comment as if to turn the conversation's lead to her hostess. There was a noticeable, awkward silence.

Finally, Mary Sue spoke and as she did, her complexion flushed. She was fighting an embarrassment of terrible dimensions. "Mrs. Jamison, I was wondering if you could help me. It's about my husband. He turned forty years of age two years ago and is getting sillier and sillier, if you know what I mean. Now I trust him to a point, but I also know him....."

"Mary Sue, I am shocked! John has never ever mentioned anything like that about your husband and he usually knows about everything like that that happens within the Company."

"Oh, I know that and I am not talking about what he's done. I am talking about what he is going to do."

"I am sorry, I don't follow you."

"Let me get to the point. It is this girl Caroline O'Brian. Two weeks ago I visited the office to see Dad and she was there. She looked at me and I knew. She has decided to attract, let me be blunt, 'seduce' my husband."

"Oh, really, please........"

"No, listen to me, I am serious! I know that your husband and Caroline are going to be the most heavily involved in the takeovers. They will be spending tremendous amounts of time together. I wanted to talk to you about the girl. Meg, she is a tremendous threat to you and me. Haven't you felt those same feelings?"

"Heaven's 'No,' of course not! I just met her last Friday and John has rarely mentioned her. She seemed nice enough. My husband did say that she is the most ambitious female that he's ever met, but also said that he didn't hold that against her. He says that she is very well educated and also very efficient. I seem to recall his using the word 'cold' to describe her. Doesn't she go out with that nice pilot?"

"Yes, she does, but he is just wasting his time on her. He's too dumb to realize that he's common fodder for her dreams. Lawrence laughs at him and he too speaks with great respect of the young lady's

80

abilities. Lawrence has told me that Ms. O'Brian considers Mr. Hughes a project of some sort. The dumb idiot doesn't know that he serves some lesser role for her."

"Oh, I imagine he knows, when he thinks about it. Have you talked to your father about it? Surely, your father could help you."

"Mrs. Jamison, I am the only whole human being in my family. I am that way because I never, ever go to my father for help. If I did, it would be a life with a god on one's side. Life wasn't meant to be lived like that."

"Then how are you so sure?"

"I just know it. My dad calls it an 'anal twitch'." She laughed, ·"That's a 'deep gut' feel. I call it 'deep seated' women's intuition. I know as sure as I am sitting here that my husband is a dead duck."

"Why don't you discuss it with him?"

"You must be joking! He would then think it was his idea! No, you don't put ideas like that into Lawrence's head. Look, what I want to ask is that we form a partnership. If you ever hear anything about my husband, you tell me. If I hear anything like that about your husband, I will tell you. Perhaps we can forestall or prevent the situation."

"You are most serious, aren't you?"

"Mrs. Jamison, my father is successful because he can sense reality when others miss the point. I sense that this young lady could destroy both your and my families."

Meg looked across the table at the earnest young lady. It was obvious that she cared and totally believed. Meg had no such worries about John. He was totally, almost boringly monogamous. Besides, he wouldn't dare. Obviously, this Caroline O'Brian was a threat to this apparently hard working and caring mother of four boys. Meg wondered if Mary Sue really cared for herself or if she was attempting to save a role model for her sons.

"Fine, Mary Sue, I will agree. I will also hope that your fears are ungrounded. I am sure your husband, with your fine family, is totally loyal and trustworthy. I also think you may overestimate Ms. O'Brian. Can you imagine the pressure she would feel if her boss, your father, found out about it? No woman with that ambition would dare such a flagrant affront to your family, to your father's grandchildren. I can not imagine an ambitious female having any personal relationship with her immediate business associates. Even I, who have never been in the corporate world have heard the saying 'that one can either work a secretary or love a secretary, but never both.'

"I just can not conceive of any situation where Caroline would attempt to seduce your husband or any of her peers and know that she had a future at Arrow Corporation. She is too smart for that."

"Mrs. Jamison, you are judging the Caroline O'Brians of the world from your own personal values, not hers."

Sitting on the edge of a hotel room chair, Caroline leaned forward to tie the last strap of her high heel. Still reclining in a rumpled bed, lay John Smedt of the investment banking firm Arlington, Bothell & Hyde. Caroline had not planned to end up here in Smedt's room, but her thoughts had suddenly focused in the hotel lounge. After suffering through an all day Sunday flight to New York, she had not been invited to Aaron Goldstein's last legal briefing with his New York partner. Only Turner, Arrow and Massendale were invited. Aaron Goldstein's implication that she and John were not now among the trusted was obvious, although Caroline had thought that the guilty must be Aaron or his law firm. They were the only ones subtle enough to set up such a secret move, a move to make an additional two hundred fifty million dollars that was now obvious, but untraceable as to its origin.

To kill some time in the hotel before she could see Arrow to confirm the Monday and Tuesday schedules with him, she had accepted Smedt's offer to meet for a drink at 7:30. Perhaps she had made a mistake by taking a quick shower and changing out of her tan skirt into more becoming evening attire. From the onset, Smedt had projected electricity. He had been discussing the merger with a look that she sensed as that confident male look of dominance with a new female acquaintance. As they finished their first drink, Caroline had begun silently enjoying all the possible ways in which she could dash Smedt's entire evening, entire month if she were lucky and good enough.

Then, something had changed Caroline's mind. It was not their quietly relaxing together that had Smedt aglow, it was not Caroline's presence at all. Suddenly Caroline found that it was the subject of his incessant conversation. Smedt simply glowed of personal interest. He was spending his reward as surely as if he already had it and 'it' was considerably more than his bonus from Arlington, Bothell and Hyde. Smedt glowed of power, not just new found wealth.

He had appeared every bit too sure of himself, too much as if he were the conqueror. Caroline looked at her watch. It was only 9:30 and perhaps the confidential lawyers meeting to which she and Smedt had not been invited was over. She hoped that this evening would be worthwhile to all, including her contribution. Well, it was time to put her hunch to the test. "Jonathan, I can't help feeling sorry for your wife, you are such a bastard!"

Silence, she had changed the tone of her voice and Smedt's blank look belied a mind a bit slow in moving. "Caroline, my dear, don't you worry. We have a perfect understanding. I understand and she doesn't know."

"That's not what I meant. I was thinking of when I had to tell Arrow how you have arranged a position in the targets' stock. It's your ass, job .... the whole shot! Now that I have a way of covering my source - I can say that you told me in the sack. By the way, I feel that we can make you return any profit that you might make, even if you should go to jail. Don't look so shocked. The secret must have been difficult to hold in..... you must have been very uptight. Do you feel any better now?"

With her sweetest smile, Caroline slipped on her jacket. With a toss of the head and a deep laugh, "Well don't you have anything to say?"

"You are the bastard!"

Caroline walked to the door. "Don't get up, I was just checking the linen."

"Hey, wait a minute! What do you mean 'when' you tell Arrow?"

"Why do you ask?"

"Come on, give me a break."

"Alright, I suppose that I do owe you something, but not much. I just found out late last night and I didn't have a chance to discuss it with Phillip today. He came in on a different flight. I plan to tell him soon, after his meeting downstairs ...... unless you can help me find out more than just the fact that you have all your net worth tied to it."

John Smedt swung his legs over the side of the bed. His contented, conquering smile of five minutes ago was lost in a wild look as his mind raced for a way around this witch. God, it was like being bitten by a snake in your bed! His stomach felt squeamish. She had to be bluffing. She couldn't know, yet she did. Could he call her bluff? No, he had already admitted guilt with his hesitancy.

"Look, Caroline, my position is only small time. Sure it's 4 million, but that's not even close to the 400 million dollars that someone else has invested the past weeks. I think I have a lead on that. Let me tell you what I know and you could forget my spot position. I'll dispose of it tomorrow. No one will ever know."

Caroline walked back into the room. Suddenly, the room felt small and stuffy. Surely, there must be more to life than having to put up with balding forty year old men. She sat down and smiled....and waited.

Smedt continued to look at this new woman who now sat waiting, waiting, "O.K., I get the message, you want me to talk. Look, I have to make a living and I think that I can really help you. But you have to help me out too. I thought my path was untraceable. How did you get a source? You are lying aren't you? You don't know."

"John, take my word for it. I know."

"O.K., I will tell you. This has to be larger than either of us. I will tell you only, but you have to tell me your source, how you made the guess or found out and you have got to promise never to name me as your source." Suddenly, John Smedt was frightened. He sensed himself somehow as a small fish that had suddenly been thrown into a larger pond. Now he was about to make some noise that could get him noticed by whatever lived in that larger body of water.

That, thought Caroline, would be quite a story. How to cover the idea of a source? She did not want to destroy this man completely. The truth was that until she had tried the thought as only a chance an hour or so ago, she only had the gleam of Smedt's eyes in the hotel lounge as he talked of the impending acquisitions. He was the source.

God! Men were such asses. Put them in a position of an indiscretion and they'd follow to form one after another. Women didn't keep secrets because they did not want to, men did not keep them because they couldn't.

"Alright, I will sit here and listen for five minutes. You tell me what you know and give me time to check the facts and I promise that if it checks out, I will tell you the source."

"I can tell you in two minutes. For several years I have been using a London brokerage firm while funneling the money through Swiss, Netherlands and then Netherlands Antilles bank accounts and investment firms. Its all small time stuff in my accounts. Nothing big, nothing too noticeable. I guess I got greedy on this one and invested a bit too much. Hell, how'd I know that someone would step in for 5%!

Anyway, in no way should it be traceable. The Government doesn't have any idea what's happening and I don't know how you found out. Hell, half the time I don't even know where my money is, it's that complex.

"Well, anyway, a month and a half ago I was in New York at the Princeton Club in the second floor dining room when I saw Aaron Goldstein talking to my Netherlands Antilles agent. Now my Antilles agent is reknown in hidden circles. He is just simply the best at what he does that there ever has been. There was no reason for Aaron to be talking to him. And I will be honest, I first thought Aaron was onto me. But I asked the agent straight out the next day and he knew what was riding on it. He told me that the discussions pertained to only the parties present. It was their personal deal, that my account had nothing to do with it."

"Why is the Netherlands Antilles so important?"

"Hell, Caroline, don't you know that?"

A shake of the head was Caroline's response. Unlike most of those with whom she competed on the corporate ladder, Caroline was not afraid to ask questions or to admit the lack of knowledge. Surprising to the timid, she was also one of the few who continued to learn.

"O.K., the U.S. and the Dutch have a tax treaty. When it was signed it allowed for tax free intercountry transactions, that is, I won't double tax your corporations if you don't double tax mine. Someone slipped up or someone wanted to slip up. The U.S. has several territories that it wished to have participate, such as Guam and Puerto Rico. The Netherlands had places like the Antilles, little chunks of jungle set in the Caribbean

"For tens of thousands of investors today and well over twenty-five thousand U.S. corporations, the Netherlands Antilles is important because the U.S. Treaty doesn't require a 30% automatic withholding tax on dividends. You see, almost all dividend checks sent to foreign countries have an IRS requirement that the dividend paying company withhold 30% and deposit it with the U.S. Government, just like withholding on your paycheck. That way, the U.S. Treasury is assured of being paid its taxes. Well, the Netherlands Antilles investment company that holds my stock doesn't worry about reporting to the U.S. It also does not worry about paying any taxes on my gains because that's a bank entry paid out to a Netherlands company, which in turn holds the stock for another bank in another European company, all protected by their respective tax treaties."

"Won't they force you to pay taxes at sometime?" asked Caroline.

"No. The trick is to get your gain into a country where there are ineffective penalties for tax evasion. It is very difficult for most Americans to realize, but in most European countries, it is not a criminal event to evade taxes. You don't get sent to prison. You get just a slap on the wrist if you are caught. And it is a simple trick in Europe not to get caught, hence there is no risk. The trick is to set it up so that if the IRS traces the transactions, they are perfectly legal - which I might add, they are."

"You mean the U.S. allows this? What about the insider information that you are using. I know that that is blatantly illegal."

"Caroline, you are getting the IRS mixed up with the SEC and the various stock exchanges. There is a huge difference, believe me. Not paying taxes is an IRS problem and they have a hundred thousand people assuring that we all pay our fair share. Because of their manpower, you need to be very careful. Insider trading, that is taking a gain on stock because of information that you learn by being 'on the inside' in some transaction, is under the jurisdiction of the SEC and they have only a handful of people watching over this type of thing. In fact, if you want to know the truth, the SEC has one major computer program keyed to flags that the market has long ago figured out, with a few young lawyers who don't know the right questions to ask. The New York Stock Exchange does only a marginally better job of policing itself.

"In all, the SEC and the Exchange don't have more than 200 people looking into trading and most of them can only do it part time. Believe me, Caroline, unless you call me out, I will skate through."

"Why shouldn't I report you?"

"Because I am only small time. Look, you can blackmail me, this I know, but I will be able to afford it. But look at the big picture. Someone has gone out on the limb for 400 million dollars. It has to be Aaron. I just know it. 400 million dollars, think of that! None of you besides Phillip Arrow has that type of money. Also, think of the magnitude of the effort! Someone is stealing a quarter of a billion dollars from other investors. Compared to that steal, I am only a small time crook."

"Sorry, John, the story's not good enough." Caroline stood up and flagrantly adjusted her pantyhose. She again made the motion to open the door.

Smedt blanched. God Damn tough broad, he thought. Inside he smiled a bit. At least he had the chance to set her up and she was ready for the sale. "What would be good enough Caroline?"

"Oh, I don't know. Something more, the whole story doesn't mesh."

"Of course not. You interrupted me. You see, Caroline, it was exactly six weeks ago tomorrow that I saw Aaron and my agent. You can check. You should also be able to find that it was a threesome. They were sitting with someone from Arrow Corporation." John Smedt paused to let the moment magnify. "It was John Jamison."

Caroline stiffened. John Jamison! What a perfect sleeper! He could be the one, he just might be! He had set everyone up all along, surely he could not be as dumb as he appeared. His background and education did not fit that image. "Alright, John, I will check it out. If what you say is true, I will work something out with you." With those words, Caroline walked to the door, slowly opened it to check the hall, and stepped out into the early evening silence.

She hurried down the hall to her room to quickly write a note. She had him! She would dismantle John Jamison tomorrow in front of Phillip Arrow. At the same time, she would take care of Aaron Goldstein. But what if she were wrong? There was too much to lose. She had to try the message as a check. One couldn't trust a bastard like John Smedt!

The two and one-half hour meeting had not gone well when a waiter brought Aaron Goldstein the note. He quickly read it and hurriedly folded and stored it in his pocket. It was interesting, but right now he had to pay close attention to the ranting Lawrence Massendale.

"Do you mean to tell me that there is a degree of clientness? That our relationship is some sort of disease, a love affair that you can turn off or on at will? You have the audacity to use two hours of our time to discuss our most precious secrets and then suggest that you are going to withdraw from this assignment. We will go to unknown lengths to report this perfidy. Expect the Bar, expect a suit, expect ....."

"Excuse me Lawrence," interjected Phillip Arrow, " I just want to get my facts straight. Aaron, we have worked with you for some time. You have now brought in this senior partner who, you say, is a

Managing Partner. He informs us that your office, with other of your partners, has had a close historical relationship with the Cardinal organization and that the Cardinals have come to you and requested your firm's assistance in fending off our tender offer. He also states that in such cases your firm has a customary right of representing the firm to be acquired, the more defenseless entity, so to speak. Is that correct, Aaron."

"In the overall context, that may be how you understand it, but........"

"Just say 'Yes' or 'No' you slimy son-of-a-bitch!"

"Massey, Massey, calm down," hastened Phillip Arrow, "I apologize for him, Aaron."

Phillip Arrow had spoken with his calmest, most assured voice, the one he used when he lied. His mind was racing over his son-in-law's outburst. Surely he could not have made up "clientness as a disease" on his own. Massey must have heard it in law school. It was a wonder that he had remembered it.

"In a nutshell, Yes. Mr. Arrow, please know that we have struggled with this ever since our other partners brought up this issue two weeks ago. The potential for conflict of interest is staggering. We recognize that all your material and information supplied to us is proprietary and confidential. I assure you that it will be destroyed or returned to you. As you have heard, I will not be involved in my other partners' work in any way."

"Jesus, you'd think we were born in a cabbage patch you squirming little ....."

"Massendale, shut up! This is a business situation and there will be give and take. How can we talk or even find out if negotiation is possible with your insulting these people?"

"With all due respect, Old Man, what is there to negotiate? The tender offers are out, the SEC filings are submitted. These sniveling rats have made it impossible for the Cardinal deal to proceed. They will have us tied up in courts for years. We can't bring in a new law firm at this late date. And without the Cardinals, I doubt if you can bring in the other two. It's finished, over, you're through."

Aaron Goldstein quickly countered, "Oh, I believe that you are being far to pessimistic. The other two are quite attainable. What I would suggest ...."

Arrow interrupted, "If you don't mind, I would like to think this over in quiet silence. Why don't you take Massendale across into the lounge and talk that possibility through. If you don't mind, I have one other matter to go over with your Managing Partner. Aaron, it was a pleasure working with you. I think a lot of you and your work and am sorry that you were caught in a bind like this."

Phillip Arrow watched the lawyers walk out of the room, leaving the door open. He stood up, groaning from the pain in his hips, and walked over to close the door. Before turning, he began his preplanned speech, "Sir, we have been playing ball for many years. Let me play a bit of hardball. I have known that Shaffer, Schwab & Meyers has been on the Cardinal team for sometime. Yesterday, I checked with the person coordinating my defense against your defense." Arrow turned to view his antagonist. His preamble had been met with disbelief.

Arrow returned to the table and picked up a single typewritten sheet that he had conspicuously laid before him at the start of the meeting. "On this sheet you will find a listing of your ten top corporate clients, in rank order, based on revenues for the past three years. Interesting to my analysts was the fact that the Cardinals did not make the top ten. They were twenty-third with Arrow Corporation a distant ninety-second. You will also notice a check by each of those top companies' names. That check signifies my having talked with each of their chief executive officers, checking to see if union pressure has been suggested regarding your representation of them as their counsel. All are aware that they face some enormous problems, potentially brought on by you tomorrow when Shaffer, Schwab & Meyers....or, should I say, if Shaffer, Schwab & Meyers is not present as my counsel.

"For your information, we did have complete access to your computer system and I might add, I find your accounting disclosure most interesting. Like most partnerships today, you have some terrible manpower problems. I have yet to see a firm grow past the five hundred employee mark and be able to successfully solve the division of profits problem. I suppose that Johnson & Higgins comes the closest, but you are just not coping well at all."

Arrow's audience was silent. "Now I would expect that even though it is late, you might call one or two of these fellows. I'd suggest Henry and old Simon. They both work at all hours, even a Sunday night like this. You can discuss the fact that various pension trusts, union included, today own 37% of all U.S. corporations' common stock. In fact, it is 50% for these ten large companies. Think of the problems that they will incur when their stock is dumped onto the market tomorrow morning by the union trust funds in a frenzied sale along with various rumors. Their stocks' prices will all drop drastically, indeed, they will become immediate acquisition targets.

"I would also suggest that later tonight, you inform your friends, the Cardinals, that you believe their best approach is to accept our tender offer. Make up any reasons you can think of, just make them stick. Also tell them that from tomorrow morning on, you are going to be solely representing Arrow Corporation simply because it is by far the best for both organizations.

"I might also add that this is the real thing. Those ten clients of yours are facing massive disruptions to their stock prices and are obviously vulnerable to corporate raiders like myself. I doubt if they will fence with you. Just asking them may be enough to make them decide to get another corporate counsel. Skadden, Arps and Whactell, Lipton will undoubtedly be much stronger and richer firms after tomorrow unless you cooperate."

The Managing Partner of Shaffer, Schwab & Meyers finally spoke, "Of course you realize that we exist only to serve. If there has been some confusion, I apologize. Of course we will represent you, if what you say is true, and 'Yes' I will call just Old Simon. May I say, Phillip Arrow, that I am surprised? I can think of only five or six men in America who wield the type of power you just displayed."

"Well, now you know six or seven. May I buy you a drink at this late hour?"

The hour was even later and many telephone calls had been made since Phillip Arrow had fired what he thought was the first round and was sleeping the sleep of kings. Three thousand miles away Everett Lacey tiredly looked over the data pulled from Blarnef and Blarnef's files. He desperately was searching for a visually sighted lead. His program had discovered nothing. Sixty miles to the north, Meg Jamison fitfully slept having earlier heard from her husband who was planning to take in a Broadway show if he could find one to waste away a boring evening. John Jamison hadn't, he too now slept. The Massendales were neither yet asleep. Mary Sue sat at her desk wondering if she had made a fool of herself with Meg Jamison. If Lawrence should ever hear of her worries, she would never hear the last of it. Somehow, she knew that she had already failed. Caroline O'Brian would be more than difficult competition. She was a tough, young foe.

At that moment, Caroline did not feel "tough." She had been wrong! She had taken a risk and failed. She was trained for neither. Her corporate training allowed for neither risk nor failure. She had been...........

Caroline sat at her suite's table with an open pad and indescribable drawings penciled across words and lists. Caroline was steaming mad. Lord, she had made a fool of herself! What Aaron Goldstein must have thought when she invited him up to her room. With what she was wearing, he did not even have to undress her. What a smirk he had on his face, like it was some big joke! The little jerk had been silently laughing at her while he let her let him take advantage of her. The little bastard! The God Damned jerk!

Caroline's mind tried to visualize the small body of the man. She could hear his fast voice, the whine, the incessant and expected demanding. Goldstein was so disgustingly Jewish! Wouldn't anybody ever openly talk about why Northern Europeans have historically despised the Jews? They are repulsive! Give a Goldstein a chance, allow him to get a hold and he would maximize his position. They have no honor! They just don't know how to play fair.

He had laughed at her. She had used the same line of reasoning that had worked with John Smedt. When she had told him that her sources had discovered his connections with the Dutch Antilles, that she knew he was working with someone from Arrow Corporation, he had laughed at her. When she had told him that she knew he had purchased stock, he had denied it. Then he had told her that he knew that Smedt used that agent, was this incorrect information coming from John? She had seen him pose and dress, laugh at her, and recite the way in which she could check to see whether he had indeed purchased stock through the Dutch Antilles. He had played the role she had earlier played with Smedt.

Caroline had had to use the John Jamison card. What had he been doing with John Jamison? Goldstein had shook his head. Didn't Caroline know that Arrow Corporation had two offshore insurance companies, one in Bermuda, the other in the Cayman Islands. It was the latter that used the Dutch Antilles agent for legitimate investments, that he was the best investment advisor in the Caribbean, and that everything he did for Arrow Corporation was perfectly legitimate? Did she need a primer in Arrow Corporation's off-shore captives?

91

Caroline had been caught. Yes, she knew of the risk management setup. It was like all the other large U.S. corporations. Arrow Corporation did not have to worry about overpaying for insurance because it owned its own insurance captive. While accountants and the IRS would not allow a deduction or expense for self-insurance if paid to a subsidiary in the United States, the rules were reversed if your subsidiary resided outside the national boundaries. For multi-national firms it was a breeze to get the deductions. Others, however, used Bermuda as an easy offshore corporate post. The more sophisticated and daring used the Caymans. Frank Turner had originally set it all up and there was little to it other than bank accounts and the transfer of funds. Since it covered insurance and there was not that much to do, it fell within the function of administration, hence John Jamison's present adminstrative role.

But she still did not understand why Aaron was with Jamison. Hadn't he been assigned the potential mergers as his sole project? He was not working on captives or insurance.

The question had been met with Goldstein's derision. Did Caroline really believe that an acquisition could be made with no money from the acquiring corporation? Arrow Corporation had had to come up with some funds of its own. Phillip Arrow's answer had been to tap into his offshore insurance captives' reserves. Borrowing money from tax free trusts had been a stroke of genius in Aaron's mind. This was money deposited in accounts for which a tax deduction had already been taken. In effect, the U.S. Treasury was paying for one half the acquisitions. With later tax reductions for increased depreciation from the write up of assets, the IRS would, in fact, help pay for over 80% of the acquisitions.

She could still hear Aaron's whine as he went out the door, "Believe me Caroline, I wouldn't be buying the targets' stock. If I was involved, I would be selling."

The phone ringing brought Caroline wide awake, it was Dane Hughes. He had just driven in from the airport.

"Caroline, sorry to call you this late, but I am just checking in. Arrow had us go over the Lears with a fine tooth comb. Say, is it too late to get together?"

"Yes, Dane, I am in bed and tomorrow may be my toughest day. Why don't you be a darling and get some rest yourself? If nothing comes up I will be glad to see a show with you at say.....ah.... you call for me at 7:00. If I am not here then, I know you'll understand. Business comes before pleasure. Good Night, Darling."

Caroline put down the phone. Perhaps Lawrence Massendale would still be up. She dialed and he was awake, "Lawrence, I was hoping that you were up, would there be a chance ...."

"Caroline, boy do you need to be brought up to speed! You wouldn't believe the meeting we had tonight. That slimy, sickly, crawly little Aaron Goldstein and his boss canceled their engagement with us. Can you believe it? A major New York law firm pulling out on the last day and the last hour! Then Arrow sends me out of the meeting to dialogue with the son-of-a-bitch and the guy tells me to get lost and takes off. Then Arrow calls Frank and me together and goes over the scenarios as if nothing has happened. I ask him 'What about Goldstein?' and he tells me that there is nothing to worry about, that it was just a misunderstanding, that the Cardinals are in and so is Goldstein. Shit! I have been sitting here racking my brain trying to make sense of all this. It is driving me crazy."

Caroline tried to calm her retort related to Massey's use of the term, "boy".

"Oh, Lawrence, there has to be an answer!" Caroline's mind raced. Aaron had treated her like a past client, maybe she could get a rematch. "Look, perhaps two heads are better than one. I am not dressed for the lounge, even if it were open at this time, but you could come down to my room. Say in about five minutes and we can think about this together."

Caroline could feel her adrenaline pouring again. She walked into the suite's powder room and touched herself with perfume. Why not, she thought? Something had to replace the memory of Aaron Goldstein. Perhaps Massey would somehow give her what she needed. She just could not strike out on all this with this batting order. She would use Massey like a change of pace. Smedt was a curve ball and Goldstein a high fastball. Damn that Goldstein!

What Aaron Goldstein needed right now was another drink. He silently looked out the window of his downtown office with his Managing Partner sitting to his right in the new day's early light. Neither had gone home, both would soon sleep in their offices. The lead partner's news had been the most shocking. Somehow, that damn Phillip Arrow had switched the forces! It would make an interesting topic in a few hours at the daily partners' meeting. Aaron had been

93

warning these men for months not to underestimate these Westerners. Yet like most of his peers in New York, his partners looked down on people from the West. One went to Los Angeles or Chicago to make money. They were outposts for those not quite able to compete in the East. The truly sharp could both make money and live in New York, that was a sign of intelligence and ability. If you wished power rather than money, you lived in Washington, but that was the only exception.

Aaron loved this view of the City in the early morning. No wonder so many of his peers could live their work. Manhattan was a world unto itself. His clubs were his family, his business associates were those with whom he competed, played and loved. There was no such thing as being tired when one could touch and smell the wealth and power of owning and running the World.

And with power comes control, thought Aaron. That was the reason for his exhilaration. Both he and his senior partner had thought that they were in control of the situation. Arrow had surprised them both. Of course, it was bound to happen that someone would tap their computer system. Neither had thought, however, that someone could get to their word processing and accounting billing systems. Now that it had been demonstrated, it was easy enough to believe. Say "Good by" EDP Manager, your job won't last past 10:00 AM and say "Hello" to not trusting California people around Shaffer, Schwab & Meyers' computers. That too, could have been foreseen. The West Coast was years ahead of the East in terms of computer technology.

And then there was Phillip Arrow. Had he ever gotten to Aaron's boss! Yes, Aaron could feel his blood running freely even with no sleep. What a competitor Arrow was! It would be a struggle, but they would have to teach him a lesson. Perhaps the other major New York law firms would assist. Arrow probably had their secrets too. Compared to this invasion of privacy, the pending acquisitions were nothing. Arrow would pay for his present success. One doesn't screw with Manhattan lawyers!

Aaron smiled. He would have to face O'Brian again in the morning, that would be interesting. My, he had made her go through the paces. Had she been in on the Arrow switch? No, totally doubtful, she would have played that card too. Aaron had been totally truthful, he had not been buying any of the targets' stock. Caroline just didn't know enough to ask the right question. What Aaron was doing was preparing to "sell short" rather than the traditional "buying long." What that meant was that he would agree to buy stock of any of the targets where he knew the acquisition was going to fail. This "buy" would be at a future date and like all short sales, he would, in effect, "sell" as of the prior date when he first made the deal with the broker. This backward selling, buying was perfect. Lord, he would have made a bundle on this deal if only one of the acquisitions would fall through and have its stock price plummet! Damn! It didn't look like it would be the Cardinals.

Aaron stretched and took the last drink of scotch. Women would never be successful in the business world until they understood how it worked and there was no way that business schools would ever fill that role. One had to have experiences. O'Brian would never be invited to those types of parties. Lord, it was easy to compete against a rigidly trained, narrowly disciplined Catholic bitch! He wondered if Turner knew that Caroline was Catholic. If there was one thing that Aaron could not stomach, it was discrimination of any type. Frank Turner's incessant remarks about Catholics were repugnant.

6

Monday

Dane Hughes awakened early, 3:00 AM by western time and 6:00 AM eastern, but in a way, it was 3:00 AM in Manhattan also. Dane often wondered at a populace that normally ate dinner at 10:00 PM, arrived at the office at 10:00 AM for morning coffee, a large, long lunch, and did not really start working until 6:00 PM. The 40% of the nation's people that lived within 300 miles of Manhattan didn't live like that. What was it about the island that created such a different culture?

Thinking that there was no chance of an early breakfast in that most New York hotels only began serving at 7:00 AM, Dane casually glanced into the hotel restaurant. John Jamison sat alone at a far table. Walking over to him, Dane asked, "Mr. Jamison, would you like some company this morning?"

"Absolutely, Dane, please sit down. I am surprised that you are up. Don't tell me that you are another poor farmboy too. I sure know that you aren't an Albertan farmboy, though. Once you get the habit of early rising, it is tough to beat."

"No, I'm a Virginian town boy. Do you get up this early often?"

"All the time. You saw my home the other day. By the way, Thank You, for that trip. I have to leave the house at 4:30 each morning to beat the traffic. Even so, it still takes over three hours. We moved up there before the 55 mph speed limit. That thing has almost killed me. You should see the Ventura and Hollywood Freeways jammed packed at 5:30 AM. It's amazing that the roads in California don't just wear out. Well, what are you up to today?"

"Nothing, Sir. I am on 'hold' should Mr. Arrow require someone flown somewhere. Today I plan to wander the City and pick up some theater tickets."

"Which show? Hell, it doesn't matter. Do you think you could get me one or were you going to go take someone?"

"Yes, I was planning to take Caroline ...."

"Well, don't let me get in your way. I can fend for myself. I have to admit to feeling pretty self-confident these days."

"Oh, that's alright, Caroline won't mind. In fact, it might be nice to break the tension. You two will have to promise not to talk business, though. Today you work, tonight will be relaxation."

"Thanks for reminding me. I had better get going. Massendale and I are opening Aaron Goldstein's office this morning. We've rented a full communications setup, the works, and are taking over one of their conference setups. I saw it early last night, but we are to triple check it to make sure that all systems are go by 10:00 when the fat hits the fan. See you!"

With a broad smile, John Jamison lumbered off. Dane thought he should be ashamed of himself. He bet that Jamison was a nice guy if you should get to know him. A farm boy from Canada! Who would have guessed? Dane had once been to central Alberta with its small towns spread like flowers across a countryside, each about one day's buggy ride apart under the towering Rockies. No growth, no change, just nice farming people trapped in a timewarp. So that explained John Jamison!

Two hours later, Phillip Arrow looked across at John Jamison. He would have to bring him along slowly. John had had all the courses, degrees, shared and suffered through many corporate experiences, knew the words to say at seemingly the right times, yet did not have the foggiest idea of what was going on. Moreover, his new found position apparently created the courage to ask questions to illustrate this fact. Looking around the room, Arrow relaxed a bit. At least all the other sharks were present. O'Brian with her quiet aggressiveness, Turner with his smell for the jugular, Smedt with his smell for money, and Goldstein. Lord, that had been close! If it hadn't been for

98

Lacey...... Looking at the last member, his dumb wit, argumentative, over-educated son-in-law, he started, "Let's summarize the coming day's activities.

"First, we have had some good news. The Stock Exchange may suspend trading in the three targets' stock as of the start of trading tomorrow morning. The Interstate Commerce Commission will call an emergency session to review our plans. As some of you know, we have members who were informed over the weekend and who will see that our side is, how shall we say it, 'adequately and accurately' presented. The Justice Department is expected to comment at 11:00 AM. I have been told the gist of the draft of that release is that there will be no antitrust problems. In other words, we have a free hand. You have all seen the full three pages of the tender announcements published in the *Wall Street Journal* last Friday. Full filings with the governmental agencies began last Friday and continue today. For those interested, we have filed lawsuits in three states this morning to prevent state security laws from being used as a reason to bring a suit to stop the tenders. Since we are dealing with entities engaged in interstate commerce, there is little chance, especially with past U.S. Supreme Court rulings, that state laws would apply.

"Beginning in one hour, we will have three consecutive one hour visits from each of the targets and their legal representatives. As you have heard, the Cardinals have been using this office to prepare. My information has it that the Blue Jays have been working here in town all weekend with their friends and they too are ready. The only mild surprise is that the Oriole Chairman will visit us personally here at 12:00 before lunch with, I understand it, only one assistant. Perhaps we will have one easy acquisition out of the group.

"Just keep in mind that we are willing to enhance the tenders, change them to straight cash for up to 100% for each of these companies. That keeps it simple. It will soon be up to the arbitragers to contact all the stockholders of the targets' stock and offer a price at a premium over the present price. From past experience, we have found that 'cash talks' and we would expect to easily gain more than 50% approval from all the stockholders.

"However, that is not our goal. In reality, we wish to use cash to only purchase 49% of each of these companies, with pieces of paper with names like warrants, debentures, preferred or common stock for the other 51%. This is important for us because we would then be in an accounting position to sell off merged, rather than acquired assets, with far more favorable accounting and tax treatment. It also is important should we wish to spin-off any of these company's subsidiaries as independent corporations to isolate their liabilities. I am thinking of retirement benefits or non-economic recovery positions. 49% cash means it will be non taxable, non dividend spinoff of assets to our stockholders. Otherwise, we will have to wait for five years. Even more important, we want to gain immediate control of these companies. We have the possibility that if left on their own, the management of these companies could create liabilities that would make the acquisitions totally unattractive."

"Sir, could you give me an example? And why would they want to do that?" It was John Jamison, who felt extremely important in his new role. Both he and Phillip Arrow held chairs specifically reserved for them at each end of the conference room table. All others sat against the far wall, leaving the side nearest the door open for up to at least six visitors.

"Yes, good question! In the past we have had acquired firms sign poor labor contracts, sign-up for poor or unnecessary leases, grant their retirees health insurance benefits, use up all their cash or tie up assets for a long term. As to why they would do such a thing as take a business position that would be disadvantageous, indeed ruinous to their companies over the long term, I can only speculate. It might help you to know that all these actions are planned at Arrow Corporation should an indefensible acquisition tender offer ever occur. I would gladly ruin the Company before I let someone take it over. I would scorch the earth from here to the Pacific."

Jamison continued, "But how are we going to convince them to do anything but fight us to the death?"

"Another good question. We have the IRS on our side. You see, John, if only 49% cash is paid for the stock, the deal will be non taxable to the targets' stockholders. If we pay 50% or more, it becomes a taxable transaction. What we will wish to do is to open negotiations in an attempt to make it better for their stockholders. It will be very difficult for them to refuse our cordiality. They have a fiduciary responsibility to serve their owners, their stockholders."

Arrow smiled at the looks of disbelief on Turners and O'Brian's faces. A management that would sacrifice their jobs so that the stockholders would benefit was an unbelievable phenomenon to the two of them.

Jamison was flush with his control of the conversation with Phillip Arrow. "Well, then, at least we are now to the point where we can drop the use of the names of birds."

Arrow looked at Jamison. He would have to bring him up short. "I don't believe that that is what I want, John. We are going to have to convince these people that they are now part of a new company, that their old companies are dead. Let's continue to use those names and make a point among the executive staff of never ever again uttering the names Southern Pacific, Burlington Northern, or Union Pacific."

"Mr. Arrow," it was Aaron Goldstein. "My partners have had the Cardinal people here since 6:00 this morning. They tell me that the Cardinal President and his staff would be willing to talk to you now."

"Please, by all means, invite them in."

John Jamison watched the Cardinal management file into the room. It reminded him of a meeting he had arranged with top Japanese managers and Los Angeles executives last year at Arrow Corporation. Frank Turner had represented Arrow. The U.S. business leaders, most from California, had sat to one side of a room such as this and the Japanese to the other. One of the first questions that the Japanese asked was, "How do you motivate your people in the United States?" Frank Turner had interrupted a prestigious Los Angeles bank president to shout, "We tell them to get their ass moving or it's out the door!" For some reason, John sensed the same type of cultural difference in the room this morning.

It was the Cardinal President who started the action, "Phillip, we understand that you have us at a disadvantage this morning. We had only originally agreed to this meeting here because we believed that Shaffer, Schwab and Meyers would represent us. Since they won't, we will make the meeting brief and tell you that we will resist you in any way we possibly can."

"I am sorry to hear you say that. As you know, this is just a preliminary meeting. We have four weeks in which the tender must stay open. Who knows, perhaps we will find something that will cause us to not go ahead with the purchase.   What I had hoped was that we might find some common ground in these twenty business days where an agreement could be reached, where the two companies could be blended without any hard feelings, and where the personal suffering could be kept to a minimum. I would hope that you would share our

101

concerns."

"You are right, I do. But I am at a loss for suggestions right now. It seems that you know all our secrets. The only alternative I see open right now is to have the management group offer a higher tender price and then attempt to find the assets in the corporation to produce some leverage to borrow these funds."

"Uh, excuse me, Sir," it was Aaron Goldstein, "as you may know, from a reading of your Corporate Charter, you have the right to borrow funds on your Company's assets only for internal expansion or capital acquisition. Those monies can not be used for purchasing of either your or another company's stock."

"You people have totally failed us! How dare you use information like that, information that you gave me in a report just two weeks ago as possible things that have to be amended by a proxy vote, and then turn around and use it against me! Have you no ethics? With all due respect to you Phillip, I must tell you that I will hound this firm of Shaffer, Schwab & Meyers to Hell for what it has done this morning."

Arrow smiled, "I have had that same thought myself."

Aaron Goldstein slowly shook his head. "Sir, I assure you that the work of my partners is unknown to me. We absolve ourselves from conflict of interest by giving you back all your material. You have our assurances that I have not talked to those who were representing you before this morning. And Sir, may I be blunt? In two weeks, Arrow Corporation will hold over 50% of your stock. You do not have a staggered class system on your Board where only 1/3rd of them can be replaced each year. In four months you will be part of Arrow Corporation. All your Board seats will be held by Arrow Corporation nominees. I would advise that you seriously consider joining them on a friendly basis."

The Cardinal President stood, "Over my dead body!" The man quickly rose and was followed by his people as he stormed from the room.

Arrow spoke first, "I have some telephone calls to make from the side communications room. You all keep yourselves available. I understand that the Blue Jays will be here at 11:00. Let's all be back here by 5 minutes to the hour."

All left the room except for John Jamison and Caroline. Jamison was feeling good and Caroline had nowhere to go. "Caroline, since we are just sitting here, could you go over what a management leveraged buyout is. I take it that that is what he was talking about."

Five minutes to the hour, Jamison thought he understood the principles. "In essence, it's usually a scam. A management team either gathers together information that a company can't live without or runs a good company into the ground while somehow convincing a Board that they should stay on. Then when things look desperate, they go to the Board and suggest that they would be willing to pay more than the stockholders' value for all the outstanding common shares. After the Board affirms the possibility, they go to a bank or source of money, say a pension fund or insurance company, and convince them of the fact that the company is really strong. They borrow the money on the assets of the business, assets that have been there but are perhaps hidden from the stockholders' view. The Board approves, they tender for the stock, and then make the company profitable again. You say that most management tender offers are fully paid off in three years, interest and principal. It sounds like cold robbery of the original stockholders."

Caroline raised her hands. The Blue Jay management team was walking into the room. This time several additional outside legal counsels were present. Extra chairs had to be brought into the room.

Again, the target management spoke first. "Phillip, you can't be seriously interested in our Company. Please tell me that you made a mistake in that tender offer last week."

"No, Stephen, I did not."

"Well, we can't believe that you are serious. You have played Hell, with our about to be initiated new stock offering. I might add, that in case you did not know, we, along with your other targets, were successful in blocking the cessation of trading of our stock tomorrow morning. For your information, all your targets' stocks are up about 5 points after an hour of trading. I suppose that I could thank you for raising our stock's price, both today and over the past two months."

"You're welcome, but let me get to the point. We think our idea of a large rail company to be unique and workable. We would be most interested in your joining in our enthusiasm. For your information, it would be your management team that we would look to to handle the entire organization."

"Well, thank you, that is very flattering, but I am sorry. We have other plans."

"Might those plans include pledging your assets and selling off a subsidiary? If you don't mind, I'd like to read to you a telegram that I received last night. It reads, 'Confirm agreement between my Company and Arrow Corporation for the assignment of an option regarding rail services and assets.' Here, you might wish to read it. I have a telephone in the next room where you might check it out."

The room was silent. Caroline looked at the packed side of the room. She thought that she could actually smell their fear. All the confident smiles had disappeared, the seating postures had changed.

The Blue Jay President handed the telegram to the nearby legal counsel and slowly walked into the side room and closed the door. Several minutes passed with no one speaking. Finally he returned and sat down slowly. "Would you please review for us your plans for the new organization and how my people would fit in? I would be especially interested in hearing your ideas on management contracts, severance, and the like."

This time it took John Jamison ten minutes to sort through his thoughts and quiet his heartbeat. Arrow had specifically pointed him out and introduced him as the new President of the Rail Division! The group had asked at least twenty questions and then left. Wow! Arrow was really going to pull it off. Again, Caroline was the only one left in the conference room. John Jamison asked her, "Is that what you call killing a White Knight?"

John Jamison was secretly pleased that Caroline had stayed in the conference room with him during these breaks. Perhaps they would have a comfortable working relationship. What he did not realize was that Caroline chose not to subject herself to small talk in the lobby or the hall with any of the three gentlemen who took such care to not look at her this morning. Didn't these creeps know that the sure sign to experienced people such as Turner and Arrow was the total disassociation that they were showing? If only they would return to their usual silent and secret learing looks. God, men were so dumb!

"Yes, John. Their St. Louis friends were the White Knights who were going to ride in to save them at the last moment. Like most knights, however, they fight for pay. Phillip simply outbid the Blue Jays for their services. That's the problem with knights. Don't let that group fool you, however. It's the type that appears to agree, that nods their head, that has found the best defense."

"What is that?"

"Oh, come on, Mr. Jamison! You, especially a man with your

104

experience and an entire Personnel Department of his own, should know the best personal defense when someone is trying to tell you what to do or how to improve your performance. You pretend to agree, you nod your head, and you say very little. It's a common tendancy for the speaker to think that the listener is agreeing when really what is happening is passive disagreement. People who openly disagree, who argue, who yell and scream can be worked with. It's groups like this one that can cause the problems. You heard their questions regarding contracts. Can you see having those people in a surly mood working for you? That whole bunch has to go."

"I think I see what you mean."

The receptionist looked in the door. "There is a strange little man out here with another man who looks like an ape. He says that he has a meeting at 12:00. Shall I show him in?"

Caroline jumped up. "No, give me four minutes exactly and then bring him in."

Jamison wanted to laugh at the pair as they entered. The Orioles looked like a shoe-in. The President hadn't brought a lawyer with him, he just had a bodyguard! Jamison could hardly wait for Phillip Arrow to start his sales pitch. That was to be delayed, however. The funny little man made a point of introducing himself and his companion to each and every person at the table. Only after the introductions with friendly handshakes and an amazing amount of small talk did he return to his seat. All around the table, everyone felt as if they had gotten to know one another, let alone the Oriole President. Never in Jamison's memory had this group of Arrow executives, as individuals, displayed so much friendly warmth with one another.

The funny little man sat attentively and responded with politeness. He sat patiently while Phillip Arrow skillfully approached him regarding a friendly acquisition. Both Massendale and Turner broke in to add words of encouragement. The introduction of John Jamison and the description of Caroline's role were met with smiles and nods. Finally, Phillip Arrow ended the presentation, "Well, that's it in a nutshell. As you know, I have admired you and your organization for years. You have perhaps the finest railroad in the entire Country. We would be most appreciative of hearing your views."

The President nodded his head and took out a half torn airline ticket folder, folded inside out with a few pencil scratches on it. He slowly returned it to his pocket. "Thank you for your interest in my Company, I believe in the scheme of things you call us "Orioles." Orioles, Blue Jays, and Cardinals don't live together, did you know that? They don't even frequent the same part of the Continent. No, I think what you are talking about goes against Nature.

"You see, for the history buffs, my Company is really not a public company. Oh, I know that the stock is held almost exclusively by the public and that the stockholders can vote me out, but they haven't. Indeed, my family has directly or indirectly been part of the Oriole management for over a hundred years. Heck, I have never worked for anyone besides my Daddy. Mr. Jamison, I look at you and I smile. I can't quite picture what it would be like with you as my Boss. No, John Matthew Jamison, I suspect that it would be best that you get on a plane this afternoon and fly back to Santa Barbara to your beautiful wife, Margaret, and forget this foolishness before you get hurt.

"Phillip, I look at you and think of your two boys who are out of the business. That was real smart of you. I have kept mine in and I think it robs them a bit. Anyway, what have your boys got between them, three granddaughters for you and of course there's Mary Sue and her four boys? Mr. Massendale, you have a lot to be proud of. I bet you didn't know that your third son's team won the soccer game yesterday afternoon. I know, I saw him myself. Your son was a bit disappointed in that he did not score a goal himself, but I told him he played a fine game. My what fine boys and what a pretty, red haired wife! Gee, it was fine to be standing in the sun in San Marino. I really enjoyed the day. Even went over to the Huntington Library before I flew here, they have the finest Japanese garden in the States. I never miss it when I visit that part of the world."

"Sir, are you trying to......," it was Lawrence Massendale, who sputtered, he appeared to have lost his saliva. He looked to a raised hand.

"No, no, I am not trying to say anything beyond the fact that I sort of like the status quo. You know things are pretty peaceful around my Company and I would like to keep them that way. Now I know that you have four weeks to see if you really want to do this. I would most fervently hope that you discover that you don't want to collect an Oriole. I will admit to you that I have no defense if you have the type of money I think you do."

With those words, the not so funny little man started searching

106

through his pockets. "Where did I put that thing? Ah, here it is. Well, I suppose that we will be going. Phillip, as a parting gift I thought I'd give you this. You might mention to your friend, who I understand is recovering from sky diving, that I believe that his son has only two children and that his niece has none.' The little man gazed around the room to let his words remain as an echo. He nodded to the only female, Caroline, "Ma'am," and turned to leave. Caroline blushed at his intense acknowledgment.

As Phillip Arrow watched the two walk out of the room, he felt through the envelope that had been given him. Opening it and dropping the contents on the table, he knew what he would see.

A laser nozzle, part of what Arrow knew was a device possible to penetrate the Lear cockpit glass lay on the table before him.

Outside the door to the office of Shaffer, Schwab, and Meyers a simple question was asked.

"Who would you wish?"

"I like the one at the end of the table."

"Not Phillip! That's right, I agree, it is to be Mr. Jamison. Be thorough now, no roughing up or light stuff. Either he is to be a cripple for life or no more. No lesser message will do. Phillip Arrow is a very stubborn man."

Phillip Arrow was indeed a stubborn man, but he also was a thorough man. Within minutes he had dismissed his people. They would meet again tomorrow at 10:00 AM. Each had his or her assignment. He encouraged each of them to enjoy the City and forget the last visit. Overall the sessions had gone very well.

Returning to his communication room he had made three calls. The first was to his internal security group. "Plan Red" was in effect and his family would disappear for a week at his expense. Not knowing how to deal with a problem was one thing, allowing oneself to present himself as a target was insanity. The second call was to a grandfather of two grandchildren who undoubtedly had a similar plan of action. This particular grandfather was most upset at the Oriole's audacity, but only stated that of the Orioles' 50,000 employees, there existed an army of toughs that could easily match any army of his own over the short term. Finally, Arrow called Everett Lacey. The call was automatically relayed through the various locations where Lacey might be and finally found him fast asleep in his Westwood apartment.

"Lacey, can you concentrate?"

107

"I doubt it, but I will give it a try."

"There have been some new variables entered into the scenario. The Oriole President has to have a plant on my staff, probably in Corporate Air. The Orioles have threatened my grandchildren's lives and claimed that they have their personal schedules even to the point of visiting a soccer game yesterday. It really surprised Massendale, I tell you, I doubt if he's ever been to a game himself." Arrow stopped himself, he was still shaken. He knew he was rambling. "To the point, the Orioles are in our nest and I want to know 'how' and 'why.' Any ideas you may have would be appreciated while my security people look into it."

"Beats the Hell out of me at this moment, go on." The ache of lack of sleep and the walls of his apartment made him forgo the usual "Sir."

"Second, I think your computer search should have another entry. The Orioles knew of some individuals of interest related to our unions. I would like to run their records against three unions. Also, if you can get access to the FBI's files at this time of day, I would like to see if there are any connections."

"Any chance of you just telling me who your personal union trust fund contacts are so I can simplify my work?"

"What makes you think I have personal union trust fund contacts?"

"Anything else?"

"Yes, perhaps you could see if the FBI has a list of 'hit men' available for hire by folks like the Orioles and whether there has ever been any connection between anyone on that list and the Birds. Try the name 'Omega' and call Omega's files, you'll find my protected number to be MG38. Let me give you the names of the unions."

As Arrow noted the names, he thought of how cool a customer Lacey was. All these were impossible tasks. With Lacey's limited resources, he would have to get help and that would cost money. It would be natural for Lacey to mention the fact.

"Sir, I hope that you won't flinch when you see my bill for this month's services."

At least he is human, thought Arrow as he hung up without answering. Arrow felt satisfied, at least he could still forecast a reaction or two. Why hadn't he seen the Orioles' battleplan coming?

In California, Meg Jamison was also unaware of a coming battle. Although it was Monday Noon and time for lunch with the girls at the Club, she was on hands and knees scrubbing moss and dirt from a brick path at the side of the house. A radio was on and she matched the tunes as she leaned body, arm, and soul into the task. It was good to wash away the grime, it was good to sweat out one's body, it was good to clean away the past. Beads of perspiration ran down her face, her halter was stained by both dirt and liquid and her guarded knees were crusted with mud. She barely heard the doorbell.

Walking down the path to the side gate, she spied an express mail carrier with a large package. It was from New York! Could John have sent her a present? She hurriedly signed for the package and walked to the still cool backyard. How could he have done it? He would have had to find a shop open on Sunday. Would that be possible? He kept talking about spending money, money that they had never dreamt possible. She tore away the express service wrapping and there lay a beautifully wrapped white package with red ribbon.

Meg was smiling. She would make herself work for this present. She placed it down on the patio table. With luck, she could return to it by three o'clock when her chore was completed.

It was four o'clock when she did return. The sun had almost left the recessed patio. What Meg had done after finishing the path and brick steps, which now shone bright red, was to again postpone the moment. While a glass chilled in the freezer and a double martini cooled in the refrigerator, she took a quick shower and then a scalding hot bath. Alone in the privacy of her home, she dried her hair, put it up in a bun atop her head, and pulled on a simple thin silk smock.

Padding with barefeet to the freezer to retrieve her glass, she then at last, sat down on a white patio chair before the ever so infrequent present. Until John had purchased her car last month, he just never did this type of thing. Meg stilled a hidden fear. Where was her husband getting all this money? How could he be so sure that the money was there?

She slowly pulled away the red ribbon while tasting her drink. What a beautiful afternoon it was with the cumulus white clouds now hiding the sun! Tearing the paper, she saw another present, then a card, and then two very high spiked black shoes with thin laces. The dirty old man! This was so totally unlike John. Perhaps his new job would change his personality, perhaps he would loosen up a bit and be more fun. Meg looked at the shoes. Perhaps this might be going a bit too far, she had heard stories and seen friends' husbands suffer

.

109

through a delayed adolescence. Was John entering his silly season?

She opened the envelope and gasped. A typed note with three thousand dollar bills. "Visit Capicio and buy their lowest cut, sexiest black dress" was typed on the note. Three thousand dollars! He must be going crazy in his old age. Perhaps Mary Sue Massendale was right. Could it be that he was attracted to Caroline O'Brian and this was a defense mechanism for him? She had seen it before with other women's husbands. At first temptation, they looked to their wives for protection. Could this O'Brian be throwing herself at John....and Lawrence....when did she have time to work? Meg smiled, poor John. She lifted the shoes and then slowly put them on. If they fit, wear them, she thought. She stood, they did fit ..... barely. Why couldn't John ever remember her size?

Meg then opened the smaller present. Barely scanty lingerie and old fashion nylons and thin black lace garters. Really, John! A second envelope was enclosed. More money? She placed the note by the glass and walked into the bedroom. If she was to be silly this afternoon, she might as well try everything.

Minutes later she returned to their private patio without her smock, clad only in her gifts. How excited she felt! She could see the ocean, but surely no one could see her. She had to admit that she felt very much alive, and "Yes," a trifle bit smug for a lady about to turn fully into her late 40's. She opened the small envelope and two tickets for the new, totally sold out, play in Los Angeles fell out, the one that John knew she wanted to see. How could he have been fortunate enough to get such good tickets? She opened the card.

It was minutes later. She sat crying in the chair. Crying and mad, it wasn't fair! Damn him! Damn Frank Turner! How dare he tell her he was picking her up in a limousine on a certain day at a certain time! How dare he! How dare he! Why hadn't she suspected? Why hadn't she known that she was to be attacked so unsuspectingly?

That question has often been asked before attack or conflict and on this early spring evening, nothing was different. Everyone was at peace with the world. Everett Lacey had been awakened to the telephone call after just falling asleep after another 36 hours working at the computer. His only response had been to roll over and go back to sleep. When he was to awake in 10 hours he would have grave difficulty in recalling all parts of the conversation. In New York, it had been an evening of electronic flashes and conversations that lacked sense, but gave direction. John Smedt's investments in the Orioles were being liquidated. On the other side, Aaron Goldstein's portfolio was poised to sell short once the Orioles had appeared to crest or when a call came to trigger the action. There was no reason to sell short when the Orioles stock was still rising. Aaron Goldstein was most pleased. Lawrence Massendale had been frightened until absentmindedly told by his father-in-law that "Plan Red" was in force. His wife had not returned his call.

Dane Hughes found himself escorting John Jamison and Caroline from a boring dinner after a poor Broadway play. Caroline had paid him no attention. Caroline was dressed "to the nines" and Dane felt a definite guilt for not wanting to share her with this older man, now so sure of himself. Jamison could not stop talking. Caroline appeared not to be able to stop smiling or touching him. "Yes," Caroline would "love" to walk up to a piano bar that Jamison had frequented twenty years ago. "Yes," Dane would be glad to tag along. Caroline's hugging of Jamison's arm had finally gotten to Dane. He let her other arm go and drifted behind the couple. At least this way, apparently deep in thought, he could look at Caroline's legs as she walked along.

Again, there was no warning. As they approached an alley, two tall dark bearded men with small, dark revolvers stepped out in front of Jamison and Caroline. Not a word was spoken. Just the motion of the weapons pointing toward the alley.

Caroline was on John Jamison's left. She immediately complied with the silent order dragging the complacent Jamison along. Dane stood still. Why did she do that? Why would anyone walk into a dark alley? Here, Caroline, here is the place! We have got to make them rob us of our money here in the light, please! One of the two men had followed Jamison and Caroline into the alley, the second angrily motioned to Dane. Ah, what the Hell! thought Dane, as he followed them into the darkness.

The darkness and the smell hit him at the same time. He fought for control. New York was attacking them on all fronts. How he hated this false town built on the sweat of America's working people. There was no chance of police. Hell, these guys might even be the police!

Dane's night vision was excellent. Night flying, night combat experience, and a habit of walking at night might have combined to allow his eyes to adjust so that he was able to see the knife. The thug who had followed Caroline and John had stopped them and pushed them against and facing the wall to Dane's left. Dane's escort was pushing him toward that same spot. With Jamison's face to the wall, he could not see the man behind him, the shifting of the revolver to a pocket, and the drawing of a shadowed knife. Only Dane saw the movement

It was then Dane reacted. Again, if questioned, he could not recount a reason. The fact recognized in his self conscious was simply that a knife had no place in an alley robbery where the robber already had a revolver, no place at all.

The other revolver pushing in his back told him where that weapon was. In a quick turning action that would force a shot to the outside toward the other's companion, Dane followed with a straight uppercut, a quick desperate blow, aimed within the arch of his spin to finish twelve inches, up through and beyond the man's jaw.

The pain of it all but crippled Dane, but there was no time to review his damage. Continuing the spin, Dane lept for the raised knife about to descend into Jamison's back. Dane's leap was from too far a distance. As the hand descended, Dane crashed into the man's knees. The black knife tore Jamison's coat on the right as his momentum carried the arch of the assailant's swing in that direction. Dane was more stunned than his opponent. He had planned to crash into the man at the waist and carry him to the ground. Now he lay free with the other man close to him on the ground in the black darkness. Dane rolled away from the area of the man with the knife.

"Move, move, get out of here!" Dane heard himself screaming as Jamison and Caroline still stood facing the wall.

It was John Jamison who took Caroline's hand and pulled her away from the wall. Hurriedly, he pulled her along the side of the alley with the light. Dane saw them moving toward the entrance as he raised himself to his hands and knees. At the alley's entrance, they stopped and peered back into its dark recess.

Dane looked again. Framed perfectly in the light, Caroline and John Jamison appeared frozen in time, squinting back into the darkness, like ducks in a shooting gallery.

Dane was so shocked he could hardly move. Two men down on the ground, both larger than he, both armed, and with every intent to kill them. The one to his right was surely not hurt, Dane had just hit his knees. He probably still had the knife, let alone a revolver. Ahead of him toward the alley's entrance where the couple stood, the figure of the second attacker raised himself and slowly lifted his revolver. He was carefully aiming at the gaping John Jamison.

On all fours, Dane somehow charged. His only training from that position had been as a high school lineman. As he hit the man taking aim, he did not hear the crash of the lunging man and knife which descended on his vacated crouched position. A shot rang off the brickwall next to Jamison. Only then did Jamison move to push Caroline away from the lighted entrance of the alley, toward the lighted intersection and apparent safety. As they started to move, they were joined by a sprinting Dane Hughes who greatly hastened their pace. After a block and a half at a desperate run, they hailed a cab. Dane had first pushed Caroline into the taxi, then Jamison, and he himself followed. Caroline hid her face on Jamison's left shoulder.

"Here's the address Cabby, take us back to our hotel."

"Oh, come, come, Dane, we must visit that piano bar." Jamison was gasping for air, but his body felt totally alive. He had a flush of excitement on his face.

"No, no, John, take me back to the hotel. What is wrong with you Dane! You almost got us killed. That man shot at us! Why did you start a fight? They only wanted to rob us, what's a few dollars? Did you have to play that big man stuff, are you that sick with your male inflated ego that you have to play cops and robbers? You are crazy, do you know that? I know that you have been jealous of John all evening. Think of what you just about did! Think of it! Not just me, you almost got John killed and ruined all our Company plans. Oh you dummy, you big dumb ignorant, hormone controlled idiot!" cried Caroline.

As Dane guided the Lear out onto the runway, he tried to remember every word of that speech. Had she or had she not used a swear word when she was frightened? He thought not. Dane smiled at the mood of his sole passenger. On the return to the hotel while Jamison bought Caroline a drink to calm her nerves, Dane had called Frank Turner. In two minutes Turner had him in Arrow's suite where the decision was made to take Jamison straight from the bar to the airport. His luggage would follow on the next flight. Arrow had muttered something to Turner about informing a "bird" that Jamison had taken his advice and returned to Santa Barbara. Then Dane was wished "God Speed." Turner had ridden down the elevator with Dane and delivered the order personally as Dane called for a fresh copilot.

113

The last sight Dane had of the hotel lounge was Frank Turner sitting down to what looked like, what appeared to be, the finishing of John Jamison's drink with a still shaken Caroline O'Brian.

7

Tuesday

"**M**eg, Meg, I am home!" John Jamison had just entered his front door far from fresh from a trip delayed by a stop in Chicago and Dane Hughes fighting of 140 mph headwinds for five hours across the continent. The early morning sun was just starting to warm the hill behind his house as the taxi drove him up the drive. He was still furious with Hughes. It was obvious what had happened. The simpleton had been trying to show off for Ms. O'Brian and had turned a very ordinary situation into a dangerous one. As a result, John Jamison had to miss what were surely to be memorable meetings in Arrow Corporate history. And to think that Frank Turner bought Hughes' story, a story that Hughes could not wait to tell! No one at the meeting who was listening to the last target's President could really, seriously think he had threatened John Jamison! No one had ever wanted to harm him, let alone kill him!

When Meg heard her husband's voice, she could barely move from the hall where she had been again staring at the present delivered the previous day. The note again lay open, along with the money and the clothing. How long had she stood there frozen? A minute...ten...twenty minutes? What was wrong? Oh, John! Why have they sent you home? Was it something you said? What could he possibly be doing home, he was not due until the end of the week? Perhaps the negotiations had fallen through. That's right, that was surely it. Hurriedly she closed the box and put it back onto a high shelf. "I'm in here John, here I come."

Exactly one large pot of coffee later, John had talked himself out. The story was rather remarkable, for the part that he had seen at least. They were assured to have at least two of the targets safely acquired. The third appeared also very possible, if only people would let time take it course. Upon his leaving, Frank Turner had stressed to him how important he was to their plans and if there was only just a slight chance of his being harmed, both he and Phillip Arrow concurred that he should be careful. Meg looked at her husband as he talked. He was flushed and confident, a new man that she had so rarely seen during times of introspection such as this. "Yes," he had performed well at the meetings. "Yes," they had introduced him as the new Rail President. And "Yes," the meetings with the targets were complete for now. He only briefly touched on how Hughes had fouled up his week.

Meg could not let the obvious slight or the reason for her husband's return remain unexplained. "It appears that Mr. Arrow believes that you are in some danger. Don't you think that you are making light of what could be a dangerous situation?"

"No, of course not. Now Meg, don't do what you always do when I talk about my work in a stress situation. You always take the other person's viewpoint and argue with me. That's just not fair."

"John, I think that all wives do that. It is partly for stimulus and partly to protect their spouses. Could Dane Hughes have been right?"

"Sure, someone tried to hunt us down in the middle of New York. Meg do you have any idea how difficult it is to get from one place to another in that City? I just don't want to discuss any more about it. Don't let's talk about it. Now, what do you think of the new job? What do you think of your new husband?"

"John, please listen to me. You have had a unique opportunity and a supreme compliment. You have succeeded beyond our highest dreams in terms of promotions and achievement. Let's stop a moment and think what our lives will be like with you in your new role. What price will you have to pay, what price will I have to pay? This job will change our lives, probably change the place where we live. It will just change us. Do we need that? Don't we have enough money and don't we live in the perfect place?"

"Meg, you sound as if you don't want me to take the job. Don't you know it's 'up or out' and I want to stay 'in' right now?"

"John, you are on such a high from all this that you can't see everything clearly. First, you almost get killed and all the while you are fascinated by a job that could, indeed, kill any man."

"Me not see? It is you who are not listening. I said it is 'up or out' and you don't seem to understand. It's my job, my only job!"

"I know that! But think of it, do you really want this job?" Meg knew that she had to force the issue now. Shocked by the morning, her stomach now churned for she believed that her husband was probably mistaken in his interpretation of the events in New York. She leaned over to inspect the coat. The cut and rip were real. What was wrong with a man who could not see clearly because he wanted something so badly? Was this a common human trait or just part of male fantasy?

"Well Yes, Meg, I do. I want to be looked up to, I want to do well for you and the girls. Why do you ask? Don't you want me to be doing this? I don't think that you are being reasonable. You sit here in this house on the hill and think that it all just occurs. There is no one who guarantees you the right to play cards at a Club, have the money to buy groceries when we need them, pay for the girls' education, and have money for our retirement. If I left Arrow Corporation at age 51 we would have absolutely no pension. It is the next ten years where those values build. I just don't think you rational. Again, I ask, don't you want me doing this?"

"No, John, I don't. Please try to look at this from my perspective. We can do fine without Arrow Corporation. Perhaps that boy Dane Hughes was right. I don't trust any of those people and even if I did, I don't think you are right for the job. John, don't look at me like that. I think you are too good to be put through the stress of a job like that."

"Dane Hughes was just showing off for his girlfriend, Caroline O'Brian. What she sees in him, I can't imagine. Say how is that new car of yours running?"

"John, you are not listening to me. I want you to 'not' take that job!"

"Oh quit it Meg!" John Jamison had yelled across the table at his wife. Her shocked look was accompanied by a draining of all the blood from her face. "Oh, Meg, I'm sorry, it's just that I am very tired and don't know what I'm saying. Let me be honest. If you and I had had boys perhaps I could be like other men and live my life through them. You have your girls and all I have is my professional career. If we had had sons..."

"Oh, John..."

"Sons, sons, sons," mused Everett Lacey as he reviewed the list of variables that Phillip Arrow had given him. He thought it strange, the Arrow boys weren't even connected to the Company. Lacey was doodling at the computer. He couldn't face the task of again reviewing the results of five days of full computer search and tens of thousands of dollars worth of utilization. The score was still zero to zero. Another entry, Massendale and Massendale, now there would be quite a law firm, thought Lacey, as he decided that he might as well add the name of the daughter.

Lacey was discouraged. He knew that he had to start from ground zero. He had missed something or there was nothing to be found from these computer maturations. He would start with Hughes. Why hadn't he listened better? What did he have that was solid? Lacey had gone back to his doctoral training. One first had to define the question. Then one had to carefully examine all the evidence.

Lacey looked at his written list. He had written just two questions:

1) Why does a union official (and Lacey knew that he would soon discover the man's name) wish Arrow Corporation to purchase three railroads and assorted subsidiaries?

2) Who directed Blarnef and Blarnef to purchase the targets' shares two months ago?

Lacey looked at the list. Could the two questions be connected? The telephone interrupted his thoughts. He knew that they were related.

"Lacey, Hughes here. I see your message left here on my door. What can I do for you man?"

"Dane, I need some help. Can you come over? I'll buy you a beer and ask you some questions."

"I am one bushed guy Ev, I just got in from New York. Tell you what, I have been sitting and sitting. Why don't you drop by and we'll run out to the beach. Can you ask the questions while we walk? Otherwise, I think I might go to sleep on you."

Forty minutes later, Dane Hughes and Everett Lacey were walking north from the Santa Monica pier under the cliffs of the City above. It was a warm, blue morning - the dark blue of the ocean to the left, the light blue of the sky above, both cut with an arrowlike peninsula of cliffs that announced the meeting of the Santa Monica Mountains and the sea. Lacey had gone to some lengths to fabricate a story. He told his friend that he had to know the reason for his having lost his job, that he wanted to know why he was fired. Dane had voiced his support and unsuccessfully tried to comply.

"Dane, that really doesn't assist much. Look, I really need some help. I have got to know who that man in the plane was. My being fired by Arrow has to be tied into that conversation, I just feel it." Lacey had been sticking to the truth even in a fabricated story. "You never saw the man? Was he young or old?"

"Never saw him! I would suspect that he was old. . . and powerful. He spoke with the authority of someone from the East, no accent, more like a D.C. type than Boston or New York. Believe me, I am trying, Ev. I can recall our conversation about this conversation over at the Turner's the other night a whole lot better than the actual words. Maybe it was the adrenaline that came after hearing them, it seems to have washed all the words away."

"What were you thinking of right before you turned on the listening system?"

"It must have been about Caroline. She gave me Hell the night before. That's right. . . . Arrow was saying that he didn't know why he had let him coerce him into this."

"Dane, what do you really know about Caroline?"

"I know that I love her. I know that I would die for her. I know that just that 'off the wall' question pisses me off?"

"I did not mean it that way. It is just when I search her personal files, I find a girl raised in Philadelphia by a maiden aunt who is now dead, that her parents were killed in a car crash when she was twelve in upstate New York, that she went to private church schools and then Vassar and the University of Michigan."

"So?"

"So, I don't find the clutter that most have in their files. Important little things that are always there about top staff people, like who paid for her education. . . . all those things are missing. But then that, I suppose, is Caroline. . . no clutter. Now let's get back to what the man said about someone coercing Arrow, "Did he say 'him' or was he referring to the union or a group of individuals?"

Dane was still riling at the random inference regarding Caroline. It was obvious what Lacey was doing. He had done it before. In his nice

119

way he was saying that Caroline was not the type of girl for Dane, that she was too well educated, too ambitious, too successful in the business world. Why didn't Lacey just lay off? Caroline must see something in Dane also. Lord knows that she was difficult to know, but she did give him some return of his affections. And of one thing Dane had no doubt, he was her most frequent and really only steady companion. Tired as he was, he decided to forego a retort. They had argued about it before. "He used the word 'you' if I remember correctly. If my memory is serving me, I think that that could have meant either him or a group."

"Good, good, go on. Try to remember what came next." It was three miles later after they had made a turn for the car with a tired man that Lacey interrupted him again. Most of that time had been spent in silence as Dane valiantly racked his memory. Lacey broke the silence, "Go over that part about the Company name again and who was it who mentioned 'legacy'?"

"It could have been either of them, maybe the man first. He wanted Arrow to use . . . . . let me get this right by your rules since he did not use any name other than 'Pacific' . . . the name Southern or Union could have been two inferred names, those are the two acquisition candidates."

As Everett Lacey drove home after dropping off the exhausted Hughes, he recounted each of Dane's words. His thoughts strayed as he drove to his feeling of pleasure in driving in Southern California in a company car. When, he wondered, would Arrow Corporation's Personnel Department reclaim it? The Company still paid all expenses. Technically, it was only used for business purposes. A small monthly deduction from his paycheck in December, offset by an accompanying bonus, supposedly covered his personal use. This $20,000 per year benefit granted tax free would be greatly missed. Working for a corporation as an executive was not such a bad life. As a single man, he enjoyed being part of the group that caused the annual April rape of the Tax Code. It was his only break as an otherwise defenseless single American in a time when the average working man labored from January 1st to June 22nd for the Government. He wondered when all Americans would rebel? When August 22nd was the date, September 30th?

Lacey looked at the neon signs calling for use of buses and car pools that appeared every mile along the Los Angeles Freeways. The Mayor's relatives obviously owned the sign company. Millions of dollars had been squandered because the City and California State bureaucrats did not listen to their genes. For millions of years man's ancestors walked and stalked in silence, not speaking, with thoughts that were turned on low, capable of picking out only unusual motion. The hunter, thought Lacey, is not constantly thrashing about. Instead, he finds a place to sit and for hours only his subconscious recognizes his surroundings. Lacey looked around him. All the other vehicles had but one half alert occupant. All had drivers who were lost in thought, yet ready for the unusual motion. Driving on the freeway is the modern hunting rest, thought Lacey, man naturally hunts and drives best alone.

Everett Lacey forced his mind back to Hughes' story. It was only a fragmented account, surely much was missed. As Dane slept the morning and afternoon away, Lacey dissected the conversation into single word variables and added them to the ongoing computer program analysis. Perhaps his search was going to be unsuccessful, but at least it was going to be thorough. Lacey now knew that he was forcing his work. He was tired. In times like these he knew that one made mistakes. What could he have overlooked, what was he overlooking now?

In New York, a group of six tired individuals sat around a conference table cluttered with press clippings, full page announcements published in the *Wall Street Journal,* prospectuses and other copies of material filed with the Securities and Exchange Commission and other government entities, and other notes and papers. Phillip Arrow had gone over each and heard the various reports. He then turned to John Smedt, the investment banker, "Does the firm of Arlington, Bothell & Hyde have any major concerns at this time? I do not want to overlook even the smallest of possible problem areas. Is there anything that bothers you?"

John Smedt nodded his head in the affirmative. His slow shuffling of the papers before him warned those present that he intended to take his time getting to whatever the subject might be.

"Well Yes, let's review what we have done. In all three cases we offered to purchase up to 100% of these companies' shares, with the provision that in the event less shares are tendered, we will purchase those shares unless less than 49% are offered for sale by their holders. If that occurs, we can walk away. You, however, have instructed us to try to purchase exactly 49% of each company's ownership after this month is over. That is going to take some expensive fees to pay off the transfer agents, but it can be done if we get lucky. And in at least one case, we will still have to request a special stockholders' meeting.

"The less than majority ownership means that we must trust that there will be at least another 2% that will agree with us - as there always is, to gain majority control. Then we will give them paper, that in Arlington, Bothell & Hyde's and the targets' investment bankers' opinions are equivalent to the cash value paid for the first shares, for the remaining 51% ownership.

"This is a classic two tier or two step approach where the second step will undoubtedly be less costly to Arrow Corporation. Thereafter, you will get the accounting and tax treatment that you discussed yesterday."

Lawrence Massendale interrupted, "In a way, we could have done the same thing by gradually buying up the stock. What it amounts to is a quick theft of control with junk on the back end."

"Yes, but what bothers us is the hostility that we saw yesterday. These people may not be able to prevent us from the takeover, but they can stall us and the process may not be 'quick.' It could be months, years before we have completed these transactions. Arlington, Bothell, & Hyde would strongly recommend that you consider the possibility of purchasing up to 79% of the outstanding shares and demanding that all changes and merger steps be taken immediately."

"John, your fee is partly based on cash paid. Don't you think there is a conflict of interest in that recommendation?" Aaron Goldstein chuckled and obviously enjoyed sinking the knife.

"No more, Aaron, than you being paid a fee based on the legal and court time and the hassle that these people will be put through. I might also note that if an offer is hostile, you double or triple your daily rates. In cases such as this where real hostility exists, you have been known to quadruple your rates and get away with it. Don't talk to me about 'conflict of interest' or 'commissions'. These folks have to get back to running their businesses. They don't need all this."

"You are damned right!" It was Frank Turner and he had been uncharacteristically quiet all day as he sat next to Caroline. "It is always easier to make a marriage than to make a marriage work. For your information, both Phillip and I will be visiting the targets on our own the day after tomorrow to get the ball rolling."

122

"I would strongly advise against that. . . . ," interjected a suddenly clearly shaken Aaron Goldstein. Were these Western barbarians ever going to quit surprising him? That was just not done!

"I know you would," continued Turner, "but what you people don't realize is that the questions that will decide this are not the price or terms, it's the autonomy and authority that the acquired firms will retain. These people are worried about their honor, not their stockholders' pocketbooks. We have to focus squarely on executive compensation, benefits, and prequisites. But they need to also know that their operating philosophies fit, that their policies, practices and procedures will or will not change. They've got to know what types of professional challenges await them. Even if all these things don't occur exactly as expected, they are the keys to selling, coopting these people."

"Still, at this delicate time . . . . ," Aaron Goldstein continued to look terrified.

"Aaron, calm down." It was Phillip Arrow. "You have to realize that these executives are not so much worried about Arrow Corporation's controls, as they are about the other rail lines. We must allay their fears at this time or the transactions will never be completed successfully. But we thank you for your concern, a concern which Massey shares. Now, do you have any other major concerns at this time?"

"Yes, let me review the potential anti-trust problems we face. First let's review the laws that exist starting with the Sherman Anti- Trust Act and the Clayton Act, both of which could be applied. Then we have a major concern with the Williams Act of 1968 and the Hart-Scott- Rodino Act of 1976. These Acts were passed especially to deal with tender offers. You see before you notifications regarding them submitted to the Federal Trade Commission with copies to the Department of Justice on Monday.

"We will have a host of interest in Washington. We expect both the Interstate Commerce Commission and the Federal Trade Commission to be interested. Our clock should be running on their 15 day time period in that all our material should have been accepted, and has for one exception, by this time today. I might add, I especially appreciate the brevity of printed material found at your Corporation. Finally, of primary concern is the Commerce, Science, and Transportation Committee of the Senate and the committees of the Judiciary and Energy Committee of the House of Representatives."

"Aaron, we know all that, you are underestimating us again. We have explained to you that from the Senate on down, we believe Mr. Arrow has taken care of the issues," replied Lawrence Massendale. Massey quickly caught the flush spreading over Goldstein's neck. It was time to put this arrogant little Easterner in his place. It would also be good to remind everyone that he too, was a trained lawyer. He continued,

"Just so that we are on the same track, I might remind all that we could be attacked in the courts both by the targets and the various state governments. It used to be that one would file suit in a home state to allow the application of state law. We must remember that federal courts can use federal or state law, while states can use only state law. The federal jurisdiction wins everytime that interstate commerce has an 'impossible burden imposed' to quote the Supreme Court. Today, state laws are basically meaningless, although we have filed action to prevent their use."

"Massey, what is your point?" It was Phillip Arrow who looked up from the papers he had been reading. "Massey, what is your concern?"

"My concern is their Boards of Directors. The Oriole Board is like that of Arrow Corporation. The outside directors are extremely weak with just enough of them to form a committee here and there on audit and compensation. I imagine that most of their meetings are also only by telephone and that they get wined and dined four times a year with all fees paid for their presence. They are a legal bother, a rubber stamp, and nothing more.

"The Blue Jays and Cardinal's Boards are an entirely different story. Seven out of every ten board members are not management employees. Both Boards have distinguished outside members. You find university presidents, church officials, civil rights leaders, nationally famous retired government officials, bank and insurance company executives. These are very knowledgeable people. In many ways we should be dealing with them rather than the Cardinals or Blue Jays' hired management. They are just not hired bodies necessary to fill chairs. Their Boards will ultimately make any decision regarding these acquisitions."

"Massey," replied Aaron Goldstein, "that is exactly why I like your chances with them. Relax, you know how the acquisitions will be treated by those Boards. The outside members will be asked to meet as an independent group with all insiders absent. To do otherwise would open them all to the claim that any vote was taken only to preserve the jobs of the present management. These outside directors will have the well being of their stockholders as their primary concern. These men are accomplished businessmen. They will look at a tender offer of 60% over those companies' expected common stock price and ask themselves how many years it would take to get to that level. I would expect their vote to be 100% in favor of the mergers."

Frank Turner laughed, "That will mean that the final full Boards' votes will be 70% for and 30% against when they bring back that recommendation." Turner obviously loved the thought. The picture of these rivals being sent up the river for a Turner sacrifice by their own Boards obviously excited him. He could not cease smiling.

It was Massendale's turn again, "I do not see how either of you two can be so sure of how their Boards will vote. Outside members might see much more than just stock price in their list of items to consider."

"Excuse me, Massey," Phillip Arrow wished the conversation back on track, "it seems that you lawyers are always looking for a degree of certainty while accountants are looking for accuracy, and I might add, that neither are found in the real world. We will face those problems only when we must." Turning to the other lawyer, "Now I believe the original question was, 'What are your concerns Aaron?'"

"Well, our concern is this. I was informed just a few minutes ago that the targets' counsels have informed the Government that they don't believe that such an effort could have been done without extensive written plans and the Government agrees. I have been informed that all researchers must sign affidavits with statements as to the full disclosure of written work completed at Arrow Corporation. I would assume that this would be Caroline and Everett Lacey. To be blunt, they do not believe that you would take on such an acquisition either so quickly or with such a scarcity of written material."

"Lacey is no longer with Arrow Corporation," voiced Frank Turner. "Someone had the opportunity to tell him of his fate over the weekend before I had the chance to fire his ass myself for his insubordination last week. My people tell me that when he came into work yesterday, he did not comment. He just looked them in the eyes like it was personal or something.

"Don't worry though. I'll officially can his ass when I see him!"

All eyes looked to Turner and most smiled. Turner glanced quickly at Phillip Arrow who was also smiling. Good, he thought, he had served Phillip Arrow well. He could not help but add, before Aaron spoke again, "You all leave the dirty work to me. One of these days it will be a pleasure to have someone like John Jamison assist me."

Aaron let the lie take its time to stink up the room. He continued, "So I have been informed. What I would suggest now is that Caroline and her legal counsel get down to Washington D.C. tonight and spend the day with our people to insure that the various offices believe the material to be complete. In the meantime, we will prepare documents here which Everett Lacey can sign. To facilitate matters, we need him here, no later than tomorrow. With luck, he won't have to go to Washington. Caroline, you can sign blank affidavits today and be on your way."

Frank Turner looked searchingly at Phillip Arrow. Arrow held up his hand, "Fine, fine, I will call him and have Hughes fly him back here tonight. In the meantime, Massey, you and Caroline get down to D.C. and meet with the Shaffer, Schwab & Meyers' people."

Caroline couldn't help looking at Massendale who, in turn, was looking at Arrow who had returned to reviewing his papers. In turning, she caught the knowledgeable eye of Turner. Had someone been talking?

Caroline waited for Massendale in the hall. "Massey, do you want me to make the reservations? We could take the train if you would want to see the countryside."

"That's not the type of side, I would like to see, my Dear. Yes, by all means get us down there, but as quickly as possible. What is it, I think the Hyatt is right next to Congress, that would be the place to stay."

"I don't know what you are talking about Mr. Massendale, would it be a left or right or a front or back side that you would prefer? And if you would, why don't you go find something surprising to look through as an aside?"

Both smiled at the other as Frank Turner walked past. They waited until he was out of range of hearing.

"No, you come with me. I know just the place unless you are embarrassed. We have a few hours to waste." He took her arm with an air of ownership totally insensitive to the despair of his companion over his selection of lodgings and his obvious lack of understanding of his body communication. She was silently thanking the fact that Phillip Arrow had not yet passed by as he left the meeting room. She would have to do something about Frank Turner. With Lacey gone, Caroline knew that she was now at the bottom of Frank Turner's pecking list.

It was two hours later when Ev Lacey's telephone rang. Phillip Arrow repeated the request and Lacey concurred. He also quickly volunteered to call Hughes and arrange for the trip.

"How soon can you leave?"

"Not until 9:00 PM my time. That's O.K., I will sleep on the way back and be fresh tomorrow." Lacey was silently thinking of the tired Hughes and the lack of desire to fly with an exhausted pilot.

Arrow added, "How are you doing on that search? If nothing is hot, could I request that you continue to look at possible defenses of the targets? I would be very interested in what they have been doing since late yesterday and as of today. By the way, I used your material yesterday with great success and it is much appreciated. I believe that we stopped the Cardinals dead in their tracks. It was obvious that the Blue Jays had another defense, a backup, that we did not touch. It was the Orioles that I misread, they had planned the old fashion approach, to just say 'No.' By the way, did you find anything related to the FBI files?"

"No Sir, but my search was incomplete. Those files aren't accessible like they were. They have placed a mini like ours, I think, in between their lines and it was doing an automatic back search. We weren't traced, but the Government is getting sophisticated. Well not that sophisticated, their equipment is still second grade, low bid stuff, but with the decrease in costs and the increase in technology available, they have machines that are now just 5 years behind rather than 10."

"What specific advancements have you made on the search for that stock purchaser who is using Blarnef & Blarnef?"

"None, absolutely none."

The silence showed much. Arrow was obviously upset by Lacey's brevity. Corporate chief executives rarely get a non answer. Even if the respondent is totally ignorant, all can sense that a leader likes a non response least of all. It is better to fabricate any story and be caught at it. Being caught eliminated the total zero that goes by one's name. Often, it is better to have a large negative sum in a leader's mind. Most often, Lacey knew, they forget the actual score and only remember the fact whether one scored or not.

Lacey smiled at the receiver and held it away from his ear. He expected a scream of frustration. Finally, he asked, "What will you do when I find out who it is who bought the stock?"

"That is difficult to say, Ev. As you know, legally, there is a lot of fuss but it all gets back to the Dirks Case. The Supreme Court ruled that a person who gets information from an insider becomes an insider only when the information is given improperly, that is, when it is disclosed for the insider's personal gain or reputational benefits. If this is a case where someone is giving it away just as gossip, then it will be tough to make anything stick. That decision was in 1983 and ever since then, the Government has been wary of the ability to prosecute any corporate executive unless he makes a tremendous amount of money on the theft."

"Will you prosecute?"

There was silence on the phone, was Arrow waiting for him to speak? Lacey changed the subject, "Sir, I also checked the data base access that you called 'Omega.' Is that what I think it is?"

"Yes, it is the formalized record of espionage and acts of violence taken by U.S. and European companies against one another. It was started after World War II to prevent prolonged series of violence among competitive companies. One's responsibility is to report such acts no more than 24 hours after they occur. Members then vote to confirm their understanding or approval of the act. Random or misplaced violence is met with sanctions. We that use them think of them as a national service firm, much like a CPA or national law firm. I too checked their records via a terminal here in New York. Did you see the work of one of our targets?"

"I saw that. Indeed, I found the Oriole's record of whom they hired, when the attack occurred, the reason for the contract, and whether or not it is continuing. Just so we agree as to the facts, it is. Jamison is the recorded target for a strike late in the week. What are you doing, is he protected?"

"I believe so. We have complied with the Oriole's request and I will discuss it with them in person the day after tomorrow. I sent in the request to have the sanction delayed until we have talked."

"Sir, I still do not understand Omega."

"It is the way in which we police ourselves as modern corporate citizens. Think of the corporation as a human individual. We record our actions for our peers' review. If force or espionage is ever excessive, condemnation and economic sanctions will occur. It is business'

128

civilized way of controlling industrial violence. You might note that except for the Japanese, who now refuse to join, there has been little intercompany violence and very little espionage since the early 1940s.

"In our case, the Orioles were allowed a free shot by the Omega members. We have insulted them in the most serious manner. We would have been taking away their freedom. Jamison should be safe now. I will confirm that by phone and in person on Thursday."

Again there was silence. This was not the world that Lacey had learned of in his graduate school. Finally, Lacey felt he had to speak. "Sir, I understand that Arrow Corporation is alive with rumors about Richard Smith's disappearance. Do you have him on some type of special assignment or should I take a look at his records too? I already looked on the Omega files. There is no mention of him."

Lacey waited for an answer and then looked at the silent earpiece. Arrow was obviously thinking of something more important.

Lacey did not want to drop the topic. "I always thought that Smith was a fine, thorough man. I always thought that he knew far more than one should expect. He could take only a few facts and see a pattern and guess what was happening. He had just the type of thought patterns that allow one to solve a computer program problem. Did he quit too? Was it the same type of resignation?"

Arrow still did not reply. Finally, he spoke to Lacey with mild distaste, "I know all that, I am the person who put him in his position and, 'No,' he did not resign. It looks like he just disappeared. I've been told that his wife started screaming last Thursday morning and accosted Massendale at Turner's party Friday night. I just read my forwarded weekend mail today and found a letter from her. Did you see her at the party that night? She wrote that Massey spent only a minute with her and had our security people kick her out into the street."

Ev Lacey's mind was racing. It sounded like Massendale. And it sounded like Arrow. He had the policy of opening all his own mail and allowed no secretary to even cut open the envelopes. His employees knew this and whereas it was impossible to see or talk to Phillip Arrow, getting a confidential letter to him was no problem. Somehow, he had always found time to read his mail. "Yes, Dane Hughes told me."

"Mrs. Smith now has the police involved as her husband didn't come home over the weekend. It seems that he dropped his car off at a repair shop a mile from the office. He may or may not have walked to work. He didn't sign in and no one seems to have seen him. Perhaps something happened to him on the way to work or perhaps he took off with a girl friend. I understand he was quite a womanizer. He could not let a skirt pass without a special acknowledgment."

"Did he have a special lady friend?"

"That I don't know. Not to change the subject, but what progress have you made on the source of last Thursday's newspaper leak?"

"None, whatsoever. I am assuming that the leak was planted to drive up the stock price. Blarnef & Blarnef doesn't care if you purchase any railroads. They just want the price to go up."

The silence over the telephone told Lacey that he had again violated the Cardinal Rule of dealing with a CEO. He should have lied about making progress just as everyone else did. He instead brought the subject back to the missing Smith. "Do you want me to concentrate on Smith for a bit?"

"I have asked Frank to take care of it. I doubt if he does. It is bothersome. We don't need police walking around Arrow Corporation this week just because Smith had a weakness for pretty women. No, you stay away from the Smith disappearance and concentrate on the tasks that you have assigned. Turner will handle it."

At that moment Frank Turner was dealing with the problem by calling John Jamison who gladly answered the telephone to end the argument with his wife. "Jamison, I want you to have your people take care of a problem. Last Friday Massendale had his evening partly ruined by a Mrs. Smith who was upset because her husband ran off with some little skirt. Now that I have heard Massey's side of it, I am really pissed! That witch has no class."

"Yes Sir, I heard about it when I called in. My people have fully cooperated with the police who have now left the corporate building. It is my understanding that Mrs. Smith says that her husband is dead."

"How the Hell would she know that? All she knows is that if it were a death, Richard Smith would be worth three times his base salary and annual bonus with double that if the death were accidental. As you are well aware, Arrow Corporation is of such a size that we act as our own life insurance company. There is no way on this Earth that we are going to pay that ugly little broad one dime, let alone seven hundred thousand dollars. I want you to make sure that Smith is officially suspended for not appearing for work. Cut his salary off and send her a final check. Make sure that the legal department has a full file on him. I never thought he was worth a damn anyway."

"Yes Sir, I will get on it right away. I was thinking of driving into the office anyway. It would be best if I took care of this personally. I will hopefully talk to Mrs. Smith today and explain the Company's position so that she fully understands."

"Just make sure you handle it, Jamison! You will undoubtedly get similar tasks soon as the Rail Division President if you are capable." Turner waited for Jamison's response. None was forthcoming.

"Speaking of wives, how is your wife taking your new promotion? Tell her 'Hello' for me, will you? I will see you Friday to fill you in on our discussions. Hold yourself open for a quick trip on Thursday and let's see, also plan for a Friday/Saturday trip one week from now. I will want you to visit all our Atlantic subsidiaries for a final check."

"Yes Sir, I will and my wife sends her best to you, I am sure. See you soon." Jamison hung up the telephone and felt greatly relieved. Now he could enjoy five or six quiet hours on the freeway. He could escape. In a week's time, perhaps he could leave early on his trip. A few days away might give Meg a chance to come to her senses, time to think about his success in a more logical way.

Jamison knew that Turner's interest in his wife was not casual. He had often sat with Turner discussing management transfers. If the wife was not willing or acceptable, the man did not get the promotion. He knew that Meg was acceptable, it was a question of her willingness. Damn! Why was she so selfish?

8

Wednesday

It was afternoon before the lawyers had finished with Everett Lacey. Affidavits were signed, questions asked, and materials reviewed. Having only been given a stale sandwich for lunch and no breakfast, he was hastened across the hall to a large conference room. Phillip Arrow rose to shake his hand. Lacey looked for Lawrence Massendale and Caroline, but neither was present, it was just going to be Turner, Smedt, Goldstein, and Arrow.

Lacey remained standing. He fought off the nausea of the time zone changes and lack of sleep and food. "Gentlemen, what can I do for you?"

It was Arrow who answered. "Ev, I know that before you chose to leave us, you were working on acquisition defenses. For everyone's knowledge, I would like them to know that as part of our severance agreement, you have agreed to finish up a few items such as this morning's work for which I thank you. Now, for these people's benefit, I would be most interested in your views of what the targets might be up to at this time. I might mention to the individuals here that when I called you yesterday, I asked that you quickly review the targets' computer records, their correspondence from their word processing systems, and the telephone records of their outgoing calls. We would be most interested in your views since we have you back here today."

"Fine, I would be glad to oblige. Where shall I start?"

"Try the Blue Jays," answered Aaron Goldstein.

"Alright, as for the Blue Jays, the review of their files shows a buildup in cash over the past few days. A review of their banks and other financial contacts leads me to believe that they will attempt a selftender, that is bid and buy up the stock we have offered to purchase."

"Why didn't they do that in the first place," interrupted Frank Turner.

"I think I can answer that," replied Phillip Arrow, "The White Knight that I contacted and with whom we talked, at quite a fee I might add, out of being so knightly, was a close personal friend of several of the Blue Jays' management. The rights of first refusal and other ties were never meant to be used. They believed their first approach all that was required. Please continue Everett."

"As you know, our....excuse me, your tender offer must under SEC rules stay open for a period of 20 days. In that time, present holders of shares tender them and we can then purchase them after that period. A company doesn't have that constraint when buying its own stock. It is covered by a lesser rule with a period of 10 days."

"14-d-8 and 13-e-4 respectively," interjected Aaron Goldstein. He appeared to want to do something to earn his fee of $ 450 per hour.

"A company can offer to tender for its own stock and must keep it open for the shorter time. This makes it possible for the Blue Jays to offer a higher price than ours, purchase the stock, and take it off the market. For example, I expect their tender offer to be completed by the week's end and that tender offer to be published next Monday. That means they will have effectively removed a significant portion of the available shares from the market a week before we are allowed to purchase any of their stock in three weeks. This will mean we, excuse me again, you will have to offer to pay a higher price."

Frank Turner asked, "Then you think that they are trying to drive up the price?"

"Only partly. This is something a high cash, low debt company like the Blue Jays can do. After they do, however, they should be a lot less of an attractive acquisition candidate being thus loaded with debt. Perhaps they are trying to undermine your financing."

"Good luck to them," voiced John Smedt.

"He does have a point, however," countered Phillip Arrow. "If we had insufficient funds, this would hurt us badly. Aaron what do you make of this?"

"The results will be a shrunken net worth for the Blue Jays, new debt, a loss of cash, and they have probably exhausted their borrowing capacity. As we discussed with the Cardinals, the Blue Jays could be precluded from doing this by some prior agreement. Unlike the Cardinals, their charter and bylaws allow it, along with any indentures found in the SEC Disclosure Inc.'s search. Whether they have leases or bank credit agreements that forestall this, we have no way of knowing.

"A tactic for us to use would be to bring up the subjects concerning the business judgment rules, state laws, and fiduciary responsibility issues. In effect, all they are doing is perpetuating management control."

Frank Turner asked, "Isn't there a possibility that they could be accumulating a block of stock that they will turn around and sell to another White Knight."

"Yes," answered Goldstein, "but a bidder under SEC definitions is anyone who makes a tender offer or on whose behalf a tender offer is made. They would be wide open if they do that. They also have to worry about qualifying to continue on the Stock Exchange."

Phillip Arrow waved to end the discussion of the target. "Our course is clear. If they won't agree to a friendly offer, we will just wait them out. They can't vote their acquired shares for they will be Treasury Shares. That makes any shares we will purchase even more potent as far as voting rights. What did you find out about the Cardinals, Mr. Lacey?"

Everett Lacey looked at his notes. "They look to me like they are about to swallow the 'poison pill'."

"What type of a poison pill?", asked Frank Turner.

Aaron Goldstein stepped in, "Frank it is preferred stock. The Cardinals have the right by their Charter to have their Board create preferred shares and distribute them to their shareholders as a dividend. Say it's one preferred share for every forty common shares."

"It will be one for twenty," corrected Ev Lacey.

"O.K., one for twenty. It will probably be convertible to twenty common shares at the choice of the holder, so in effect it will represent 50% of the Company. Say the dividend rate is 14% and keep in mind that a preferred stock dividend is not deductible for tax purposes.

135

Essentially, they are taking out a loan from their shareholders for which they get no funds, but on which they have to pay a doubled interest rate. It is ruinous to a company, but allowed by the SEC because the stockholders benefit greatly. In effect, it is a huge annual dividend that in reality, most companies can not really afford. And of course the IRS loves it. They tax dividends at 70 %."

"Sounds to me as if it is going to poison the issuer," added Phillip Arrow. "If they do that, it certainly will be poison to any potential White Knight. It will destroy all their cash flow. It also all but precludes any White Knight alternative for the Cardinals. Maybe that's O.K. too. I have never seen a White Knight who did not become a Black Knight in time."

"Yes Sir, but I don't think they have that in mind," stated Lacey as he again took control of the conversation. "What this is is a blank check that the corporate bylaws and state regulations allow as a last gasp anti-takeover measure, so I would expect the worst. I would imagine that these preferred shares will carry restrictions such as stating that a 90% vote of approval of preferred shareholders is required for any purchase of over 25% of their stock and that one must offer 100 % cash at the offered price for all shares. No two step purchase would be allowed. Also, the preferred stock would have the right to elect at least 1/3rd of the Board members of the acquiring corporation."

Again Phillip Arrow held up his hand, "The answer here is not to have a second step if they do this. We have offered cash for all shares, preferred and common if we have to. We will go to the full 100% cash offer if necessary. Now I am very interested, Mr. Lacey, what did you find out about the Orioles?"

All at the table turned their attention to Everett Lacey, "The Orioles are tough, Sir. I haven't found much, but I have a clue. It is a clue based more on the lack of evidence than on any findings. I don't think you will like what I have to say."

"Go on."

"I think we will see a 'Pac-Man' on Monday."

"God Damn you Lacey," yelled Frank Turner, "there you go using that phony New York acquisition jargon. Keep it up and you might get a job back here if you would care to put up with the whores."

"The Orioles are going to turn right around and eat you up Frank," answered John Smedt. "They are planning a tender offer for Arrow

136

Corporation shares. And why not? They are just as large financially as you are."

"Thank goodness," said Arrow, "it's just what we have been waiting for. It will mean millions of dollars in savings to us."

"We have?" wondered Frank Turner aloud.

"Yes, we will be using equity, probably preferred shares of our own for the second stage of the tenders. The higher the price of Arrow Corporation shares, the easier it will be and the less costly, I might add, to complete the purchase of just the other two targets."

"Yes Frank," laughed John Smedt, "this may turn out to be a case of front end loading with back end trash."

Ev Lacey looked at Phillip Arrow. "Sir, I don't know how sure of themselves they can be. I did pick up the fact that they added some Golden Parachutes several weeks ago. It does give you some idea of their strength, however. All corporations that I know of added parachutes years ago, the Orioles finally just did it last week."

"Thank you Mr. Lacey," interrupted Aaron Goldstein, "but this will be very expensive under the Tax Act passed in June of 1984. Any Golden Parachute that would allow them to escape to freedom with extra money will have a 20% excise tax tacked on top of the tax rate of 50%. Moreover, there will be no corporate tax deduction allowed for these payments. This extra money for a top management who think they might be going out the door could be very costly."

Frank Turner suddenly came very much alive. He did not wish to miss the chance to note that Arrow Corporation had never enacted any Golden Parachute provisions although he had long suggested that it do so. He turned to Aaron Goldstein, "I think we had better go over all the shark repellents you put in for us several years ago. We may need them with these Birds. What did we do? We added a super-majority provision where an 80% stockholder vote is required to approve any two tier offer, we added a staggered Board where we have three classes of Directors, each with a term that ends on a different year. How do we stand against all these other defenses we are seeing?"

Phillip Arrow knew that Turner could not resist coming back to the subject of Golden Parachutes at Arrow Corporation. Turner was the type that would never be paid enough. Like most greedy men, he always hungered for more. So Arrow interrupted, "Excuse me, but that won't be necessary. I will be talking with the Orioles in their nest tomorrow. I don't foresee a problem. In fact, let's not worry about the

Orioles, let's instead worry about Boards of Directors.

"In one respect, I don't see the Orioles as a problem. Their Board is controlled solely by their Chairman. The result may be bad for us today, but at least we don't have to worry about that Board. They will do whatever the Chairman says.......just like mine, I might add. The other two are more of a puzzle. Does anyone have a reading on them?"

"I suppose that I would have the best," ventured Aaron Goldstein. Both are fighting with the problem where a management who serves on the Boards, the 'inside directors,' that is, have a conflict of interest. If they vote against the offer, they will be questioned as to the reason. Did they do it to save their jobs or were they thinking of their stockholders? We have heard that both Boards have asked to meet without inside directors present because of this. Consequently, we can expect that their managements will be out of the final decision making."

"Great news," shouted John Smedt, "no outside director will put up with any funny business......."

"Unless he is Arrow Corporation's type of outside director," volunteered Everett Lacey.

"I am still going to get a chance to fire your wise ass," retorted Turner.

"Gentlemen, please," asked Phillip Arrow. "I just can not agree that any of the Boards would exclude their management members. I just don't see this as a time for any company to have its most knowledgeable and valued members on the sidelines. John, is not it correct to assume that they will be most concerned with the value of the 'backhalf' of each offer and how it is valued? Our tender offer is very vague. Inside directors will be much needed and much used."

"Absolutely," replied Smedt, again glad to speak. "Their Boards will be working from a broad outline of options. It will be the management who will or has been arranging the specific defenses. I expect that the total Boards will work from a broader outline."

"Describe that outline."

"First, the outside directors will know that as controlling votes on the Board, they can give in and accept your offer and recommend it to stockholders who will then surely vote that way. Second, they could attempt to make a contact with you or ask their management to do so. Their goal would be to negotiate a better deal with us, such as all cash

138

or a more attractive bit of paper on the back end. Third, of course, they could seek a White Knight that one of them might know that their hired management does not. Almost all Boards share knowledge."

"John, if I can be blunt, all that is bullshit," voiced Turner. "Those guys won't give it the time of day. No outside director takes his work seriously in this day and age. Any good consultant can earn $2000 a day consulting giving advice. Look at most directors. They will spend 30 days per year or so working with a company for....what is it with these two......"

"Twelve thousand dollars a year," ventured Lacey.

"That's right," angrily responded Turner, who wished that he could have remembered that fact without giving Lacey a chance to show off his mind. "Twelve thousand. The average director is worth about $400 a day. Companies get what they pay for. Those outside directors have great liability.

"I disagree." It was Goldstein who had taken on a command tone. "While tender offers are governed by federal laws, basically the Williams Act, a director's response is covered in most part by state law. Both in Illinois and New York, directors are deemed to owe a fiduciary duty to a corporation and its stockholders. A lesser statute in Washington also reads the same. All are required to act as prudent businessmen reviewing the offer in good faith and in a manner consistent with the idea that a corporation is organized and operated for the benefit of its stockholders.

"We have already seen one case this year in Delaware where Directors who sold a firm for too little have been held personally liable for the difference. They have to come up with the difference out of their personal funds.

"Let me be blunt. I know that you, Mr. Turner, have mentioned Golden Parachutes several times. Those are for the benefit of a certain class of employees. As such, they are wrong unless they benefit the stockholders. Outside directors are aware of this.

"Believe me when I tell you that the outside directors will have their legal counsels telling them that only after due consideration and only after identification of valid business reasons should they oppose the offer. Only then will a business judgment rule shield them from liability in connection with a decision to oppose an offer. It can't be done today in a knee jerk fashion. They would subject themselves to great liability. Not everyone has Unocal's guts!"

"Liability to whom, their grandmothers?" Turner could not believe that Arrow was even listening to this crap!

"I admit that most suits thus far against directors have failed. The courts' definition and latitude to decide what is or is not prudent business judgment have not been very precise. But you miss my point. It is not that a suit against an individual stockholder will or will not be successful. It is that most directors don't have the time or are unwilling to risk their estates for a job that pays a measly grand a month. Believe me, they will be listening closely to their counsels."

"You also have something going for you that we haven't discussed yet," added John Smedt. "Think of how the average stockholder is viewing this. They are confronted with an offer that they can not refuse even if they think it is inadequate. If a stockholder should not tender his shares during the next days and enough other stockholders do, he will be left taking only what we give him on the back half. Only those who tender now will end up with cash. If ever any stockholders needed a Board to protect them, it is now. They will otherwise end up with whatever trash we decide to throw at them on the back end."

"That is a good point," replied Ev Lacey. God, how he loved this type of meeting. Why was it that he would never have a chance to have a true place in this type of world? "But it should also be pointed out that there is another alternative open to stockholders other than tendering or waiting. They can simply sell their stock during the next four weeks on the open market. It is the easy thing to do to cash out 100% at the market price that is 5 to 10% below the tender price. That difference is what the arbitragers are willing to risk on your shafting, er .... discounting them on the back end.

"I might add, Mr. Arrow," continued Lacey, "that the market appears to be taking your tender seriously. If the market price today is any indication, then the professionals believe that the tender will go through and that you will be quite fair on the back half."

Phillip Arrow smiled. He had indeed noticed that the targets' stocks were this morning selling close to the offered tender prices. "That is one way of reading it. If I can believe what I read in the newspapers, there was a meeting back in Los Angeles where we discussed perhaps going up a bit in price to get a target's cooperation. I just think that these people have read the newspaper and think that the ultimate

140

prices will be higher than any price mentioned thus far."

Suddenly the room was silent. The reference of the continuing leaks to the newspapers was an open accusation. Frank Turner was smiling. Thank God that Arrow had finally put the dumb Coon down a notch or two. Who did he think he was explaining to them what an arbitrager's role was? Who was it who did not know of these modern pirates who infested the financial waters like leaches? He couldn't help asking, "Do you have any other observations before you leave, Mr. Lacey?"

"Well, yes I do. It should interest you to know that all of you are now being investigated by the top acquisition detective agency here in New York. During the last three days a team of what must be dozens of men have been interviewing past employees of Arrow Corporation for any dirt that they might find. It is a bit of a charade, but they might get lucky. They are paying a cool $2000 an interview with an agreement to remain silent. Here is my check, which I will soon give to charity."

"Well, you son-of-a-bitch, what did you tell them?" Turner blustered the response before he thought. Damn! He was letting this Black get to him.

"Enough to have the investigator go through his whole line of questions."

"Alright, Everett, tell us," responded Phillip Arrow with a tired smile. So Turner had finally gotten to Lacey! It was to be expected. Lacey had already briefed Arrow on the detective agency's search. Lacey's response was just to keep Turner off his stride. There was no reason for Lacey to be discussing this with this group now. He was human after all, Turner was starting to wear him down. No doubt about it, Frank Turner was a master of his craft, thought Arrow.

"Well, Sir, they are developing several tacks. They ask plenty of questions about Mr. Massendale and allude to the fact that he did not pass the Bar. I believe that they are trying to look for background to claims of faulty drafting of the tender offer or the like. A complaint might be that Arrow Corporation has made false representations. Interest in Caroline takes another tack. They are asking a lot of questions about her father or lack of father and his possible indirect or direct ties to union racketeering or organized crime. As you know, that could lead to an allegation under the Foreign Corrupt Practices Act, the record keeping part, as a tie to the Racketeer Influenced and

141

Corrupt Organizations Act."

"Shit, Lacey, you are sounding like Goldstein! Have you ever thought of studying law rather than just mouthing the words? We all know that Caroline is a bastard, what else is new? What do they say about Goldstein or Smedt here?" Frank Turner had decided that it was now or never. He was going to go after Lacey with a vengeance.

"They are asking no questions about them, just the Corporate officers of Arrow. I suspect that they already know that the two of them are bastards."

"Please, Everett, tell Frank what they are asking about him before he dies of curiosity." Phillip Arrow knew that he had to cut the meeting short. This was getting nowhere.

"Well Sir, the only other two about whom questions are being asked are you and Mr. Turner. Jamison, I take it, is so clean that they don't even bother. They are suggesting that you are a homosexual and will attempt to develop the theme that Arrow Corporation does not have adequate top management. About Mr. Turner, they are being more personal. They are wondering about the rumors that he likes to sleep with small furry, deranged female dogs."

Lacey couldn't help himself. It just came out without thinking. Earlier he had told Arrow of their interest in Turner's roving eye for wives of other men. In the moment to reflect, he wasn't sorry for changing the story. Turner looked as if he were about to have a heart attack. He would let Arrow close the meeting.

"Mr. Lacey, this has been very entertaining and I thank you. Before you catch the TWA flight from JFK to LA, I would wish to talk to you in private. Gentlemen, that should fairly well conclude our work here in New York and I thank you for the help with the Exchange people and the security analysts. I will meet with the others tonight at dinner and Aaron, since Massey isn't here, I would appreciate your presence when I meet with the newspaper people in an hour. Since over one-half the major acquisitions today are made by an unsolicited cash tender offer and bid, I don't see what all the excitement is about. We must play down any rumors of hostilities. Once such rumors start, we find that they often become more than a reputation, they become a reality."

In Washington, D.C. a similar discussion regarding reputation was ongoing. "Massey, what about my reputation? I was sidetracked here in your suite last night, but don't you think I should go up and see what

142

my room really looks like?" Caroline and Lawrence Massendale were seated in his suite's sitting room looking out over a Washington D.C., green and pink in the cherry blossomed awakening of Spring.

"No, no relax. We have had such a bitch of a day. Can you imagine being sent over to the Department of Labor auditorium to meet that group? Did you see the roster of Department Heads on the wall? Of the fifty six or so, only two were white. One had the audacity to wear big black glasses. I saw no Orientals or Hispanics. It looks like Labor in this City is just one color. I wonder if they have an EEO program? Where was I?" Massendale had stalled. He felt as if his brain were fried in the humidity.

"Look, I will order some drinks for the room. You just relax and let me make a few calls."

Caroline smiled at the stumbling brain connected to a voicebox. She heard him ordering the drinks as she walked into the next room. It should be safe to leave him here for a few minutes she thought while she visited the bathroom. It seemed as if her entire day had been spent in protecting them from his misspoken words. Under pressure, she had found that his voicebox and brain appeared to not be directly connected. As she returned, she heard,

"Phillip, it's Massey......Yes, our day went well, very well. Without regard to personalities, we are doing very well.....why am I calling then......Oh, I wanted to report that I just had a call from Blarnef & Blarnef's attorney and I just returned it. No, I don't have the foggiest idea how they found me."

Silence, then, "Yes, that's right. They wanted to tell us that they would/are totally supportive of our tenders. They even asked what they could do to help us. I told them to call the targets on their own, if they wished. Better yet, I suggested that they write each of the target's Directors on their own. I then asked them how it was they were holding shares in all our targets.

"Yes, yes, that's right. They said that they had always held shares in the railroad industry and that most of the shares had been owned for years. That it was only several months ago that they increased their holdings by a percentage point or so and broke over the 5% reporting requirements for the 13-G filings. No, they just said that they'd increased their transportation and natural resource holdings by a per cent or two and dropped their corresponding utility and banking investments. That it was just a strategy thing.

143

"Yes, yes, I believed him. After all, Phillip, the man I talked to is a member of the Bar.

"What, you have never heard of an investment firm directly writing board members? Of course it is not done! But there always is a time for a new tack or two. Come on Old Man, admit it. Blarnef & Blarnef have already done their damage. Now it is our turn to use them a bit for our purposes. Of course we can trust them!

"And if I might add, perhaps you were a bit off base in accusing anyone of violating your trust so to speak, last Wednesday. I thought it was idiotic at the time to think that anyone would think that an Arrow Corporation executive would cheat on his Company or that our New York agents would be so stupid........Hello.......Hello......Hello!

"My, my, Caroline, I believe he has hung up on me or that was a very loud cutting off of the line. You know, there are times when I think I could do a better job of running Arrow Corporation than its founder." Lawrence Massendale was straightening his tie. He had to say something, no matter how stupid, to hide the embarrassment of Arrow's breaking off their conversation.

"I agree!" Caroline broke into laughter. The look of quick shock had turned to a blush spreading up into Massendale's balding head. "Don't look so surprised." Caroline continued to laugh at the obviously very startled Lawrence Massendale.

"You do?"

"The reasoning has to be clear to anyone, especially our older Board members. Think of what they would do if Arrow died."

"Oh, I am sure that he has instructed them that Frank Turner should take over."

"I am not so sure. Frank is a very narrow manager. The Corporation is too large to be run by just an operator or an entrepreneur like Phillip Arrow. It needs a total man, understanding of all functions, and in today's world that includes law. Can you think of a company so diverse, as much in need of sound legal decisions? Every decision that Phillip Arrow makes is basically a legal decision. No, I think you would be a perfect replacement."

"What about the research that shows that companies headed up by lawyers or finance people do not fare as well as those headed up by operations or sales people? There has been a history of lawyers taking over and their firms or companies then quit growing. We lawyers are always looking at the reason why companies shouldn't be doing things

144

rather than why they should. The one thing I know is that I personally hate risk and I think that I would fall into that trap."

"So should an Union Arrow Corporation. It is too large an entity to be betting everything it has on any one gamble. Think of what Phillip is doing! He is betting his entire corporation on these mergers. There is no way that he should be doing this. There just is no reason why we should be so overextended."

"You are right, Caroline, I can't think of any reason for doing what we are doing. Men like Arrow are motivated by wealth, power, and status. Arrow has enough wealth, I don't even think he likes money. He spends very little on himself and always thought that it ruined his sons. He has total control of Arrow Corporation. Union Arrow will be too large to control, he actually could lose his feeling of power with this move. It has to be status, but status with whom? He has all the personal recognition that he will ever desire. Indeed, he shuns publicity these days like mad. Look at the fight we went through with *Forbes* to keep his name out of their magazine."

"Well, you are his son-in law. If anyone should know, it is you."

"Hell, Caroline. I am married to his daughter and I don't even know her! These Arrows are strange packages of flesh and genes. Maybe they are not human, maybe they are from another planet." Massendale wanted to put some distance between himself and his wife. Perhaps Sunday and last night had not been just a chance thing. Could he get that lucky again? Lord, she had been ignoring him all day up until now.

Caroline had sat beside Massendale on the sofa. She felt his hand begin searching through her jacket. She shifted her body. Massey was such a paradox! At some things he sounded so simple, with some he was so good. She looked at him as he absentmindedly gazed out the window. He had her attention. Did she have his?

"It's too bad that you ordered those drinks. I don't know what your father-in-law is after. I just know that it is fun to be along for the ride. We just know that he has to be searching for something too. We are all searching in a way, aren't we?"

Dane Hughes was also searching. He again found himself walking the streets of Manhattan. An unseen hand was pulling him toward the alley where the piano party had been stopped. He had to see it in the daylight and when he arrived at the alley's opening, he wondered at this silently tugging curiosity.

145

The alley opening was narrower than he remembered. Garbage sacks were piled six feet high in long rows that looked like cords of wood in the northern forests or bales of hay on the western plains. The grey building walls were sludged with soot. Broken beer bottles were strewn across the sidewalk. Dane looked around at the garbage and up at the buildings which surely held thousands of inhabitants. The thought that any city would be sparkling clean if its residents simply swept the street in front of their homes entered his mind. If it was that bad on the street, what must the alley be like?

It was worse, much worse. Garbage months old lay against the walls and blocked the far end of the alley. It was in the one clear spot where the attacker had forced Caroline and Jamison to the wall. Could they have known of this place? Could he, or they, live in one of these buildings? What did Dane really know?

Standing in the alley in the grey daylight, Dane only knew something was wrong, very wrong. He could feel, touch, and smell it. No one would stand in this offstreet alleyway. The two had been expecting them. Other businessmen had passed their hiding place. The two had to have been professionals. No one had been asked for money. The men's actions had been swift and sure. The request had been a quick death search. Into the alley, pocket the revolver, take out the knife, swing the arm, all before Dane was even in place. Dane recalled the man raising himself to shoot Jamison, rather than turning back into the alley to assist his friend. The man had left himself open to the slight chance of attack from behind with his slow, careful, sure trained action and aim.

Dane's mind was filled with questions. He walked down the street to the corner telephone booth. He would attempt to call Caroline. Perhaps she had seen someone who had been listening to them at dinner. Had they talked about the piano bar at the theater also? He thought not.

He knew they had not. There was no answer. Dane let the phone ring for minutes and then walked back to the alley wall to put his hands against the bricks much like John Jamison had done. Dane had seen three people sitting close to them at dinner while they discussed piano bars. There had been two elegant sixty year old ladies and a fifty-five year old gentleman with a cane. Dane could picture the man limping toward the restroom......and the telephone.

Say that the man had heard the name of the bar and placed a call to the men so that they could station themselves along their path. Would the two have had to know New York or just walk toward the bar? Living here was not necessary, just probable. What had actually been done? The answer was plain. Sixty seconds had been expended on the attempt to kill Jamison. Damn quick work!

Dane looked around. He had knocked one of the men over to that littered spot and the other back on that glass. No wonder, they had been slow in responding. Soon Dane found himself picking up bags of garbage and looking in the trash cans. It took him only minutes of throwing sacks to find what he subconsciously knew was there. Wedged in against the wall at the bottom of a stack of plastic bags were green camouflage jackets and two pairs of large trousers. Dane looked at the labels, Marshall Field. He looked at the material. The suits were of the two hundred dollar hiking, hunting outfits sold to the wealthy.

Dane could picture the men dressed in these green and black clothes that night. Was there a Marshall Field in New York or were the gentlemen from Chicago or the Midwest? No words had been spoken, no accent given away.

They had to be men for hire to kill Jamison. Were they also to kill Caroline and himself? He did not know, but he had to call Caroline, now, fast! Perhaps he could get Massendale if Caroline were not in. She had to know.

Moments later he was at the phone. "Hello, hello, Caroline is that you? I thought that I had called Massendale's number." Outrage answered his statement.

"Yes, yes, I am sorry. I didn't think. I know that you are sitting working on a hard problem and hate to be interrupted. I am sorry. I am calling because I am in New York at the spot where ......"

It was two minutes later that Dane hung up the telephone. Totally frustrated and many times interrupted, he knew that she did not believe him. Would he have any better luck calling John Jamison? He thought not. One thing was certain. He had flown his hours this week. Arrow had two extra pilots with him and Dane was not needed. He would deadhead back to Los Angeles with Lacey tonight on TWA, even if it were at his own expense. Perhaps if he visited Jamison with his wife present, he would be able to convince them to be extremely careful. Perhaps if he was lucky, he would again see the two who had attacked them and shot at Caroline. Of one thing he was certain. The

147

two were now in California. They had failed in their first attempt and if they were professionals, the only way they would be paid would be when they completed the assignment. He had to see John Jamison soon.

John Jamison had to escape. He had spent the day yesterday on the freeway. Today there was no escape. His wife would not leave him alone. Why couldn't she see his point of view? Why was she so against change?

Change! Jamison had seen the resistance to change in his family, in his work, at play, at the Club, in the Church. The human spirit did not like change. It resisted change like a disease whenever that change led to a comfort level the same as, or lower than, that that had existed before.

Sure this was to be a change, but it was a change for the better. He looked across the table at his wife, "Meg, I think I will take a walk up in the hills."

"Fine, I will go with you. The exercise will do us both good."

"I thought that you only liked to walk on the beach, that the snakes in the hills......"

"Come on, let's get our walking shoes on, John. It will do us good. We talk better when we walk....or is it that you listen better?"

It was five minutes after they left their house that the disappointment came. The two pest removal specialists who had entered the Jamison household had not brought enough incendiary to do the correct job and they knew it. Why didn't California people build homes like they do elsewhere? Why this low rambling affair with rooms connected only by outside hallways? In the North, East, and hot and muggy South and Midwest, square two and three story structures required only four corner plants and a center incendiary setup for good measure. What they had brought with them was enough only for the bedroom areas. At least they could get started even if they had to come back.

One man climbed down from the small attic crawl space. Hell, there wasn't even a crawlspace under the floor. These damn houses were built on concrete and the rug and thin wood cover would not burn at all, even with the new chemicals they were using. Quickly the central consumable radio igniter was activated. With luck, they would be able to finish the job tomorrow and ignite it that evening, two days ahead of schedule. To Hell with the original plan and clearances! To

148

think that they would have to drive down into LA to pick up more material! What a waste of time! But if that is what it took to make a living, they would have to do it. Ten minutes later they were gone.

High on the hill above, the owners of the redwood home were having the same thoughts.

"Meg, I am fired if I don't take this job. It's what I have to do to make a living."

"It is not that at all. Be honest with yourself, John, you want this job more badly than me, the girls, our home, the life we have made for ourselves here in the community. Think of the church choir, the friends that we have made, your love of your boat and ocean fishing, California wine, sunshine and our quiet, warm living. Oh, John, you are kidding yourself with your dream of power."

"No, that is not true. It is you who will not be honest, who will not change, accept risk or pay the price. I think you live in a fantasy. We are broke if I quit. No one will hire a 51 year old man,"

"We could sell the house. We would have some money. We would not have to start over."

"But I would be through in corporate life. It would be like retiring."

"Then let's retire. We don't need this. John, listen, it is not the money that we need."

"You are right, Meg, it is not the money at all. It is quality of life and matters such as my status. I have never had any recognition for my years of work. Now you are asking me to turn my back on it. Have I asked you to move? Have I asked anything of you? Where is your risk in this? Just stay on for the ride. For the first time since grade school I get the chance to be a leader. 'Follow him whether he goest,' remember? Please Meg, I beg of you, please cooperate with me on this job just this once. Believe me, I know what's best. Whatever the costs to us, the reward will be worth it."

"Isn't being a leader a natural thing, John, or at least different than being a manager? You have always been a manager, now you are proposing to play a different corporate role. You have said that a leader is charismatic, unpredictable, and a risk taker. That isn't you, John. You administer, you are an administrator. How can you be certain that this is what you want?"

"Meg, I am totally certain. I would die for this chance. I would kill for it ... no I wouldn't kill, but you know what I mean. This is the best thing to ever happen to me in my whole life. Please trust me."

"John, I trust you. How can you be so sure? Aren't those things of which we are most certain, the matters on which we are most often totally wrong? Please think of what we have. Why do we have to improve on this?" Meg spread her hands. The full view of the Santa Barbara coast spread out before them in the late afternoon sun.

"Meg, there is no standing still in life. One either grows or recedes. This will be good for us, believe me. It will be the best thing to ever happen to us. Please trust me."

"I trust no one!" In New York, Phillip Arrow had answered a question from Everett Lacey.

Arrow was finishing a complete debriefing of Everett Lacey's work. He judged these six days of work as major accomplishments. Lacey was solving problems right and left for the Company with his efforts. The strange thing was that Lacey did not realize it. Arrow thought it best not to inform him. There were many people who one overpays in any corporation, thought Arrow, but there are few that are underpaid. Those few, however, offset all the others' shortfalls. The trick to making profits off humans' efforts is to pay all the same. Contrary to modern business school lore, Phillip Arrow had found it best not to overreward or praise outstanding performers. To do so was to push them out into the job market. There were always to few potential opportunities within any one company. One had to take great care with types such as Lacey or they would be lost to competitors.

Ev Lacey broke his thoughts as he ended the review of the $400 million unauthorized and apparent insider stock transaction. He had asked Arrow who he least trusted. Rebuffed, he had continued and now concluded, "In a nutshell, Sir, I don't know who it is."

Arrow looked sharply at Lacey's despair. Could he be a quitter? Perhaps he just needed some fuel to charge his batteries.

Arrow had to break the silence, "Then let me go over the alternatives for you, Mr. Lacey.

"First, let's consider Goldstein and Smedt. They were chosen, in part, because we know that they both cheat in a controlled manner and never in any way hurt a client company. Their targets are the common public whom they take advantage of through offshore investments and agents. Caroline came to me the other day all steamed up over John Smedt's stealing. I had to tell her that we knew. After all, his Netherlands Antilles agent is on our payroll. Where she became knowledgeable about Smedt, I do not know, although I have a suspicion. And then there is Goldstein who plays the same game, but most often the other way around. Like real life, he goes both ways."

"You don't mind?"

"No, it allows us to know what we are dealing with in terms of outside personalities. That knowledge equates to our control. The chance of them taking a full position of 100%, the chance of them establishing a four hundred million dollar position, is slight. I would give that possibility to more than a 10% chance of occurring.

"I also discount the outside third party who heard about this second hand and who then developed a constant pipeline of information. Like most successful corporation executives, none of my people have the time to form or preserve any close friendships ... that is, if they had any to begin with. I doubt if any of them talk to their wives about their work with perhaps the exception of Jamison and Massendale. The only new person that you should perhaps check out is Meg Jamison. I had forgotten how pretty she is and I have yet to meet a beautiful woman that could be trusted. Unlike her husband, she did not become an American citizen and retains her Canadian papers if my files are correct. Call her and all other third parties no more than a 5% chance, however.

"That leaves 75% to apply to four corporate executives, Turner, Massendale, Jamison, and O'Brian. Also, I might include you as an additional suspect to bring the list up to eight."

"Me?" His insertion on the suspect list at this late date caught Lacey by surprise.

"Don't look so shocked. I am trusting that it is not you, but I can not be sure. If you find no one, your suspect score will rise to 25% as I believe that you have only a 50/50 chance of being successful and if you are the one, a 50/50 cut of the 50% chance that would find you unsuccessful. Overall, right now I place you with a 5% possibility with the rest divided up among the other four. It could go up to 50 times 50 or 25% if you are unsuccessful in your search.

"Come, come Everett Lacey! You would be thinking the same way."

It was a few very silent moments before the smiling Arrow continued, "Of the four, Massey is the least possible candidate. Mary Sue tells me that she knows that it is not him, that she can tell whenever he lies. I think she can and she has never told me an untruth yet."

Lacey's lack of any reply bothered Arrow. He continued, "No, I do not think it is that nervous young ass even though I wish it were. He just doesn't have the balls although I swear sometimes he is not as dumb as he sounds. Give him 5%.

"Then there is Jamison and I know that it is not him. there is no way that it could be. Give him 2% and make Massendale an 8%. Forgetting Mary Sue's lack of taste at age 22, there is something ... a lot of things that I have never liked about Massey.

"That leaves 60% that has to be divided between Turner and O'Brian."

"Would you divide it 50/50?" queried Lacey. "I know that it is not Caroline. I would have given her only 5% so that leaves Turner with 55%. He has to be the best candidate."

"I wish I could agree, but two things prevent it. First Frank Turner is the perfect economic, amoral corporate man. It is the ancient paradox of art. Art and science mix. Art and economics do not. This is a work of art. Frank lacks the finesse. He is a void when it comes to art. In fact, it is more than that. When he was born he was born with no sensitivity, no compassion. Think of him having an arm cleaved off. He has no appreciation of any art form.

"Second, there are his ethics or what you and I would call his lack of ethics. That is why he is where he is as my hatchet man. His ethics are those of the Eastern Business Schools, the ones in which he was trained by our Nation's best business minds. I don't see him as immoral or criminal. Everything he does starting with brushing his teeth in the morning has to do with furthering the good of the Company. No, Frank is totally honest and totally moral man within his amoral, if you can call it that, lifestyle. Pure and simple, he has the modern corporate value system.

"I suppose you could describe him as a barracuda. They cut and consume anything in sight with no thought. That is Frank, pure and simple.

"One needs that type around to survive in the modern business world. They are my guard against all the Harvard and Wharton MBAs who are trained to work like that who don't work for me.

"Why I can remember the day when we did not have to use lawyers, contracts, or pieces of paper. A man's handshake was all that it took. But I ramble ... was it Frank. No! This purchase of stock hurt the Company and that does not fit into Frank's value system.

"Caroline may be poorer, but if I look at the facts, I regret the day I gave her the promotion to be my Assistant. I sense that I fear her, that her latest transfer was to rid myself of a threat. I would put the split of the 60% at 10% for Turner and 50% for Caroline."

Arrow looked at Lacey's disbelief, disbelief that was written across the man's face. He decided then not to tell him that his daughter, Mary Sue, had also picked out Caroline. Yes, there was something wrong with O'Brian. Mary Sue was not often mistaken. It was the Laceys of the world who always depended on facts who most often made the critical mistakes.

Arrow's mind pictured his daughter and he smiled at Lacey. Yes, he had been right. If anyone would stumble on who it was, it would be Lacey. And that, after all, was what was important.

9

Thursday

Ev Lacey had not turned on his computer screen when he arrived home at midnight suffering from a jet lag brought on by passing through six time zones in less than 24 hours. As he crashed to the bed, he admitted to himself again that the two gin on the rocks at 43,000 feet had not helped. He felt just as bad as the last time he drank high in the clouds over the U.S. Would he ever learn?

A brisk jog, situps, and then a hard run followed by a shower and a breakfast almost brought him back to the living. The sun had long ago risen and Lacey felt an urgency to check on the work at his new office. But as he was about to go out the door, he could no longer resist. He leaned over the table and turned on his home computer's screen. Two entries later he was reviewing his Arrow Corporation program's summary results.

There it was!

A correlation of .83 and 5 exact trace matches. The buy of stock at Blarnef and Blarnef had the name "Massendale Trust." Who would believe it? Lawrence Massendale, what a sleeper!

Lacey ripped off his coat and began to trace back through the codes to see how the computer had found the matchup. His heart was in his throat. He would first look at the Trust. No! It wasn't Massey. It was the trust of the Massendales' sons with Mary Sue Massendale as trustee! Mrs. Massendale! Arrow's only daughter had ripped her father's company off to the tune of a quarter of a billion dollars! His job was over so soon! Only a bonus was to follow. He marveled at his computer program. When the answer came, it came so quickly!

He sat back. How could "she" have gotten the information? That was easy, Massey was a notorious talker. But how did "she" get that much capital, where could she have accumulated or controlled the 400 million dollars that was originally invested? No one person could raise that much money. Surely, she must have had help.

Slowly, Lacey worked back through the history of the trust. It was a non reversionary income producing trust with assets proceeding to 4 similar trusts for her sons' children, if any, upon Mary Sue's death. Mary Sue Massendale was the singular, lone trustee. Lacey backed through the files to the original date of the trust. It had started with a gift of 1% of Arrow Corporation stock given to any future children of Mary Sue's by their future grandfather at his corporation's inception. Twenty five years ago, that stock had been worth one million dollars. Lacey looked to the most recent Arrow Corporation proxy. The trust's holdings were not listed. The two sons still held their stock, but not Mary Sue.

She had sold her stock, probably directly contrary to her father's wishes. How could she have dared to do it?

Lacey methodically reviewed the history of the Arrow Corporation proxies. Mary Sue had sold her shares in Arrow Corporation fifteen years ago at the age of 23. He reviewed the trust, she had become the trustee upon reaching the age of 21. He thought, let's see, her oldest child is 14 and she is 38. Her change of the trust assets was made at age 23 after she took full charge of the investments. Ev traced the history of the one million dollars. It read like a textbook in investment management. Several times she had stepped in to purchase Arrow Corporation stock and several times she had sold, all at the right times. At no time had she held the shares for longer than one year. Because of this, the SEC reporting was incomplete. The last trust record showed eighty-four million dollars or an after-tax return of 24% per year. There had been only two losing years. Amazing!

He then turned to the second tracer key. The Blarnef and Blarnef investment in the targets was from a pool of combined investments using twelve different investment sources - probably various Blarnef and Blarnef trust accounts. Lacey checked the size of the investments.

156

Only two others were of the size of Mary Sue's, indeed they were a bit larger. He followed the first source back to the largest Los Angeles bank, taken out of their Commercial Department and approved by the Chairman of the Bank. He pulled up those files. Yes, the loan used the Massendale Trust as collateral. Amazing! Mary Sue Massendale had put her children's entire fortune on the line, the product of her investment appreciation of fifteen years. Lacey penciled out the dollar value of the trust at this point with the potential tender offer prices. After taxes and the paying back of principal and interest, Mary Sue had at least tripled her money and could, by year-end, have two hundred million in her trust with just this one loan. What nerve! What ability for a housewife......Lacey checked himself. He couldn't help himself, funny how he saw only the Arrow grandsons when he thought of Mary Sue.

Lacey then checked the second other large account. Again, it was a loan from another major California bank. He then checked the security recorded. Again, what double nerve! She had used her trust's principal for the second time as collateral. Was this the source of collateral for all the other accounts that also looked like borrowed money? If it was, the full 250 million in appreciation could be hers. With her other investments, she could have over three hundred million in the trust after taxes, perhaps more. With the loans, she could have six hundred million!

Lacey returned to the printer. After turning it on, he sat at the keyboard before hitting the print command. Was this what he wanted to do, was his job really over? When he delivered this news to Phillip Arrow, he would effectively be out of work, albeit with a large bonus. Would Arrow pay him? Yes, of that he was sure. But did he want the money? Hadn't Arrow asked him other questions, had not he, himself, identified another primary question? Why would the unions, or why would the union executive, or why would anyone coerce Phillip Arrow into purchasing the rail lines? Lacey did not want to stop that search. He reached over and shut off the printer. Phillip Arrow could wait and if he knew the truth, he would probably want to wait.

Besides, his bonus was based on the total of the fees that he had collected. Lacey smiled. That thought settled the matter. Funny thing about management incentive plans. They usually produced just the opposite of what was expected.

Lacey wondered aloud if Mary Sue Massendale knew the reason

why the acquisitions were taking place. He doubted it. She must know only what her husband told her and on that knowledge was building her fortune. Could Massendale, himself, suspect? Lacey doubted it.

Ev Lacey sat looking at the second trace. The computer software had found Mary Sue Massendale because of her Social Security number and the match to an old reported trust number. Once that number was entered, the program had cut through the data like butter. If he could find this answer, so could others. One just had to know the right questions to ask. He looked at the Blarnef and Blarnef files. The dummies had used the actual numbers so that in report season, some rookie clerks could easily get the work done with the required reports for the Internal Revenue Service. Lacey tested the write capability of the Blarnef and Blarnef system. It was positive! The last digit of Mary Sue's identification number read as a "9"; he inverted it to a "6." Now no computer, while matching data, would stop in this investment pool. Ev looked at the other investments in the pool. Could they also be Mary Sue's? He put in a global change of the number sequences. To Hell with it, he thought. She'd have to look out for herself if she had other trusts in existence.

Everett Lacey got up from the desk. Hours had fled by and he had just enough time to get to the office to check on his new people. He would have them concentrate on the identification of the union executive and take them off the search for the stock purchaser. First they must find out who it was and then why he was pressuring Arrow. And he would take a special look at Frank Turner. If he weren't involved in the stock purchases, he might very well be connected with this man. They sounded a lot alike ...... almost like a son and his father.

It was early morning and Frank Turner thought that even the Blue Jay's headquarters receptionist looked tired. They must have been working here all night, he thought. She looked terrible and totally mystified by his introduction. Did he have an appointment? Impossible!

"Just tell him that Frank Turner, Executive Vice President of Arrow Corporation is here to see him."

The receptionist called the President's secretary, who in turn came out to hear the request herself. Sometime later the flushed older lady came down the stairs to say, "I am sorry, but he is unable to a talk to you right now. Perhaps you could call back."

Frank Turner smiled and handed her a note that he had just written, "HAVE COME TO DISCUSS CESSATION OF TENDER OFFER - MUST SEE YOU OR IT WILL CONTINUE". He handed it to the secretary and wished her well.

Five minutes later he was introduced into a conference room with the Blue Jay President and his legal counselors and advisors. Turner counted nine associates. "Good Morning. I was wondering if we could speak alone?"

"I don't believe that that would be appropriate, please state your business."

"Sir, I believe we have gotten off on the wrong foot. This hostility is not wanted by Arrow Corporation at all. We have not even had the time to tell you how important your Company was to our plans." Frank silently noticed the audience's reaction to the use of the word "was." "Mr. Arrow has been assuming that your Corporation would control the other rail lines as in our outside assessment, you have by far the strongest management team."

"Please get to the point!"

"Sir, I am trying to," replied Turner as he silently thought of this man walking out of this building in three months, naked, if Turner had his way. "What I wanted to show you is a supplement to the loan material submitted to the SEC with our tender offer. As you know, we had to identify the amount of cash available for the purchases and that number was twelve billion. What I want to show you is an Appendix which increases that amount to twenty billion. I might add that we are now anticipating that you will present a tender offer for your own shares by this time next Monday. As you have the timing advantage to step in behind us and purchase early, we thought that you might ...."

"Excuse me Mr. Turner. I specifically gave you our time this morning because of your note concerning the cessation of the tender offer."

"That is correct, Sir. I came specifically to discuss the termination of your selftender offer, not our tender offer. I did not write that it was the Arrow tender offer on that note."

"Are you attempting to threaten us, Mr. Turner?"

"No, no, no! I just want to try to prevent the damage that will occur to your organization. Please, we think a great deal of your Company and its management. I believe that you now know that if this were to be a bidding war, Arrow Corporation will easily win. Please think about your people. With that I leave you, but there is one additional item that I will mention. I would request that you contact Phillip Arrow by tomorrow noon if a friendly merger could ever be considered. Your position is important to us because it will influence the way in which we talk to the other potential merger partners."

"What about the other companies?"

"You have my word, should we complete a merger, your Company will run them with complete autonomy."

"Could we have that in writing?"

"Absolutely. We would also want to make certain that your people are adequately protected and compensated. Please understand, we know nothing about running a railroad. We will leave that all up to you. Now I have to run and I do thank you for the time."

A half a continent away, Phillip Arrow was shown into the Oriole President's office.

"Good to see you again, Phillip. I am sorry I had to be so crude the other evening, but I had to get the message across to all your people. I see that you have checked with Omega and they have sanctioned my indiscretion."

"No, that is alright. Thanks for picking someone beside myself, I am too old for that type of thing. My, it is nice to be here in this part of the Country!"

"Phillip, what can I do for you?"

"I have just been thinking along your lines and came here seriously considering talking about the Hatfields and the McCoys."

"I am mighty glad you didn't. If you had, I would have had to let loose my dogs before you left the office and had a chance to set up. I hope that you don't think that your family's secret retreats and vacation locations are unknown to us."

"No, I have been thinking along other lines. What is it that I would be doing if I were you? I have concluded that what I would do is start a tender offer on Arrow Corporation stock. Yes, I am guessing that you would be putting that together. I am here today to keep us from such a battle and repeating a disaster like the Bendix, Martin Marietta, Allied Corporation affair." Arrow had tightened the fist in his lap. Only certain of his pilots, top executives, and security force knew of the locations of all his family's retreats. He had known that there was something wrong with his air or security force. Why did not he listen to his senses? Was he getting old? He was clearly upset and he knew

160

that he could not show it. Negotiations were at a deadly, make or break position.

"Of course, that is more than a guess."

"Yes."

"Well to be blunt, Phillip. After we kill away your spore, I would want to get my hands on Arrow Corporation and kill it dead. I would close down good plants, sell off your subsidiaries, wipe Arrow Corporation from the face of the map."

"Please, please, I don't believe that will be necessary. I am sure that we can work something out."

"Like what?"

"Your forthcoming tender will be very embarrassing to us. As you know in our tender, we have the ability to withdraw ours if a second occurs either on the target or on ourselves."

"Yes, that is where we got the idea."

"I am concerned with the other two possible acquisitions. If you come out with this highly manipulative approach on Monday, they will effectively have 4 days to repeat your actions should we withdraw our tender. What I need is time. Rather than your going ahead in haste with the expense of a full filing of an Arrow Corporation tender, I would ask you to wait until the Thursday of that week. That would be almost two full weeks after our original tender. That will give us the breathing time we need. Until then, we will just proceed with pushing your stock and raising its price a bit."

"You expect me to believe that ......do you think we live in a cabbage patch out here too? What prevents you from cheating that next week?"

Arrow was caught in quick thought. Where had he heard the 'cabbage patch' quote in the last week? Was it from one of the targets? No, it was in the Shaffer, Schwab & Meyers' weaseling meeting. So this little old man had Goldstein or his partner on his payroll...... surely, it couldn't be one of Arrow's people. "Yes, I do. I will give you my word and shake your hand. That should be good enough."

The small little man sat silently staring across his old and cluttered desk. Arrow looked around the dingy room. Compared to Arrow Corporation's modern facilities, this office and the other offices of the Orioles were straight out of the 1930s. The picture was obviously that of frugality. The Orioles told all their employees that money was tight. Arrow knew that the Oriole's Chairman drove a 1973 green Ford

161

stationwagon. There was no fat on the Orioles. They were by far the most dangerous foes that he could encounter. Finally, his opponent spoke,

"It is, Phillip, it is. What is it that Sir Thomas More said in Man for All Seasons? 'You don't keep your word and your life slips through your fingers,' something like that. The way to view this, I suppose, is that this is a double 'greenmail.' We both will be responsible for the bidding up of each other's stock value to the benefit of each other. I really like the idea, Phillip. I have used greenmail before where I have bid on a company only to have them buy their stock back at a favored price much like the Disney fiasco. I have, however, never ever contemplated playing double greenmail. Only the common investor can be hurt. I like it......that is the way it should be."

Phillip Arrow rose and the men shook hands.

It was later that afternoon when the final meeting occurred when Frank Turner talked with the Cardinal President and his twelve advisors. Turner felt exhausted from the time zone changes and the tension. As he looked around the room, he noted the dark red carpet and the walnut paneled walls. Were all railroad headquarters of this decor?

"As we have told you, Mr. Turner, we would look forward to totally controlling the Division. Will we have complete, full autonomy?"

"That is correct and we recognized that your major concern is the operations of the rail entities. We will, of course, be most interested in the return or profits and the control of cash."

"What you are saying sounds good, but it is a generality. We would like to get down to specifics.

"First, we want to be assured that for at least five years our compensation plans will not be altered. If they are in anyway, we would all have severance packages that could be triggered on an individual basis. Included in these contracts would be acceleration of the exercise of all stock options, full vesting in all retirement plans, cash payout of deferred bonuses, a week's severance pay for each month of service, forgiveness of stock option loans, housing loans, and thrift account loans and continued entitlement and usage of all prequisites and health, life, and disability benefits until the severance period ceases. All these items mentioned would not, I repeat, would not be accompanied by any non-compete agreements."

"That will be acceptable. We will put it in writing. We must insist

162

that everything be in writing," answered Frank Turner.

"Then there is one exception to the above. We want a guarantee that all retirement benefits will be maintained, including the retiree health benefits."

"Arrow Corporation sees those as your largest unfunded, unaccounted for liability."

"It is if you forget about the Railroad Retirement Fund. Which reminds me. We have an additional deferred retirement supplement for executives. We would expect this plan to continue. Any change in the plan would require a full lump sum payout."

"Agreed."

"Second, we would want no interference in whom we hire or fire. We would expect most of the other targets' staffs to go, but we want your assurance that our fine team stays in place. Just to give you a background on our people and the team we have in place here......"

Frank Turner's mind drifted off. This man couldn't be serious! The league rules say that you can only have twelve players, fella. We are merging the Boston Celtics, the Los Angeles Lakers, and the Philadelphia 76ers. Did he really think that just one team would stay in place, that the other teams' best players would be waived? Frank's eyes caught the man's questioning look as he ended by saying,"........do you agree?"

"Yes!" replied Turner. He was still picturing cutting Larry Bird or Dr. J to keep a rookie Laker forward. He wondered what the man had been saying, what he had agreed to. "We will put that in writing too," Turner added. Why not, he thought. There was no harm if he did not know what it was he agreed to. He tried to concentrate on the speaker.

"Third, we have a considerable capital expansion program going on here. We want your approval that all capital programs will continue for the ten year period for which they are planned."

Well, thought Turner, at least he was going over the core of the future problems. "Please, please, I thought that all this was clear. We are not merging your companies to shut them down. We want, we would expect that you would actively pursue your expansion plans. We have no intention of minimizing your planned efforts."

Turner was hoping that his expression was holding. He had taken three courses in his MBA coursework with two refreshers since then to refine his skills. The School called them "Negotiation Training Seminars" and "Enhanced Sales Speech and Presentation." Minimize,

Hell! He was going to close the expansion programs down and sell off the partly completed work at a Fire Sale. What Arrow Corporation was going to need was cash to pay off the interest on the money it had borrowed to do this deal. If they were lucky, they might have some left over for the principal. That damn Arrow was crazy, what a premium to pay! This guy was even crazier. Was it a trait of company presidents?

Turner looked around the room. All but their top operations man believed him. The operations man would have to be the first to go, unless he were their natural leader. Then he would transfer him before the crucifixion. Lord, it was easy to kid a kidder! Corporation CEO's are the easiest people in the world to con. Most corporate leaders wouldn't recognize the truth if it hit them in the face. It was the price paid by those who surrounded themselves with people who always tried to please them.

Dane Hughes drove his sports car into the Jamison's drive. He knew that the Vice President of Administration would not be pleased. John Jamison was not going to be an easy sale. It had been a long three hour commute from West Los Angeles. The Coast Highway had again been clogged by autos and debris from two slides. As pretty as the bluffs along the Santa Monica Mountains were, they were no more than the remnants of a river delta, now raised sixty to two hundred feet above the coast line. Each year this caked mud rock advanced an inch or two toward the Pacific Ocean. Each year the progress claimed its share of the cliffs. As rainwater seeped deep into the ground, it served as a lubricant to the deep pressured rock. And with its movement, came the movement of trees, houses, and the people who inhabited them. Someday, what he knew as Los Angeles would be claimed by the sea.

Driving up, Dane had reflected on the slowness of the movement of the cliffs compared to the pace of humans. Nature measured in years, tens and hundreds of years. Man measured in seconds, minutes, and hours. Living in these mountains by the sea, one could blend the two. Perhaps that was what the Jamisons had found so far away from the City of Los Angeles. Perhaps they were escaping the tide of humanity into which John Jamison was so surely about to throw himself.

Too soon, Dane found himself awkwardly standing on the Jamison's doorstep unannounced. He should have called, but if he had, he would have been refused an invitation. Under his arm, he carried the camouflage coats and pants he had discovered in New York. Surely, when Jamison saw them, he would be forced to think and prepare for another attack.

It was Meg Jamison who answered the door with a surprised, welcoming smile. "Mr. Dane, what may I do for you?"

"It is Dane Hughes, Mrs. Jamison, please just call me Dane. I wanted to know if I could speak with both you and your husband. And may I say that I am most impressed by your house. It is beautiful up here."

"Thank you, I love it too. I have the rare opportunity in life to live in a home that I truly love. Uh...John is down at the Club. Have you been down by the Biltmore and may I invite you with me? I was just going to meet John for lunch."

Dane felt uncomfortable in his t-shirt and slacks. Meg Jamison was dressed for a fashionable luncheon, tailored dress, matching shoes and purse. He had heard that this was the way in Santa Barbara, dressing up to go to the grocery store, beach club, school, or gas station.

"I am not dressed. Look, I just wanted to give him these clothes and discuss an incident that happened this week. I would look pretty silly going to lunch and just carrying a bunch of men's clothes I wanted him to see."

"Just take the jacket and leave the rest here," Meg answered. She quickly silenced his protests. Taking the clothes, she placed them on a chair by the door. Taking the enraptured Dane Hughes by his arm, she led him down the path to his car. "Good, now let's see, if you drive, I can ride back up with John."

As Dane's car pulled away, a green truck bearing the name of a local plumbing firm made its way down the hill from its parking place and turned into the driveway.

Two men hurriedly walked toward the back of the house carrying bags filled with their equipment. Their key quickly opened the back door and they jogged through the halls to the attic crawlspace opening. Exactly seven minutes later the charges were set and connected with powdered paths to the already installed consumable igniter. A quick tour throughout the house assured them that nothing had been disturbed. One man waited at the back door. The other did not return.

A "hiss" brought the waiting man to a quick crouch at the livingroom door with a revolver drawn. His companion was looking at the clothes left on the chair by the front door. No words were spoken.

The labels of the one coat were inspected. Both nodded to the other and the single coat was placed back on the chair. Two minutes later their truck was gone.

Ten minutes later that same truck was parked at a gas station's telephone booth. One of the men was thanked for his very unusual checking in with his controller. It was very fortunate, indeed. No fire was required tonight, the two were to live, an agreement had been reached and no lesson was required. Yes, payment for a completed job would be made in full this afternoon. As for the clothes and the pilot, that was their mistake. He was not to be harmed. One did not contract with careless men who tried to compound mistakes.

When told, the second man resisted the drive to LAX and the return to Chicago. He wished to stay for the evening. It was only the loss of the potential service payment and the chance to catch the early United flight that made him relent. That, and the fact that they were leaving the incendiary charges in place. Their bombs might go off at any time depending upon a stray radio wave. That was doubtful though. They would be passing again. "Yes," it was unfortunate that they did not foresee this. They could have wired the receiver to the electrical circuits of the house. Now they had to rely on the consumable batteries. It made for an hour argument as to the shelf life of the units. "Yes," they would have to do something about the pilot. He had had his string of luck with them that night. If only they hadn't been under orders to attempt not to harm him or the girl. Indeed, they had been informed that they would be terminated if either of the two was unnecessarily harmed. That was then, though, now it was a personal matter.

Meg had taken Dane on a brief tour of Santa Barbara. Now they were walking into the dining room of the Beach Club. John Jamison was sitting with a gin & tonic looking out over the Pacific waves. He did not see them approach as the glassed panorama of the ocean had fully captured his early afternoon attention.

"John, look who I found! It is Mr. Hughes and I have invited him to share lunch with us."

Dane saw the surprised look, the rejection, and the disagreement with the luncheon invitation in Jamison's face. "Hello, Mr. Jamison, and thanks again, Mrs. Jamison, for the invitation, but I have to hurry back to Los Angeles. Perhaps just a quick lemonade would do."

Jamison quickly took Dane up on the refusal. "Fine, here I will get

166

it and your usual for you, My Dear?" Jamison wrote the order on a card and handed it to a passing waiter. "Now, what can I do for you - Say you've been back to New York again this week - any message for me - what's going on back there?"

Dane looked at the now attentive face. "No Sir. I don't know what's happening. They asked me to fly Everett Lacey in Tuesday night and I deadheaded back. To the point, I took a day off and told Arrow my nerves were raw from too much night flying."

"I bet! That flight Monday night was no fun. Now in retrospect, don't you think you were a bit half-cocked?"

"John!" Meg Jamison was startled and embarrassed by her husband's tone of voice and its cutting criticism.

"No Sir. That is what I wanted to show you. Here's the jacket of one of the two men who attacked you. I found both sets of clothing in the alley. They are the type you can pull over a suit."

"You went back to the alley and just happened to find our robbers' clothes? Ho! Ho! Ho! That's too much!" Jamison laughed with glee. He was on his second gin and the idea of Dane trying to vindicate himself amused him. When he stopped laughing, "What did the police say?"

"Sir, I did not go to the police."

"Then what is this, Dane, some sort of a game? Look, if you are serious as you claim, the least you could have done was bring in the police."

"No Sir. I don't see that doing any good at all. The reason I am here is to tell you how I read it. I believe someone was sent to kill you and perhaps all of us. I also believe that just because you escaped once, does not mean that you will be safe forever. I would expect that they will try again and if they do, they will do it soon and right here in Santa Barbara."

"Right here in this seat?"

"John, be serious." Meg could read Dane Hughes' seriousness. As usual, she thought her husband missed the point. "If he only has a chance of being right, why should we take it? What would you suggest Mr. Hughes?"

"Leave here, don't go back to your house. Just get in your car and go to a random hotel for the weekend."

"We could do better, John. We could drive up to Arrowhead and stay at the Hemstrom's."

"Oh, come off it Meg! You are getting carried away by this man. One, Dane, thank you for coming. I now believe that you honestly believe that that man tried to kill me, though I can't see how anyone could have seen anything in that alley that night. Two, if they are professionals, nothing that I can do will stop them. Three, I don't recognize the coat. It could be anyone's. To tell you the truth, I thought they were both wearing brown. So please, please, relax, both of you. It is a beautiful world out there and we are meant to live in it peacefully. Personally, I plan to spend some time this afternoon on my boat."

Dane Hughes looked across the table at Meg Jamison. He had heard that it sometimes happens, but it was new to him. No thoughts passed between their eyes, just concerns, softness, worries, fears, and caring. He felt like part of a river of emotion and then it was gone.

Meg Jamison had looked away to the seagulls skimming the waves. She too had felt the flush of feeling that passed between them. She relaxed. It had been a Biblical death knell to her. "Dust to Dust," she had quickly thought. The ocean would remain forever. Justice would prevail over history. Life was but a wave to ride. She looked at her husband. John Jamison was smiling at the thought of his boat and the afternoon ahead of him. He, too, was at peace with the world.

A full continent away other minds had also turned to thoughts of the sea. John Smedt was feeling tremendous, totally exhilarated, doing what he loved best, looking at boats. He smiled, not truly boats. He had entered the period of few men's lives when they could look at real ships. Few could visit these yards and walk aboard any craft with the money and the willingness to spend it that he now possessed. He knew right where he was going. He had earlier heard of the Danish craft sitting at the end of the walkway. As he walked beside it, his only thoughts were of his awe. What a marvelous craft!

"Ahoy there John Smedt, what are you doing here?" A startled voice he knew yelled to him from out of the sun above him.

No more shocked was his reply, "Aaron, is that you? What are you doing here looking at my love?"

"I thought Caroline O'Brian was your love."

"Never! I would rather walk the plank than spend one more moment with that cold fish. Why are you ruining my day? Again, Sir, pray tell me why you are standing on my ship?"

"I was thinking of buying it."

168

"On Guard, you Knave!"

"Come on aboard, they are serving Manhattans. It is a great way to sell a three million dollar craft."

After a full tour, the two sat watching the harbor. "Then you too are fairly sure that the tenders are going through."

"Absolutely, I knew it the moment I had to put the financial package together. Twelve billion was no problem. Hell, I smelled fifteen billion then if Arrow wanted it. Those targets are just not going to be able to refuse. It is all over. Arrow is pulling his strings and the birds are about to drop dead."

"Even the Orioles?"

"Yes, I think so if Arrow really wants them. What has he ever wanted that he hasn't obtained? But in this case, I think the mouthful may be too large. He probably only wants two bites, he can pick up the rest later."

"John, tell me, don't you sometimes think back on 1968 and remember? To think that the SEC had no rules on tenders before the end of the 60's. We were dead as an industry for ten years before the Congress stepped in and made it possible to consolidate the industry of America."

"No, I don't think of the past, only of the future. Are you going to have any trouble with your fees?"

"Don't we always. They will bitch and moan and make us prostitute ourselves, but in the end, they will pay." Aaron Goldstein was silent for a moment. They watched a seagull flitting atop a mast and then another that joined it. Aaron continued, "Any idea of when? We are guessing six months."

"Better damn well be sooner! I am telling my partners it's payday in four months. With our new financial services owner, we have a push on cash management."

"You are not telling me then that you will collect the full two hundred million fee?"

"Hell, no! C. H. on a chimney. I am not that stupid. It will be as low as ten cents on the dollar."

"I agree. You can't very well get a jury to agree to a fee that large for a few week's work. Either way, we will both do fine. I calculated our usual billing rate based only on the time spent up to a few days ago. My Firm's bill should only be sixty-five thousand."

"I know, instead it will be over one hundred times that amount. I know. We do the same thing that you do just to keep track of who's earning his keep. I am sure it's the same, you take a man's salary and multiply by three. One third is for salary, one third for overhead, and the last one third for partners' profit. Looking at it from our work to date, we have just eighty-three thousand in the projects. Shit, and we have the nerve to ask for two hundred million!"

"You never know, John, one never knows until he asks. Anyway, you will have another bonus coming. Don't look so startled, Caroline O'Brian told me and she is probably telling everyone."

"That bitch!"

Caroline carefully tiptoed across the carpet. Lawrence Massendale softly snored in his afternoon nap. Clothes lay strewn everywhere. It had been an early afternoon celebration. The morning had seen the FTC and the Interstate Commerce Commission drafts. Arrow had been right. No agency was going to prevent the acquisitions. They were wired!

She selected a proper business suit and low heels. Her evening date was special and she looked forward to seeing him. When dressed, she finally faced the inevitable conversation, " Massey, Massey, wake up! Your plane leaves from Dulles in ninety minutes."

Slowly Lawrence Massendale, III came back to the living. He brushed his hair across his balding scalp. "Wow, did you ever knock me out! I like that side, I think I am going to stay right here."

Caroline forced back her frown. "That's what I asked you to do. Just because your wife expects you home tonight, doesn't mean you have to do everything she wants and nothing I want. Please stay with me for the weekend. I promise to make it very interesting, if not exciting."

"You know it is not like that. Mary Sue is a very suspicious person. I swear she knows what I am thinking most of the time. If I don't get home tonight, she will suspect something." With each word, Massendale increased his pace of dressing and packing.

At this accelerating pace, thought Caroline, he would be gone in thirty seconds. "Oh, Massey! Don't kid yourself. She suspects something already. Just the way you talked to her on the telephone today gave you away."

Massendale stopped packing his luggage. "What are you talking about?"

"It is her father's trait that she has. She looks for a change in one's

170

behavior. It's obvious. Phillip is well trained in it, Mary Sue does it naturally. It is not much of a trick, but only one out of a thousand people can do it.All you look for is a change in people's behavior."

"You sound like you think you can do it?"

"You bet, I was trained by a man who was very good at it, my father's brother."

"When did he die?"

"He is not dead. It is my parents who, unlike your parents, who are deceased. When did you say you had to leave?'

As Massendale rushed to the door, he leaned over to give her a kiss. At least he was tall, thought Caroline. "Now don't forget what we talked about, Massey. I don't think it too impossible at all for you to be the Chairman of the Board of Union Arrow Corporation."

"Come on, fly back with me and we'll talk about it."

"No way, I am going to spend two days walking the City and seeing my girl friends. Now get going! Don't bother about checking out, I will do that Sunday."

It was thirty minutes later. Lawrence Massendale sat across the avenue from the hotel. He was staying until the last possible minute. The driver claimed a 6:00 flight was still possible. Massendale burned of jealousy. He knew Caroline had chosen the conservative business suit for his eyes, that she was going to change and meet some male very special to her.

He had been around people long enough to know when they were excited about a coming event. Caroline had all the signs. Who was he?

Just as his taxi driver insisted upon moving, the hotel door swung open and Caroline, dressed as he had left her, walked out. With her was an older, no perhaps the same age lady. A car door opened. Two youngsters shyly hugged her. Massendale looked to the car's driver, a slight grey haired man of sixty-five. Massendale lay down on the back seat and told the driver to get going for Dulles. Damn, he was such a jealous fool! He should have known.

10

One Week Later
Thursday
April 25, 1985

Tomorrow is the day! Tomorrow is the day. Phillip Arrow repeated the thought. Tender offer rules required targets to respond within ten working days of the official start of the tender. Only the Orioles had announced their plans. The newspapers were full of articles regarding their new tender for Arrow Corporation. Counter tenders were popular with the press. The 'Pac Man' name for the counter move undoubtedly helped in building this interest.

Arrow smiled to himself. His staff and Goldstein and Smedt were in dismay over his seeming disinterest in the Orioles. Only he knew of his handshake with the Oriole President. It was good to know that confidence and secrecy still meant something in this world. The Oriole President was a good man to have on one's side. Together, they would watch Arrow Corporation's stock rise like the Oriole's had two weeks earlier. In another two weeks, they would both walk their separate ways. Yes, the Orioles would fly their separate way, only the Blue Jays and the Cardinals would be left in the net. Hopefully the Arrow common stock earmarked for use for these other targets' purchases would be selling at a considerably higher price than it opened for this morning before the Oriole's tender. All thanks to the Orioles.

The suspense as to the Blue Jays' and Cardinal's responses were beginning to tell on both himself and his staff. The chess game of the past two weeks had been a frantic move and countermove. So much to do and with actions so fragmented! It took real concentration to focus on the action at hand. He knew he must concentrate to remember what his guests had just said.

Phillip Arrow looked across the table at his national accountants. The annual report of Arrow Corporation required one of the national accounting firm's letters of approval for reasons related to Arrow Corporation's listing on the New York Stock Exchange. For this reason, and this reason alone, Arrow put up with this accounting firm's outrageous annual billings. Up to the date of the tender offer, he had not shared his plans with any of their senior people. Now, he felt that perhaps he should have. If everyone was stealing from him on this, he should have given his accounting firm a chance. They were true professionals. He motioned for the senior partner to continue.

"As you know Phillip, if a transaction is such that two companies and their shareholders simply combine their interests, this is called a 'pooling.' We would just add the two financial statements together and leave future earnings and cash flows unaffected. However, in any combination where it more closely resembles the acquisition of one company by another, we have different sets of accounting rules and it is treated as a 'purchase.'

"Purchase accounting requires that we allocate the purchase price to the assets of the company acquired. In doing so, these assets must be recorded on your books to reflect the newly established value, that is to reflect the amount that you applied to them. Whenever the purchase price exceeds the book value of the assets of the acquired company, an asset write-up will be made. Generally, an asset write up will lead to higher depreciation. Any excess that exceeds rational amounts is simply called 'goodwill' and sits on the books as such. The goodwill will have to be amortized over time This will mean higher depreciation and amortization charges to Arrow Corporation and hence lower future earnings as you report them."

"Correct, I understand that," sighed Arrow.

"Yes, we expect that you do. But we should also discuss the fact that there are separate rules for tax accounting. An acquisition of stock or assets will be treated as a taxable transaction if it is not

174

defined as a reorganization. Should you purchase more than 50%, plus or minus some discretion related to the concept of 'control,' the purchase will be taxable to the acquired company's stockholders. For the Company's standpoint, the basis of the assets will be stepped up in the same manner as with an accounting write-up. The end result of the step up in assets values will again be higher depreciation, lower income, and lower tax expense. Hence, the cash flow of Arrow Corporation, excuse me, Union Arrow Corporation will be improved. This way the U.S. Internal Revenue Service will help you in the purchase."

"That assumes that the targets will or will not agree to a sale where their stockholders' benefit. For stockholders to benefit, a tender has to be for less that 50%, that I understand. But if I am not mistaken, the scenario you described is not quite the way we have structured the acquisitions," replied Arrow.

"Correct, you have formed three 100% wholly owned subsidiary acquisition companies. The assets purchased will receive a write-up for accounting purposes, but not a step-up in basis for tax purposes. If the case arises where you purchase less than 50% of the stock for cash, the acquisition company will be able to record a new tax basis for the purchased stock, but the assets of the acquired company will remain unaffected. In the second step of the acquisition, the acquired corporation will be merged into the newly formed corporation. Since this is a pooling, the tax basis of the acquired corporation's assets will carryover to yours. There will be no step-up in basis. This is a triangular arrangement and allows us the freedom to select the best possible tax and accounting relationship possible. Put simply, we are escaping paying tax on previously taken depreciation. The Congress just has not caught on yet."

Phillip Arrow held up his hand, "I have had that explained to me a hundred times and it still sounds pretty confusing. I think that I barely understand it. No wonder the United States Congress allows this manipulation. How can they pass legislation on something that they can not understand?

"But please, Gentlemen, please understand that I care little about Arrow Corporation's reported earnings. Please arrange all the your accounting and the work with my financial people to emphasize cash flow. We are going to have some tremendous interest costs. All I will want to do come next year is be ahead of the game in cash available. I have a loan that I wish to pay off as soon as is possible."

"Surely, Mr. Arrow, you don't mean to stress cash flow 100%! As you know, we can take some aggressive actions, but it will hurt your earnings per share and hence your stock's market price. You could become open to a tender offer yourself."

"I will take that risk. Surely, Sir, you can understand me when I say '100%' and 'emphasize.' I grow weary of having to explain myself."

"Yes Sir, we understand. We just want you to be aware of all the implications and possibilities. Again, we have people available and we would like to recommend that twenty of our people come in here for the next two weeks and study every possible alternative open to you at this time."

"No thanks. Please don't try to sell me management consulting work at this time. I know that you have a quota. Don't waste my time. Now, have you gone over, this morning, the totality of your two week study of the target companies' available financial information?"

"Yes Sir. We have exhausted every aspect. You can not find a more thorough examination. We take great pride at our Firm to have the best analysis and accounting review techniques. Moreover, we put our best people on these type of reports. No stone was left unturned."

Phillip Arrow sighed inwardly again. What made these people think they always had to sell and never admit to a mistake. How many clients like Arrow Corporation had they misled? Arrow found himself speaking again, "I note that you did not comment on the change in self insurance accounts in the footnotes of both the Cardinals and the Blue Jays."

Arrow watched the experts hurriedly open the reports and hunt for the section to which he had referred. It constantly amazed him. After 40 years in the business world, he had learned only one thing for sure. Never trust an expert to do your work for you. He continued, "I would want you to check for something called a 'VEBA,' a Voluntary Employee Benefits Association. It allows one to prefund all of a company's employee benefit, and take a tax deduction a year early. The prefunded assets sit in a trust, a tax free trust that earns twice the normal rate because of a lack of tax. In effect, the Government pays a great part of any large company's, who chooses to use a VEBA, employee benefits ."

"Sir, we understand. We recognized the VEBA and we don't see any concern. All they have done is changed 'current taxes' to 'deferred taxes' and not affected their earnings one iota. By the way, VEBA accounting will change as of December 1985." It was clear that the accountant had been caught offguard. Sweat had broken out on his forehead.

Phillip Arrow shook his head. "You have not been listening. I could care less about accounting earnings. What this does is require another prefunding before the end of the tax year before any tax deduction can be taken for the present year. I expect that we will want to use that cash for other purposes. I also expect that we will be faced with having to 'catch up' with the taxes deferred. We are talking of being damned if we do and damned if we don't. I calculate the cash flow required to be either 300 or 400 million dollars. Check it.

"By the way, I asked to hire your firm's best people for the past two weeks. I would have expected that you would have caught this. I trust that there is nothing else that your Firm has missed. Now if you have nothing more, please get out of here and leave me alone."

Arrow watched the men quickly depart. He knew that some young junior accountant was about to learn an important lesson. Arrow doubted if any of the men present had spent more than twenty minutes on the numbers. They obviously farmed out the work to their more junior, less well trained staff. To think that for their service, he paid millions of dollars a year in fees!

Down the hall from Phillip Arrow's office, the same cost control concern was being voiced by John Jamison. That would cost us hundreds of thousands, uh .... six hundred and eighty thousand dollars at a minimum. Please, Mrs. Smith, you don't seem to understand the situation as it appears to others. We have terminated your husband!"

Jamison looked across at the angry woman. As a conflict avoider, he had put this interview off for over a week. Smith's wife was exceedingly plain, he thought. No wonder Smith was known to look at other women. Who could blame him? She was wearing an old cotton flowered dress, black laced shoes with low heels, and had straight black hair, cut short, with glasses that did nothing for her features.

What a boring woman, he thought. She had just sat there and listened to him. Three times she had asked the simple question about what she could expect from the Company. Her husband had been terminated, fired! Didn't she understand that simple fact? John Jamison had decided that she was simple minded. As he again repeated the Company's position, she interrupted him.

177

"Mr. Jamison, I don't want you to underestimate me. My husband was a corporate manager here in charge of security. He was a college graduate who met a nineteen year old girl with a Hispanic accent who was graduating from the University of Cal Berkeley with a Masters in Political History. I was Phi Beta Kappa and have earned both another Masters in Greek literature and Latin since that time. We have no children, so I spend my time taking care of our ageing mothers and working with local community charities."

"You don't look Mexican."

"My father was and I am. Our Hispanic ancestors have been Californians since the middle 1600s. I might also note that while your ancestors were in their caves, my mother's Indian ancestors were highly civilized. My father's peoples plight is that they are born in a terrible climate in a resource poor land. Differentiate for me please, the difference between the Mexican population today and the Irish of the 1800s. However, that is not why I mentioned it.

"From your eye contact, tone, and words up to this moment, you are just trying to endure this conversation to go on to something that you consider more important. So let me be specific. One, I have asked that my counsel draft the appropriate suit and interrogatories to learn everything that Arrow Corporation was involved in up to, during, and since my husband's disappearance. We were extremely close. I know that he is dead. Nothing can change that. All I want from you is the legal and proper payoffs in the case of his death. Your alternative is a suit that will cost you millions of dollars in cash flow and thousands of hours with the disclosure of your corporate secrets."

Suddenly Jamison was frightened. Turner had suggested that if he couldn't handle a Mrs. Smith, he couldn't handle a Rail Division Presidency. His stomach turned as he felt the nausea. He would have to pull his act together and take control of the situation. He only knew the game too well. Twenty-five years in the corporate setting had made him as good a game player as any. Too bad that this lady's problem had nothing to do with that game.

"Well that takes the cake! Mrs. Smith, please understand that I really must be going! A plane waits for me now at the airport to run out to Kansas City to look at a potential new Division Headquarter's site. Even though I am in a hurry, I will take the time to personally escort you out of this building. How dare you! How dare you come in here and threaten me or the Corporation! What do you know of cash

178

flow? We have all the cash we will ever need. That's not the question. The question is, do we legally owe you any money? The answer is 'No'!"

"Mr. Jamison, with the official firing of my husband for not showing up to work, you violated your moral obligation to me!"

"Don't give me any moral obligation arguments! What is moral to you not be moral to someone else. Now get out of here!"

"May I ask that you discuss this with Mr. Arrow?"

"No, you may not! I wouldn't bother Phillip Arrow with something so trivial. No, I and I alone am responsible for employee benefits. You have gone as far as you can in this Company. We have assurances from the Police Department that they are also through with their search and that they also consider you a crank."

Getting up from his chair, John Jamison took the woman's arm and escorted her to the door. Smith's wife looked up at him as he led her into the hall and to the elevator to the front lobby "Thank you for your valuable time Mr. Jamison. You are correct about your concepts of morality." As she walked away, John Jamison turned toward the men's room. He hoped that he would arrive in time.

Across town to the north and east, a morally startled Mary Sue Massendale looked across her patio table at the man sipping on an ice cold lemonade. "Why Sir, that doesn't sound ethical. Are you accusing me of fooling around where and when I shouldn't?"

"No, I am not suggesting it. I know it. Let's say that I have pictures of all your activities. I even know your schedule. You sometimes sneak out after 2:00 AM in the morning while your husband is sleeping. Other times, you will stay out and work late."

Mary Sue Massendale knew that she had to be careful as she looked across the table at this quiet man who exuded calm strength. Her senses told her that he was also unpredictable. After a pause to look at him, she answered, "If you call it work. Those would be the nights when he doesn't come home. Have you noticed that they are suddenly more frequent? I know that you know. Did you know that I knew that someone has been watching me for the past two weeks? May I ask if it was my husband who put you onto looking after me? Does he suspect?"

"No, it was not your husband. I, if you don't mind, don't believe that your husband would ever think that you could be involved so heavily, that you have been earning money on the side. Don't worry, I

179

didn't come here to tell you that I might tell him."

"Well, I am glad. Please let me get you some more lemonade."

He watched her pick up his glass and walk across the sunlit patio and through the kitchen door. A pretty lady, he thought, if she would care to dress up and fix her unruly red hair. Obviously, she was a working mother. Walking through the house from the front door to the patio in back of the house, he had seen her morning cooking in progress. Clothes lay on the table for sewing, an ironing board stood in the middle of the family room. He could hear the sound of a washing machine and a drier in action. She obviously used no domestic help. Where she derived the energy to do more than the drastic work load forced on her by her four boys and husband, he did not know.

He began to think of her as a person, an individual with her own personality and not just a caricature of a powerful man's daughter. What did she really have to live for, be proud of? She had a perfect house, a seemingly perfect husband, a marvelous father, and from all reports, well mannered, beautifully adjusted children. Why did she have all this hidden hunger, this greed, this passion for screwing around?

As she walked back out the door, the thought struck him. Did she have the avarice that her father was reputed to have in his early business career? Could she kill? She had had ample time to put something in his drink. She knew that he had her dead to rights. His telling of her arrangement of the affair would probably ruin her, her family, and perhaps her husband. Would she kill? He looked at her smile.

Mary Sue Massendale looked at the suddenly blank faced man whose complexion had just gone a shade lighter. "Do you mind if I take a sip of this first? I should have fixed a glass for myself, but I was too interested to return and learn how you traced me."

An hour later, Everett Lacey had told his story. He had marveled at her questions and her knowledge. He now sat in a small alcove off the master bedroom looking at her microcomputer and examining her telephone hookup which she correctly called a "modem." Following her lead, he walked to the garage to find the printer which was placed a distance from the sleeping quarters. While the terminal and computer took little space, the high speed printer looked enormous next to the tennis rackets and surfboards. Finally, he followed her into the living room. She had been waiting to cast the telling questions.

"You believe that you have hidden the only possible trail that could lead to me? I had thought that everything was covered, that I could not be traced, but you found a way."

"Yes, I believe that all traces are now obliterated. I went back into the files and changed the middle number of the identifier rather than the last number. Thinking about it, if I were to do it again, I would have the computer check only the middle numbers for a match. It is the obvious thing to do to modify the first or last number."

"Then may I ask what you are going to do? My SEC lawyers are preparing the formal filings now should they be necessary. However, as you have probably seen, I am divesting my accounts of all the targets' stocks. During this 28-day waiting period their stock is still trading. The stock price is 2 or 3 dollars below the tender price because of the risk that the acquisitions might not go through. Arbitragers are buying up all they can because they are betting that the acquisitions will occur. I, on the other hand, don't mind selling at a 55% profit rather than the full 60% premium. This way, no one will ever know that I held the stock. Moreover, I won't have to put up with taking any trash on the back end. My father told me about trash when I was eight years old."

"Mrs. Massendale, I am not going to do a thing. That is not why I came here." Everett Lacey carefully looked at the struggling Mary Sue Massendale. He had caught her in her indiscretion. Perhaps she was as vulnerable as she had ever been in her life. He could sense that she would do whatever he asked.

"Then you want money?"

"Mrs. Massendale, shut up! My problem with women is that they always talk and never listen for more than two minutes. Don't insult me! My ethics can not be questioned!" Ev Lacey paused. Mary Sue Massendale sat silent. She was willing to listen. Her apology was explicit, if unsaid. Lacey continued, "I have another story to tell you. I need your help. From looking at your work, I think you have the ability to increase my potential for finding an answer by an exponential of 10."

"I am sorry. I apologize. I promise to be quiet and listen." Mary Sue immediately recognized the falseness of the first promise. She hoped that it did not cast a reflection on her other statements.

Another hour passed as Lacey traced through his search for the reason for the acquisitions. It was obvious to him that the daughter did not really understand her father. She felt only his past youthful avarice in her blood, the thrill of the hunt. She had not seriously considered the reason why Phillip Arrow would risk all on this merger of railroad companies. Perhaps the father she knew was the one of her youth. Like many, she might not have thought through to the fact that people change over time. Her father was a different man from that man she had know in her teens. Time had changed his motivations. Lacey could see his points take hold. Phillip Arrow would never have ventured, bet everything, on three old railroads at his age of sixty seven.

As he finished, her questions became more specific. Lacey found Mary Sue's mind working along paths that he had inspected. She was forming her own hypotheses. The visit ended with a quiet fizzle. There was suddenly nothing more to be said. She would be thinking about it and 'Yes' she would be glad to inspect the items that he suggested. Would he be willing to have her examine his research design? Perhaps he was missing something. Feeling it strangely like another insult, he found himself unusually reluctant in agreeing to her visiting his office next Tuesday.

She walked him to the door. "I am sorry that I have insulted you twice today Mr. Lacey."

"Twice? Uh, just another question or two. How did you establish the override to have your own files on that system and was it you who leaked the news of the tender offer to the press?"

"It is IBM equipment. Personal computers have not been their game. If you look at the hardware you can see that it takes just a thin wire between two nodes, software was not involved at all. That is why you have made no progress in that area and had to ask the question. As to the latter, of course. My goal was only to see the stock price go up. Both then and now as reinforced by your visit, my hope has been that the acquisitions do not occur. It will be bad for Arrow Corporation, bad for the target companies, and bad for the Country."

"You must then question me, my values. I am the one who planned the acquisitions." Lacey was also thinking other thoughts, or better put, analyzing his feelings. His time was up. His bonus depended upon telling Arrow before he found out by himself. If Mary Sue felt the same, she would soon confess to her father. It was strange that she had not brought up his further divulging of her work to others. Why would she not broach that subject? Lacey knew time was short. If he were to tell Arrow, it had better be now.

182

"Please, Mr. Lacey. I just want you to know that I think you a very moral man. Now please get out of here before my husband comes home. He will question my morals."

But at that moment, Lawrence Massendale was not going home and in no position to question his wife's morality. He instead was just returning from a lunch that started at Noon and had lasted for hours. His heartbeat quickened as he entered the main lobby. Caroline would return a few minutes from now using a different door. They would both have to work late to make up for their absences. Hopefully, no one had noticed.

Massendale felt wonderful. In an uncharacteristic manner, he smiled at the receptionist and wished her well. That feeling quickly disappeared when she greeted him by name and a tall U.S. Marshal leaped to his feet to introduce himself. Moments later as Lawrence Massendale rode up the elevator to the executive suites, he silently cursed the more than pretty receptionist. Like most Los Angeles headquarter offices, the reception area was manned by the prettiest, most buxom female that could be hired. Personnel called it their Double E requirement. This one would have her walking papers within the hour.

Still minutes later as he read the federal complaint brought by Mrs. Richard Smith against Arrow Corporation under the Civil Rights Act of 1964, he was doubly troubled. How the Hell was he to know that both the Smiths were part minority? Smith was a God Damn American Indian who looked like an Italian! Jesus, and that dumb John Jamison didn't know! Even worse, he was on his way to Kansas City. What a dumb place for anyone to go! The idea that the Rail Division should have a headquarters there was reason enough to bring suit under the Civil Rights Act. Just flying there would be a violation of anyone's civil liberties. How could he fire the big boobed blond broad in the lobby? This was getting to be a damn inefficient place.

His office door burst open. Frank Turner charged into his office. "They have bit, the Cardinals are fried chickadees! It's you and me, Massey, you and me."

"Frank, it is 'you and I'."

"That's right, Baby, you and me. Phillip wants to see us in forty minutes. We are personally to handle the Cardinals with John Smedt at an all day negotiation session beginning tomorrow morning at 8:00 in New York."

"What about your and my boss, Phillip Arrow?"

Frank Turner paused a moment before answering to look at Lawrence Massendale, III. Turner could sense the fear in the room. Was Massey trying to hide something? What had he been doing when he came into the room. "He is holding himself, O'Brian, and Goldstein free for the Blue Jays. They are sure to come chirping today or tomorrow. It's just you and me, Massey. We are to pound out the details, telex them to Arrow, and when set, sign up the Cardinals."

"It won't be that easy," replied Massendale. He appeared clearly shaken. It was also now obvious that Massendale's blood pressure was rising from the flush of his skin. As nervous as Massey usually was, Turner sensed that he had better put him at ease. An executive who freezes up at a critical time was not what Turner needed either today or tomorrow. Damn, this Massendale was a little old lady!

"Don't look so uptight, Massey. It will be a breeze. It's their Board. They are sending their management in to the battle to get five dollars a share more. They have already approved the motion to recommend the tender to their shareholders. That is that, all shareholders will sell their stock if the price is increased by five dollars."

"You can't be sure of that." Massey felt that he had to slow Turner down. He was on one of his emotional binges. "How would you know that?"

"Oh come off it Massey! You don't think Arrow went into this without a few spies. He's been paying one of the Cardinal's top management to pass him information for the past two weeks. Hell, the guy is so scared, he would do it for free!"

"Is he that knowledgeable about their Board? Only three Cardinal executives sit on the Board and it ....."

"No, no, no, Massey. We've their Board covered through Smedt. You must remember that his firm, Arlington, Bothell & Hyde was purchased a few years ago by Security Financial Express. It just happens that Express' President sits on the Cardinal Board as an outside member. He is phoning Arrow a report every night."

"Surely, he has suggested that he remove himself from all considerations. The conflict of interest ....."

Turner was now becoming agitated by the conversation. "Bull, the conflict! He is not a lawyer. His company is going to make a fee of one percent on the Cardinals. The only thing he wants is for us to pay a higher price."

184

Turner knew that he had not turned the conversation. Massendale's knees were jerking. Turner doubted if he could even stand up. The way things were going, Massendale would soon have to try and run to the bathroom to keep from messing his pants. He had to quiet the man down.

"Massey, look, maybe we can wait and plan an attack after we meet with Phillip. I am sorry for breaking in here like this. And to change the subject, did I interrupt you .... whatever you were working on when I came in here?"

Right in front of his eyes, Massendale turned a higher color of red. Turner's quick reaction was that he had stamped on an accelerator rather than the brakes.

"It's that rude, arrogant Smith lady. She is convinced her husband is dead. I understand she saw Jamison earlier this morning and finding no satisfaction, slapped this suit on me."

Turner looked at the desk to where Massey was pointing. "So what is the problem? We are sued ten times a day. Why should that bother you?"

"It is the way she is going about it. Murder is not a federal offense, it is a state action just like robbery, assault, or the like. No one is tried for those crimes, can be tried for those crimes, in a Federal Court. The only time a murder comes up in Federal Court is like say, in Miami, where the state won't charge hit men for the Mob because of the Mob/State connections."

Turner was confused by this rambling. "I don't understand."

"That is when the Feds step in and use the Civil Rights Act. The murderer is found guilty of violating the victim's civil rights and sent up for ten years. The verdict and testimony is then forced on the State Court."

"Hold on! You have used some phrases I don't like. You said, 'when the Feds step in' and 'murder.' You make it sound as if you think she has already been to the Justice Department and has their interest or promise of assistance."

Massendale had not thought that far yet, but it did sound reasonable. "Yes, that is what I was implying."

He watched as Turner reached his desk, picked up the Corporate Directory, and thumbed through its pages. The directory contained both home and office numbers. Turning the phone on Massendale's desk, he quickly dialed.

"Mrs. Smith, this is Frank Turner of ..... no, no, I don't want to
talk to any lawyers, not even my own. Mrs. Smith, please let me
apologize. I think that you have talked to two of my people who have
had their instructions mixed up."

Turner raised his hand to Massendale who was about to voice a
rebuttal. "Yes, yes, we, of course, will cooperate. How much was it
that you requested ..... a basic $ 680,000, I see. Did you include the
double indemnity increase in case of an accidental death ... yes, I see,
what about prorating and adjusting for his increased bonus this year?
You would want to be paid that prorated bonus, wouldn't you? You
had not thought of that? Also, what about your legal fees up to this
date?"

Frank Turner was standing and smiling. He was undoubtedly at his
best, the place he wished and was trained to be, negotiating. "I will
tell you what. If you agree to repay us should your husband reappear,
we would be glad to pay you that amount .... slightly more if you
follow my calculations. Tell you what, I will have someone type it out
and draft a one page agreement. You sign it and the check will be
yours tomorrow."

Turner stood smiling at the frowning Massendale. "Interest? No, if
you repay, it will just be the flat amount. We will forget about any
interest. Yes, it is a pleasure doing business with you too .... and
please Mrs. Smith, know that our thoughts and prayers go with you."

Placing the phone's receiver in its cradle, he angrily looked at
Massendale. "See that that is done in two hours. Get your whole staff
to do it if you find it necessary. This is just what we don't need and
God Damn it Massey, don't go over my head on this to Phillip! I'll
have your ass along with Jamison's if you do!"

Turner again noticed Massendale's coloring. He now looked paler,
as if the pressure were lifted. "See you in ten minutes in the empty
conference room at the end of the hall."

As Turner turned to leave the speechless Massendale, the empty
conference room, unknown to them, was occupied. Dane Hughes had
caught sight of a harried looking Caroline O'Brian preparing for the
meeting. Stepping into the room, he took a chance on catching a
smile or two.

"Caroline, Hello, can't stay, have to rush, my you are looking
ravishing, I miss you, I need you, I want to meet for dinner tonight,
or perhaps fly to Vegas and get married. Answer 'Yes' to one or all the

above."

Caroline had felt her body stiffen. What did he want now? This was her worse time. She was behind for selfish reasons and she most despised being interrupted when she was making a list. Even so, she could not help returning a smile. At least Dane proposed now and then. He had at least one redeeming characteristic.

Dane then surprised her by turning and yelling into the hall. "Now Lacey, where did you go? Get in here and say Hello. Just because she had your fat ass fired ....."

Again, Caroline couldn't refrain from a frightened smile. The shy face, then body, of Everett Lacey appeared from behind the door's side wall where he had chosen to stand unseen.

Dane kept the conversation moving, "I just found him sneaking off the back elevator a minute ago. Well, say Hello the two of you."

"Hello, Caroline."

"Hello, Everett."

"Come on Ev, sit down and let's chat with this young lady for awhile. I want to tell you both something, might as well do it all at once."

Lacey looked at Caroline and in a flash knew that he could not tell Phillip Arrow of his daughter's work.

Everett Lacey slowly sat down at the table. He found his heart racing even more. What would occur if others should find him here? He had wished to have an emergency chat with Phillip Arrow. Dane had caught him sneaking up the back way. To hide his purpose, he had allowed his friend to place him at a table with Caroline. Stupid, Lacey! That was "very stupid," again thought Lacey. He watched the suddenly attentive Caroline O'Brian. Yet, he knew it had not been dumb. He had wanted to be stopped.

Yes, he thought, to tell Arrow would be to play the games of the O'Brians and the Turners. Screw you, Phillip Arrow, your daughter is worth ten old men like you! She has her life in front of her, yours is only history. Why ruin a young woman to save an old man?

Before Dane could again speak, Caroline spoke and voiced a question. "Do you know Everett that I really miss having you here? You were a fresh mind in a wilderness. I find it difficult to stay mentally active, something like being alone. By the way, what are you doing here, now?"

"Caroline, he is on a secret mission that only Phillip Arrow knows about. Now be quiet and listen to me." Dane Hughes caught Caroline's startled look. He did not often take the lead with her. Lacey's face was a blank.

"I wanted to brief the two of you that I believe I know who the two were who attacked you and me that night in New York."

"Oh, Dane ...." Caroline's bark of exasperation was cut short by Everett Lacey.

"It was Kevin Heike and George Andrews. Both are paid mercenaries hired for special purposes by a service firm headquartered in Chicago," interjected Lacey.

"You know their names?" Dane Hughes was staggered, then he saw Caroline's grin. She knew Lacey was kidding.

Before he could respond, there was a loud shout. "Lacey, what the Hell are you doing here?" Frank Turner had entered the room followed by Phillip Arrow. "I have been waiting to see you again. I personally wanted to tell you how personally disappointed we all were in your behavior both before and after you left the Corporation. You must have felt like a real crumb for the way you acted. I can still hardly believe it. Arrow Corporation gave you a tremendous opportunity and you blew it! I ......"

"Frank, sit down!" It was Phillip Arrow who uncharacteristically had raised his voice. "Ev it is good to see you. Has anyone told you that we miss you around here? What do you hear about the Cardinals and the Blue Jays?"

"I hear that the Cardinals have voted to sell and that the Blue Jays are probably going to try to stick it out hoping that you don't get 50% of their shares tendered."

"Yes, I believe that may be true. We are hoping that they will give us a call today or tomorrow, however. I am holding Caroline and Aaron free for them. Frank and his friends are going to have to handle the Cardinals. It is the Blue Jays that are bothering us."

"I believe that their Board is meeting again this afternoon. I would not hope too hard, Sir. It looks like you will have to go for 75% of their stock to demand a special Board Meeting to gain control of their operations." Lacey noted that Phillip Arrow had neglected to mention the Orioles. The press was filled only with stories of the Oriole tender.

"I fear that you may be right. Right now, however, I have to plan for the best so if you two don't mind ...." Arrow gave Hughes and Lacey a brush of the hand.

188

Both Dane and Everett stood up and walked toward the door. As Lacey was turning to squeeze by a startled Lawrence Massendale, Dane ventured, "Caroline, see you tonight?"

"Sorry, Mr. Hughes. I fear that I will be all tied up tonight." She immediately wished that she had watched her words. Massey looked like he was about to faint. If they could get this meeting over within an hour, they might ...."

Frank Turner solved her problem. "Let's get going. I have a ten o'clock flight out tonight and a heavy date before then. I would like to be out of here in double time."

Meg Jamison sat in the back of the limousine. The miles had so quickly melted away. She knew that she was not more than twenty minutes away from the Arrow Corporation headquarters. She looked at the inside of car: luxurious felt covered seats, a dividing one-way polaroid glass shield between the passenger area and the driver. She could see him, but he could not see her. She had found that the partition was also sound proof. To talk to the driver, she had to push a button to lower the divider or use another to access a microphone, speaker system. A bar sat in the center of the limousine's back open area, with a seat to each side, all facing the back seat on which she sat. Behind and on top of the bar was a video monitor. She had inspected the movie library in the compartment in the back of the front passenger seat. All were hard core pornographic films if her judgment was correct.

She again looked at the note. Three items were written. It was her choice again. She could either fix a dry, chilled martini, she could either sit in the center of the back seat when he entered, she could either slip the lace in his pocket or not. All were her choices.

Meg looked at the autos now streaming from the City in the opposite direction the limousine was heading. Work was over in the City Center. Most were going home to rather standard, average American lives. What had separated her? What choice had she made that now found her in this spot? What differentiated her life from those she passed?

Riding in her dark, air-conditioned world, Meg had spent the last hour viewing what she only knew at the "Valley." A long ten mile wide depression, that led west and north from the small mountain range that separated it from downtown Los Angeles, now housed close to four million inhabitants. It had to be one of the world's largest

189

suburbs, all connected by freeways that made its parts but minutes away. Fast roads seem to have created a fast culture.

She had heard that over one half the households contained a divorced adult. Marriage was not a strong institution in Southern California, yet how much less strong than in other modern places of the world, she wondered? It was a simple lesson. Material focused societies did not create human bonds. Family focused societies did.

The thought drove her back to the present. What was it that she was focusing on, material or family? Her husband was as excited as she had ever seen him and yes, she did enjoy sharing his success with him. It was really her fault. She had not found a way to deal with a problem that she should have solved. Leaning on or sacrificing John was not the answer. She would keep her eyes open, surely there was a way to stop this maniac Turner. She again looked at his adolescent note.

They were her choices, all three. Yet, hadn't she already made those choices? She looked at her expensive low cut dress, her shapely legs and the very high heels. No one had caused her to have her hair done beautifully, be ready for the limousine when it pulled up to her home. Indeed, she had run to it only partly so that no neighbor would see it parked there for any length of time. No one had made her feel tight and young in getting ready for the show. No one had made her take such care and forced her to wear her best perfume.

No, no one could make her do anything. Frank Turner was right, the choices were hers. She pulled cautiously at the bottom of her dress and inched it slowly up her legs. No one should be able to see her. In slow motion and as her body trembled, she saw her hands unsnap what had been her most surprising present. If this is all he wishes me to wear, she thought, it was an easy enough task. No one would ever know or see the difference. Could she make his drink extra cold?

She was shocked when the limousine stopped. The time had passed so quickly. Where had her time to prepare gone? The back door quickly opened. Frank Turner stepped in and smiled at her. She was sitting in the center, she did have a drink ready. He pushed the button to lower the divider. "Driver, we have plenty of time. Please drive up through Beverly Hills over Laurel Canyon and into the Valley. I would like to stop at a nice bar around 8:00. We would need to leave at 9:00 so that you can have me at LAX for a flight at 9:30 sharp.

You can drive the lady back to Santa Barbara from there. Now drive easy!"

As he had begun to talk, he had felt Meg's hand slip into his coat pocket. He had also heard her gasp regarding the canceling of seeing the show. Tough! As he raised the window dividing that world from theirs, he felt in his pocket. The material felt warm and soft, the glass handed to him, ice cold and hard.

11

Two Weeks Later
Thursday
May 9, 1985

F rank Turner entered Phillip Arrow's office. He had been on the road for the week and had talked to Arrow but twice, the last to be called back for this special morning meeting. He quickly saw that Arrow wore a large smile on his face, much like the cat that had swallowed the mouse.

Sprawling on a chair in front of Arrow's desk, Frank Turner asked, "What's up? I can't tell you how upsetting it is to be called back here like this. You can't really expect me to be effective when you are jerking me around."

Phillip Arrow looked over his desk and smiled to show he paid Frank's comments no attention, "The Blue Jays have finally seen the light. Their President called yesterday afternoon and requested a meeting this morning. With the tender offer period expiring this afternoon, he is finally hedging his bets. Most of his shareholders have accepted our offer if the preliminary reports are correct."

"So, how much stock of his do we have to buy?"

"I would suspect that it will be 79% of all his Company's stock that will be tendered, perhaps more. If you have kept track of both the

Cardinals' and Blue Jay's stock, you would have seen as much as 20% of their shares trading each of the past weeks. They no longer have many old time, long term holders. Most have sold fearing that the Blue Jays' resistance would queer the deal and that the stock would drop down to where it should be."

"Do we have to buy all of it?"

"According to the terms of the tender, Yes. If they had not resisted, we would have been able to arrange for a 49% purchase like the Cardinals. We will have to treat them as an acquisition and we will be able to use merger, spinoff accounting only on the other. More important, it triggers tax purchase accounting. We will have 60 days to pay tax on the recaptured depreciation, investment credits and the like. That will mean an additional billion dollars in cash."

Turner gave Arrow a wry, amused smile. It was typical of Arrow to attempt to have him worry about matters that should not cause concern. "So what's the problem? We have a credit line for up to twenty billion."

"No we do not! The credit line was only for the purchase of shares and for no other purpose. That wasn't made clear to me in Dallas. Now Smedt tells me that the monies borrowed can only be used to close the mergers. Severance, taxes, and expenses come from us."

"Hold on! Smedt told me just the opposite. I heard him say it many times in our earlier conversations."

Arrow nodded his head toward this selfconfident executive. "So did I. Our tender prospectuses contain the same statements. Our problem is that we only have a letter of understanding. The actual loan agreement will be signed early next week. The New York banks have shifted their signals. How do you read it?"

"It looks to me like they are planning to put the squeeze on us. But so what? All banks do that. We are just going to have to play like Hell with our cash flow to stay above water for a couple of years."

Frank Turner waited for Arrow to reply. As he waited in vain, his mind reviewed the numbers of the cash flow projections. It would be tight. Any more surprises and they would need to borrow heavily to cover cash flow shortages. Who would loan to a company that already had ten billion in debt?

Frank knew that he could not be left with the last word on any major problem left open. "So why call me? I was to handle the Cardinals and you, the Blue Jays. By the way, where are our legal counsels?"

Arrow smiled across the desk at the arrogant, demanding first lieutenant. "I have asked that Massendale and Goldstein sit in the end conference room. If they are needed or if we have to ask questions, you can run down and ask them. The Blue Jay people will sit in the side conference room and it will work the same for them. There will be just the four of us."

"Four?" Turner looked suddenly startled.

"Yes, I have also invited the Cardinals' President. There seems to be some problem with his perspective of the future. It seems that someone has promised both the Cardinals' and the Blue Jays' Presidents control over the other. I want to straighten it out from the start. It will either make or break us, of that I am sure. It also gives us a chance to make the Cardinal President a part of the family. He can have a chance to see what it feels like from this side of the table."

Frank Turner took no notice of Phillip Arrow's rebuke. Turner knew that he kept sane by not letting anyone's words bother him. To his knowledge, he had not accepted the possibility that he had done anything wrong since the day he had run down his baby sister on his motorbike.

"Anything that I need to know before they get here?" Turner was now, in fact, suddenly steaming mad. Was the Cardinal President to become a competitor of his for Arrow's Chairmanship so quickly?

"Yes, several things and then you fill me in on how the Cardinal situation is going. First, the detective agency that the Blue Jays hired has turned up some type of information that is embarrassing to us. I want to know what it is. Second, if any deals are made on compensation like those you made with the Cardinals, I want to be part of it. How you could ever agree to five year, non cancelable, no competition clause, and elective termination choices with a lump sum payment of five times annual compensation, I will never know. I want to be part of the decision making process before you send it to me on a platter asking for a make or break decision."

Frank Turner looked bored. Silently talking to himself, he wondered whether Arrow could have arranged the deal with the Cardinals that he had. It had taken two days of non stop negotiations to have the Cardinals come over without a fight. There was no sabotage there. Hell, they were even letting Turner make decisions within their company now as if the merger were completed. That would not be

195

finalized for three months. As the Cardinal President had said, "It's over, it is time to go on and run the new company." No, he doubted if Arrow had ever gotten that bruised, been in a situation that tight, ever done as well.

Arrow looked like he had lost his train of thought. "Oh, yes, and then there is a question of a national headquarters. From what Jamison found in Kansas City, St. Louis, Memphis, and Chicago, I think Kansas City is our choice."

"It is?" It always burnt Turner to have Arrow use such freedom with his 'our' inclusion. What a dumb decision! Turner held back his comment. One did not take the Boss on over the little things, only the big major things over which one's life was at stake. If it was Kansas City, so be it. The fact that his wife, Mary, had grown up there as a young girl, of course, had nothing to do with it.

Arrow did not answer the question. Finally Turner spoke again. "What about our counsels and the rest? I still would have expected that you would want both Massendale and Goldstein in this session."

"As I said, I have them standing by, Massendale, Caroline, Goldstein, and Smedt. They tell me that you put Jamison on the road again, but nothing is harmed with that. He can miss this bloodletting. Ah, there is the phone signal, both Presidents are in the outside office. Let's go out and greet them. Don't worry about the rest of our people, they will do fine cooling their heels."

At that moment, only one of the five in the conference room was thinking about "heels." Lawrence Massendale could see Caroline's legs clearly. He was wondering if either John Smedt or Aaron Goldstein thought Caroline's heels round too. His thoughts were interrupted by Aaron Goldstein. "Let me get this right, Lawrence. You have the audacity to call me up yesterday afternoon to demand that I fly across the continent to sit quietly in this stuffy room?"

Caroline answered for him, "That is correct Mr. Goldstein. But then you don't really care how you earn your money, do you?"

"You are correct about him," answered John Smedt, "but I am more particular. I think that this is a damn outrage!"

"Please, Gentlemen, you must understand," answered Massendale who was feeling more sure of himself with each new day, "the first part of the meeting is a sales job, nothing more. Phillip and Frank Turner are meeting with both the Cardinal and Blue Jay Presidents. It is to set matters straight and influence the Blue Jays to cooperate with us. The Blue Jay President knows that he is dead. It is just the manner in which he is going to die that is open to negotiations. I can see what Phillip is doing, I would hope that you can also."

"God Damn," shouted Goldstein, "how can it be that I have to put up with such dribble? You don't even know what you are talking about. The Blue Jay President has probably just set this up as a preliminary part of a legal suit that he is about to slap on you. Dumb, Lawrence, dumb! I can't imagine allowing myself to be part of this?"

"Then why don't you just walk out, Mr. Goldstein? We would be glad to see you go. I am sure that Mr. Massendale can handle all the legal questions." Caroline leapt in to protect her new knight. The tone of her voice was not lost upon either Smedt and Goldstein.

Aaron Goldstein angrily tugged at his briefcase and pulled out some papers. He would be damned if he would answer the bitch. Whatever was happening down the hall was damn important! He should be sitting in on that meeting right now.

The meeting was twenty minutes into its start before even a vague hint of business was covered. Six baseball teams were discussed, as were the weather and the clogging of air traffic. All were necessary parts of the corporate friendship dance done with all new acquaintances. The four were about to discuss serious matters. It would never have occurred if a female were present. It had been a dance of males.

"Just to start, Gentlemen," asked Phillip Arrow, "may I personally hear your ideas of how this new company should be organized?"

The startled look on the Blue Jay President's face brought Arrow up short. He continued, "Please, I understand that you came here under no obligation. I ask the question only because I wish to start with no misconceptions."

Phillip Arrow looked at the men. Frank Turner had his sincere, business school smile on his face. The two target Presidents' faces held wry looks of disbelief.

"I was told," answered the Cardinal President, "that I was to be in charge of all the rail operations. I understand," nodding to the agreeing Blue Jay President, "that the same promise was made to my friend here. One of us had to be lied to, or perhaps both of us were misled."

"No, no, I assure you," smoothly covered Phillip Arrow, "that there was no intention to mislead anyone. Let me tell you that I see having three divisions, with the each of you as a head. You will be copresidents." Arrow caught the startled flash of Turner's anger. Surely, he thought, as he was about to continue, Turner knew that he was pulling their legs.

"If we go ahead and have you join us, Sir," nodding to the Blue Jay President, "we would want you on equal footing with the other Presidents."

"That is exactly why I came here this morning. I wish to know exactly what 'equal footing' means. I have seen the Redbird's severance agreements, the agreement not to touch the employee/employer savings plans, and the large bonuses that you granted in lieu of stock option acceleration with my friend here, but I would have to have the specifics in my case."

The Blue Jays President appeared to have obviously given in to the pressure. He was a beaten man. Arrow sensed it from the man's use of the term "Redbird's." This man was willing to play the game.

"That is not the type of 'equal footing' I was talking about. But before we get started," added Phillip Arrow who had turned his attention fully toward the Blue Jay President, "I was wondering........ if we do reach an agreement, would I get to see a copy of the New York detective agency's report on me and my people?"

"What report?" answered the Blue Jay President.

Phillip Arrow did not respond. He instead coldly eyed the lying railroad chief executive officer. Both of these Presidents were going to be gone in some span of time. Hostile takeovers usually saw management disappear in two weeks. Friendly takeovers took two years. Phillip Arrow knew that the end result for each in several years would be the same. But right now, he had to work with them. This was going to be a difficult negotiation.

As if to read Phillip Arrow's mind, the Blue Jay President added, "Is it necessary that both these other two executives sit in on our discussion. In light of Mr. Turner's track record with us, I have little interest in negotiating with him around. Indeed, I would just as rather go home and talk to a female deranged dog."

Phillip Arrow knew that the man would be pushy. He already knew that Goldstein and Smedt loved Lacey's female dog story. Half of New York probably knew by this time. Give this type an inch and they will take a mile. "Too bad. You requested the meeting this morning. I am at your pleasure. If we can not work out some type of mutually satisfying working relationship, I will use my 79% voting rights of your stock to call a special meeting and denude your corporation of you and your management within the month. I don't wish to do that, but I will if necessary."

The two combatants stared at each other. Arrow knew that he was not going to lose this round, but he knew that he had lost one already. The man wouldn't lie about the detective agency unless he had that service totally covered. It had probably been a verbal report. He would probably never hear its full story, but by the man's tone he had something. Perhaps he would not be able to use whatever he had discovered. Arrow smiled again. He had learned long ago that there was nothing wrong with having a skeleton in the closet if his opponents could not use that knowledge. Silence enveloped the room as he waited for the man's reply.

"That sounds too close to a threat, Sir! I don't like to be threatened. Let me say this and you can get on with your business. Last night my Board requested that I come here and agree to a friendly merger. I refused, submitted my resignation dated one hour from now, and am here only to introduce my replacement. I wished to at least begin this meeting to see if you were sincere. If you think I would ever buy that bull about three copresidents, you are crazy."

In stating the latter, he had turned to the Cardinal President, who was an obvious friend. Surprising to all, he next turned to Frank Turner. "You are crazy too if you would accept any copresident position."

The Blue Jay President rose and walked to the door. Calling a junior man into the office, he quickly introduced a brash, young man who looked something like Frank Turner as his temporary replacement until Arrow had appointed a new Chief Executive Officer. He smiled at Frank Turner's snarl after he had mentioned the young man's brief work history.

About to walk out the door, he again turned. "Just for your information, the Board also approved ten year severance and lump sum contracts for the top forty executives of my Company last night. Since you do not yet have ownership of our stock, I am still in control as is my Board. If you were wondering what you were going to do with the three hundred million cash we have sitting in the bank, don't bother. Checks to all executives are being written today. This will take care of all stock appreciation, deferred salaries and the like. Of course, there is a non-compete and SEC questions. To solve those problems, those forty top members of my management have also submitted their resignations effective at the end of the week. I wish you all well with your negotiations. If there was something more violent I could have done, I would have very much liked to have done so."

Violence at that moment was on others' minds in Chicago. Dane Hughes and Ev Lacey waited in their rented automobile for the exit of one of the two men identified in the Omega file accessed by the code number of Phillip Arrow. The moment stretched to minutes and the minutes to hours. Both Dane and Lacey had seen the man enter the house in the mid morning and Dane was only partly sure that the individual was one who had attacked him.

Lacey kept wondering why he was in on such a crazy scheme. He had found no relationship between the attack and the union other than it occurred during the same time period. Lacey knew he was grasping.

Their plan was simple. Once the man left his residence, they were going to enter and search it. Lacey had surmised that the man must have a sophisticated work order system. Since the order for services went in via telephone communication lines to a central computer via clients' terminals, it only made sense that Omega employees took their orders via similar terminals. Records and access codes should be found in the house.

The hours wore on and their conversation died away. If it takes a heap of living to make a house a home, thought Lacey, this guy must really enjoy his home. Their mistake was that they expected him to be gone during the daytime. Here was a type who obviously worked during the night. Lacey felt his clothes begin to stick to him in the sultry early afternoon heat.

Everett Lacey had plenty of time to ponder his dispair, the depths to which his investigations had plummetted. The union trust fund, the union leader connection was a fizzle. There was no way it could have ever worked. Yes, considerable pressure could be applied to Phillip Arrow and the acquisitions could have been forced. But how could a union trust fund leader ever profit from such actions?

There was no conceivable way that the union leader could have easily benefited by this move. Dane was right. In a way, the acquisition of the debt plagued, Congress backed, railroad pension fund liabilities protected Arrow Corporation from its own pension debts. Although greater in debt, Arrow Corporation was now more protected. The mergers really were not advantageous to the unions. The unions should have been opposing the mergers. Crazy!

Lacey had seen that the unions also used Omega. As a diversion, he had decided to assist Dane in his crazy scheme. Obviously, the Orioles had hired the man who lived inside. Of that there could be no doubt. Perhaps, just perhaps, he had also worked for the unions. There had to be some connection.

It was six hours later when a shadowed figure left the house. The cramped, sweating bodies lifted themselves from the car's seats. Chicago had been at its sultry, humid best. Both men felt as if they had lost twenty pounds. Hughes knocked on the door. There was no answer. Standing back, he viciously kicked it in. No one noticed. If they had, no one would have cared. Two men kicking in the door of a vacated residence were not abnormal for this part of Chicago.

Lacey entered the house first and Dane followed. Closing the door as best he could, Dane turned to find Lacey quickly surveying each room. Clean, the house smelled of pine and cigar smoke.

Their waiting and effort had been in vain. No records of any type were found in the house. A single computer terminal and screen sat next to a telephone. There was no printer or paper records. Turning on the terminal, Lacey watched it wipe its hard disk clean of all records. Obviously, he had tripped its system guard. He should have depressed some key on the keyboard when he turned on the power. He turned to join Dane in his silent futile search. It was as if a body just ate, slept, and watched TV in these rooms. Few clothes and utensils were found. They had sweated in vain.

Lacey knew that he was to find no clues as to other assignments related to the targets, no ideas of any connections with union leaders and as desperate as this had been, it indicated the dispair   he felt in ever finding the reason for Arrow's merger insanity. For the first time, he felt perhaps that he should give up. If it weren't for the new energy and ideas of Mary Sue Massendale, he might very well go back to L.A. and chuck it in. At least Phillip Arrow still did not know about her. Now, if he could just calm Dane down before he really found trouble.

Dane knew he was to have no revenge, no reward for his efforts. He thought of his desire to pursue these men. As a civilian, he had never been attacked. Were these men a sign of his mental sickness or was it that he felt foredestined, that it was to be either he or they, that they were to meet again on perhaps terms far more unfavorable to him?

They slowly walked from the hot rooms into the even hotter late Chicago afternoon in silence. The two friends had not spoken to each other once during the last hour. All that waiting had been for nothing.

The thought was repeated two thousand miles away. All that waiting for nothing. Four dispirited people sat in the ever stuffy conference room as the evening approached. For nine hours they had been on call for the Arrow summons. Instead, Frank Turner had visited thrice to ask technical questions and in the latest trip, to ask that they review a handwritten agreement. Turner had been in the finest of spirits. He knew how grating it had to be to the four of them to sit as inferiors on call, not included in the historic events of the Company. The worse they looked, the better Turner appeared to feel.

It was another hour later when he returned to the room for the final time. Phillip Arrow followed him into the room and spoke, "Thank you all for your help. It was much needed. We could not have done it without your being on hand."

Turner could not believe the blank stares. It was too good an opportunity to miss, "Yes, you all helped us a lot today. I want to say 'Good Job' to each of you." Looking at them, he thought that Smedt and Goldstein were about to explode. What a great day, he thought, what a great day and it was not over yet!

"Well, Sir, what happened?" Caroline could not stand the suspense. She was excited by these two calm assured men.

"Caroline," replied Arrow, "the Blue Jays are going to cooperate. There will be no more opposition. There is only one small detail. Their three hundred employee count at their corporate headquarters will be cut by forty plus executives within the next few days. It is for us to get in there and see what is happening, move what we can to our headquarter site, and......."

"We can't do that!" It was Massendale who had his first chance to add something for the day.

"Maybe not," responded Frank Turner in that Arrow was coldly staring at his son-in-law, "but we are surely going to try. If you are worrying about the fact that the merger will not be effective for three months, don't. The Blue Jays already have new officers."

"Who?" Caroline knew that she was going to like the answer.

"Caroline, you are to be their new Executive Vice President, Jamison is their President. Those roles will fit with your new division

202

titles and responsibilities. What it does mean is that we have to get the Kansas City operation going next week. Are you ready to move to Kansas City?"

"Kansas! Oh, God, Phillip, are you becoming senile?" Massendale couldn't believe that a decision had been made. When had there been a discussion? The Old Man was becoming more of a martinet everyday. The idea was crazy as a loon's.

Arrow rose from his seated position. His mouth was tight and complexion flushed. He turned and walked from the room without saying another word.

"You have real style, Massey, real style," lowly whispered Turner. "Where do you pick up your sense of timing?" Laughing, he left the embarrassed, tired, mad, angry potpourri of emotions. These mergers had made a mess of Arrow Corporation executives' spirits. Turner loved it! The day had perhaps been his best ever! He turned toward his office. He still had time to kick ass for a few minutes before he had to hit the road. It was time he exercised a little control for the day. If not, he would quickly lose his touch. Today was one day where he did not wish to lose his edge.

Meg Jamison guided her yellow Mercedes down the coastline of Malibu. She should soon reach the address that Frank Turner had sent her. Again, cash had accompanied his invitation. This time, however, the note had stated only the time, the address, and the request that she use her imagination. It was like a progressive date. Turner expected progress, yet he did not wish to give up the concept of reinforcing her recognition of the Jamisons' need of a salary.

Meg had carefully reviewed the note and the contents. She had then sat for hours and retraced each word and action of Turner's in their previous two meetings. What was he after, what did he really want?

Meg had the window down. It was an early summer day along the coastline where the Santa Monica Mountains stretched down into the sea. She saw miles and miles of surfers, more surfboards than seagulls. Was this Turner's idea of mature surfing? If it was, it fit her analysis of his actions. Like the surfers, Turner would never go in the water if the waves were tame, if the water was too inviting. What the Turners of the world liked were the large waves, the rough water, the unexpected, the unconquerable.

The first realization was that Turner was not like her husband. As simple as that sounded, it was a complex realization for a woman who had lived with only one man. After awhile, all women believe that men are like their husbands. John was a friendly dog, Turner was a mad dog. Turner's mind was a frightening maze. He had to have some alternate goal other than a romp in the hay; she could sense it. If it was to make her cold and her husband unhappy, he was surely accomplishing his task.

She caught herself again covering the single question upon which she had focused her attention. Yes, she was correct. She no longer thought about her husband when thinking of her conflict with Frank Turner. John was off in Kansas or Missouri or someplace today. He was even further than that away in her thoughts. This battle was between just Turner and herself.

The second realization was that there would be no stopping these meetings on her part. She had sold out. After the first time, there would be no refusal on her part. She had made the choice to further her husband's, and more truthfully, her family's future. She was a high paid unwilling prostitute, nothing more. For the first time, Meg understood the depth of despair that good women the world over have experienced. Morality was not a test that could be so lightly given.

The third, and final realization was that only Turner would put a stop to these meetings. Meg reached to touch the packages on the seat next to her. She had purchased the clothing only this morning. It was then when she was sure what she must do.

Lost in thought, she almost passed the open gate with the number of her destination. Driving down a narrow driveway, she passed a second fence to arrive at a stark white, red tiled beach house. No other car was present, which was as expected. She had purposely arrived two hours early to prepare herself.

Meg slowly got out of the car and reached for the packages and the hanging skirt and blouse. Clad in a grey sweatshirt, baggy pants, and tennis shoes she felt hardly glamorous.

Walking up the path, she removed a note pinned to the door. The house was theirs for the rest of the day, the door was open. She looked around at the setting before entering. A beautiful blue sky, dabbled with white clouds spread across green trees that hid the two fences. She could hear the roar of the ocean waves. Unused to entering a house alone and uninvited, she tried to settle her heartbeat. Finding that impossible, she turned and forced herself to quickly enter.

Forty minutes later, she had toured the entire darkened palace.

Every chance she had, she opened windows and blinds. The darkness of the rooms almost allowed the comic nature of the decor, furniture, and equipment to pass. In the clear light of day, it appeared as it was. Sick, California sick! How many mirrors on ceilings had she seen, handcuffs on bedposts, an actual torture rack, closets full of light gowns and heels, drawers full of plastic packaged paraphernalia, a library supplied by a teenage maniac, movies with thousands of titles yet just one subject, video cameras, hot tubs, a full bar, a kitchen packed with food. She wondered who would find time to eat.

Time was running out and she had much to do. She took out the quarter cut, barely supporting bra, the thin blouse that cut low, would still hang straight down from her bust, thin garters, skirt, and four inch heels. She could barely stand on the latter, but she could and for the short time, she would suffer.

A full hour later, she had dressed and adjusted her hair. As she finished shaking extra cold martinis, she heard the door closing. Frank Turner walked into the living room with his confident, dominating air. White slacks and a blue sportscoat set off with a pink handkerchief in his pocket made a dashing picture of a California man. He looked like he had had a perfectly marvelous day.

"What's this! A drink ready for the tired man? Mrs. Jamison, you do know how to treat a fellow. Hey! Let me take a look at you. Wow! I like that, and that, and especially that."

Turner had walked up to her at the door to the kitchen area and accepted her offered drink. His free hand slid over the thin fabric covering her bareness. She steeled herself, she could not flinch as she felt herself naturally responding. Meg took his hand and led him toward the couch that looked over the waves.

Meg suddenly felt selfconscious holding his hand. She fought off the urge to remove her grip. She looked out the windows. Curtains to the right cut most of the afternoon sun, while the open window to the left looked down the beach. They could see joggers on the beach, not more than forty yards away, who, in turn, must have noticed the two sitting down on the couch. Meg again fought off the urge to pull that window's curtain. Was Frank Turner an exhibitionist?

"Say this is great, I have been thinking about this drink for the last hour on the freeway."

"Is that all you have been thinking of? I have been thinking of all this for days, ever since I received your note."

"You have? Mrs. Jamison, I am shocked!"

"Yes, you don't mind my being honest from the start do you? I have been thinking of our.....you know, other two times. I want to be honest, I enjoyed them very much. You are like a disease in my mind. I just can't get you out of there." Meg's left hand was busy. In a deft motion, she had accomplished what she wished. "How do you like your drink, is it smooth enough?"

"Uh, yes, it is smooth enough. Mrs. Jamison, what has come over you?"

"Oh, it was a long trip. I suppose that I have had too much time to think about us. Are you hungry?"

"Uh, yes, I am."

"Well, I fixed the drinks. I think that you should fix the hors d'oeuvre."

Turner looked out at the waves. Two passing walkers stopped and looked up before turning away. The roar of the waves began to fill his hearing, his ears and head. He tried to sit still without moving. A sudden change in his position would be a sign that she had the upper hand. He had to gain control of the situation. Could he change the subject. "Those are some really sexy heels you have there."

Meg Jamison looked up. She knew that Turner had a passion or two. All men had sex fetishes of some kind she realized. Frank Turner's was probably shoes, she would have to remember that and use it. She had been told that high heels were still the most effective male attraction device. There couldn't be any other reason women wore them.

"Here," she said reaching down and taking one off and handing it to him, the other going on the coffee table in front of them, "what do you think of them? They told me that they were the rage."

"Uh, very nice." What was it felt Turner? Was it the lady, the waves, or the drink? Damn, he thought that he had more control than this. He had just walked in the door ten minutes ago and she was controlling the situation. He felt cornered. He was an attacker and what attackers fear most of all, he knew, was to be attacked. Had she thought it through that far?

He let the moments pass.

"Mrs. Jamison, what has gotten into you... what ⋯ has come over you? Why this sudden change of attitude?" asked the smiling but still startled Frank Turner.

Meg Jamison sat squarely on the sofa slowly sipping her martini. "I thought that if I were especially nice to you, that perhaps we could do this more often. I mean, I would like to see you more often. In a way, I am already coming to depend upon you."

She could see him struggling with her proposal. A Frank Turner did not like to be owned or used, only to use and own others. It had been a shot low and across his bow. He looked more like he had been shot in the stomach. She wondered at his stamina. He looked very fit, but he was, after all, over 50 years of age. If she could break him, humiliate him, even if she paid a price, it would be worth it. It would be a long time before he would ever care to put up with this much punishment again.

"Come on," she said, "I expect that you have seen this place before and I need someone to explain some of these things to me." She slipped on her shoes, took him by the hand and led him across the room to a door to one of the bedrooms. "I have two things that I really want to try before I leave, that Chinese basket being one of them. Some can wait, of course, I would think that you might invite me back here again."

Hours later as the clock was running out on the day, Meg found herself back on the road heading north to Santa Barbara. Her body was sore and bruised. Frank Turner had turned mean. It might take her days to recover. She again rolled down the window and thought of her nagging begging to see him next week. It would take him weeks to recover. Perhaps she had seen the last of the bastard! Score one for Meg Jamison, or at worst, call it a draw with someone who knew only about winning.

12

Three Months Later
Friday
August 9, 1985

Phillip Arrow sat in his office with his chair turned away from his desk. He was looking out over the smoggy face of Los Angeles. His thoughts strayed to Kansas City. How he would like to live there! But that was impossible, clearly impossible. Arrow looked at the stock market report he held in his hand. For the first time in his life, people around him saw him as truly frightened.

He had often told people that his definition of an entrepreneur was a simple test. Had the man ever risked all on a venture, where he had much, and all of it was at jeopardy? Had he ever lived with that fear, both day and night, that gnawing at his gut, that knowledge of certain ruin? If he hadn't, he wasn't an entrepreneur. Yes, he, Phillip Arrow had been scared in his early days, but he never remembered a time when he should have been more scared than this.

Arrow Corporation's acquisition of the Blue Jays and Cardinals had progressed to its conclusion in orderly steps. Unknown to Arrow, John Smedt and Aaron Goldstein had essentially been correct in their assessment months earlier on board John Smedt's new ship, which had been rechristened, "The Bitch." After running the price of Arrow

Corporation and the Orioles' stock price to record levels, the Orioles were allowed to fly free.

The two step mergers affected with the other two rail targets were completed with Arrow Corporation securities in the second stage valued at over twice the dollar amount originally anticipated. Hence, Phillip Arrow was able to purchase the two targets for essentially no premium when viewed in dollar values existing on the first day that the tenders became public knowledge. It was just that Goldstein and Smedt would never know how sure a bet it had been.

Phillip Arrow believed that he owed the Orioles a tremendous debt of gratitude for their mutually terminated counter tender offer. If rumors were correct, the counter with the Orioles was also true. The Orioles had just opened tenders on two Eastern rail lines using his tactics as a guide. They would never have been able to do so without the Arrow Corporation's tender inflation of the value of the Oriole stock. Soon there might be just two major U.S. rail lines, Union Arrow and the Orioles. That was the good news!

Arrow looked at the article he held in his other hand. The newspaper leaks had started again. For the past three weeks, a constant stream of disclosures had been printed, all pointing to one fact - Union Arrow's stock price was overinflated. Corresponding record drops in the Company's stock price had occurred and were continuing. From a high of $260 a share at the time of the mergers, the price had been more than cut in half. Early reports were that it was off another six points after early morning trading today.

And although the mergers had concluded, not all, in fact little, was going well with the newly merged firms. Earnings of all entities were down. Frank Turner had had to be reassigned to the original Arrow Corporation subsidiaries as their profits were suffering substantially. Like children left unattended and neglected during the acquisitions, these units were quickly falling apart at the seams. Turner had returned his attention to units over which a suddenly dispirited and apparently disinterested Phillip Arrow gave no notice. For the first time, Arrow had given Turner a free hand in running these subsidiaries.

And while earnings were down in the original subsidiaries, they were also remarkably deficient in the newly acquired companies. The Cardinals' group was in fact losing money for only the third time in their over a hundred years of history while the Blue Jays were barely breaking even. Both groups were invariably compared to the Orioles, who were showing record profits, much to the consternation of all.

Arrow knew that the financial causes of these sudden dramatic decreases in the new corporation's earnings were due in large part to the tremendous interest costs associated with the debt taken on with the purchases. A secondary cause was not as worrisome. With the purchase of these companies, all the assets had been increased in value to match the purchase price. Amortization and depreciation were increased with the resulting impact on accounting income. The latter, however, was only a paper loss. It paled in comparison to the annual billion and a half dollars in interest expense that had to be paid on a monthly basis. With earnings down, the new Union Arrow Corporation had significant cash flow problems in meeting these payments.

This cash flow deficit had not been helped with the target companies' golden parachutes. As anticipated, no deduction had been allowed for the over 400 million dollars in cash payments made to departing target officers. These monies, along with VEBA funding and other hidden 'time bombs' had claimed close to a billion dollars in unexpected cash flow. That amount neatly complemented the similar unanticipated billion dollars due the IRS for the Blue Jays' intransigence and the consequence of the recapture of depreciation.

However, just as overriding a cause of the financial downturn was a paralysis in management decision making. Violent conflicts over management authority were in process. As a result, information and communication within the organizations were at a standstill. Grown men fought over territory and the definition of their domains. Few decisions led to no actions. Financial growth had ceased. And then there was an even greater problem. The Company was being destroyed from within.

And none admitted to the sabotage. Cash management was in a shambles. To meet an expected moratorium on capital expenditures, huge outlays of funds had been prepaid by the targets' managements shortly before the "change of control" to cover costs of finishing projects. In some cases, prepayment of projects had been accomplished to assure their initiation. In every corporate department of the acquired companies, hasty efforts had been made to prepay or expend monies that might not be available in later months. Union Arrow profits at the mid year were only 20% of what had been expected.

Arrow looked again at the Rail Division earnings. There was some cause for panic. Damn the Staggers Rail Act that allowed greater freedom in setting rates without ICC approval! The last thing he needed at this time was competitive pricing!

This shortfall in profits had become known two weeks ago. As a public company, Union Arrow's quarterly profits had to be made public. As a consequence and far more important, the price of Union Arrow Corporation's common stock was dropping dramatically. Selling at $186 per share on $ 8.87 per share in earnings at the start of the tenders, the stock price had suffered from both the reported poor earnings and dilution caused by the merger. In purchasing the companies, Arrow had increased the number of Arrow Corporation (now renamed Union Arrow) shares outstanding. With the rail divisions either losing money or just making up for Arrow Corporation's original subsidiaries' downturn, it appeared that Union Arrow Corportation's earnings for the year would not match those of the original Arrow Corporation. $8.87 in earnings per share now became, at best, $ 5.00 per share with the decreased earnings and the increase in the number of shares outstanding.

And rather than selling at a price earnings ratio of 21 with its rare mix of natural resources and transportation like the old Arrow Corporation, the darling of the stock exchange had apparently lost its glamour. It appeared that the PE was heading toward 7. The investment community now looked upon Union Arrow as a railroad company. The result was a disaster to the Company's stock market price.

Yes, and he could not help but feel that the leaks of information to the press were having their effect.

Phillip Arrow knew that Union Arrow's stock could drop to $ 35 per share and one analyst was forecasting a low price of $14. This would produce an equivalent market value of the now increased number of shares equal to a total value of only 1/7th of that with which Phillip Arrow had started. Indeed, with 130 million shares outstanding, Union Arrow Corporation was now considered a potential acquisition candidate itself. A candidate, that is, if any acquiring company wished to spend $ 2 billion in cash for a company with another $ 10 billion in debt.

Arrow privately hoped he wasn't playing it too close, that his plan was correct.

Common stock market wisdom was that no company or individual

212

would have such a death wish. If the mergers looked this bad from the outside, Arrow knew that they were even worse. He could see a year next year where the Company made nothing at all.

Up until now, Phillip Arrow had not been concerned with his new Company's stock market price. He could envision no raiding company wishing to take on such a huge burden. Arrow assured himself that his people concentrated on the fundamentals of the acquisition: the organization, the people, their pay, and the control of the capital expenditures. He made a specific point of not getting to know much about the new Division's businesses. At an age over sixty-five, he had known that he would have to depend upon others to know the business. He was willing to pay the price of allowing others to make mistakes in learning how to control the businesses within Union Arrow. Seemingly disinterested to his staff and outside observers, he had forced his 67 year old body away from the final merger activities. It was a task for younger men and women.

As the final merger steps had taken place, he uncharacteristically took some time for himself; first for a trip around the world reviewing potential acquistions, then several weeks were spent on reviewing trusts, wills, estate planning, his charitable Foundation, and his grandchildren's future. He had wished to spend special attention on his children's children's trusts. He believed that the time was necessary because of the needed counseling with his grandchildren's parents. Together, they would set a limit and develop a plan using the assets of the trusts he had set up for them years ago. Each grandchild was to have an education and a first house, after that they were on their own. The rest of his wealth would go to charity and his Foundation, the rest of their trusts were to pass on to succeeding generations.

His sons had cooperated, but he had had difficulty with Mary Sue. She had said that it was not his role. She was a tough negotiator. As Trustee of her children's trust, she refused to allow his meddling and he finally gave up feeling fortunate to have found an old IRS asset valuation. Legal counsel upheld his daughter. All insisted that he remain outside the trust's workings to preserve its tax status. He had threatened to exclude the trust and grandchildren from his will to no avail. But then, with Mary Sue in charge, he knew he had little to worry over. From the original money and his continuing contributions, she had told him that she had greater assets than either of his two sons. The five-year-old report he reviewed showed that she had averaged a 21% annual rate of growth for the first ten years she had managed the trust.

Lord, he was proud of his daughter! If it weren't for the mess that the Company was in and if it weren't for her husband, his silly son-in-law........

Lawrence Massendale, III was hooked solid. It appeared all he could think about was Caroline O'Brian. In church on Sunday, in his drive to work, at home over dinner, at the office during the workday, his mind was drawn to her. He admired the way she carried herself, her self-confidence, the spirit that she displayed. There was no wonder why even his father-in-law had first noticed and then promoted her. She was totally deserving of her new and active role in the Company. Her work performance had to be rated as "excellent."

Massendale had had to admit to himself that his merger performance, from a professional side, had been shabby. The truth was that he just did not care. The results were so totally predictable.

He had even varied his position a time or two because of Caroline's recommendations. After Frank Turner announced that the new Arrow Rail Division headquarters was to be in Kansas City, he had resisted that decision. When Jamison had come to him and suggested they attempt to change Arrow's mind, he had agreed to the effort to convince Phillip of the advantages of having such a subsidiary corporation staff close by in Los Angeles. Caroline had taken him aside one day and had locked the door in the furnished but unused spare executive office. Obviously, she was right. His disagreement was basically caused because of the fact that they would be seeing less of each other. It did appear obvious once she pointed it out. There could be no chances taken. His fascination had to be kept secret. They couldn't ever again meet like that in the Arrow headquarters. Kansas City was a correct decision.

Caroline had moved the week after the election had been made, a date that preceded the actual merger of the three companies by months. He had never been so lonely. If this was what love was about, he now knew it for the first time.

And one day while reviewing the Kansas City office's phone calls with their automatically printed record, a confidential telephone company listing of the individuals' names called by Arrow executives, he had counted the times that John Jamison called his wife and the number of times Caroline had called him. She had crept even to

Jamison in frequency. It was at that moment that Lawrence Massendale first thought that perhaps this attraction was truly mutual. Lord, how he loved that girl's company!

And Caroline O'Brian appeared to love Kansas City. She had immediately found an apartment within walking distance of the new office. Being that close, she dispensed with an automobile and kept her excursions from her condominium limited to shopping for groceries. She could do her other shopping in Los Angeles or New York. Caroline finally felt as if she were beginning her productive business life. Her days and hours were filled with work and more work. No corner was inaccessible to her. She visited with employees, reviewed reports, projected numbers and made decisions. Yes, she made decisions! John Jamison did exactly as she pleased, planned, and requested. In a way, he was a tame Lawrence Massendale.

The distance that separated this married man from Caroline made her acutely aware of her fascination for Lawrence Massendale. She had charted his strengths and weaknesses many times. He was past the point or phase in his life where he would wish a spouse to bear children. He knew the organization to which Caroline had decided to dedicate her life as well as anyone. She could talk with him about business at any time. And damn it, she had to admit it! The man knew how to make her feel good. He could talk business all the time.

Indeed, Caroline felt that she had no other interests in her life and wished it so. Conversations with a Dane Hughes concerning art, politics, the theater, or sports now totally bored her. She had been often taught that to be successful in business, one had to throw heart and soul into the battle. This was what she had committed her life to do.

Yes, Massey fit a perfect role. He was a conduit of information from the headquarters office in Los Angeles. Without Massey, she now felt that she might be shut off from those now distant decisions that controlled everyones' lives. Although Arrow Corporation was now, in truth, 2/3rds a rail line company, major decisions were still made in the West. And best of all, she could control Massey.

The one exception that Caroline allowed herself during these three months was to occasionally see Dane Hughes when he flew into town. She was deliberately cooling their relationship, although Dane occasionally continued to supply her with accurate insights into the Company.

Caroline had to admit, there was no comparison between a Dane Hughes and a Lawrence Massendale. Hughes was now boringly middle class.

Dane Hughes had no such belief. He only felt lonely and estranged. Tired and frustrated, he felt as if he had flown the world over during these months and indeed, he had. Phillip Arrow had taken an around the world flight and Dane and his copilot Hank LaBear had handled most of the flying duties. Arrow had taken the trip to review new acquisition candidates. It appeared that Union Arrow Corporation's next target might be outside the United States.

Dane had sorely missed Caroline. He missed the way it had been when Caroline was but a few minutes away. Now she was hours away and almost always busy. How could he have any chance to further their relationship when he was always dragging around after Phillip Arrow he wondered?

He knew that their relationship was slipping through his grasp. Absence does not make the heart grow fonder, this he knew. He was under no illusions. He knew that if he had grown up in Texas and worked in Alabama, he would have most probably fallen in love with a Southern girl. With four billion people on the earth, surely there must be another woman who would excite him as Caroline did.

Yet, in his several flights with John Jamison to Santa Barbara on Fridays and then back again on Sunday nights, he had envied the man. Jamison's wife would meet Jamison on arrival and bring him back to the airport at the weekend's close. Dane could sometimes not stand to look at the couple. Why was it that Jamison had so much, a family, a wife, a home, when Dane really had so little?

Surely, if Caroline could see what he saw when he visited Santa Barbara, she would feel differently about a home and a family. The Jamisons had everything going for them.

Jamison felt he had almost, but not everthing, going for him. He had been the first to move to Kansas City, recruit an office staff and set up what he called the "Neutral Site." Two months had been spent in visiting all members of both acquired companies' management. Countless hours had been used in preparing organization charts and manpower profiles, other countless hours had been spent in reviewing operations and salary costs. These summaries were sent back to Frank Turner in Los Angeles and his ideas were forwarded back, usually through Caroline O'Brian. He could envision the smile on Turner's

216

face as he "X'd out" the individuals' names. Jamison had quickly learned. Crossing out names from a chart was not the same as telling a man to his face that he was terminated. Turner had left all that pain to him.

With his move to Kansas City two months ago, the real work had begun. To date, over one thousand staff employees had been terminated. John used the word "terminated" because that's what Turner desired, but then Turner had no feelings. John looked upon himself as a buffer between this harsh reality and the world in which the Rail Division's management worked. He hastened to use the substitute terms: "early retirement," "voluntary resignation," and "rejected transfer" whenever possible. He found that most individuals who were displaced could be explained away by noting that their talents and interests did not appear to match their new job responsibilities.

John had moved by himself to first scout the City and have the freedom to devote all hours of a day to his job. Alone, the fact that his job took sixteen to eighteen hours was not resented by a wife who would have been newly relocated to a community and desired to share his time. It gave him the freedom to spend dinner and breakfast hours with his people and meet far more of them than if he were living with his wife.

Thus far, these eating meetings were proving most worthwhile. Most individuals loosened up while eating or drinking. He found and discovered much. His survival thus far was a result of taking this information and placing the people where they did not wish to be, where he had learned that they would not fit. If a man wished to move, he was kept in place. If he wished to stay, he was immediately asked to transfer.

John's problem at the moment was that this approach took time. As successful as it was, he was barely half way through the Turner and O'Brian list of required terminations and all the easy ones had already gone. Daily, he was dealing with more and more difficult situations and people.

And then to be honest, there was his personal life and his toughest long term problem of all.....convincing his wife to sell their Santa Barbara home and move to Kansas City.

Meg Jamison was refusing to move. For four weeks she had rarely seen her much traveling husband, then came the indiscriminate choosing of Kansas City as the Rail Division headquarters site. With

217

college-age girls coming home for the summer, she had refused to move to Kansas with her husband in May. John had wanted to attempt to sell the house on their own, although the Company would have agreed to purchase it. The only price they had offered was low enough to assure a resale within a 90 day period. Meg had refused to allow the house to be put on the market. She had been much relieved to learn from her divorced friends that although a husband could buy a house in California by himself, he could not sell one without a spouse's agreement.

Meg knew that with the coming of Autumn, she would soon have to make a choice. Her husband was obviously doing well. He had exuded success on the two weekends a month that she saw him. Even those weekends, however, were spent in California. She had refused to visit Kansas City. Subconsciously, she knew that she could not be asked to make such a choice regarding moving without an elaborate Midwest marketing effort by the Company. As long as she put that off, she could postpone any decision.

She could not understand how the individuals who had moved were so happy with their decisions. Perhaps corporate types are the gypsies of the modern age, she thought. Perhaps they consciously make friends only within a company so that a move is an easy matter. Or perhaps they were people who had no friends.

She was sure that was the case. She had never ever heard of her husband speaking of any of Frank Turners or Phillip Arrow's friends.

How often her mind had used the profile of the "corporate man" during the past months. She was coming to believe that there was a stereotype personality that grew out of the corporate form. Her husband appeared to be becoming more and more plastic everyday. Soon he might be exactly like Frank Turner. Did all corporations inadvertently mold their human players into some new type of creature?

Frank Turner had deranged her mind. She now lived in fear. It appeared that her strategy had been a success. He had not called since they met at the beach in Malibu. That fact did not negate the fear that was now present in her life. She dreaded telephone calls and somedays she left the mailbox stand unopened. Turner was an evil man.

Frank Turner did not feel evil. If anything, he felt he was in Heaven. Frank Turner was in his element. He loved this type of work. It was artistry. The cutting of an organization down into a profitable,

218

functioning, healthy specimen took a fine hand. What dinosaurs they had purchased! If only he had more time to devote to the new Rail Division! He damned the Phillip Arrows of the world! Arrow had given him the original Arrow Corporation subsidiaries to run. Turner just did not have the time to devote to Kansas City. There were disasters everywhere and he truly believed that he was missing the fun.

Frank loved most of all the canning of corporate deadwood. He was exhilarated by the interview with a thirty year employee who believed that he was indispensible. No one is too old to learn the basic lesson of life in an organization, believed Turner. Put your hand in a pail of water and see how important it is to the bucket. Note its size and place in the pail. Pull it out quickly. There will be a tremendous splash. But return three minutes later and take a look. The water will again be calm. It's as if you never existed.

Frank looked upon the two rail companies as overfilled buckets. The job was to see that the unnecessary fillers were cast aside, for Arrow Corporation was on the edge. With close to a billion and a half dollars a year in interest expense, it had to produce cash. All subsidiaries' operations were reviewed and tightened, salary increases were forestalled, benefit plans were curtailed, promotions frozen and good people were, of course, leaving in droves. Frank welcomed the drop in payroll costs. But Damn, it just wasn't fair. Jamison got to have all the fun!

John Jamison had written Frank Turner, with copies to Caroline, at least six different letters on the subject. Arrow Corporation was going to be hurt by the "Bright Flight" over the long term if Jamison's assessment was correct. A company's people were a resource. All the good people, those with easily employable skills, were being sucked away by higher salaries, greater challenge, and better, more enjoyable working environments. Only those with flaws were staying on, only those who had absolutely no willingness to take a risk or no place to flee. The good ones weren't waiting for the ax, they were leaving like groups in a retreating army. There were other times to fight, other companies to pledge one's life to and fight for. In the long run, Union Arrow was depleting its human resource assets at an accelerating pace.

Frank Turner's response was terse. Unless there was a successful short run, there would be no long run of any type, failure or success. And there was no room for failure in Frank Turner's life. One did not invest a career to have a failure. No one connected with Arrow

Corporation was allowed a failure. If one failed, his "ass" was out the door - just like Lacey's.

Everett Lacey did believe that he was both a failure and a success. Over the past four months he had added four new men to his staff. From his Los Angeles consulting office, they had rung the available data bases dry. There was just no way that he could deduce a cause for any union's action from the data present. Thousands of corporate and union relationships had been examined. The only positive result was the discovery of various heretofore unknown corporate problems of those new companies analyzed. Lacey had a two-man sales force on the road to solicit these companies as clients while he planned for the day when his Union Arrow consulting billings would no longer be paid. Surprisingly, his sales force was successful. Now, Lacey had other clients. His workload was creating long hours and undreamed of stress.

His staff had identified five probable union trustees for whom Phillip Arrow could be laboring. After a thorough review, he had told his people to concentrate on only two of them. The principal reason for their selection was that these organizations were part of the Omega group that Arrow had asked him to check.

With painstaking slowness over a one hundred day period, his people pieced together the various unions' strengths, leaderships, histories and interlocking boards of trustees. Lacey was finally able to narrow his search to just two suspects. He was getting close.

Lacey had labored under the disadvantage of not knowing the specific labor union and had long not understood the reason for Phillip Arrow's not disclosing the individual. As the days and nights of labor wore on, he developed a theory that he finally accepted as fact. Disclosure of this individual by Arrow, if ever proven, was cause for the total destruction of the Arrow clan and empire. There could be no other reason. Arrow could lead Lacey to the source, the name, but he must operate under some rules or pledge. Phillip Arrow was bound, like all participating members of Omega, to not reveal the names of the other participants when known.

Union Arrow Corporation operated with over one thousand labor contracts. None of the original three unions that Arrow had given him were connected with the Corporation in anyway. Lacey had finally concluded that this was Arrow's way of pointing him toward union files without violating the death pledge. Finally, Lacey had concentrated on just those unions that had unfunded liabilities in the billions. Since 19 out of every 20 union trusts in the United States were underfunded, any more liberal criteria would have given infinite possibilities. There had been a time when Lacey believed that he had just a slightly better chance of pinpointing this target individual than did the majority of union members have of collecting their full retirement pensions.

In retrospect, Lacey knew that his problems were minor. It was only a project that might or might not get completed. There were so many loose ends, that perhaps they could never be tied together.

He compared himself to Phillip Arrow. Arrow Corporation's stock was going down the toilet. Everett had plotted the earnings and stock prices with his forecasting program. He could see Union Arrow at a loss and its stock selling at $15. And on whom would the blame focus? Lacey knew that it would not be Arrow, Turner, Massendale, or O'Brian. The "fall guy" was going to be John Jamison. Not for a million dollars, thought Lacey, would he have wished to be in Jamison's shoes.

Yes, he was probably going to fail, but it would be only a shadow of the Jamison plunge. And with this failure, there was, of course, some sunshine. Lacey had come to know and admire Mary Sue Massendale. He now found himself showing up early at his office downtown and staying late on the off chance that Mary Sue would drop by or give him a call. They thought alike. He knew that it would be a disaster to be married to someone like that, but she was great to work with. Her active mind made it enjoyable to get up in the morning and drive downtown to work.

Mary Sue Massendale felt the same, yet she could not understand the lack of mercantile enthusiasm in this man, Lacey. Did it come in the blood? Were you either a businessperson or not a businessperson at birth? Lacey just did not seem to see the total picture.

Take for instance, his forecast of Union Arrow stock price. Clearly, it was going to fall, but not to $15 as Lacey suggested. At some point, a speculator would step in. If a person such as Phillip Arrow, who owns a substantial interest in a corporation....even if it is only 7% (but enough to effect control)....is susceptible to anything, it would be "greenmail." Someone would surely step in and purchase a block of Union Arrow stock at 20% to 30% above the forecasted, rock bottom low. They would then turn around and make a faked attempt at gaining control, clearly enough to hassle an owner/leader like her father and prod him into irrational action. Like Disney, Union Arrow could be blackmailed into repurchasing a block of stock far above any present market price.

It was only a question of what everyone felt would be the rock bottom low. Mary Sue had easily penciled it out. Her father had expended over 15 billion dollars for the two targets. Over 8 billion had been straight cash at the front end of the tenders plus over 2 billion more in merger costs. The Blue Jays had required 20% in Arrow stock and the Cardinals, 51%. In total, slightly more than 17 million shares at the pumped up price of $260 had finalized the acquisitions. With 130 million shares outstanding and an annual interest expense of one and a half billion on the borrowed funds, the new Union Arrow stock was expected to have earnings per share of slightly over $13.00.

That, however, was not to be the case. The original Arrow Corporation subsidiaries were lagging and the Rail Division was a disaster. Earnings per share were now forecasted at $5.00. That, however, did not account for the one time acquisition costs that would be expensed during this year. Mary Sue could easily see where Union Arrow Corporation could show a loss by the end of its fiscal year. Holders would have to quit worrying about valuing the stock based on a PE. Any multiple times a zero would equal a zero.

What would be the low price? That was the billion dollar question. Mary Sue knew that she could not be wrong. She had liquidated all her trust investments. The trusts now held only cash invested on a day to day basis. She chose $20. Her trusts would purchase Union Arrow stock at that price, in whatever amount of shares that were available. She had over 790 million dollars available through equity and loans in her children's trust along with her personal private funds now housed in the Caymans. With luck, she could purchase 40 million shares.

It was true. Her father was getting too old to run the Company. If anyone was to run him out of the active management, it was far better that she do it than someone else. Indeed, after it was all over, he might be able to rationalize it as a clever manipulation of stock to bypass federal and state estate taxes. At the least, the Company would stay within the family.

13

Monday
A Month Later
September 10, 1985

John Jamison sat at his oversized corporate desk in a walnut paneled office that overlooked the skyline of Kansas City. He absently stared at one of the two chairs placed at the other side of his desk. He was, in fact, looking down upon the chair. Like many corporate managers, he had early in his career learned the many nuances of office layout. Jamison's chair rolled on a two inch pad of plastic. He was always in the position to look down on those with whom he must talk. For the friendly or selling conversations, he would move across the room to a large mahogany table surrounded by six chairs. For the authoritarian discussion, he would remain where he was. As discussions progressed in directions favorable to his position, he would often get up from his desk and move to the table.

This morning he would stay seated where he was. In a moment he was about to discuss the present charitable programs and activities of the two acquired rail lines with their crusty old administrative officers.

Somehow, someway, the days had faded into the late summer and his mind drifted to his wife still back in California. Meg continued to stall regarding any serious consideration of a change of residences to

Kansas City. Jamison admitted to himself that he had not pressured her. His comfortable apartment living allowed him to spend sixteen to twenty hours a day at his job.

He hadn't been home for a weekend in a month and he was, today, both lonely and tired. But at least this week would be different. Meg was flying out from Southern California today. After weeks of gently begging her, she was finally going to look at the three houses that he had found as potential Jamison residences.

It was a good week thought Jamison. He could see the new colors on the trees below. Kansas City would be at its best. Meg had better decide soon. Winter would soon be upon them.

Jamison was both confused and hurt by his wife's new attitude toward him and his job. It was as if she had gone through a change in personality. When home, he felt as if he were almost despised. When away, his telephone calls were met with dispirited responses. What was wrong with her? Plenty of other American wives moved with their husbands. Even if they had not had a move in twelve years, there was nothing new or unusual about this situation other than the level of the job that Mrs. Jamison's husband held. Could she actually be jealous of his success? Their children were raised and away at school. There was just no reason for her procrastination. He felt that he would have to be tough with her this time.

The buzzer on his speaker phone interrupted his reverie. "Yes," he was ready for the two gentlemen. "No," he did not wish to be disturbed by any incoming phone calls unless they were from Turner or O'Brian. This meeting was going to be disturbing enough. Both men to whom he would speak were alike. Both had spent over thirty years with their once independent railroad employers. Both had risen through varied administrative positions, been present when each company's systems and cultures were being established, and had a deep loyalty to the old companies that were no more. Both were fifteen years his senior and now ready to retire. Jamison suspected that they stayed on now only out of their loyalty to the people with whom they worked. Jamison knew that these men's perceived roles were to minimize damage.

Over the past months he had also fully come to an understand that his role always conflicted with theirs.

"Gentlemen, come in and sit down. You know, it is a pleasure to see the two of you come in like friends. Just think that only a year ago you were competitive enemies."

"Mr. Jamison, we have known each other for over three dozen years. As you know, we set up the systems to share all information between our companies. We developed our friendship long ago."

"Oh, I forgot. Uh, let me get to the point of this meeting. Both your companies have had a history of being deeply involved in community affairs. I believe that you both have had a corporate giving program. In one case, this amounts to a set schedule of two percent of before tax profits. In the other, the percentage varies from year to year, but overall, the amounts are about the same. You both also encourage your people to be active in community affairs. In one case, there is even a formal program. Every individual who holds a management position is expected to give at least thirty minutes of his or her time to community affairs, church, school, boys or girls sports, hospitals, boards or the like. In the other, there is a liberal use of time-off. If I had a son playing baseball, for example, I could take off early to manage the team. And what else? Uh, both of you require your salaried personnel to contribute 2 % of their salaries to your community charity funds.

"We have carefully analyzed these and other of your programs, as you know. The gift program is especially disconcerting. Caroline O'Brian, who recently joined your Corporate Charity Committees, reports that a large amount of management time is spent on approving the recipients of the gifts, gifts which at two percent of before tax profits, are not insignificant. She has calculated the cost of the management time and the time of all the volunteers spent on this and the other community activities and ...."

Jamison was interrupted. "You aren't going to tell us that you are thinking of modifying these programs? When we agreed to merge, these programs were specifically discussed and it was agreed that they would be retained. Our involvement in the community is not solely altruistic. We gain great goodwill. On the other hand, you have to realize that a corporation is a legal individual or entity also. There is such a thing as corporate responsibility."

John Jamison held up his hand. It seemed as if both men were speaking in unison. He had to cut them short or he would only end up in an argument.

"Oh, I agree! But you have to see this for what it is. What we have here is a conflict in corporate philosophies. The old Arrow Corporation believed that it was up to the individuals to give of their personal time and funds, not corporate time and funds. Charity begins in the home, not in the office. As you know, we have historically had no such programs at Arrow Corporation."

"Alright, forget the comments on philosophy, Jamison! What about the later merger discussions? You were there! I know! I can remember your assurances. Don't tell me that you are thinking of modifying these programs. It will go far beyond a time savings or the saving of money. What you are talking about is the changing of the way in which our people think of their Company. You will be changing the corporate culture."

"I know I was there. What you don't realize is that I was new to the job and did not have all the parameters established. And 'No,' I am not talking about changing the programs. What I want, effective as of this date, is the total cessation of these giveaways."

"I won't ...... we won't do it."

"Gentlemen, gentlemen, think about it for awhile and then get back to me, say the day after tomorrow at 9:00 AM. Also while you are at it, I want to discuss the alteration of the health benefit packages for both present and retired railroad employees. Bring me your thoughts on these. Basically, what I am interested in is whether all the companies can have the same programs so that we can more easily transfer people from subsidiary to subsidiary."

"That was also discussed and agreed to at the original merger sessions. If you are thinking about changing to the old Arrow Corporation plans, that would be a drastic cut in benefits to our employees. You don't even have a plan of medical coverage for your retirees."

"I know, I know, but you gentlemen assume too much. I am just asking you to give me your ideas. We won't be making any decisions regarding those programs Wednesday, just nailing down the specifics on phasing out the charity programs."

As Jamison watched the two men walk from the room, he sighed. When was the last time he had seen a friendly face? This place reeked of fear and loathing. Did not these people understand his position? He was just doing a job. At least he had the potential to talk to someone friendly fairly soon. Meg should be getting on the plane now in Santa Barbara. Please, please, he thought, don't let me see the look of loathing on her face.

Meg Jamison was indeed ready to board the plane. A suitcase, a travel bag, and a suit bag sat on the runway as Dane Hughes walked up to her having just landed his sparkling white Lear with its insignia of an arrow at the Santa Barbara Airport.

Dane greeted her with a sure sign of pleasure. "Mrs. Jamison, how are you? I understand that you were to be my sole passenger."

"I was? Hello, Yes I am fine. How are you? What do you mean 'was'?" Meg Jamison could not believe it! Could it be true? Could she postpone the inevitable again? She suddenly felt like a free woman, a convict given a reprieve. She felt as though the weight of the world was lifted from her shoulders.

"I am sorry. Coming down, we lost two fuses..........our two radios don't work. We are going to have to fly over a mechanic to look at them. The fuses shouldn't be a problem, but I am bothered by the reason why two fuses blew out at the same time. There is no room for error eight miles up, we had best have it checked."

"What about me?"

"Oh, I'm sorry. It looks like we can fly you out tomorrow at this time. I won't be piloting since I have a Phillip Arrow flight scheduled on Wednesday, but we will get you there. Did you drive down or take a cab? Here, let me help you with your bags.

"My, it's a beautiful day! What I would give to walk on the beach on a morning like this rather than sit here all day watching mechanics fuss around."

Meg Jamison later was to try to recount her reply asking him why he didn't take that walk and her volunteering to join him. Dane had gratefully agreed and walked back to arrange the day with his copilot. It wasn't that he was needed. The earliest they could think of a return was estimated at 2:00.

A quick drive home to store her suitcase, hang her dresses, and change into casual clothes followed. A hamburger at a shacky little restaurant and a long walk resulted. So on a beautiful summer day, she found herself in shorts and barefeet striding along the warm California beach with a smiling, carefree man who seemed to have no worries in the world.

"Mr. Hughes, if I can be curious, why aren't you married?"

"That's simple, she won't say 'Yes!' Lord knows I have asked her often enough during the past few years."

"It wouldn't be Caroline O'Brian, would it? I know that my

husband talks about her a lot these days." Dane had smiled and nodded his head. "She must be crazy. What's the matter with her?"

Dane was feeling relaxed and easy. Strange how walking on the beach was so unnatural. If it were natural, one should have one leg longer than another. "Uh ......, I suppose that it is because I took the early role of being her Father Confessor. Good Old Dane Hughes, if you have trouble, come to me! For some reason, it just has put a damper on the relationship. She wants to discuss everything, but share nothing."

"Are you Father Confessor to others?"

"Sure, my best friend, Ev Lacey, who was fired from Arrow here a while ago, and I talk alot. Hell! There is not much that goes on around the Corporation that I don't know about, not that I can understand it."

"Do you want to be my Father Confessor?" Meg had to talk about the impending move to Kansas City. Subconsciously, she had made the decision to stay in her present home. John would have to choose her or live apart. She hadn't talked openly about it yet and wanted to use Dane to try it out. She knew from experience that an idea once presented verbally, could be better understood by both the listener and the speaker.

"Do you mean about you and Frank Turner?"

Walking alone on the beach in the past, Meg had often thought about what a fine target she made for someone sitting in one of the cliff houses with a rifle. For a moment, she thought that her daydream had come true. Her knees sagged and she had trouble continuing walking. Stopped and staring at this man, who looked her straight in the eyes, she slowly recovered her control.

"How did you know?" Her thoughts were tumbling. If this relative stranger knew, how many other also knew? Turner was just the type to tell everyone. Oh Lord, she wanted to scream! Help me!

"Ev Lacey and I were sitting on the side patio a few months ago and heard Turner put the rush on you. There wasn't anything you could have done. I don't know if that was what you wanted to talk about, but I had to tell you that I knew. You see, it is my confession. For months I have been kicking myself for not coughing and breaking up his act. I was wrong. I am sorry."

"Oh, I am sorry too. If you had, the rest probably wouldn't have happened." Meg could feel the relief surge through her. Frank Turner had not told, he could not, would not do such a thing.

"He's still bothering you?"

Again, Meg had been talking of another subject. She was about to discuss the change in her husband and the grief between them because of his new job. His question swept her back into the tide of emotion. It released a dike to a flood of pain.

"Yes, three other times. The first was clever, nylons and accessories along with thousands of dollars cash and a note to wear black and be ready for a black limousine, a show, and late dinner down in Los Angeles. It was one of those cars with a cocktail bar, a large back seat and complete privacy from the world and the driver. The limo picked me up and he met me in LA. We instead rode around Los Angeles until he caught a flight.

"After the second time, I thought I had convinced him that there would be no more blackmail, that it was over. I did not hear from him for months. Then he sent a photograph.......a terrible photograph of me taken in Malibu, some more undergarments, and wrote to wear red. That was two weeks ago.

"The only problem was that it wasn't Frank Turner who picked me up and rode down and back with me. I live in fear that he will call or write again. I know that I will do what he asks. Does that sound too terrible?"

"No, that just sounds like Frank Turner. Mrs. Jamison, let me be blunt. I think that you have your priorities mixed up. Your first priority should be to look after yourself and forget about looking after your husband. In a way, you now treat him as a child, as if you have to make sacrifices for him to survive in the world. In a major way, women like you rob men when they do that. One has to fend for himself........or herself in this world to be truly alive. I don't think you are giving your husband the pride of failing when he has tried his best and lost. That is a better feeling, believe me, than winning."

"Oh, I don't know if I totally agree with you. You can't live alone in this world. I need my husband, I want him to be happy. I don't think you know how fragile John is."

"Is he happy now? Are you happy? Look at you, look at this beach! What I can't understand is your moving! Here I am to pick you up today to fly you back to probably look at three or four houses that your husband has picked out and I bet you don't really want to move. Hell, you have been walking for a hour and can't even make yourself talk about it."

Dane picked up a rock and tried to skip it over the waves. He watched as Meg Jamison showed him how to do it correctly. Looking west, Dane could make out the outline of the coastal islands. He had heard that they were barren, water starved areas of rock. Strange, so barren a land could exist so close to so much plenty. Strange, so barren a choice for life could be found in such richness. Meg motioned for him to continue walking with her.

"You are right. I can't quite imagine moving and having no friends. As a young mother, it is probably alright because your children and their schools will help you meet people. As a newly married, the world is before you and you have your old school friends that so quickly fade away when you have children. I just don't know how I will meet people back there at this stage of my life. John will have his job, so he will be kept interested and busy. Me, I picture the rest of my life spent wandering the halls of a big house in Kansas or Missouri."

"Then don't move, don't even bother going back to Kansas City tomorrow and have to argue or be tempted. Tell your husband and Frank Turner to both 'Go to Hell!' Meg, it is your life, the only one you will ever have. You know the best advice I have ever heard? It's this, there are three important things that you do that shape your life. The first is where you go to school, this you may have no decision over. The second is whom you marry. That will set the tone of your life and to picture it, you must look to that person's mother, father, home life and their attitude toward children. The third is where you live. Period!   What one should do in life is settle down where one wishes and then try to make a living. Forget standard of living, that will be better measured in terms of quality of living, and that is decided by the community in which you live."

"No wonder you are a Father Confessor! Have you ever thought of going into the ministry or teaching high school? You would be excellent at it."

Dane grinned. Perhaps this was good for the both of them. He knew that for many reasons, the company, the sea, the air, he felt immensely better. "Yes, now that you mention it, I have. Bet you didn't know I had a teaching degree that I have never used. I have thought about it. I never knew a child I didn't like. It is the parents that bother me.

"Well, Mrs. Jamison, I don't think we will settle everything today and it's time we turned around and walked back to the car. I have to be getting to the airport. Whatever's wrong with that aircraft had better be fixed. Phillip Arrow doesn't like excuses and I don't want to have to give one to explain why he can't ride in his favorite plane Wednesday morning."

Everett Lacey knew that Phillip Arrow didn't like excuses, so he had none to give. "Look, Sir, I just don't have the foggiest idea of who owned that $400 million of stock that was purchased by you for $640 million in the tender offers. My suspicions all along have pointed toward Frank Turner. I just know it's he. I can taste it and I think you can too. I found that Smedt and Goldstein made money on the deal, but you say that their small amounts do not bother you. I now know that you knew from the start that they would steal from you, but it was a known theft which you could control.

"And you are the last person to suspect. You would not have done it because, in effect, you would have been costing yourself money. Caroline doesn't have the financial backing yet, she is not mature enough to control or raise that type of money. So it has to be either Massey or Turner. Massey has three or four checks. He has a wife who is your daughter. She would know and I have talked with her, just as you have. Moreover, I can't imagine who would have bet that type of money early-on on only Lawrence Massendale's word. He often thinks he knows the story, will tell it, and be totally off the mark. No, the answer still has to be Frank Turner, but I have no proof, not one bit of evidence."

Phillip Arrow sat at Lacey's kitchen table. Lacey's apartment was a mess. Computer paper, manuals, printouts and equipment were scattered around a living room and dining area. Lacey had hooked up a terminal on a direct line to Arrow's Executive Information System. For other work with another hook-up, four retired FBI agents worked downtown at "The Lacey Company," a new consulting firm that appeared to its competitors to be doing very well. Phillip Arrow made no comment. He knew that Lacey was lying and he wondered why.

Ev Lacey broke the silence, "Sir, I somehow know that Richard Smith's disappearance is connected to this. I would like to look into it if you don't mind."

It was as if Phillip Arrow had not heard him. "Could you fly out to Kansas City with me on Wednesday? I think time is short and I may need your help there.

"I think your project is about over. Someone else has started leaking information to the press."

"Sure, I would be glad to. I do have one piece of information though, something that one of my men found the other day." Lacey had to change the subject. It was obvious that Arrow knew he was lying to him. He had missed his chance, just as he had missed Arrow's slip of the tongue.

"What's that?" Arrow was deep in thought but had caught the look in Lacey's eyes.

"Remember the Oriole search and the concern at the time regarding potential 'hit men?' My man was checking telephone calls out of the Corporate Air Department during that period and found several patterns of calls during the time preceeding the tender offers. He checked the number in question and it was a disconnected number in Houston. Then he checked the long distance call record of that number when it was in service. Someone had rented an apartment in Houston, installed a phone, and had all calls to that location, call-forwarded to the Oriole office. It was all automatic. The phone never even rang in the Houston apartment."

Lacey had paused and Arrow had turned to face him. "You have my attention, go on."

"The phone that was used is the one at the airport in the pilot's room over by their restroom. The person had to be a pilot. There is no way that anyone else could have made that many calls from a room reserved only for use by Arrow corporate pilots."

"But you don't know which pilot?" Lacey shook his head. Arrow looked out the kitchen window at a view of an alley and other apartment houses. He shook his head and continued, "That is a problem I can solve. I will replace every one of them."

"Sir, I don't think that it was Dane Hughes, but I can't prove it."

"That's too bad. He will be the first to go. I'll have it all done in three months and we will damn well give each new employee a lie detector test and a loyalty contract. I'll be damned why the lawyers won't let me give any present employees such a test. No, it has got to the point where you have to fire people before you can work on your security. I should have done it when the Oriole President inferred the source. I knew then that there was a bad pilot."

It was then that Arrow created the clue that had Lacey calling to find Dane Hughes with a message for him to drop by as soon as possible. Within the week it would provide the key to answering all his questions.

"Greed and avarice Mr. Lacey, greed and avarice."

"Is that the only way to motivate men, Mr. Arrow?"

"Heck no, Everett! That's just the first level. We set up compensation schemes to motivate men, but money doesn't work half as well as fear. And if you really want something better, find some hate. Hate is the best motivator of them all unless it's family preservation."

Arrow stood to leave. "At sixty seven I was sure of only one thing, the *Bible*'s right, 'the people is grass.' Remember that, Everett, I will never tell you anything more important. 'The people is grass'." He again smiled at Lacey. Everett Lacey now looked totally confused.

As he left the apartment, Lacey made a last ditch effort to persuade Arrow that Dane Hughes' job should be spared.

"Where is your proof, Everett? Show me and I will keep him. Right now look at the evidence. He is the pilot I try to use, the most knowledgeable about my and others' corporate travel, the most likely to have overheard something. He has to be the key suspect."

Close by in LA, a small group of executives were about to have their opinions and suspicions also confirmed.

From reviewing the profit numbers and the effect on cash flow as illustrated by the computer printouts, the decision had to be made, he decidedly had to be terminated. Frank Turner sat at his desk in his Los Angeles office and contemplated the coming termination of John Jamison. His replacement would not be available for another three months. They had to move out the more obvious, proficient, and deserving candidates to prevent a total railroad employee backlash when they promoted a puppet. Could Jamison last that long?

He had called Caroline O'Brian back from Kansas City to discuss Jamison's performance and asked that Lawrence Massendale also sit in on the meeting. Terminating a company president often became technically sticky, and he would need legal support. Depending upon what O'Brian reported, he would fly back there tomorrow to review Jamison's performance himself. Let's see .... he had a meeting with both Goldstein and Smedt to finalize the payment of acquisition fees. Perhaps they could fly along with him. They would be closer to home once the meeting was over and then they could fly onward from Kansas City.

Frank Turner called his secretary to usher in Massey and the bitch. Turner looked at his calendar. Good! It was the 10th, that meant that

O'Brian would be wearing her Scot outfit. Turner wondered about her accessories, were they also plaid? He would bet that they were white with plaid lace....probably something very special. Perhaps he should change his tactics and forget about wanting to terminate her. Perhaps he should try to dominate her!   With Caroline's being around the Los Angeles headquarters only once or twice a month now, she was almost becoming bearable......or was that bareable? Turner looked at his notes. That's right navy blue blazer with matching white and blue medium heels.

Caroline had been gaining confidence. She walked in and took the lead. "Frank, good to see you. Let me get to the point without any smalltalk so I can catch the 6:00 back to the Midwest. This guy Jamison is a real turkey. We could have made a Hell of a lot more progress if we had anybody else in that position. Even a stuffed doll would be preferable. I rant and rave to Phillip, but he doesn't seem to care. It's as if he put Jamison in there so nothing would happen. The subject of this meeting is not that John Jamison should be pulled off the assignment, but how we go about convincing Phillip Arrow that that is the case."

Lawrence Massendale seconded her motion. "I have been watching his performance myself, Frank. Jamison seems to be a man with a devil on his back. When you see him, just look at his complexion. He looks like a person who has been working twenty hours days. There is obviously just too much pressure for him."

"Come on Frank," added Caroline, "we all know that he was the wrong man for the job. Phillip seems to have some love affair going with the man. What he sees in him, I will never know."

"Caroline, we have to proceed carefully. Eliminating someone from a top corporate staff is always very sensitive. Remember the trauma associated with Lacey? If you remember, that took my approaching Arrow at the right time and in the right way. Your idea of convincing him on merit is to storm in there and force your opinion. He just doesn't work that way. You plant seeds and let them germinate in Phillip Arrow's mind. You don't plow the field everyday."

"Well, he is driving me crazy. The deal was that you were going to be back there most of the time, if you remember. You have left me alone with an idiot who has now turned morose, self-doubting, and is totally insecure. Lord, he needs his wife out there! Perhaps he will have more balls once she gets there. I understand she's flying out

234

there today. Jesus, he's mush without her!"

"Caroline, calm down. I have an entire other company to run if you remember. Can Jamison last for a bit longer?" asked Turner.

"Not if you want the type of profits that you do. Look, the year is half over. Either we cut the costs or they will eat up our cash flow for the rest of the year. By this time John Jamison should have shut down their marketing, cut salaries and benefits, closed off all, rather than just part of their research, advertising, repair and maintenance and other expenditures. He is so reluctant to try to weasel on contracts. He feels that just because there are signed consulting, advertising, lease, and supply contracts that we have to abide by them. Hell, he is so moralistic! No one ever taught him that contracts were the reason why we have lawyers. Half the time they are to write them, half the time they are to break them. The dumb smuck!"

"Well, you are finally talking about something Phillip Arrow will listen to, that is the failure or success in making profits. Here's what I want you to do. Prepare a report of the budgeted cost savings and actions planned to date and illustrate the shortfall. I am surprised you didn't already do it. I will discuss it with Jamison on Wednesday morning. Massendale, I need some help here. Give me the forms necessary to document what is happening. We gave Jamison a Hell of a lot in the way of prequisites and compensation when he went in. I want there to be some way that we can get out of it. I don't mind paying a severance, but it has to be within bounds. Now get out of here! Caroline, if you need a ride to the airport at 5:00, I am going that way. Thanks for the report, even if it was only oral, I liked what you said. Don't forget the written analyses. I will need it within 24 hours."

Caroline eyed Frank Turner suspiciously. This was a new Frank. She could sense it. Perhaps this old man was finally going to try to get into her plaid laced panties. With a great show, she slowly lifted the report from her briefcase She would let the silence build the tension between them a bit.

Finally she spoke, "I thought you'd request such a written, rather than a 'verbal' report and already had it developed as of the month's end. I think you will find it interesting, revealing, and complete and certainly better than any 'oral' report I might give you." Caroline greatly enjoyed this game of wits and looked hard at Frank Turner to see if it caused him to rise. Caroline found instead that she was looking at a frowning and saddened man. He hadn't even listened to her. She had to continue,

"You're such a cold fish, Frank. You don't look like you are enjoying yourself this time. What's the matter?"

"Caroline, don't think that this is any fun. Usually when one cuts a peer at the corporate level, the individual is as good or better than you are. Then it's fine. Setting Jamison up for a termination is like shooting fish in a barrel."

"Frank, come on Old Man, we haven't fired anyone at the Corporate level in years," voiced Massendale.

"Bullshit! They just resign instead and we go through several a year. Look around you, Massendale! Who do you see who was here seven years ago? The average tenure at the corporate level, even for CEOs, if you have ever read *Forbes*, is five years. Who did we have go last? Ah, Yes, it was Lacey a few months ago, or did he leave before Smith disappeared?"

"You really enjoyed screwing Lacey, didn't you?", added Caroline.

"Sure, didn't you? With Lacey it was a pleasure, a real pleasure."

"Because he was Black?" Lawrence Massendale wished Caroline would watch her language. She was never prepared for the male counterthrust. He had to interrupt this game of words. It was obvious that he was not included and in no way did he like the way that Frank Turner's eyes were now viewing Caroline's open jacket.

"Hell, No, Massey....because he was good! Don't you realize why I have been so successful. The rule is never to have anyone on the corporate staff who is a complete man, who could take your place. Look at this place, who would you promote to take my spot? Look at you, Massey, you don't have one person on your staff worth a Damn! Hell, the good corporate people are always weeded out by those on top of them! It is the rule of corporate survival of the fittest."

"Speak for yourself, Frank," argued Massendale.

"Oh cut the crap, Massey! We're no different than other men. We do it because it is natural. Look at Phillip Arrow, himself. He has no real replacement. In his mind, each of us has a flaw that would prevent us from becoming Chairman of the Board. That's why so many corporations go outside when it comes time to find a top man. Or contrarily, why a replacement president from inside a corporation so often fails. The corporate evolutionary process either leads to bright flight or firing. Why do you think I screw around so much with other

236

men's wives? I need a flaw, Massey!"

Massendale still looked unconvinced. Turner had to add an insult, "The successful middle management corporate type is the man who keeps his head low and is invisible. It is not the place for a superstar. Good men, yes, but not great men. At the top, we are visible so we need a single fatal flaw. Do you follow Massey? Do you identify?"

"You keep talking of 'men'." Caroline had risen and started to walk out of the office. "Don't you think you are missing a point?" asked Caroline. She would be damned if she left Massendale undefended.

"You are a man in your mind, Caroline."

Turner looked at the both of them. He had obviously insulted the gender of each.

Without a reply, Frank Turner watched them stalk out of his office. Jesus, she was too much! Yes, it might be an interesting pastime. He dropped the report in the waste basket heading for Henry. This was his usual procedure for all correspondence and reports coming to his office. He kept no files. Perhaps someday O'Brian would learn that reports and the written word will ruin you. He sat there for ten minutes picturing her lingerie. Yes, he knew that he had been wrong. Someone like Caroline would find far more plaid to wear.

As Caroline walked down the hall, she thought she hadn't accomplished a thing. She stopped. She would wait for Lawrence Massendale. Jesus, Frank Turner was too much! What an old-fashioned dinosaur, what a history lesson! Fly two days, use all that energy, just for a fucking 15 minute meeting on an issue which could be covered by a conference call! He was nothing more than an old time manager who did it all with personal meetings and intimidation. Didn't he know that with 200,000 employees one couldn't rely on personal meetings? She could do a better job than Turner anyday.

She waited for Lawrence Massendale to catch up with her. "Massey, I'm all but bushed. Why don't we sneak off for a couple hours to review the situation again and then you can take me to my plane. You can be my White Knight, you'll be saving me from Turner and we do have a lot to review. I would like your feelings in one important matter."

"Caroline, I can't. My wife is coming in to see her father and then drive me home. I really want......oh, speak of the Devil. Here she comes. Just don't worry, it won't be much longer. I have finally gotten everything ready."

Mary Sue Massendale's knees buckled. She saw her opposition

down the hall talking with her husband. Would she be wrong in approaching them? She knew she was. Massey did not like to have her near him at his work. He was too sensitive about his son-in-law status. She was getting nearer. She could see the girl's confident look of ownership.

Caroline O'Brian looked straight at the approaching woman without a qualm. She was probably doing her a favor. Indeed, she believed that she now stood as Massey's only ego reinforcer. This woman could buy any man she wished, but she could not buy this one. She had tried, but had found someone too tough. Caroline knew that she had won! She had won with her mind and body. It was a complete victory.

Mary Sue began her forced smile. She quickly thought of her brown business suit and low heels, no match for this stylish lady. Had the four boys caused her to let herself go? Or was it age? Why were there suddenly lines in her face, where had her figure gone? Gravity and age were making it impossible to compete. Perhaps it was time she reviewed her wardrobe and appearance. How could she think of superficial things like this when there was more to life? The work that she had been doing for Lacey was what was really exciting. Perhaps she could review her latest findings mentally as she drove her husband home. She would let him talk. He would never know. Non computer types never experienced that all capturing mental stimulation.

From the sudden change in Caroline O'Brian's posture and facial expression, Mary Sue immediately caught Caroline's chosen defense. Not now looking at the approaching woman, Caroline had turned to Massendale and changed the subject of their conversation. Mary Sue saw the startled look on her husband's face. Surprised, he couldn't stop himself from barely nodding to his wife and turning in apparent awe to respond to Caroline. Mary Sue had caught every word. She. could not help but smile as she reached her husband's arm. Caroline O'Brian was good!

"Then you don't think, Mr. Massendale, that I would be out of place to suggest that my compensation be increased.....that I just go in and ask Phillip for a more fitting salary?"

"Oh, no, I didn't say that, Ms. O'Brian. You must know that your job has been carefully evaluated by our job evaluators using a point factor system that looks at responsibility, skill, and effort required. I suspect that he will say that you present salary reflects both internal and external equity."

Caroline turned to Mary Sue Massendale to acknowledge her presence. "Hello, Mrs. Massendale. What would you suggest that I do?"

"I would suggest that you tell Phillip Arrow that the Company's job evaluation system was created in the 1940s and represents an example of discrimination built into a management system. No woman will ever be fairly rewarded for her services until jobs are evaluated on a sex free basis. To do so, one needs to do away with measurements such as experience, education, physical effort, and the like unless they can clearly be shown to be job necessary.

"You must realize that most modern companies salary administration systems are nothing more than elaborate camouflages of what is blatant discrimination. They are simply systems that continue the status quo.

"But what about the job market and competitive rates?"

"Setting salaries in 1985 based on what was paid in 1984 is an accepted practice and has been so in America for two hundred years. You used 1977 rates to determine 1978 salaries, 1944 wages to determine 1945, ad nauseam. Arrow Corporation does what most all U.S. companies do, they perpetuate the discrimination of the past. Sometime, you should look closely at this Country's history of wage rates, Ms. O'Brian. You can see the perpetuation of the effects of the long denial of women's suffrage and slavery.

"And while you are at it, don't let anyone tell you that they are only matching competitive trends. What companies do today is outrageous! You find the most competitive of companies sharing all their pay information with even their most bitter opponents. If Union Arrow were to set its prices like it sets its pay levels, everyone would be in jail for collusion."

Lawrence Massendale saw his opening. "Ho, ho, ho......you really asked the wrong question there. Mary Sue, you don't know what you are talking about. If you are against market pricing of jobs, you are against the competitive market. If you are against the competitive market, you are against capitalism. If against capitalism......"

Massendale let his voice trail off. Caroline was looking confused, still trying to follow Mary Sue's responses. She was not listening to him. He looked at his wife. She also wasn't listening. He knew that he had to speak again. "I apologize, Ms. O'Brian, but it was your fault. Get my wife started on pay equity, ERA and comparable worth and she will never be quiet. I suggest that we drop this topic right now and go our separate ways. All I can say, Ms. O'Brian, is Good Luck! Please tell me what happens."

Taking his wife by the arm, Lawrence Massendale walked her toward the door. Wow, had that been close! Where did Mary Sue get her crazy ideas? She sounded like a socialist. Wasn't Caroline O'Brian something? Could she ever think on her feet! Yes, and he was sure she would......she probably would hit Phillip Arrow up for a raise the next chance she found. Perhaps he could talk her into staying for the night and doing it in the morning. It would be great to hear what Arrow said.

Could he get rid of Mary Sue and stay late again after his wife had made a special trip in to pick him up? Perhaps he could, if he didn't stay too long. Then Caroline could fly with him tomorrow. He would have to be home before Mary Sue went to bed.

That was it! He would go all out tonight for the both of them. But first to get rid of his wife. He would have to approach this very carefully.

14

Tuesday

Phillip Arrow looked at the corporate news releases yet to be sent off to the newspapers. He would have to correct each one himself. So much to do before he caught the flight to Kansas City! Slowly he sank deep in thought regarding the first problem confronting him this morning, his people's inability to obtain a copy of the detective agency's report. He did not notice that the tan clad figure of Caroline O'Brian had entered his office. Incredulous, he was wondering what price would be necessary to buy the detective agency staff....if the manager/owner was one of those few that could not be bought with money.

"Good morning, Sir. I hope that I am not disturbing you."

Phillip Arrow had jumped at the sound. It was obvious that his nerves were on edge these days. For some strange reason, the detective agency's report was eating at him like a cancer "Oh, no, Caroline, no.......please come in......what may I do for you this morning?"

"Phillip, I wanted to talk to you about my salary."

Phillip Arrow reached into his drawer and pulled out his check list. Five items were typed on the left hand side. Labeled "Performance," "Potential," "Cost of Living," "Head Hunters," and "Last Increase," he jotted Caroline's name down on the top. It was a habit that he had picked up as a young man, one that he knew that he should have dropped. Still, it gave him some entertainment in these boring compensation discussions.

"Well, O.K., Caroline. I am at a disadvantage. What was it that you were making?" Arrow had carefully chosen his tenses. One allows a negotiating opponent a win at the start. It makes their later failures more acceptable to them.

"It is $ 80,000 and as you know, my job is worth considerably more. My last raise was almost a year ago for $ 10,000." Caroline noted that Phillip Arrow had checked the paper in front of him.

"Phillip, if you look at my performance, I certainly believe that I warrant a review right now. I have accomplished all the goals that you have asked of me. What I have done, I have done well. As you very well know, with Frank spending most of his time on our original subsidiaries and with John Jamison being a bit slow on the uptake, most of what has happened in the Rail Division has been at my instigation. Speaking for myself, I think I have done a Hell of a job!" Caroline noticed Arrow making another check on the paper in front of him.

"But that is not what is important. It is not what I have done, but what I can do in the future. The experience of the past months has been invaluable. During these next months I will be worth considerably more to you than in the past. You know as well as I that I am just starting to realize my potential."

Phillip Arrow smiled at the latter comment. He could score two checks whenever a salary increase requester mentioned the specific category's name.

Caroline was growing frustrated at the lack of response from Phillip Arrow. He had not said a word! He just sat there with a pencil in hand and a silly grin on his old face. She knew that she should make him talk, but she wasn't through with her arsenal of arguments.

"As you know, Phillip, I have been forced to maintain two apartments. With the increase in cost of living that we're experiencing again, I am actually earning less than what I was earning here just four months ago. I calculate that the impact on my cost of living has been on the magnitude of 15%." Phillip Arrow scored another two checks on his pad.

"Finally I might note, Sir, that I have a fair idea of what my job is worth. I must receive two unsolicited telephone calls from executive search firms every week. The salaries that they are talking about far

242

exceed mine and those salaries are for jobs with far less responsibility."

Caroline knew that she had to shut up. It had been the most one sided conversation in her experience at Union Arrow Corporation. "Well, Sir, would you consider my request for a salary increase."

Phillip Arrow looked at his score sheet. Caroline had scored only seven points although she had hit all five categories. His hard and fast rule was to never give an increase unless a score of 9 was recorded. "I am afraid not, Caroline. As you know, we have a salary increase freeze on. That goes for everyone in Union Arrow, including myself. I am sorry."

Caroline jumped up to stand in front of his desk. She had to see the slip of paper he had just looked at. Had he summed up a score? Damn, he had covered it with his hand. "Sir, I don't like that response, I don't believe that it is either fair or appropriate."

Halfway across the continent, the same response was heard at exactly that moment. "Mr. Jamison, I don't like what you have just told me. I don't like it one bit."

John Jamison looked at the mature man before him. He had just read the man's personnel file. Father of three children, ages 22, 20 and 18, he also held a Wharton MBA and an exemplary military service record. His performance appraisals had been the highest of anyone in the railroad and he had been tagged as a potential chief executive officer. As an operations man who commanded huge loyalty from his people, he had been the perfect man to promote and move to Kansas City. Countless employees had stayed with the railroad during the past months because this one man chose to trust in the future and accept the new ownership. Frank Turner bragged of identifying the man's stature with his employees at first sight.

But Jamison also had to look at the O'Brian report with its pencil marks showing Turner's review and approval. The man was far too independent. He could not be controlled. Turner's original recommendation, to move him to the compromise headquarter's location of Kansas City, had been made partly because they could separate this individual from his "power base." Terminating him in Kansas City was a completely different story from firing him in the geographic area where he had worked and lived for some twenty-five years.

"If I might, I'll try to discuss this rationally. Three months ago you asked me to move here. I sold my house at a loss and suffered selling costs that the Company doesn't pay. I rationalized it because of the

243

large stock option grant that was offered me. If I am terminated, those options are worthless. My wife did not want to move. She had to leave all our friends. The main reason we came was that we have our three children in Harvard, Stanford, and Yale and we can just barely afford to live as it is with the tuition being what it is today. My children will all have to quit school and I will lose my house. My ability to find a job around the Kansas City area is totally limited. What you are talking about is ruining my children's and my wife's lives, just not my own. I gave over twenty years to this Company. I am too young to collect anything from the retirement plan. What am I suppose to do?"

"You will do what you have to. We expect that you will leave immediately. We have found that if we allow terminated employees to stay for any period of time, they infect the other employees. Please go back to your office, pack your things, and leave today. You will be paid until the month's end."

"That's no severance. Even the clerks get a week's salary for every year of work."

"I am sorry. I have no control of that. Severance is reviewed on a case by case basis. Policy and decisions are made by Arrow Corporate back in Los Angeles. Please do not create any problems. You don't know how tough this is on me."

"If this is our last talk Mr. Jamison, let me have my say. Perhaps you will use what I say to do better by other of my peers. Arrow Corporation parachuted managers from its subsidiaries on top of our own management without any explanation as to why or what is to be achieved. I know the reason why. It's because you all don't know what you are doing. We have been told we must achieve goals without any reference to our actual resources. None of you know what is possible. You are trying to wring out profits over the short term just to make the parachuted in management look good. You all assume that the acquired lines will follow Arrow Corporation's rules, yet none bother to tell us what the rules are. I really wonder if you have any. You assume that we have a top operation when problems exist with which you tell us we can not deal. There is no analysis or appreciation of our employees' talents and no attempt to capitalize or build on what we do well.

"No wonder our budgeted profit contributions are slipping. You are quickly, not slowly, destroying the Company that I love. Now you are taking actions that will probably destroy my family and myself."

244

The individual rose and walked to the door and turned. His remarks had been met with silence. Jamison could not even look at him. "Tell me, Jamison, what would you do in my shoes?" With the question unanswered, he left the office.

Jamison groaned as the door closed. He had to do it, he just had to. Frank Turner had called yesterday and said he was flying in this afternoon to discuss his progress. His progress! Not the progress of the Division or the blending of the acquisitions. Jamison knew that he had to pay the price and go through the stack of actions that he had been putting off. They were forcing him to do it, he had no choice. From his perspective, the major problem was that the Company was suffering from an accelerating "bright flight." For those that did not flee, he was told to terminate. What a reward for the man's loyalty!

At least he would get some relief tonight. He was looking forward to seeing his wife even more after her delay of yesterday. When one was happily married, one had at least one solid rock of loyalty on which to rest. He hoped that the departing man's marriage was as strong as was his. He would never be able to go on if Meg gave up on him. Having a solid wife was God's greatest gift.

Lawrence Massendale looked across the breakfast table at his wife. She was in one of her infrequent soft morning moods which occurred about once a month. No sharp commands had been given. The four boys had been allowed to escape out the door on their way to private school without reprimand.

It had amazed Massendale how fast his boys were growing. All were at a point where they didn't need a mother or a father, just someone to cook their meals, wash their socks, and soon to hand them the car keys. Mary Sue excelled at all aspects, including some that he would admit that he should have shared, and she seemed to enjoy it. He had tried many times to hire a cook or a maid to assist. It just wasn't right that their house should be the only one on the block without live-in help. Mary Sue would have none of it, she wanted to totally control her nest.

Massey looked at his breakfast. Sausage, melons, french toast and syrup, hot coffee and orange juice. He would eat slowly and wait. No one important would be in the office today. Caroline and he were flying first to Chicago and then to Kansas City. Arrow was going to follow later this afternoon with Turner also flying out separately this morning. They would have an Executive Committee meeting of the

Board in Kansas City on Thursday. Turner would have a recommendation on Jamison ready by then. How he looked forward to seeing Caroline even though he had seen her just yesterday! He could not refrain from thinking about her. Even with his wife, he fantasied the switching of the two. His thoughts were interrupted.

"Lawrence, you know how I told you last night that I really, truly love you?"

"Uh huh."

"Well............" the doorbell rang. Massendale sat rooted in his chair. Thank God his bags were in the car! "You are eating, Honey," continued his wife, "I will get the door. It is probably one of the neighbors."

Massendale waited and sipped his coffee. Low voices sounded from the front of the house. Then the door shut softly. Mary Sue walked into the kitchen with papers in her left hand, tears ran down her cheeks, sobs racked her body.

"It was the Marshal's office. These are divorce papers. They say you are suing me for divorce. Oh, Lawrence, how could you! How could you? After what we did last night. You never stay around for breakfast. You knew he was coming. What about the boys? They need a father, more than that, they need a father figure. You are a model for them. They will most likely copy your life in theirs even if it's only subconscious. They'll blame themselves. Oh why, Lawrence, why?"

"We live long these days, Mary Sue. It used to be that one would marry for passion, a young family, and an early death. Now people marry for passion, marry again for a family, and marry again for their retirement years. The latter is something new. Tell me truthfully, do you want to share your last days with me? I sure as Hell want something different!"

"Lawrence, that is just a speech written by a modern psychologist. Marriages are all the same. We have so many memories to share. Have you found someone else? Who could have more common goals than you and I?"

"There is no one else. I have got to be on my way. Please call our family law firm on this. You will notice that I used a new lawyer for myself. He is the meanest individual divorce lawyer in Beverly Hills. I think it best that you explain it to the boys first. I will send someone for my clothes when I get back."

A surprised and shocked Mary Sue Massendale watched her

246

husband hurry out the door.

Meg Jamison was so shocked that she could not think. After the Arrow Learjet rolled up to pick her up at the Santa Barbara Airport, Frank Turner had disembarked to help her with her luggage. She was so stunned, she lost her ability to speak and only barely heard his words. Meg felt that his sureness drained her of her self-confidence. Two sure-talking pilots whom she had never seen before were introduced before they were locked away in the cockpit as her husband had described. She was then introduced to two additional gentlemen, a Mr. Smedt and a Mr. Goldstein. Meg again felt an embarrassed terror. She had dressed to meet John at the airport and was determined to entice him back to California. Now she felt these two men undress her with their stares. At least they were there. She thought of flying East with just Frank Turner as a passenger and shuttered.

Frank Turner grasped her arm like he owned her and showed her to the back lounge. He said that he wished to discuss business with the two men in the front, larger chairs and asked if she would sit at one of the table couches. As she was seated, he folded out the table to show her a conference setup where four men could easily sit at a six foot long table to discuss a project, complete with a slide projector and overhead screen on the back bulkhead/toilet wall and door. Meg folded back part of the table so that she could move about with ease. As the flight began, she could not help but hear the conversation. As the discussions continued, the voices of the men rose.

"I will be damned if I let you screw my Firm like that Turner! Our arrangement is a signed contract and non negotiable."

"Nothing is non negotiable. Let's look at the facts. It has been five months now and neither of your Firms have been paid a dime. You are all on to other clients now, our work is past, it's sunk....done. What you are facing is a long court case with all sorts of charges, counter charges, and expenses. The contracts were signed in Los Angeles. If there is a case, we would want it handled in downtown L.A. and we would ask for a jury trial. Have you been to one lately? Do you want to meet the people who are supposedly your peers? No, as they say, the ball's in the Arrow court and I suggest that you accept our offer."

"Turner, you have got to know that neither of our Firms will ever work with you again. You lack the type of ethics we find necessary in our clients."

247

"Oh, I think that you will work with us again. The fee we are going to pay you will be only a third of the original anticipated, but still a tremendous amount. You will be tempted, as you always are."

"I doubt it. Let me tell you something. In most cases, I could talk my partners into accepting something like this. They are, after all, practical men. But what is necessary is that I recommend it. Understand? They have to have the recommendation of the contract manager and I just won't recommend it."

"I am sorry to hear that. If that is the case, please be informed that Arrow Corporation will feel obligated to report to the SEC that both of you made approximately three million dollars each on these acquisitions and that it was done by either taking a prior position or by selling short on insider information. We will report that action to the *Wall Street Journal* and your competing peers. There is no doubt in my mind that you will both be fired, that you will both have grave difficulties ever finding similar employment, and that the SEC and we will sue to recover triple any profits that you have made. Gentlemen, you face jail terms and bankruptcy. I would be careful before I made any decision not to recommend any fee settlement offer."

"You have known all along, haven't you?"

"Well, I didn't, but somehow Phillip did. He told me to tell you to think of it this way. The three million dollars that each of you will keep is really a commission for your assistance in lowering our acquisition fees with your Firms."

Meg could see both gentlemen smile and then reach over and shake the hand of Frank Turner. Their voices dropped. So that is how one does business, she thought.

Meg was feeling nauseous. She knew that air sickness was like sea sickness, a problem with the inner ear adjusting to the movement of the small jet. The picture of Marines streaming off landing craft into a hail of lead was always an understandable act in her mind. She would gladly put on a parachute. It seemed as if the walls of the jet were closing in on her. Oh, how she hated motion sickness!

She had to put her mind on something else besides her nausea. What had happened to the loud voices? Straining to hear as the voices dropped even lower to a whisper, Meg turned to look at the men. All were in the process of rising. All had been staring at her. Frank Turner led the way, walked past her and sat to her right on the couch. The second man, she believed his name was Smedt, sat down across from her. Then to her surprise, the third man squeezed himself down onto the couch to her left. Smedt folded the table down. Meg found herself trapped.

She wanted to get up and run away. Where could she go? She looked across at Smedt and then back to Goldstein. Both were smiling, but neither would look her in the eye. Then she felt the sure hand of Frank Turner high on her leg "Did you get a chance to listen to our conversation? I know you did. How could you not hear these guys cry? Did you know that they are the prostitutes of the business world? Look at them, they don't deny it, at least my definition. You see, a whore is anyone who does a task with his or her body on a fee basis payable only upon the completion of the task. Don't you agree, Smedt?"

"Come on Frank, don't stall around." John Smedt looked at Aaron Goldstein. Both were still in shock. Together, they had agreed that they would probably settle on ten cents on the dollar, not the thirty-three cents that Turner had finally suggested as a compromise! What a windfall! Screw the fact that they had cheated a bit on the side, everyone does! This more than tripling of expected revenues would make both of them their Firm's top producers over a ten year period. Both would become their Division's Managing Partners, perhaps even the heads of their respective Firms.

"What's this, a man with no patience? John, you have to learn how to relax. Don't you agree, Meg, doesn't one have to take some time every once in awhile? You know, just relax and let yourself go."

Meg Jamison couldn't answer. Her breath was gone. The passenger compartment was soundproof and she was miles above the ground. Oh, Dane where are you? (Rattled, she barely realized that she was not thinking of her husband.) Suddenly she couldn't breathe. Was she going to die?

She felt herself lifted up by both arms, moved, and heard the table extended to its full length. Her eyes were closed as she was lowered backwards. A set of hands held her arms above her head. She could not move. Another set of hands slid over her blouse. Lips touched hers. Her legs hung limp over the edges of the table. Why were her knees so weak?

Kansas City drifted by the car's window like a slow moving picture. Frank Turner had had a rental car waiting. Minutes ago, he had dropped the silent Smedt and Goldstein off at one of the three terminals and now was driving to the Arrow Rail Division office. Pretty, green trees lined the streets. She saw long rolling hills framed in a soft midsummer afternoon that had descended on the City.

"There's the building. You had better pull yourself together, get out of the fog, Mrs. Jamison! Start paying attention."

"Uh huh."

"Damn it! Who the Hell do you think you are! You sold out Baby and you have paid the price! Because of it you are more than you would ever be without having done so. Cut this off-center, spaced-out shit! When you walk into this building, you will be the Queen of the Company. What I do is to keep you humble, what you do in there and out in Kansas City is that you keep them humble."

The car had stopped. Meg did not reply, but instead quickly got out. She noticed Turner's smile at her quick action. He was looking for some response, some life. If she could, she would at least try to be human when she saw John. Oh, how tired and nauseous she felt!

"Come on, we will go up the executive elevator." Frank Turner walked over to a small elevator by the garage door. The elevator's car was waiting. The door opened quickly. "You either have to have a key or know your office door's code number," he explained.

For some reason, Meg saw the world in bright vivid colors, magnified in brilliance. She saw him punch in the numbers, the last two of the five had been 31. That's about right, she thought. He is about 55 years of age. That year would be his birthdate. Somewhere she had picked up the habit of also using her birthdate on combinations that she had to remember. She supposed that most people did.

Meg was introduced to her husband's new secretary and while she waited, she inquired as to Mr. Turner's birthdate. It was 1/11/31, an easy enough number to remember.

"Honey, it's good to see you. Come in here and let me close the door." John Jamison had suddenly appeared. He looked older as he crushed her body to his.

"John, John, you brute! Just behave yourself. My, what an office! Oh, look at the view! No wonder you don't call more often."

"Don't call often! I have been burning up the lines to try to get you here. Gee, I am glad to see you standing here! You will love this place! I have found three homes that might do. You can't believe how inexpensive they are compared to California. Everyone likes it here. I know it's a little hot today, but......"

250

"John, I'm tired. Do you think you could take me to your apartment?"

"Apartment, Hell! I have rented the finest hotel suite in town. Look, I have three more conferences left yet today. Would you mind taking a cab? I already had your bags taken from Turner's rented car and the cab is waiting downstairs. I promise that I won't be long. I will see you soon. We have a ton of things to discuss. I think that I have changed a lot during the past month. I think you will like it a lot."

Everett Lacey climbed into the copilot's chair on the evening flight to Kansas City. Dane's Lear was the second Arrow Corporation flight to Kansas City today or the third, if one counted Massendale's round about trip through Chicago. Although he enjoyed flying, Dane was wondering at the waste, the expense of corporate flights. Wasn't he just a bus driver for others' ego trips? He had been thinking that he would have enjoyed to fly and talk to Meg Jamison again. He was also admitting that he was glad that the Lear basically flew itself. Phillip Arrow had turned to reviewing his paperwork after an intensive hour discussion with Lacey. The cockpit door was again closed. Lacey looked at Dane and asked, "Have you been listening?"

"Sure, how could I help it? Damn interesting stuff." It was only a half truth. Why was his mind on Meg Jamison?

"O.K., help me sort it all out. You tell me what you heard."

"Again? Alright. I heard you tell him that you had found out who purchased the stock. And he said that he knew you knew and that he had known since you found out about it several months ago. You asked him how he knew and he said it was obvious when you were lying. That there had to be some good reason for you to hold back on him and that he thought he knew.

"You asked him what those reasons could have been and he said that there were probably two. First, you were not satisfied with just this answer. That you wanted to find out not who did it, but why all the mergers were occurring and what union leader was coercing him. Second, the only real reason for your not telling him was that it was someone near and dear to him and that you feared how he might react when told. He then said that he could only think of one person who might elicit that response from him and that you did not have to discuss it any further."

Dane turned to look at Lacey. He, too, wanted to see his face when

251

he answered the question, "Is it the daughter?"

"Go on with what you heard, it could be one of his sons."

"I have got to tell you, Everett, I really admire her. He then reviewed the merger and asked if you had found out the real reason for his being coerced into taking these steps. You reviewed your work and said that you had the name of the union chief who was forcing his hand......or that you had two names, but you were sure it was a guy that I have even heard of. He didn't reply, but I take it that he nodded his head in agreement."

"He made no facial expression and I really had five names, we just got lucky and selected the best two candidates. But you missed the main point. Think for a minute about how he knew that I knew he was being 'coerced.' That would be tough to put together from a computer screening or review of my past work."

"Damn! Right now he probably expects everyone, especially those people at Arrow with whom you talk."

"There aren't many of those, Dane. Go on."

"Arrow then said that the real reason for your coming to Kansas City was that he knew the answer was there. Either it rests with one of his people or with some high executive of the Railroad Division who has survived and been feeding his union friend information. He told you that he now knows for sure, even though it's just a feel, that the union chief had all the information on what is going on and is the source of the stream of damaging news stories that are now drastically affecting Union Arrow's stock's price. He then added the corker!"

"Go on."

"He said that you had to accelerate your research, that it would all soon be over for him, that he had seen a couple of moves that could only mean one thing, that he was soon to be forced out as Union Arrow's Chief Executive Officer. He then said that you had earned your termination bonus, but that he wanted you to keep on the same track of inquiry and that if you found out who the source of the leak within the Company is, he would double your bonus.

"And if I might add, it was then Lacey that I thought you overdid yourself. You said you wanted it tripled and I'll be damned, but I think he agreed! Did he?"

"Yes, he did. Dane, I sure as Hell hope you never tell anyone even a fraction of what you know. You would need a triple bonus then too. People get killed for this type of information. That's what had to have happened to Richard Smith."

The cockpit was silent. Dane's mind raced back to the disappearance of the Arrow Security Chief. "That means it has to be one of us in the Company - either you, Arrow, Turner, Massendale, Caroline, or Jamison. Arrow could not seriously think it is one of the Rail Division's people. They were not around then."

"He doesn't and doesn't seem to care.

"Now let me slowly go over some facts for you and I will let you help me sort through them. There exists a union manager who controls vast amounts of money. He directs, coerces Arrow into these acquisitions for reasons only you, I think, have heard. You once told me that the union man claimed that none of his staff knew what he was doing. That makes me think that he is either working for someone else, with partners at least as powerful, or is doing this on his own."

"Working for someone else? Like who, the Arabs, the Chinese, the Russians?"

"Or the Mafia, the U.S. President, or Argentina, who the Hell knows! All we do know is that it appears that one of the five Arrow executives is connected and I don't know, I need to know how. I think I was lucky and guessed the union man's identity this morning. Now that I know who to go after, I can penetrate their files in depth. I will have to do it quickly. Once done, they will know. There will be a ton of explaining to do."

"Well, if he's the one and he is the man I dive bombed Albuquerque with, he's short and light."

"Yes, he is of small stature. How did you know that."

"Because he didn't weigh much. Ev, when I take off in this thing I can feel the weight in my hands. I know the fuel weight, I know the air density, the wind. I can feel the temperature. I felt how much he weighed. Hell, I even knew what seat he was sitting in."

"O.K., what seat is Arrow sitting in."

"Not right now. It is at liftoff as we climb out where you have the feel. Now you tell me one thing, why aren't there seven candidates excluding yourself, rather than just five?"

"Seven?" Everett Lacey looked shocked. His analytical mind was the type that did not often overlook the obvious. Counting was a basic necessity.

"Sure, you mentioned Arrow, Turner, Massendale, Caroline, and

Jamison. I would think that you could include me. I have heard everything. I would also think that Mary Sue Massendale should be included. Obviously, Massey tells her everything that is going on."

"You are right. Damn! Why am I always overlooking her?" His thoughts shifted to the bright lady's mind. What a gem she was! He wondered in this time when 50% of women worked why she did not wish outside employment. But then he knew. Children with a mother at home did 20% better on average in academics than those with a working mother. Mary Sue was fortunate that she could have them as her first priority.

Everett Lacey sat silently thinking of Mary Sue. If he felt such admiration, why was it mingled with so much fear?

Mary Sue was sitting in the alcove at the terminal next to her bedroom. The boys were in bed and she wished to get her mind off the sickness, the anquish, the misery that she felt. She had decided to go over ground that Everett Lacey had missed. If Lacey was correct, if the union leader had someone giving him information from within Arrow Corporation, perhaps they had taken a position in each of the targets to earn some pin money. It did not stand to reason that someone this close to the game could resist dabbling in investing. There had been just too much insider information to have wasted the opportunity. No one could have resisted.

Mary Sue's guess was a simple one. She accepted the hypothesis that someone was coercing her father into the acquisitions. Anyone who might have done this, might also have wished to make some safe money on investments while the tenders had been prepared. She had made money, surely others could also have ridden that train.

First, she reviewed the transfer sheets of the targets. Her program allowed her to scan the files as the computer searched for individuals who, having been identified as purchasers of Cardinal stock during this period, also purchased Oriole or Blue Jay stock.

Mary Sue knew that she was probably going to be unsuccessful. Only 20 to 30% of the stock, when traded in the United States, is registered with the companies for which the stock is issued. The majority of traded stock is held in trust by CEDE & Co. and is identified only by the bank in which the stock is held. The transfer sheets only showed large volumes registered as a "CEDE." With this being just the first line of defense for confidential, illegal transactions, Mary Sue knew that her ability to look back into the CEDE files would be limited. The greatest wonder, she thought, was that it was the U.S. Congress that set up this system that did not allow the free knowledge of who bought and sold securities. It was as if Congress wished that the knowledgeable security manipulators escape detection. But then who was she to complain? If they, the U.S. Government, were any better at what they did, she might be in jail.

The computer completed its scan. No individual had purchased stock of all three targets during the period. No matched name was to be found other than the CEDE match which pertained to over 70% of the transactions. Mary Sue turned to her second search approach.

The people at Blarnef & Blarnef had told her of their concern with an indirect tracing of her trust's massive buildup of the targets' stock. Blarnef & Blarnef traded always through CEDE & Co., but they did recognize a weakness. Large depository buildups in stock would be traceable by the banks in which they were held. Mary Sue looked at the record of buildups for the period. They showed absolutely no pattern, but then she knew that they would not.

Blarnef & Blarnef had agreed to buy the targets' stock using over twenty five major banks as depositories. A computer program traced the buildup of stock, increases and decreases in target shares, on a daily basis. The Blarnef & Blarnef approach was to average out or "smooth" these buys. Any bank that rapidly built up target stock would be shunned by them. Any bank that had a decreasing balance would be balanced out by new acquisitions. When one looked at the history, one saw level, smooth holdings by most banks. Others were also using similar purchasing programs. On the surface, it appeared that no major action in the targets' stock had taken place.

Mary Sue knew differently. All she had to do was subtract out her massive purchases and review the remainders. Knowing the Smedt and Goldstein plays and the names of their banks would also help. Ev Lacey had been invaluable here. She would be sure to subtract out those purchases and sales also. Perhaps a pattern could be shown. She quickly programmed the Fortran code and thanked her university professors for insisting that she have this early knowledge. While raising the boys, it had been her hobby, the way that she stayed informed and on top of what was happening. She ran the small program against the data bases. There it was! Someone at State Bank was having fun!

The rest, she knew, was going to be simple. Unlike the Cayman

Islands where she held her personal funds, there was no penalty for disclosing account names or owners of investment corporations in New York banks. Indeed, the U.S. Government had a right to inquire at anytime using the computer system that Mary Sue was now quickly accessing.

Yes, there was the name on the State Bank records. She too recognized the union leader's name. It was the name of a family's trust fund. Mary Sue searched the records for the names of the children. The niece's name looked somewhat familiar. Where had she heard of a woman with the name of Charlotte? Why was she thinking of Charles? Mary Sue turned off her computer. It was late and too confusing. Perhaps she should drop her other work .... Mary Sue stopped her thoughts. What was bothering her? It was the size of the trust investment ...... just two hundred thousand dollars. It was not worth the risk of being caught, too small an investment to make much of a return. Why would this man invest so little ...... unless the answer was what was obvious? He had to be a minor player. That would mean that someone was directing him. That someone had to be connected in some way to the original Arrow Corporation. Had Everett Lacey been looking for the wrong person?

15

Wednesday

Phillip Arrow sat at the Kansas City Board Room's executive terminal in the early morning. No one was, as yet, in the Kansas City offices. He called up the stockholder storage section. An "IN USE" sign flashed across the terminal's screen. He hit the keys to interrupt the other user with a message which he quickly typed in capital letters, "LET ME INTO THIS DATA SET; GO WORK ON SOMETHING ELSE EV." He tried the stockholder files again. Now they were free. Lacey probably had not slept during the night.

Strange that he should fly for two thousand miles to work on a computer that he could easily have accessed in Los Angeles. He knew that he had to hurry. Soon, scheduled meetings with each top railroad executive on an individual basis would begin and keep him busy for the next two days. He truly looked forward to his last meeting with Massendale tomorrow. The political consultant that he had contracted with for twenty years had reported the divorce filing late last night. He also reported that he could easily compromise Massendale's new attorney who was handling his side and Arrow had told him to do so immediately, for twice the amount estimated if required. The consultant had not been happy. Arrow had insisted that he do it immediately, that night if he wished their business relationship to continue. No, Arrow did not care if the other lawyer might be busy or

257

sleeping. Do it now! There was not a Beverly Hills lawyer who would sleep if the price were right.

Arrow believed that Mary Sue would be better off without the idiot and by God, would that son-of-a-bitch pay! With Caroline scheduled for the next to the last meeting tomorrow, he would have both their scalps by dinner. He would use the next full day and one half to plan for them. If they could get in bed together, they could bleed together.

Arrow's mind shifted to his daughter. Strange how that since she first became a teenager, she could not make herself turn to her father for assistance. Mary Sue had always wanted to do it on her own. In a way, he felt that she robbed him a bit of the love he was so ready to give her.

His screen flashed the summary of new purchases. Over a hundred small 10,000 to 20,000 share purchases were shown of Union Arrow common stock already this week, with all using Eastern nominees. He had picked up the pattern a month ago after reviewing some of Lacey's computer analyses. It was strange that Lacey had missed that trend, the computer had clearly found and shown it, but Everett Lacey did not recognize what it meant. Too bad Lacey's in his mid thirties, again thought Phillip Arrow, he just wasn't experienced enough to know what to look for in business at this level. When he was, Lacey would be a different man.

He advanced the picture on the screen to the total shares purchased by this collection of Eastern jackals. Damn, it was now over 20% of all Union Arrow stock outstanding! With the merger costs now affecting the corporate earnings, the overall earnings per share of the combined companies had dropped another 50% over the past month. Much of this was due to the acquisition costs, but most was caused by the high interest costs of the borrowed funds. Those subsidiaries of his, especially this Rail Division, had better increase their cash flows.

Damn, but at $ 20 Union Arrow stock was a steal!

None of this, he knew, was unusual. Most major acquisitions caused initial drops in per share earnings. It was the corresponding drop in the market price of his common stock that had him worried. Union Arrow Corporation's stock had decreased in value by 90% since the acquisition. He had seen it happen to LTV and Whittaker, but he could not believe that it was happening to him now. Arrow himself had started to buy the stock, but his holdings now stood at just 12%. Almost everything he owned was now invested in the Company. If this kept up, he would have to go to his friends in New York and borrow personally to buy more shares.

Before that though, he wanted to see how the new Chairman aspirant was going to handle the situation. He could see where Frank Turner had, himself, been purchasing Arrow stock with his personal holdings, almost up to a full one-half percent. Where did Turner get the money for such an investment? He had Frank scheduled for the meeting right before Caroline. If it weren't for that damn Massendale, Frank would have waited until last. Perhaps there was a saving grace. If he got beat around a bit by a Turner, he would be sure to take it out on Lawrence Massendale.

Damn, the system was down!

A blank screen also faced Everett Lacey. They had used a Systems' Destroyer! Incredible! He had heard of them, but never seen one in action. He tried to restart the system. It was cold dead! He could imagine the circuits of the minicomputer back in the old Arrow Corporation Executive Computer Room. He hoped that no one had been standing close to that machine.

Whoever they were at the union files, they had used a controlled power surge coordinator, much like a flash of lightning. Put any electronic magnetic instructions in a computer's core, on a disk or a storage tape, and apply a sudden burst of electricity. It wipes everything clean.

Ev had watched the programmed system destruct sequence play out at the speed of light through tens of thousands of files and programs. It had raced through all the connected files and finally ended in the system control language. It would be weeks before they had any semblance of this system restored. He smiled. If Arrow had been working with his stockholder list, he wished him well. Hopefully, there was a free standing tape backup. Any backup disk or tape with any type of wire connection or access, which was the case with almost all the files in this operator free system, were gone. Of that he was sure. He wondered what it had done to the competitors' systems that they were secretly accessing. Thank Goodness, that he had dropped the FBI access!

Someone must have been sitting there waiting for his search at this deep level of inquiry. They must have had a series of alarms. Surely, no destruct sequence of such consequences would be left without a human failsafe check. He had been running the profile of the union executive against the six Union Arrow suspects, including Dane, but excluding Mary Sue.

Lacey pushed himself back from the desk and sighed. What did he know now that he did not know four months ago? It had to be Turner, yet Jamison showed the best early correlations. What would it read with the union executive's comparison? He suspected that the union had seen the results on their equipment, he surely had not seen it on his. Lacey knew only one thing for certain, his computer work was done. If he was lucky and found out who it was, it would only be done by going over his past work. He would have to see Arrow and talk him into letting him return to L.A. today or tomorrow. Lacey knew that he was no longer safe, that someone would surely search for the individual who triggered this destruction. Perhaps he was safe here for awhile. Hopefully, no one had noted the point of access of his computer search.

It was then that the answer and thought entered his mind. He had excluded Mary Sue. It was she who had the code for the hidden files on the Arrow system. And just as important, she had made a similar search of this material. He had only talked to her last night. She had confirmed the union trust leader's name. What a feat! Now if she could just see the connection. Lacey had seen her tracks across the data that he had been reviewing. Thinking it strange at the time, he had been distracted thinking of how close this modern work was to the tracking of game by his ancestors. No, he had not progressed far on any scale of evolution. Tracking game was dangerous, dangerous to both man and woman. His thoughts returned to Mary Sue, had he jeopardized her?

Where had Mary Sue learned to hard wire a computer terminal wondered Lacey? He could not remember ever hearing of Mary Sue...... that is, unless one was talking about Arrow's grandsons. Mary Sue Massendale was an enigma to Everett Lacey. He had never ever met anyone quite like her. What a companion to take on a hunting trip!

Could those who just destroyed the system know of her unauthorized and active access? He had excluded both Mary Sue and himself from the list just now. Those individuals originally shown would have been noted by whomever had been watching his work. Would they surmize that perhaps she knew of his, Lacey's, work? Would she be in the same danger that he now felt he was? Why was he constantly

260

thinking of her these days? Was it because of her husband's walking out on her ? She had been so matter of fact when she mentioned it. What a strong lady!

Mary Sue was uncertain. She was upset. How could she be so unattractive that Lawrence would look twice at another woman? She walked down the hall from the attorney's office. Could she ever remember being so humiliated? Her lawyer had been a family friend for many years. She could swear that he had smiled at her grief. What was there to smile at when there was such sorrow?

Mary Sue was also angry. What audacity of both the attorney and her husband! It had been an outrage to see an already drafted agreement in its final copy. Twenty four hours and her signature was already on a contract that would be air expressed to her husband today. It would take days to process, but the legalities had already been accomplished. She resented the rush, but for many good reasons as described by her lawyer, she had signed the papers. Lawrence's lawyer, at least, was being most fair in taking so little. Her lawyer did not believe a better settlement possible. Indeed, he stated that he was surprised in light of his past dealings with this Beverly Hills divorce lawyer. The man was reputed to be a shark of sharks. This divorce agreement appeared unexpectedly onesided in her favor. Oh, she hoped that the lawyer was right! Lawrence would never see her good side again.

Mary Sue had asked for only one major addition to the agreement. Lawrence was to be forever shutout as a potential financial guardian for the boys. If she should die, her father and then her brothers would handle all aspects of estate, trusts, and guardianships over the boys. Lawrence was to have no possible way of getting his hands on either the boys or her assets. He was to lose much!

Mary Sue Massendale stopped at the door to the office building and looked into a full length mirrored wall. She had dressed for the morning. Admittedly, she looked better in a dress and heels than in her usual shorts and tennis shoes. What did Lawrence expect? It had to be so much more enjoyable to see an attractive Caroline O'Brian dressed each day for the office than to see his wife dressed only for housework, soccer, baseball and boy scouts. She wondered what Ms. O'Brian would look like with four sons to attend to. She wondered what Lawrence would look like if he had to stay home. Didn't he recognize the personal price that one parent had to pay to raise children today?

Mary Sue knew that she had to walk to expend her energy created by the frustration and humiliation. It was so easy to get divorced in California! Indeed, it was far easier than getting married. The only difference was that the lawyers received the gifts!

What must it be like to be a lawyer? Trained in negative thoughts and why things would not work, they lived the outcomes of such anticipations. Always dealing in disputes and turmoil, they must feel like the scum of the earth. Was this Lawrence's problem? Mary Sue tried to think of just one thing of a happy nature that a lawyer did where both sides benefited. Outside of assisting in an adoption of a child, she could think of no instance where at least one party was not gravely hurt. Negative jobs and negative training had to produce negative human beings.

When would she tell the boys? She had not been able to clearly think of a way to do it. Lawrence was gone for the week. She would do it Friday night after he did not come home. Next week, she would take the boys in the stationwagon to see their grandfather. What would her father do when he found out? Perhaps she would have to ask Phillip Arrow for help. He would have to be asked to control himself. It would do no good to have a father like Lawrence who was humiliated, destroyed, and unemployed by an avenging grandfather.

Mary Sue turned back to return to her car. She felt no different about Lawrence than if he were one of her sons. What would she do when one of them came to her and told her that he was leaving his wife and children for some dream? Had that been her trouble? Her home was a workplace and Lawrence was just one more irritating, but older, male when he was home. Had she tried at all to keep him satisfied, was that a role that women had to play? She knew he had been a target of O'Brian for months. All she had done was talk to another woman about it. She had made no real effort. Did she not have the energy or had she decided to let him go then?

Mary Sue was in sight of her car. Perhaps it had been her choice after all. She had sensed all this coming. The thought that she might have had some control of the situation, even if subconsciously, made her feel a bit better. Damn the Caroline O'Brians of the world! And damn the men who were attracted to them!

Dane Hughes was feeling much better as he waited for Caroline. He relaxed in the snug, secure booth in the darkened bar. What a cheery place! What a great place for a rendezvous! Caroline had agreed to meet him for drinks during work What made him feel so good was that she suggested that they meet early and that she would join him at 11:30, a time far in advance of the late hours he used to wait for her in LA. It had to be that she was as anxious to see him as he was to see her after all these weeks. And there she was! Dane had taken a seat across the bar so he could watch her walk toward him. Lord, she was pretty!

"Hello, Dane, you deserve a big kiss, you big brute! Yes, I will take one of those. Gawd, it's hot out there today! What a hole this is!"

Even her language could not offend Dane today. He loved her posture, the way she held her head. What a beautiful lady. "It's good to see you, I missed you."

"What, with all your flying around the world, you missed me! Do you expect a lady to believe all that?"

Dane felt the soft covered ring box that he had purchased in South Africa. Could it wait? Yes, he would not give her the ring and ask her that question in a damn bar! He reached for her hand.

She held his offered hand and asked, "And what brings you to Kansas City at this time of year?"

"Just a Phillip Arrow flight. It was very enjoyable, really. For some reason Everett Lacey is still doing some contract work for Arrow. He was on board and we talked all the way across the continent. I sure miss not seeing him around."

"Yes, he gave us some spark, but Dane, he just never fit in. I don't think his kind can ever be team players like others. What has Arrow got him working on?"

"I can't tell you, Caroline. Ev and I are good friends and we have been working on it together since the start."

"Since the start of your friendship?"

"No, since the start of the acquisition when he was fired."

"Then he is looking for who bought all that stock early on?"

"Damn, Caroline, don't do that to me. Now that is just my guess, since Lacey has never told me everything and in fact lied a bit at times. I think, however, that he is still an Arrow employee and has been on the payroll during his leave of absence."

"Sure, he receives a severance check."

"No, I mean on a consulting payroll also. He is on a project of great importance to Phillip Arrow."

263

"I can check on it."

"Don't bother, I think he is about done. From the flight I picked up the fact that there were parts he thought he'd never solve and as for the person, he's looking for, he's found her."

"Her? Did you say 'her'?"

"Damn Caroline, you are getting the whole story from me in ten seconds! You are going to have to keep that part silent until you die, I must have your word on it."

"Dane, if you have to ask, it means you don't trust me." Caroline had slipped across the couch seats to sit next to him. Her unmentioned excuse was given with a lowering of her voice so others would not overhear. She looked out across the table at the nearby tables. Dane could feel the warmth of her leg against his.

"O.K., O.K., I'm sorry! Look, I don't even know what his project's really about. First, I thought it was about finding who purchased some stock, then it appears he's not interested in that......he is interested in some union guy.....look, I know very little about it. It is just that he mentioned one thing that really shocked me. He told me that it was his daughter."

"Whose daughter?"

"Mary Sue Massendale, of course."

"Did he say it was Arrow's daughter or was that just your interpretation ?"

Dane sat and thought for a moment. "No, that is just my guess. I think for sure it is a female. Caroline, I don't question Everett when he is telling me things like this. You do that and he clams up. When he talks, I listen. What I can tell you is that he was pretty subdued, although he appears to be quite happy to be close to finishing his work. You know, like happy to see her nailed but worried about something."

"Like he is afraid of a backlash?"

"Oh, come on, let's stop talking business. What would you like to do this evening. First, let's have lunch, I have ...."

"Oh, Dane, I just can't. I have meetings all day and into the evening with Frank Turner and Lawrence Massendale, then out tonight for a quick trip back East and an early meeting. In fact, I am late now for a working lunch. I must prepare for another session with Phillip. Don't look so disappointed. I will see you next time you are in town and we will make a night of it. Now I have to run, see you then."

Dane was left in a quiet bar with the feel of her kiss. Dark bar, dark beer, dark feelings, and dark mood he thought. What could he do to make this woman want to be around him? Hell, she had not even waited for her drink to come!

Neither of the two people driving by in an Union Arrow limousine wanted to be in the presence of the other.

Meg Jamison rode along side her husband and again silently viewed the Kansas City streets. She was to take the car and meet the realtor to look at the three houses that John had found. She had hinted that she was not going to stay, that none of the houses would please her. John hadn't heard her. It was as if John were in another world, a world that was not hers.

And along with this non communication, she felt deep guilt. She couldn't stand his touching her. Obviously, he had been faithful to her during the month since they had last seen each other, could she say the same? Didn't he know the price she was willing to pay for him? Didn't he realize that the forced moving of a person from their world, their community, was a price every bit as great as what she had already paid? And what a price that had been! It was a price that once paid, put her in a different world. What world did John reside in, that of ambition, drive, success, and recognition? Meg knew hers was only that of stark reality.

John Jamison felt destroyed and humiliated. He concentrated on the scenery and thanked the fact that the trip would be blessedly short. He could never remember feeling this mentally beaten. Meg was cold and hard. It was as if he had defiled her. Why did he feel like he should be apologizing to her all the time? It was like they were in different worlds.

Their argument this morning had been brief. She was obviously going through the motions to fulfill some unwritten law of matrimony. Why should she sacrifice so? Hadn't he done his part? His job always had been to provide. Now that he was finally really successful, what did he get? Cold water, a cold bed, and a cold wife. What selfish world did she reside in, that of comfort, security, lack of change, and self centeredness? Damn, didn't she realize that he had a reality to cope with too!

When he arrived at his office, the first appointment was waiting for him. He shouldn't have tried to spend most of the morning with his wife, he thought. He would have been better off to get up and have left early. This meeting could be the most important of his career.

The two rail subsidiary division administrative vice presidents sat before him. Looking down on them, John felt it strange that only six months ago, he had held a position similar to their own. What would he do in their place? Had he ever started a working day feeling so low?

"Mr. Jamison, we have conferred on the proposed changes for the organization and what we would like to propose is that we look at all changes in a broader context."

"Exactly, gentlemen, that is what I had hoped you would say. We have to look at the long run."

"We were speaking more of the matter of communication. We believe you understand that change is upsetting to our people. What we would suggest is that we list all the changes that you desire, categorize them, and put together a program to communicate and implement them in the most effective manner possible. What we were to talk about this morning is just one element of what we believe to be a spectrum of our corporate cultures. We wish to define all of the proposed changes and then plan a process of full change with a view toward the total picture."

"I see your point. What you are saying is that it could be possible to perhaps more quickly get the job done with several shock treatment blows, taking several changes together, and then step away rather than this constant hitting you over the head everyday."

"Exactly, so what we would like is for you to sit back and give us an idea of all the changes that you have planned that will affect our people."

"Fine. I think that is an excellent suggestion and thank you for your cooperation. I happen to have just such a list here in my drawer...... ah, here it is. To begin, we, of course, will cancel the charity programs, then cancel the outside community involvement sponsored on corporate time, cut the administrative staff by another 50%, establish a salary freeze for management for two years, decrease the benefit levels including canceling the retiree health coverages, eliminate our counseling and psychiatric coverages, terminate all training programs, drop all computer programs outside of accounting, close the marketing, planning, and research departments, revise the Political Action Committee so that it is no longer a neutral support

266

group, drop all day care facilities, change the lunch programs, cancel the Company automobile program, revise the generous vacation schedule to match the original Arrow's.........."

"Mr. Jamison......."

"No, no wait. I am not even a sixth finished. I just........"

John Jamison watched the two men stand and both took envelopes from their pockets. Each handed one to him. The first man said, "After thirty years of loyal service, the Company to which I pledged my loyalty is dead. It is time I found someone I am proud to work for again."

The other added, "I must be less generous. You are the lowest type of sycophant, Jamison. You suck air without barely being able to swim. You would sell out your mother and father. You would whore your wife. You make me sick!"

John Jamison sat for minutes after the men had walked out. He could not read the letters of resignation. How could he survive without those two men? All the administration would be in chaos. They had set him up, they never wanted to help him with his work. Distracted, he did not notice his side door open and close, nor did he quickly recognize the rumbled man who had sat in front of him just 24 hours ago. The individual just stood before him, silently waiting to be recognized.

"Oh, may I help you? I thought we had discussed everything yesterday."

"My wife sent me back. She wanted me to ask if there was anyway that I could stay with the Company. Look, Sir, I have given my life to the Railroad. I have been good for it. I still have much to offer, I can think of a hundred places where I could work and save you more money than what you would pay me."

"No, I am afraid that is out of the question. Our conversation is through."

The man was on his knees by Jamison's desk. Tears were streaming down his face. "Sir, you don't understand. My wife made me come, but she doesn't really realize it. I don't think that she can handle this. We will lose our home. I don't know if I can calm her. Please, I know that I can help you, won't you help me?"

"I can't. I have been told to terminate you. Look, I will be honest. I think you are going because too many people look to you as their leader. We are doing what the North Koreans did in their prisoner of war camps, we are killing off the natural leaders. We want only our people running your Company."

"Then there is no hope?"

"None."

The rumbled man shuffled out past Frank Turner who was standing in the doorway. Turner walked into the office and over to the table to sit down. "Do you always tell the people you are terminating the Company's dirty laundry? Don't answer. I don't want to hear. Jesus, Jamison, you are a chicken shit! You are just not tough enough!"

"I am tough enough for you." Jamison was doubly sickened. How much had Turner heard?

"Maybe so, but not for that man who is walking out of here. For Christ's sake, Jamison, you are wearing his hurt all over your face! I don't even know what his story is, but it is nothing more than a result of consolidation of business, an indispensible process to a healthy economy. Jesus, just looking at you makes me sick! You owed him something more than that. You could have given him some hope, restored his pride. Hell, at the least, you could have made him hate you. He could run for years on that hate and it wouldn't hurt you a bit! No, you have to calm your conscience and try to be a good guy too. You left him no room to rationalize. Now he leaves a failure. Shit, now he just might go shoot himself!"

"What else can I do for you?"

"You can discuss these reports with me now! They are your progress reports for the past two months. All they are are a bunch of excuses, a pack of lies. You are such a Dumb Shit, Jamison! When are you going to catch on to the fact that you have the easiest job in the world? You don't even have to think. All you have to do is cut and slash, slash and cut. Instead, all you do is pencil push which you somehow think is going to keep you away from the chopping block."

"What specifically do you wish to review?"

"I don't want to specifically review one God Damn thing! I want you to get your ass in gear. I want you to fire a thousand people in the next three weeks. I mean fire! Get their asses and paycheck drain off our backs throughout the Country. I want you to make up for lost time!"

"I have been thinking of quitting."

"You have what! You can't quit, you slob! You took this job and you have to stay unless we tell you to go. Hell, everyone here thinks I am in here firing you right now. What they don't know is that I think you can make it a bit longer. You quit? We would stink your name throughout the Country. The next job you would get would be shoveling manure. Come to think of it, that would be a perfect job for you. It would be a task where you couldn't make a mistake."

"Maybe so, but it is not me that I am thinking of, it is my wife."

"Your wife. Oh, you dumb turd! Look, I thought I might have to use this so I brought it along. You have to toughen up Jamison. You have to start paying the price for your job and your pay. Your wife did! Here is a little film with audio taken at a beach house in Malibu one night a few months ago. I want to see if you recognize your wife's sacrifice, if you would call it that."

Meg Jamison had never felt so attacked. The Company real estate agent had taken her to the three houses selected by her husband in Kansas City. The woman's brashness, pushiness, and self contained air of the salesperson with the sure kill, matched the houses that she had shown Meg. Didn't John know that they needed none of this faked luxury? She wondered as she walked through the homes if the interior decorators of America had only one set of tastes. Dark green rugs, dark paneled walls, peg and grooved floors, bars in family rooms, maid's rooms that shouted the perceived inferiority of the inhabitants. Cold houses shown by cold people. Surely Kansas City had some warm homes. There must be some real people in this town.

Meg looked at the talkative real estate lady next to her. John had made sure that she was accompanied by a "hawk." Meg had had most of her friends go into real estate at one time or another. The formula was simple. There were scouts and there were the killers. The scouts were "sparrows" who acted as information leads to those few in each firm who could close sales. No sympathy was ever given. When the sparrows ran out of leads, they were sacrificed.

The cold-faced, hardened real estate agent kept talking of Meg's potential "home." Meg wondered if the lady had ever lived in a "home." They were looking at only houses. It took, as they said, "a great amount of living to make a home!" Meg knew that there was just not enough living and loving left in her to ever find a home here in Kansas City. A prison, yes, that she could find, but never a home. She had her home in the Santa Barbara hills. Didn't her husband know how important her home and community were to her?

John Jamison sat in shock. He did feel cold. He had sat quietly through the full fifteen minutes. He didn't turn his gaze from the screen, even after Frank Turner had turned the screen off and walked from the room. One hour.....then two hours passed and his secretary looked in.

"Mr. Jamison, you weren't answering your buzzer. Here is a Special Delivery that arrived a few minutes ago. I'm going home, Goodnight."

John Jamison took the envelope. He slowly opened the one hour delivery and a photograph fell out. It was an instamatic picture of a naked woman in a bathtub of blood red water. The note read simply and he could hear the rumbled man's voice speaking the words aloud, "By the time you read this note, I will have joined my wife. This is how I found her when I returned from your office. What I most regret is that I can not truly communicate my loathing of you."

Jamison slowly rose from his chair. The day had fled away. He dialed the hotel to leave a message for his room. He had been "called out of town" for the rest of the day and the evening. He would see his wife tomorrow. Reaching for a paper, he scrawled a note, sealed it in an envelope and wrote the three letter addressee's name on the face.

He straightened his desk and sealed the picture and letter in the trash bag for the security maid's pickup. He looked around the office. All was in order. He had thought of this several times before. It was now time.

There was no reason for haste, yet he knew if he stopped his motions that he might stop forever. He walked to the hall and then to the stairs. He must walk. The executive offices were on the top floor, was this the reason? He slowly walked up the stairs into the still Midwest day of the rooftop.

He knew that he had two choices, the four outside streets or the inside garden patio. He had always liked trees, ever since he was a boy on the Albertan plains. He walked to the edge and looked at the clouds in the sky. There could be no hesitation.

The air screamed past him. Strange that it was so unpleasant. Who ever liked that much wind? It reminded him of Lethbridge where they measured the wind each day by viewing its effect on a heavy chain hanging over the steps of the City Hall. He was a boy when he last felt that much .....

16

Thursday

The telephone rang early. Mary Sue Massendale was in her bedroom putting old sheets over the top of her bedroom furniture. Up since 4:30 AM, she had been busy preparing the room for the painters. A new mattress was already ordered. While the painters worked in the late morning, she would shop for the new linen and bedspread. She picked up the telephone.

"Mary Sue, this is Massey. You awake yet? Sorry about that, it is only 7:30 here....but I wanted to talk to you before you took the boys to school. Have you told them yet?"

"No."

There was silence, then "Look, Mary Sue, I know that this is tough on you and I want to tell you I know how hard you are taking it. I want you to know it is not personal. It just has to be. We are better apart. Understand?"

"I understand that that is what you are saying. Why are you calling?"

"I, ...uh, oh, I received the lawyers' draft. I am shocked, both by the contents and its speed of delivery and your signing. It is unheard of for a divorce lawyer to have final papers ready, I....."

"Lawrence, it was not my lawyer, it was yours who wrote up those papers. My lawyer went over to your lawyer's office Tuesday evening

271

at your and his request. They sat there and hammered it out and his word processing produced that final draft."

"No, Mary Sue, that is not how it worked. They must have worked all night. You signed it, did you read it all?"

"No." Mary Sue saw no reason to tell him the truth.

"I didn't think so. That was really dumb, Mary Sue. You can't do things like that. I tell you what, I will work on a change or two and send it back......."

"What change?"

"Oh, several. I can't quite see that much for child support, but more importantly, I would like to exercise some control over the boys should something happen to you. I am particularly concerned with their financial well being."

"No, Lawrence. Don't even talk about it. My father, then my brothers stand in that line. You asked out and you are out. Don't think that you can be halfway about this."

"Now just a minute! You are not thinking about the boys, you are only............"

"I am just telling you, Lawrence, that should you not sign those papers as they are written, I am going to the press on this. I know that you are after my father's job. If you think you are going to make President and Chairman of Union Arrow, you don't need me suing you and Caroline for adultery and alienation of affection. You would have a zero chance."

"How did you know.......alright, I hear you. Mary Sue, I don't like your tone of voice. You sound like you have turned vicious. I am worried about you, you sound like your father."

Phillip Arrow leaned back in the restaurant chair and placed his fingertips together in a half prayer gesture. Peering out from beneath his fingers, he could see the cigar of Frank Turner. Caroline was also partly visible as she nervously reached for a cigarette after the light breakfast meal. It always troubled Arrow, that seemingly universal human trait that expected, by right, the freedom to pollute another's breathable air. Arrow was wondering what Frank Turner would say if he urinated in the drinking water that still sat untouched on the table before them.

Phillip Arrow was tired. For the past day which lasted sixteen hours, he had met with various executives of the acquired firms. This morning he had other meetings scheduled beginning with John

272

Jamison. But O'Brian and Turner had literally demanded this break-fast meeting before the Jamison session. Obvious to Arrow, Frank Turner was going to suggest that Jamison be replaced. Arrow could feel Caroline's tenseness, her desire to interject the subject before the meal was over. Obviously, she believed that it was Turner's place to toss out the ball. Arrow enjoyed her discomfort, perhaps he could set them up a bit for their coming downfall.

"I think you two should relax a bit. In reality, it doesn't make much difference what occurs to us financially this year. The market doesn't know what to anticipate. All we have to do is hold back any publicity of any type and keep the public guessing. Our role is to concentrate on the organization and make sure it is structured correctly for the next ten years. It would also help to conserve our cash a bit."

Frank Turner interrupted, "While our stock goes down the toilet."

"It would have anyway, Frank. Even if we were turning out great numbers, the financial analysts would not believe them. No, the focus of the next twelve months should be on what we have been doing of late. We have to first look at the people available, the spots to be filled and make those choices well. If we sacrifice short term profits a bit for the long term success of the Company, so be it."

"Phillip, I wish that I could agree with you. There is just so much to do here and not all of it is getting done."

"Well then Frank, I would suggest that not everything will get done this year. We will survive. We have before and we will again."

"Sir, I don't think you understand." It was Caroline and she did not like the direction of the conversation. "There may be no profits at all with the way things are going in Kansas City."

"Perhaps that is an exaggeration," hastened Frank Turner, "but it gives you an idea of where we are heading."

"Oh, I think that I know where we are going. Caroline, I have been looking at annual company bonus plans for executives for too many years and this situation is an exact mirror. You have a desire to cut staff, cease planning, delete expenditures for penetrating new markets, stop developing new services, cease advertising or in any way building for the future. Instead, you wish to concentrate on cutting present expenses to increase near term profits. Usually, it is done because a manager's bonus is tied to these short-term profits. In this case, both of you are concentrating on covering interest expense and reducing debt, the result is the same."

Caroline couldn't believe Phillip Arrow's words, "Aren't our bonuses also tied to profits?"

"I think not Caroline. You must have forgotten our conversation at Frank's house some months ago. I said that your bonus would be based on the integration of the acquired companies. I said nothing about profit measures. The same is true for Frank."

"Well, if that is what you meant, we are still doing a poor job here in Kansas City on all fronts."

"Caroline, I agree, some of you have been screwing around too much. But you must remember that what we are dealing with is an organization of human beings of incredible dimensions. In many ways, we are like a government. And like all organizations, we are bound to fall into the rules and energies that govern all large organizations."

"Rules and energies! Oh, come on Phillip!" barked Frank Turner, "that sounds like 'space talk'."

"It could be. What I believe neither of you realize is that you can not apply the same rationale to an organization of a quarter of a million people as we did in the decentralized old Arrow Corporation that was only a third of our present size.

"Caroline, let me use you as an example. Picture yourself as an ant on a log floating down the middle of a wide, wide flooding river. Ahead is a waterfall that should you go over, surely will crush or drown you. With tremendous effort, you convince all the other ants on the log of the danger ahead. You, with even more effort, achieve a consensus of action. Then you manage to get them to do what they agreed as a consensus. All of you get to one side of the log at the water line and put out your small legs to begin swimming, kicking, and pushing the log to the side of the river. If you are fortunate, you will move that log by a foot or more. Who knows? That may be all you need to do to shift the log a bit in the current to catch on a rock!

"Put simply, one or two individuals in a large organization can have little real effect. Even hundreds of people have no effect on a company the size of Union Arrow. The organization will live on its own."

"Piss ants on a log! Oh, come on Phillip! We have a Hell of a lot more clout and control than that!"

"I don't think so, Frank. What you have been doing of late is just kicking some of the ants off the log. The organization is still drifting down its course in our society. Let me refine this view a bit. Have you

274

ever seen a river on the rise? That is what Union Arrow happens to be. We are a swollen torrent, made up of three tributaries that have suddenly run together. At first our waters will not mix. Then certain currents will develop and certain transfers will occur. Finally, after many miles and many meanders, the river waters will be homogeneous and totally mixed.

"Our problem is that we are just at our first turn of the bend. Both you and Caroline give me the appearance of being in a rowboat with the idea that with your paddles, you will stir up the waters and create just the right mixture. Let me assure you, nothing you will do with those paddles will do the job. Only the energy of the organization, as it courses down the riverbed over time, will create a sufficient mix. It will just take time."

Phillip looked inquiringly at Caroline. She had been quiet for some time. Hopefully, she was upset with his "screwing around" remark. He knew she was wondering if he knew. If she thought he did, perhaps it would speed up the process some. Arrow could tell that Frank knew and enjoyed his remark.

To Frank, though, screwing around meant little. Fornication and defecation were the same to Frank and who knows, in Nature's world, perhaps he was right. Arrow knew it wasn't the case with himself. He had shown no intimacy with any woman since his wife died. He knew that he never would. It was one of those things that he believed separated men from animals. Massendale was a slug. Turner was a rooster.

Caroline looked at Frank Turner. He was reaching for the check to pay the bill for the breakfast. He was going to forgo bringing up the termination of John Jamison. The chicken! The arrogant little sniveling bastard! Caroline couldn't believe it. Arrow was a basketcase, talking about rivers and ants! If he kept it up he would be mentioning butterflies and flowers. Damn Turner! Caroline also knew that she was at a disadvantage. Damn Arrow, he had to know! How much did he really know? Mary Sue had probably been crying on his shoulder.

Caroline was just about to voice the subject that had been the reason for the meeting. Surely Phillip Arrow would know that they had ducked their "problem of utmost importance."

Then Caroline decided that she would wait until her afternoon meeting. There she would see who was the toughest and Damn, if she was going to slide by the subject of getting rid of John Jamison. If

Frank Turner didn't have the balls, she did. Jamison was dead meat!

Meg Jamison was worried. John had not called from wherever he was going. The message had given her no clue. Getting up early because she could not sleep, she was at her husband's office by 9:00 AM. She had to talk to him. They had made their mistakes. Were they not walking through steps placed before them by some unknowing, uncaring material god? It was time to take their medicine, to fall forward as they fell, to advance their lives past this misery.

The gracious secretary let her into her husband's office. She walked over to the couch and sat down. Executive office furniture was a marvelous study, she thought. Each ascending level of the building had progressively nicer and nicer furniture. Rank was defined by the luxury of the rug, the paneling on the wall, the size of the desk, the office space and location, size of tables, the existence of couches, choice of paintings.... John's office was far nicer than any room in their house. Yet even with the large windows, the choice of walnut furniture and paneling and the blood red carpet, the room was oppressive. Was there really any difference between a nicely furnished jail cell and this?

Where was her husband? She sensed that something was wrong, the secretary knew of no trip. Dare she? Of course! Meg walked over to his desk and looked at the papers neatly stacked in rows across its top. It looked as if John had straightened up his office before he left. She turned over the single sealed envelope sitting in the middle of the center writing blotter. Nausea filled her throat. She slumped down in the executive chair to open her mail.

The note was a crushing blow. He loved her, he was sorry he made her hurt so, he felt so badly, please say "Good-by" to the girls, he loved them so. Meg was crying. Why didn't she scream? Why this - why this? What could make him have written so - her mind searched for the slight chance, could he have just gone away?

The door opened. A Hispanic maid looked at the crying woman, but asked no questions. She walked over to the desk and quickly reached for the trash bag. Thankful that no one had noticed the lateness of her morning's work, she turned.

The crying lady grabbed the sack from her and not saying a word, ripped it open. The maid hurried from the room. There was no understanding these crazy Anglo women.

Meg first found the rumbled man's suicide letter, then the picture.

What a terrible picture! He had also sent a video tape. Meg knew that she had to see it. What could this man have done to her husband? She walked across the room to the TV video cassette recorder.

Minutes later she sat stunned! John, oh John! The nausea was real now. She ran for the room's executive restroom.

Some time later, she stood applying her makeup. She then walked across the room and straightened up the desk. She replaced the trash with the suicide letter and picture in the trash basket. She opened her purse and put in the video cartridge. Slowly, she unfolded John's letter to leave it open on the desktop. Where could he have gone, what could he have done? She was in no hurry. She knew that she was too late to help him. He was dead.

In the hall but fifty feet away, two friends met. "Dane, what are you doing poking around these quarters?" Everett Lacey was on his way to see Phillip Arrow. He had finally arranged a ten minute session, just long enough to tell Arrow of his failure to resurrect the dead system and to say a farewell for his return to LA. Whatever Arrow had proposed for him here in Kansas City was just not worthwhile. Hell, Arrow hadn't even talked to him since they arrived! What had been the program?

The office corridor stretched along all the executive offices in a U-shaped pattern. Dane Hughes had just come out of the Transportation Secretary's office. He was a bit mystified. Perhaps her secretary knew where she had gone. Caroline had told him that she had to fly East in the evening. Curious, he had checked with the Transportation Office. He wished first to see when he was scheduled out and then to review both the Arrow jet flights and the commercial tickets that had been written. There was no record of any trip by Caroline yesterday. Obviously, she had purchased her own ticket. That was against corporate practice and Dane doubted that Caroline had ever violated any rules. Where could she have gone? Or had she gone anywhere at all?

"Oh, just checking up on my schedule. What are you up to?"

Dane walked along with Lacey who replied, "Going home. Do you want to fly me? I will ask Arrow, if you wish." Dane's eyes were on a white faced Meg Jamison who was walking out of her husband's office.

"Sure, sure....... Mrs. Jamison? Are you alright?"

She shook her head. Dane and Ev walked up to her. Suddenly, she lunged forward and grabbed hold of Dane in a desperate hug. A startled Dane heard her whisper, "I think John has killed himself."

Dane hugged the silently sobbing woman. "Why do you say that?"

"The letter is on his desk."

Dane followed the sprinting Lacey into the Jamison office. A startled secretary stood looking at the open door through which Lacey had stormed. Dane sat Meg down on the couch. He forced her to lie back, then raised and turned toward Lacey who had walked across the room to hand Dane the note.

"Let's go look in the most obvious places. Ev, you walk around the outside of the building. I will check the patio and the elevator shaft. I will have the secretary call Security to check the restrooms. Meet me back in the main lobby when you have circled the building. Don't overlook the outside ledges, behind shrubs........"

Lacey had turned and departed. Some time later he stood in the lobby waiting for Dane to return. Finally, he walked through to the patio. Dane was sitting on a bench.

"You O.K.?"

"No. He is back there wedged between those two planters. I guess he just ran out of courage yesterday."

"Why do you think he did it? He had everything going for him."

Lacey looked at Dane for an answer. Dane knew why he would have committed suicide. If it was good enough for him, it must have been good enough for Jamison. "I guess the price was just too high. We had better call the police."

"No, let's first tell Arrow."

Phillip Arrow sat in Jamison's office. Meg Jamison had been taken to the hospital for observation. Her one request was to fly home as soon as possible and if possible, to fly John Jamison's body to the family burial spot in Alberta. Arrow looked around him, Lacey, Hughes, Turner, and Massendale. He asked aloud to no one, "What made him do it?"

Frank Turner replied, "Phillip, he just wasn't tough enough. I told you when we started that he wasn't the man for the job."

Lacey couldn't restrain himself, "Do you mean that he wasn't a team player, that he didn't fit in, that you never trusted him, that his performance was substandard, that he antagonized his fellow workers, or any of that other crap you always say whenever someone leaves the Company?"

"You should know."

The combatants stood in anger, neither expressing the real reasons for their thirst for vengeance. Phillip Arrow sensed the killing mood in the air. It had been a long, long time since he had last felt it. It was more recent for men like Lacey and Hughes. Viet Nam had left that hidden American ability fine tuned.

Lawrence Massendale followed Turner's counter, "That picture was horrible. The police found the husband dead also. Really, Phillip, we are going to have to change our benefit plans. We pay off 100% for a suicide death, but if he had been unsuccessful and just landed in the hospital, we wouldn't pay a dime for medical benefits. They just made three very rich beneficiaries. We probably can't do anything about Jamison and her daughters, but I think we can make sure that it does not happen again. Christ, Phillip, Frank and I have been asking you for months to approve the change in that life insurance coverage....... ever since the Smith disappearance.

Frank Turner agreed, "Damn right! The next death that looks like suicide around here gets zero dollars. I will see to it this afternoon."

"Mr. Arrow, do you want me to fly Mrs. Jamison home tomorrow? We could do a first leg up to Calgary." Dane had changed the subject before a second death occurred. Arrow looked like he could scarcely control himself. Massey was in mortal danger, but did not know it. Dane had seen the killing look before. Arrow's eyes were steel grey.

"Yes, thank you, Dane. That was my idea.

"Lawrence Massendale, I swear to all my Ancestors that tomorrow at this time you are through at Union Arrow if you don't get the authorities to finish and approve their autopsy and have that body in the air with Dane. It is also your career if Hughes has five minutes of delay once he sets down in Canada tomorrow. Now get your quirky ass out of my sight. When Ms. O'Brian gets back from wherever she is, I want to see the both of you. Let's make that definite. Now get the Hell out of here!"

He then turned to Frank Turner. "Now what do you suggest?"

"We will need a transitional management for two or three months until the deadwood is cleared out and our new puppet is in place. I suggest that I stay here and take over as the President Designate until then. I will move in Steven, the Chemical President, to take over my duties back in Los Angeles."

Phillip Arrow felt old. He knew that Turner had planned to suggest this anyway. He had expected O'Brian, Massendale, and Turner to have recommended Jamison's firing today. His planned response was to have been a refusal, to say that he was pleased with John's work. He wanted that to be a surprise to all of them, as true as it was. Telling Jamison beforehand would have been tantamount to giving it away and forestalling the chance to see who would step forward. He should have told Jamison anyway. Had he killed himself last night? Who would know? Whatever the dead had dreamed, the deed was done. Arrow decided then he would drive over to the hospital to see Mrs. Jamison.

What an honest man Jamison had been, he thought. One doesn't have to be brilliant or aggressive on a corporate administrative staff, just honest and loyal. "Alright, you take over Frank. I wish you well. Lacey, will you walk with me?"

Phillip Arrow led Everett Lacey down the hall toward a small unused office. "It appears that the world of reality is running at a different pace than my plans."

"Sir?"

"Let's talk business for a few moments, then I am going to take the rest of the day off."

As they walked down the hall, Ev Lacey tried vainly to explain why it would be impossible to bring the computer system back to life quickly. Arrow was only half attentive and not at all acceptable to the idea of Lacey leaving.

Lacey had to add another idea. "Sir, since I can't use the computer, I have been thinking of doing further checking on Richard Smith. When I get back to Los Angeles, I want to look through the log of telephone messages from Henry's area. Perhaps, Smith made a call or two the day he disappeared."

"Forget Smith, Ev."

Phillip Arrow picked up the red desk telephone and dialed his office's number, an office on the other side of the building complete with a secretary and people waiting to talk to him. "Would you cancel the rest of my appointments for the day? Yes, that includes Ms. O'Brian and Mr. Massendale. I will want to see them after we fly out Mrs. Jamison. What? O'Brian is in my office now and wants to speak with me. Tell her I am glad that I stopped here and didn't walk all the way down to my office. It probably saved another death. No, don't tell her a thing. I will talk to her tomorrow. Please have my car waiting for me by the back door of the building in fifteen minutes."

Arrow placed the phone down. He turned to face Lacey. "I am about to go to my friends in New York again. I expect, however, no help. It appears that Union Arrow is now a target for an acquisition by some unknown raider. It appears someone or some group is purchasing our stock. Indeed, it also appears that whoever it is has no concern with security laws or disclosing who they are."

"And you don't know who it is? I know that there has, as yet, been no SEC disclosure. I have checked that much, at least until the system blew yesterday. You saw my note?" Lacey saw Arrow nod in the affirmative.

Lacey continued, "I also checked the requirements for reporting. If it is someone who has owned stock before or who had a partial position, they could claim an oversight. If it is just one person or group, they are going to be in big trouble with the SEC. I found only your request to exceed the reporting limits with the stock you have been purchasing.

"Then you knew that Union Arrow stock was being purchased?"

"Yes Sir. I figured that out two weeks ago. I know! I should have seen it earlier. My guess is that it is the Orioles."

"No, I don't think so. I have the Orioles President's word on it and that's better than all the written contracts I have ever seen. I also know for a fact that he is serious about acquiring those two Eastern lines. If I were the Norfolk Southern or the Kansas City Southern I would also watch out. What else do you know?"

"I know that Union Arrow is a vulnerable target. You diluted your personal ownership position by 23 % when you gave out stock to acquire the back half of the two acquired firms. When you purchased the targets, the total entity including Arrow Corporation was valued at about thirty two billion dollars with you taking just over eight billion in debt and draining cash flow by two billion. That was with your expected price earnings ratio, PE of 15. What has occurred is that the new Union Arrow has slipped down to the traditional railroad PE of 7 over the past three months on far lower than expected earnings. The stockmarket is looking at you as a railroad and not like it once did.

"The result is a market value of slightly over 2 billion with your holding but 8%."

"Not quite, it is 12 %. I have recently invested every dime I have. I have used up over 80 million dollars in purchasing another 4 %.

"Ev, the drop in price isn't really so unbelievable. It has happened

281

to most major companies that the market decides are conglomerates. It is control of the Company that I am worried about, not the price of the stock."

"How much do you control through the Savings Plan and old employee profit sharing plans?"

"Another 18 %."

"How much do you need to protect yourself? What type of cushion would you like?"

"The common rule is 30% and I have exactly that amount. But I think that this is different. We know who it is. It is the union funds who already own, I suspect 17 to 19 % before this action. I believe over 40% of Union Arrow stock has been purchased in the past two months. That would put them at 60% and my control at 30%."

"What can you do."

"Nothing that I can think of that is constructive. All I can do is plan to scorch the earth." Arrow smiled, Lacey had accepted the union idea.

"The primary problem is my Board of Directors. It would have been three years until anyone should have been able to gain control of my Board of Directors and forced me out. I had Turner, myself, Massendale and Jamison and my three children. That was a seven person majority out of the total Board of 13. The other 6 are 2 members each from the two acquired companies and my 2 friends who have served as outside directors for me for over twenty years. Practically, I have 9 votes on any matter with the acquired two companies 4 directors still being very hostile.

"The problem is that I do not believe Massendale's vote is on my side any longer. With the loss of Jamison, my control has shrunk to a 7 to 5 margin. That places me as only 1 vote away from losing my control."

"One vote? I count two and that is a lot in a case like this."

"Not if they gain a 50% position on the Board. If one of the presently friendly men are bought off, the vote would be 6 to 6 or 50% with that being sufficient to call for a Special Board meeting under the Corporate Charter that could end in stripping me of my title. They would ask that I not vote on any matter that affects myself. That would make any vote 5 to 6. And of course if something should happen to either of my two friends or Frank Turner, the result would be almost the same. The vote would then be 5 to 6 and call for a loss of confidence with my abstention."

"Can't you quickly replace Jamison?"

"Yes and I will do so as soon as possible. I am calling a Special Meeting in Los Angeles next Monday. I want you to be there. I was wondering if you would care to serve on the Board?"

"Me, Sir?"

"Yes, I would want you to rejoin the Company since your original investigation is now completed. Your position would be of a special projects nature. To set your place in the organization, you would have the simple title of Vice Chairman of the Board. I would want you to fly back with Dane tomorrow and wrap up what you have been doing. Just be there on Monday morning for the special meeting."

"Yes Sir."

Everett Lacey sat stunned in the small office long after Phillip Arrow had left the room to visit the hospital that had accepted Meg Jamison. Lacey was doubly stunned. The shock of seeing John Jamison lying dead still lay in his mind. The inclusion on a Board of Directors doubled the trauma. He thought of his hard work, the sacrifices of his mother who had raised him alone, the years of abject poverty. He had only dreamed of freedom, independence, and money to purchase food and clothing. Never had he dreamed of power with prestige. Would he be able to wear success well? Would it kill him as it had John Jamison?

17

Friday

Meg Jamison paid the taxi driver a large early morning tip and lifted her luggage for the short walk to the executive elevator. She had no black clothing, so she had dressed in her best. Wobbling on her heels, she set the two suitcases on the floor and hit the numbers for Turner's birthday. It was 6:15 AM and she had had little sleep. Phillip Arrow had been the first to visit her at the hospital. He had quickly sensed the starkness, the inhuman nature of the place, the way in which it could drive her insane. She had refused any sedative. Most of all, she wanted to think and remember.

Arrow had sent a secretary to pick up only her things from the hotel suite and had them in a new room, in a new hotel by the time he had checked her out and brought her across town. A limousine was scheduled to pick her up at 10:00 AM for the airport, but that could and would be changed.

Last night, Phillip Arrow had wanted to stay and Meg had wanted him to do so. He had been abashed. That cold man had actually sat there and cried with her! He had told her that John always operated at his best, that he recognized John's best was not well measured by the typical aggressive corporate mentality. He had also said that he was at fault. It was his personality flaw that never allowed him to voice praise as he saw it. John had never heard his support, nor sensed his appreciation for doing a difficult job with sensitivity and compassion.

Meg had sensed the ongoing change in herself as Phillip Arrow talked. The afternoon and evening had been like the ice cold water into which hot iron is plunged so that it might harden. He had come to console her. Instead, she had consoled him.

She did not know for whom he grieved. Surely it was not for John. Surely he need not have grieved for her. The precious part of her had died months ago.

As the elevator rose, she felt her anger and hatred grow. John had once repeated to her a commonly stated Arrow Corporate rule. You motivate by reward, fear, or hate and the best motivator was the latter. Frank Turner had killed her husband. She burned with hate. How dare Frank Turner to have defiled her husband's last moments!

The halls were empty, no alarms sounded as she walked toward the closed and locked door of the secretary's office that led to husband's office. A lock combination also was required at that door. Meg touched the numbers for his birthday. The door did not open. She then tried Turner's dates, still no open door. Meg tried her own birthdate and the door swung open.

She had waited to call her girls. She would do that after 8:00. She would first make a list.

Meg, sitting at her husband's table, stared at her scrawls. She could not stand sitting here next to the television screen. She stood and walked to the recessed area on the other side of the doorway. There she sat, inspecting a crystal vase that she found on the small table next to her soft, cushioned chair. She counted the ridges, not wishing her mind yet to rewake. She knew what she had to do. Search this office for any other evidence of Turner's. Her mind jumped. She could get into his office too, she surmised. Should she search his first? Did she have the time? Would she be caught? The fear of the thought brought her senses fully alive.

It was then she heard the faint buzz of the combination opening on the outer office door. Could her husband's secretary be here this early? Meg stood, vase in hand. Her husband's office door opened quickly and swung toward her, stopping only inches from her face. It then closed, with Frank Turner's back toward her, with his eyes looking toward the television video player, with his sure checking to see if the tape he had forced upon John was still there.

It had all happened in seconds. The world was crashing down onto her. She had to act.

Meg couldn't stand him. She couldn't stand the thought of their being in the same room together. What would he do to her when he discovered she was there? She was defenseless. In her mind she could feel his sure hands on her body.

With all her power she swung the vase. With all the tears of months and the hate and loathing of hours, she brought her back into the motion. She knew how to do it. Swing like Dane Hughes had said he had swung in New York, twelve inches past the spot you wish to hit. Swing all the way to the ground.

Frank Turner crumbled. Meg panted for air, her heart was in her throat. Was he dead? She could barely touch this body. Her fingers felt the throb of the heartbeat in his throat. He was still alive. Damn him!

Meg looked at the vase. Amazingly, there was no damage to the hard thick base. No damage whatsoever. She looked at the fallen man, now determined in what she must do. Putting down her purse, which somehow she still held in her left hand, she walked to the hall and down the corridor to the Mailroom door. There she found a four wheeled and two tiered supply cart. It was almost seven o'clock. She would have to hurry.

Meg struggled fiercely in her husband's office. Blood was beginning to seep from Turner's head. Please, she thought, he couldn't wake now. Not yet, Frank, not yet! She avoided the head wound and tried vainly to hoist Turner's body over the top of the cart. He was too heavy! She pulled his arms through the bottom section and then pushed him onto the bottom level. His arms and body fit, his legs dragged from the side. She bent and forced one of his legs under him, then the other. He was lying on his face and knees with his stomach down, but forced up by the bent knees. Your friend forced me to be like that, you bastard, she wanted to scream, now you do it!

Meg wheeled the unconscious Turner to the hall door. She looked down the paneled hallway, no one was there. She knew some employees arrived by 7:00, surely she would be seen. Quickly, she pushed the cart into the hall, leaving the office door open. At a pace approaching running, she pushed the cart toward the executive elevator. Its shaft was by the general elevator. Surely she would be seen! Please, she thought, don't make me wait in the hall for the elevator door to open.

The birthdate of Frank Turner was again entered and the door immediately opened. It had stayed just as he had left it! She walked to the back of the cart and pushed it into the small gaping opening just as she saw one of the adjacent larger elevator's doors begin to open. Meg rushed in and pushed the unmarked top button, the one above that for the floor she now was on.

She had a double wish. The door would not close fast enough. If the person or person turned to the left, she would surely be seen. If the button she pushed was a dummy, there was no reason for the door to close at all. It seemed as if minutes passed. No one walked past the door, no one looked in, no one saw her or the unconscious Turner.......and the door began to close.

The unconscious Turner moved a bit. Meg leaned down to see his eyelids twitch. He was becoming conscious!

The elevator door suddenly opened to the clear, clean Midwest morning. She again pushed the cart. As if it knew where it was going, it hit the hard graveled surface of the rooftop and turned toward the center of the building. In a long curve, she pushed the cart to the center court area. She could feel her light blouse begin to stick to her. Beads of sweat were on her forehead. Her heart still beat in her throat and she felt as if she were about to faint.

Was it from this spot where John had jumped? She pulled at the moaning Turner's body. She talked to the man. "You can't stand what you did, can you Frank? You wanted to make me cold, you son-of-a-bitch, well I am cold! I am just like you, Frank."

When adrenaline flows the body's functions change. What one notices when the fight or flight mechanism is triggered is oftentimes lightheadedness. The hair on one's neck does stand up, blood does go to the muscles and not the brain or the stomach, one does become far sighted and more keen of hearing. With real fright, the body can relieve itself of the weight of urine before a long run. But most of all, there is strength. The strength exists to run quickly, to climb trees, to lift large rocks. Somehow, without thinking, Meg had Frank Turner's body up onto the three foot rampart. With a heave, she had him hanging arms first over the wall.

I have only one regret, she thought, as she used his belt to shift his weight. John was awake when he fell. Get mushed, Frank. There will be no "Good-By."

Suddenly, he was gone. She heard no sound, she waited. Could a ledge have caught him? Then she heard the soft thump.

Meg looked around herself on the roof. Had anybody seen her? She looked at the nearby windows of the other high buildings, some of which towered over the roof on which she stood. She could not see through their glass. She looked at her watch. It was exactly 7:00. Then she looked at the rooftop itself, there were no cart tracks.

The cart was quickly back into the elevator, in moments it was returned to its place by the Mailroom door, and she back to her husband's office to pick up her purse. She looked at the vase, the floor, and the room. Was that all a person's life was worth, she thought, fifteen minutes? She now had time to search both offices. She would start with Frank's.

"I think we will be a few minutes early, Meg," voiced Phillip Arrow. "Hughes and LaBear will probably have a clearance and be ready to go when we get there. Massendale says that everything is ready. Your husband's remains are on board in external storage. A hearse will be waiting at the Calgary Airport and you will just touch down and go on. You won't have to get out. I understand that the funeral is next Tuesday."

The black Arrow limousine cruised down the road. Meg Jamison smiled at this man who was trying so hard. "Yes, please don't think anyone has to attend. I appreciate your sending someone up to arrange it. I have asked that just my girls and John's immediate family be there."

"Fine, I understand. Hughes will fly you up from California Tuesday morning and we will also fly your girls in if you wish. I asked that Massendale and Caroline O'Brian meet us at the airport this morning. I want them to ride back with me, business must go on you know. I also wanted Frank Turner there to see you off, but for some reason he hasn't shown up yet although they tell me his car is in the garage."

Phillip Arrow caught himself. Funny thing about a successful businessman. One somehow seemed to fit in business meetings around funerals and marriages. One did business all the time. He thought back on his marriage. Had he conducted any business that night before turning his attention to his new bride of forty years ago? He knew he had. He also knew he had worked the day after his marriage. Mary, forgive me, he thought.

The thought made him cease talking. Funny how attracted he was to this young widow. Ah, if he were only twenty years younger! Yes, it was good that he didn't explain to her why he had allowed Everett Lacey to ride with her. This was to be Dane's pilot team's last flight for Union Arrow. Over the months, the other teams would be changed, mainly by taking the acquired companies' people and letting his own go. Hughes and LaBear were his best. Yet he sensed that the outbound communication regarding his movements might well be stopped with just this one change. He would see if he were right after this trip.

"I did note that Everett Lacey will be flying back with you. He is Dane's friend and he will ride up front if you wish. Again, I apologize for Frank's absence."

"That is alright. Would you please tell Mr. Turner that I understand?"

Arrow caught something in the lady's tone as the limousine turned into the driveway, but he let it slide. Subconsciously, it was the honest statement, told truthfully which was instead one of his culture's common lies. A lie that is always told as a lie. She had told it as truth. It missed his mental flag, he was distracted. He was more aware of the silhouettes of Massendale and Caroline standing next to each other. He would crucify them on the way back. Damn, if he had ever put up with anybody screwing up on Company time!

I could kill him, thought Dane Hughes, a visibly upset Dane Hughes. Hank LaBear had walked into the private Calgary airport lounge and called a taxi. He had made two trips between the plane and the lounge. Ten minutes ago, he had walked back to the taxi area and departed. At least, that is what Dane had been able to piece together from what the lounge attendant reported.

Dane had seen him take his flight bag with a comment about washing up. He had paid no attention. It was probably no more than brushing one's teeth. Now he had two passengers waiting in the lounge for him to return. It was far too hot for anyone to sit in the Lear on the runway. Dane did not know where LaBear had gone. He just knew one thing for certain. He did not think that LaBear was coming back. Dane knew that Hank had been upset that the inside word was that Arrow was changing his original pilot force. But didn't Hank know that they were the best there were? That they were Arrow's own personal team? Had he been mad or did he just quit? Dane had no idea. Hank and he just did not talk.

Everett Lacey walked up to him, "What do you think?"

"I think that I either fly you to Los Angeles myself or we wait here for a day for a copilot."

"Can you fly it by yourself?"

"Yes, easily, but it's against regulations. I know, I know, I am the last to worry about rules and regulations. What I worry about is how strange all this is."

"Hell, I don't see anything strange about flying in a suicide's body, dumping it into a car that you will never see again, making the widow sweat in 100 degree temperature in a non air conditioned plane on steaming hot asphalt, making her think that she might have to stay with her dead husband tonight, and then making her stand in a public place feeling like screaming she's a widow. No, I think that it is just pure unadulterated torture. What are you, a masochist?"

Dane turned for the door. He was beaten and he knew it. He also knew that he was alive with the challenge of flying the Lear solo.

They were an hour out on a long curving northern route when Everett again talked to Dane. Meg had been riding co-pilot and learning to fly the Lear. Dane was determined to keep her mind off other matters and hence was teaching and quizzing, laughing and trying to reach the lady who seemed as off in the clouds at times as they actually were.

Lacey cramped himself into the Lear's now open doorway. "You know, I have been thinking hard."

"Does it hurt?"

"Yes, yes it does. Let me give you some facts that you may or may not know. First, Phillip Arrow doesn't trust his pilot corps, indeed he will be replacing them all because he knows that one of them is giving away his movements and perhaps some of his plans to competitors or enemies. Two, he suspects you most of all."

Dane face held a look that was incredulous. Like many badly hurt by other's words, he could not form a reply.

"Three, we are getting close to the end of the line on finding out what is happening. Four, Arrow, himself, had me fly out to Kansas City because he felt that he was close, very, very close. Five, Frank Turner is my choice for the Black Knight of Union Arrow and he doesn't show up today. Six, I found the data the other day, but the union burnt the circuits before I could analyze it. Or better put, they know I am getting close. Seven, Hank LaBear takes a dive in

Canada."

"So?"

"So, that means that LaBear was the leak that Arrow is looking for and Turner has a surprise for us."

Meg was now fully alert as she looked at both men. Frank Turner's name had made her nerves stretch raw. She knew that they were wrong, but surely she could not, could never tell them or anyone. "Oh, I think that that is the silliest thing I ever heard. I don't think either Mr. Arrow or Mr. Turner work that way."

Dane's mind was racing. There are many ways to blow down an aircraft. One can plant a bomb with a time detonator. A better device would use a pressure sensitive mechanism. A heat buildup capacitor attached to an engine or a simple electrical buildup capacitor would work just as well. What else? A knockout gas for the inside of an aircraft could be used. Running into a mountain or ocean would be a fine way to go for a sleeping crew. He knew that it was the most often used method to date of professionals. What else? The radios would have to go dead, everything would have to be coordinated. There could be no emergency broadcast, no clue as to sabotage.

Where would they do it? Dane immediately knew. His present flight path was abnormal, far too far north. There was no good reason to take this route. He should have questioned flying over to Seattle. Their route should first go south and then west, not west and then south. It had been LaBear who had set it up. It was a path of death.

They were to crash in the British Columbian or Washington State Cascades. Were they over the U.S. border yet? They could easily see beneath them the snow covered peaks. Dane immediately started to decrease altitude, then stopped. He would put Meg in charge with the autopilot and then make a quick search of the cabin with Everett. He asked, "Did anyone see Hank bring on anything before he disappeared?"

It was Meg who answered. "Yes, he put some groceries right behind Mr. Lacey in the cupboard .... right there."

Everett Lacey reached in and pulled out a zippered shut satchel. It was a plastic coated, round carrying case that would fit in the narrow deep storage compartment. He turned to show Dane and started to pull the ring to open the green and brown case.

"Stop!" Dane Hughes reached for the satchel. Still sitting in his seat, he reached for his pocket and extracted a penknife. He then carefully slit the side of the bag. Wires and sticks of explosives were shown. Dane's hand was steady, sweat was beading on his forehead. Lacey gulped for air.

Meg was the first speak, "If that really is a bomb, can't we just disconnect it now? Just cut all of those wires and we should be safe."

None of them could take their eyes off the slit satchel. "No, I don't think so," said Dane. "This thing is full of failsafes. See the wire and the switch here at the top. If we had zipped it open, it would go. These wires are arranged to trigger when any one of them but one is disconnected. We would have to know the sequence."

"What sort of timing device is in that box?" asked Lacey who was pointing at a small box wedged in one end.

Dane carefully viewed the box. Then he heard the sharp cut of static and he knew they were in deep trouble. The recently repaired Lear radios had just gone dead. All these things had to be in sequence. With luck, the radio cutout was scheduled for some period of minutes before their crash. Ground contact and radar would catch them without communications, a built to order explanation would occur for what was to come next. "I don't know. Leave it up here with me. You take Mrs. Jamison to the back of the plane and both of you strap in. I will give you the count of ten and then I am taking this thing down. We have to put it on the ground."

Meg protested, "Can't we just throw it out the door? Now that we know where it is, we can get rid of it."

"Open the door at this altitude and your blood boils. We are at 39000 feet and its minus seventy degrees and almost a vacuum. More important, I would bet that the trigger is altimeter related. I would also think this is just a backup. My communication wiring is gone, something mechanical is about to happen. He would have it hard-wired. Now get out of here! Drag her back there if you have to Ev and show her how to curl up."

A still protesting Meg Jamison was dragged to the back of the plane. They could hear Dane counting loudly and slowly. At the count of ten, Lacey plopped down in the co-pilot's chair. Dane was startled, "What the Hell!"

"I can't follow directions either. Besides, I am curious. There are only big grey, green and white mountains down there, or hadn't you noticed?"

In a screaming turn, tilted at 45 degrees the Lear again plummeted to the earth. "Arrow to earth" thought Dane, arrow to earth. He thought he knew what the failsafe satchel's triggering device was. Could it have been a complementing altimeter? Short range radio signals? He saw that his altimeter was gone along with his radio. Did they have this airplane so wired that they could follow it exactly in his plunge? What good were the runways in reach if they were below the critical altitude where the bomb would explode? When would the next failure occur?

Both men looked out the cockpit to the left. With airbrakes on and landing gear down, the Lear's speed and altitude was dropping quickly. Clouds covered the peaks and swept through upturned mountainous valleys. Trees were becoming visible in spaces among the clouds in their plunging spiral.

"What did you say?" Dane had heard Lacey mutter a question. Ev was now pointing to a long narrow lake. Dane turned tighter. It was a glacial trough filled with water. A high mountain cliff stood at one end and the lake ran from it to the top of another cliff that appeared to disappear down into the clouds. He could land from that end, if the clouds allowed him the visibility. Dane knew he never made a decision. It was the only high level spot that he knew of, it was their only chance.

"I just said I wonder why? Who are they trying to kill, Mrs. Jamison, you, or me? And if we knew who, would we know why?"

"Who the Hell gives a Damn!" Dane knew that he sounded like Caroline these days, but then, who the Hell did give a Damn! "Shut up and let me fly. Mrs. Jamison, you bend over back there and say your prayers. I will do my best. Sorry Ev, I didn't mean to shout at you."

"Perfectly alright, my friend, perfectly alright. Death is but a passing experience that we must all share. The Vikings thought it best to go out in style. I for one, would like to go out knowing why."

"Strap in tight. Maybe we can save that experience and plan something better than this. Landing gear up, I want to be able to control this thing with some quick speed." Dane was looking down. All he could see at the end of the lake was a white cloud bank. There was no such thing as level land down there. Even if it were level it would be covered by trees. Damn the clouds! Dane thought of his times in high mountain country when storms rolled in. Sometimes one could not see ten feet in front while walking. At a hundred plus knots there would be no chance.

He looked quickly at Lacey. "It was one of two, Turner or Massendale. Arrow is out, so is Jamison, Caroline wasn't there yesterday, Mary Sue is not clued in, Meg and I would be committing suicide."

"Caroline was there this morning."

The insult inflamed Hughes, an extra shot of adrenaline flowed through his body. They were twenty feet above tall evergreens. He was approaching from the high cliff side to first overfly the landing area. Ahead was the tall cliff below which they would see the lake and then the cloud bank. He saw it then. Damn, the cloud bank was moving in over the lake. He would have to fly into it. What was behind the cloud?

He had never doubted his ability to fly. He could feel the weight of the Lear and sense the sluggishness of the controls. Would he skip like a rock? Could he hit the slot coming back? He knew he could, he had been doing it since he was a kid playing the pinball machines.

Dane swept down over the cliff, the lake appeared briefly, and then cold, stark white clouds enveloped them. He pressed out away from the lake in a brief turn to the left and then a steeper turn to the right. He was fashioning half a circle eight, now the steep curl to the left and a straight run back to the lake. He looked at the direction and saw 90 degrees, slightly too much. The opposite of his incoming was 88, 268 minus the 180. He had to hold the right altitude with no measure to spare. He would have to feel it. Dead ahead, all he saw was white. Would his radar scope help him in these tight quarters? He did not have time to glance to see.

They would come out of the clouds only feet before the lake's cliff. Did a waterfall drop off there or were there high trees? Dane held the flaps down and checked to see that the gear was up. Could he, if he missed the slot, put the Lear on its tail and escape the cliff at the lake's end?

If only the surface of the lake were long enough. If only he did not come in too low and hit the face of a fog shrouded, hidden, forward cliff. If only he did not come in too high and hit the back of the lake with its boxed in cliff wall. If only he did not go too far to the right and hit the forest. If only this bird would keep flying.......if only a water landing were possible.

In the service, Dane had had several friends who had gone their way into the sea. The aircraft manufacturers claim that one can easily land their products in light to moderate ocean swells. They never bother to show the young Navy pilots how to do it.

Most of all, no one tells them that it takes a perfect landing and plenty of nerve. The tendancy is to come in with the nose too high, mainly because of the fear of slicing into the water. But when the nose is too high, the tail hits first, then the nose pops over, and then the craft cuts into the water like a knife heading for the depths like a powered rock.

Dane knew that he needed to hit level, perfectly level, with the Lear's belly first. Any catching of the wing engines or tip would flip them over. He also had to hit the water as close to the front cliff as was possible. If he could skip across, he would need the lake's full distance. Still, all he could see was white.

Suddenly, the lake was there and he had come in too low. But then that was not his fault. He had hit the altitude where one of his engines had suddenly shut down. Hank LaBear's work was done. Dane opened his flaps.

At full fly and going much too fast, the Lear hit the smooth lake's surface four feet from the near shore like a flat stone and then skipped again and again to settle into the water. It had all happened in seconds. Lacey and Hughes watched the lake's end and the shear cliff rush toward them.

In an eternity of dozen plus seconds, they stared the cliff into submission.

All sat in their seats as the Lear rested with its body on a narrow beach at the far end of the lake. There was not a sound. Finally, Meg began to move around in the back of the plane. It was she who asked them if they were unhurt. Both replied in the affirmative.

Dane looked out the side. They were resting, nose up, on a narrow beach which appeared to be part of a ledge that dropped off into untold depths. Ahead of them a small grassy inlet ran into the cliff wall. Forty feet of flat delta-like, grass covered land showed off a narrow stream running from a crack in the cliff's surface.

Ev got up first, "Great flying. No, better than great, fantastic, but do me a favor. Let me have only one of these exhibitions."

"No, I overshot, when it came to it, I was chicken. If the engines hadn't shut down, we would be plastered against that cliff." Dane followed Lacey out of the cockpit and cracked open the door. He looked out. The air was crisp and cold. Meg followed him out the door, clattering down the steps in her high heels. Lacey came next, along with several blankets and a bag of snacks. As he stepped from the plane, they could see it shift. Their weight in the front had been tilting the Lear forward, now it shifted backwards, almost to begin a slide out into the lake.

Ev spoke into the silence of the lake, "Funny how ever since I was a boy, I liked to push rocks over a cliff or throw rocks into a stream. I feel like helping it go."

"That might not be such a bad idea. The crash signal finder probably doesn't work and the radio's gone, but some of it may be working. Whoever wanted us down, probably is pinpointing the spot we are standing right now. They would keep something going. If they are professionals, they will have to show some evidence of their kill. They would have to be able to identify the site of our crash."

Lacey had already walked to the front of the Lear to lean against it. Hughes quickly joined him. Meg screamed, "What about our luggage! How are we going to survive?

It was too late. The Lear had slid tail first and was rapidly taking on water. They watched it slowly settle in the water. Soon, it sank to explore the unknown cliff face below the surface of the waves. It was as if the Lear never had existed. Meg again broke the mountain silence. "You dummies, we needed the luggage. I don't even have my purse......"

She was rudely interrupted by Hughes who tore into her as he ran from the ledge. Lacey, without words, was following. Right as she was, thought Hughes, he wanted to be away from the lake and in the center of the small delta when........

The water boiled with the explosion of the Lear. The bomb had been pressure sensitive. The Lear was no more.

Thirty minutes later, they were about to move off toward the other end of the lake and hopefully begin a trek down the mountain. As they stood there, clouds appeared to fall upon them like wisps of wet smoke. The mist covered the trees so that they could now barely see the other end of the lake. Thirty minutes later and Dane knew that they would have been dead.

The adrenaline had washed from their bloodstreams. They were feeling the cold and the exhaustion fell upon them like the clouds. From some source, Meg had found the strength to talk. Two silent men had seen her walk to the lake's end and with a long stick, coax the bodies of five stunned fish to the shore. There Lacey had killed and gutted them with Dane's knife. Somewhere tonight, if they could start a fire, they would have a meal to eat. The Lear's bomb and explosion had done some good.

Dane led off through the talus, large debris-like rocks that had peeled off the face of the cliff above them with the periodic freezing and thawing of water in the rock face's cracks. Salmonberry bushes sported their late summer green and red growth among this rubble.

Dane believed that there were one or two similar lakes below this one. Mountain lakes in the north are glacial cups, he knew, scoured by ancient and disappearing ice. Only in August and September would the lakes be as warm as they were now. He had seen no sign of human activity. Perhaps the lake saw no or only the infrequent visitor. With such an altitude, the fish life was small and stunted. Perhaps there was a non accessible ridge separating the lake from the mountainside below.

Meg was still talking, "Will they be able to see the Lear at the bottom of the lake from the air when it clears up?" Meg's question came from folded arms held tight against the afternoon chill of the mountain shadows.

Ev smiled at her and broke his twenty minute silence, "Next question. Dane, where to now, oh Captain?"

Dane pointed toward the lake's end and concentrated on Meg's next questions. "We could starve out here. How will anyone ever find us in this fog? How far do you think we are from civilization?"

Dane walked over to some salmonberry bushes. "Meg, relax. With this fruit and an occasional fish, we could stay alive for a month. You can't argue that we don't have enough water. Our biggest problem is exposure. You are fine for 51st Street on Manhattan on a summer day, but not so for here. I suggest that we start moving faster to keep ourselves warm."

The going was slow. First the rocks of the talus and then the bushes that grew under the evergreens impeded their progress. Laceys and Dane's shoes were not made for hiking, but only a minor encumbrance compared to Meg's heels. The men helped her over many of the difficult places. She refused to allow them to try to cut the heels off with their small knife.

They were circling the lake to the left. Dane was aware of the cliff

298

that bordered the lake. He found it not impossible to vision himself pushing through the bushes to step over the side. He felt that such an irony was not impossible. Where skill, ability, and luck had watched over him that afternoon, nothing looked over the careless man. To assist him, he wished that Ev would return to the living. Everyone of Meg's questions were his to answer. Lacey appeared to have the problems of the world in his appearance. He was walking in silence, head bowed, to think something out.

After awhile, Meg turned silent also. She still believed that this experience was unnecessary. There should have been some other way to deal with that satchel bomb. Having told these men that fact four times, she found they no longer wished to discuss it. All were silent, all were tiring as they walked in their own lonely worlds.

Finally, they reached the end of the lake. A small creek bed led to a two hundred foot drop to what appeared to be a larger lake below. They could barely make out the grey surface of the lake through the damp, cold mist. Dane sat down to enjoy one of his rare cigarettes. The other two shunned him as if he were sinning against Nature. There was no visible way down over the cliff.

It was Lacey who came to the rescue in the late afternoon haze. "Look at that tree."

Twelve feet above the ground was a mark that could only have been made by an axe. Following its direction, Dane found another and soon a third. A short half hour walk up a slope ran into a wood on the other side of the lake. A ledge was divided by a rope that disappeared over the side. It was tied to a tall tree with a scar showing the badge of a Boy Scout Troop. He shook his head. Sometimes his pioneer blood ran thin. He looked at the rope's course down the side of the mountain. What parents might say if they knew their eleven year old boys had scaled that loose rock wall to originally place that rope!

Lacey summed up the ego-shattering moment that was mingled with relief. "If ten year old boys can hike to this lake, I think we are safe."

And they were. Lacey, in the fading light, went over the side first. Dane pulled the rope up and tied it to Meg. He then lowered her over the side. After the rope was extended to its full length, he quickly followed. It was dark when they found the seemingly broad two foot wide path that led around the larger lake. It brought them to a shelter built, by its sign, fifty years ago by the CCC during the Great Depression. With the sign and the trees' Boy Scout scars, they knew that they were in the northern Cascades just south of the Canadian border. In their mid thirties and forties, they argued over the words that had formed the "C" initial that was repeated three times.

Dane knew that they were close to civilization and needlessly spoke the words. Both Ev and Meg, however, had turned to the task at hand. The shelter was awash in a sea of litter. They found tin plates and plastic spoons, but no available firewood. Finally, Ev and Dane foraged far for dry wood while Meg finished cleaning the grounds.

They ate in an exhausted silence and they ate surprisingly well. Meg's smelly fish, peanuts, raisins, and chips from the plane, and berries from their walk filled them. With the night, a breeze had started to blow off the cliffs and the water. Soon the mist and clouds departed to reveal a black, black sky with brilliant pinpoints of stars. As the night fell upon them, the stars grew more brilliant. An almost neap moon was already high in the sky, soon to disappear behind the lake's black cliff wall.

Lacey finally broke the spell. "How many men, for how many hours, have spent their time gazing into embers under these stars? Hear the cry of the loon? This cool night, this burning fire, this splendid but simple meal, and the sound of that distant waterfall are all the connections that we have to our ancestors. We have a million years of unrecorded history. All we can truly share with them is to experience their experiences, to feel as they must have felt."

Meg excused herself to walk off into the woods. Ev poked the fire. In a clear soft voice, that only Dane could hear, he said, "You or me first."

"Me," was Dane's reply. "We are in more trouble than we ever dreamed possible. If those folks are good, and I believe they are, they will have sorted out the radio signals from the Lear. They will know that no major damage was done when we came down, they will know where we landed, and from the maps they will guess where we are tonight. We should have smashed that plane up and gotten rid of it quicker.

"Tomorrow they will come looking for us. I suspect that we are three or four hours from a mountain road and that this lake serves as a base camp for a series of side excursions like we took today. It has to. Look at the size of this shelter and the usage. All we have going for us is that we are all healthy. Whoever they send looking for us will most probably meet us on the same path we take out of here. They are

300

either flying in right now or already at the point where the path meets the road. I can picture running into them on the trail. We will be cut down like sheep."

Ev Lacey stared into the fire, "Well, you know more about this than I do. Tell me, Dane, have you shared any of your and my conversations of the past week with Caroline?"

Dane looked Lacey square in the eye. How had he pulled that question out of the air? From what they had been discussing? "Yes, the last time was on Wednesday. She was off to a series of afternoon meetings with Lawrence Massendale and Frank Turner and then back East. She could have told either. Also, I think she talked to Arrow. And don't point out the fact that she did not go back East. I know that she stayed in Kansas City."

"What did you tell her?"

"I told her that you had found out who it was, that it was Mary Sue. No, to be exact, you did not tell me that it was Mary Sue. I used your word, that of 'daughter.' You never told me it was Mary Sue."

"You know that Caroline is, was having an affair with Massendale and that he is divorcing his wife, Mary Sue, as of last Tuesday."

It was obvious that Dane did not know. Dane immediately stood, turned slowly and walked off into the dark woods. Meg walked back with a questioning glance at the silence and his look of shock as he passed her. The silence continued. Meg huddled in front of the fire and had the good sense to remain silent. Dane soon returned with cut evergreen bows which he arranged with tips downward close to the fire and over which he spread one of the blankets. No one spoke until Dane broke the silence, "Mrs. Jamison, you may sleep here. I will make another bed for us with the other blanket and we can take turns sleeping and keeping watch tonight."

"That is silly. For what would you keep watch? Double the size of that bed, put one blanket down and we will use the other one for cover. I also suggest that we take our clothing off and dry it on the rack there. We are all terribly wet and cold."

"Don't you think that we will be rather cramped?"

"Yes, hurry up. I am tired."

Dane silently found some more branches. Meg Jamison walked down to the lake shore to look at the dark cliffs against the deep black lake sparkling with the light of a thousand stars. When she returned, the two men were lying under the blanket.

No one spoke, the fire played shadows on the trunks of the nearby trees. A distant waterfall could be heard. Meg had turned her back to the men who had taken off their outer clothes and arranged their shoes to dry. Dane was embarrassed, while Lacey was again lost in thought.

Something that Dane had said in his confession had bothered Lacey. He knew that he was close to the answer. Could someone close to Caroline have a role in all this? He had been wrong. It wasn't Turner. Turner was one mean man, but he was not dishonest. He had just been born with a void, a total lack of feeling, sensitivity, or empathy for any other human being.

There were too many loose ends. Where did Richard Smith fit in or was he just a coincidence? Wasn't it Phillip Arrow who said that there never, ever had been such a thing.....'a coincidence'?

Dane tried to make light of the sleeping arrangement. "This may not be such a bad idea, Mrs. Jamison, but I think you should sleep in the middle. I don't know if I can trust this guy."

"I was planning on it."

"Please, Mrs. Jamison!"

Meg Jamison stood at the bottom of the bed. She first slowly stripped off her blouse and skirt. Then she unhooked her bra and draped it over the drying rack. Finally, bending down to undo her strapped heels, she raised to also hang them to dry. Her nylons and old fashioned garters followed in slow motion and then her bikini panties in a slow stripping action that left the two men short of breath.

Meg didn't say a word, but instead walked up the center of the blanket and slowly leaned over while rubbing her body. She slid into the bed. Lacey had turned with his back to her as she walked over the blankets, Dane lay on his back. "Please turn toward me, Mr. Lacey, and let me snuggle up against you to get warm."

Dane counted the seconds. It seemed an eternity. He had counted ninety slow seconds of slow twisting movements as Meg Jamison positioned herself on the hard bed.

He barely heard her whisper, "Dane, now please turn toward me. That's right. Move close. Yes, now hold still for a moment."

A half minute of breathless silence followed. Dane complied. He felt the hardness of her upper body against his chest. "Thank you, Gentlemen," she barely breathed, "now I promise not to say another word tonight."

18

Saturday

It was early morning before the dawn. Meg Jamison traced the flicker of the burning fire on the trees above them. The men slept a sleep of quiet death. Totally exhausted, they could not see the first trace of grey to the East that surely told of the coming morning. Meg had just replenished the fire. The air had been shockingly cold. Her skin felt tight and her morning missions were accomplished. How these men slept! Hopefully they would feel as good as she did now when they awoke. It was good to be alive. It was good to feel the warmth of their bodies, better yet was the warmth of the fire on the blanket covering their feet.

Twelve hundred miles away another fire started slowly.

It was located midway in the house, by the doorway to the master bedroom. The windows were closed, the blinds were drawn. The ceiling hatch leading to the attic was shut. The house presented an airtight jar, not a natural flue. A fire could not burn in this oxygen starved area.

Yet it did. The fire burned slowly in the chemicals left to form its core. These materials needed no oxygen. Still, the redwood rafters refused to ignite against the chemicals' intense heat.

But then the fire hit the other chemical trials and raced in a streak toward the rafters. Soon they formed a solid ring around the attic

303

opening causing the moveable lid to drop to the hallway floor.

Wood began to ignite. The hallway grew smoky and what light there was first faded and then reappeared as the flames grew larger. The air, drawn in through the attic vents, became a slight breeze.

Yet, if one had been in any of the rooms at the other end of the home, no notice would have been made of the smoke. From the outside, it would have taken a skilled eye in the daylight to see the smoke beginning to pour from the vents under the eaves. Yet there was no daylight. The sun had not yet lightened this portion of the western sky.

And there was no skilled eye. It was five o'clock AM on a Saturday morning and no human eyes were turned on this beautiful Santa Barbara home that sat high on the hill.

The fire began to run along the attic rafters. The heat in the hall now was unstopable. Two bedrooms were engulfed in flames in an explosion of fire. The entire inside of the home was feeling the heat of combustion. Windows cracked. A front door exploded as the living room flashed into fire. And finally, the flames burst through the cedar shake roof to drink gustily of the oxygen rich air.

Still no one saw the flames. For ten minutes the flames burnt on. Finally, a car drove by and stopped. The driver, an older man, first thought of survivors, but could not approach the house because of the heat. He finally ran across the road to scream the neighbors awake.

It was another ten minutes before the first fire truck pulled up to the house. By that time, the redwood and cedar home was caving in to the vacuum created by the combustion and consumption. The firemen touched their hoses to the nearby trees to keep the flames from spreading. There was nothing that could be done for the structure.

Ahead of them was the task of cleaning up and searching for the bodies of possible victims. They were told that the owners were in the Midwest and their search confirmed that the home was not inhabited. It was only later morning when the officials first became uneasy. It was then that they learned that both the residents had died during the three days preceding this fire. That is, the husband had died and the wife was presumed killed in an aircraft crash, an aircraft that had carried her husband's body. Could this much destruction be unconnected?

That wife and two men lay awake watching the sky begin to lighten. They told themselves that the warmth and the rest was essential and that rising at this time would be useless. The blackness and greyness had begun clearing away to begin a day with a sky free of clouds. It was going to be a beautiful day.

"Do you think that they will find us today?" It was Meg who voiced the first words.

Neither of the two answered. It was as if they could not talk. Finally Dane replied, "Meg, you might as well be told now. Ev and I believe that we will have killers waiting for us on the trail. Our best hope is to walk out of here in a hurry. You may want to be found, but Ev and I would rather walk out unnoticed, catch a ride, and make it back to Los Angeles on our own."

"Roger," was Lacey's reply.

"Well, I think that you are both paranoiac." Meg shook her head and crawled out of the bed and walked to her clothes. After last night, she was going to make them watch her dress. "If there was a bomb, it probably was nothing more than your friend Hank LaBear going crazy. I heard you say yourself, Ev, that both Dane and he faced being replaced as employees. You two are just too crazed by your imaginations. Moreover, I can assure you that Frank Turner had nothing to do with it."

It was Lacey who summed up their thoughts, "Meg, you are really something. We admire you greatly, you are beautiful, smart, and tough in a manner of diamonds, not steel. But this world turns with a herd of people, some of whom are just plain evil. To live in it, you have to plan your course and take care to associate with only those that you choose. It is something like choosing to walk through either a barnyard or an open field. If you walk through the former, you can't help but get some of it on your shoes. We have been walking in manure of late.

"It is something like raising children. Expose them to the world as the liberal teachers suggest and they will be soiled. We just don't, as adults, remind ourselves that the learning process goes on throughout our lives. We have picked up some type of disease, perhaps by chance or for some unknown reason that we don't quite know. Whatever, it is best that we pay attention to the symptoms and stay away from people who might muck us up further."

Meg shook her head. Hughes was morose and Lacey was losing the ability to express himself. What could she do with these two crazies?

The morning breakfast of nuts and raisins passed quickly and in silence. Meg had taken charge of the food. She parceled out only small portions. In all but fifteen minutes the two men were ready to walk the trail. Meg was still at the lake's edge trying to wash her face with the ice cold surface water. Dane spoke, "Do you think that we should tell her that it is impossible to wash that smoke and grease off her face with lake water?"

"No, she has turned silent and hostile. I don't know if she appreciated your sneaking out of bed last night after she went to sleep to cut off the heels of her shoes."

"I saw that you were awake when I did it and also awake, I believe, when I finally passed out. Did you figure out what was keeping you so wide awake last night?"

"Yes, I did......I think. I was missing the boat all along in the same way for both questions. It was the lady."

"Mary Sue was responsible for bombing my plane? Why? Did she think that the slug Massendale would be on Board? Lord, Lacey, sometimes I agree with Meg."

"Sometimes you don't listen to what others and your senses tell you." Lacey stared at Hughes. Could he really trust Dane with the weight of his ideas? It was at that moment that Lacey decided not to tell Dane Hughes. Something was tragically wrong here. He would tell Meg Jamison. If something happened to him, she could carry the message to the authorities.

Meg walked from the lake and picked up the small bag of food. Striding off up the well marked path, she said, "Come on, let's get going."

The lake sat in a bowl within a bowl and it was two miles later that they rested on the top of the second hill leading to a path that rapidly fell off over the side of the mountain into a third bowl. The ancient glacier had crawled down the mountain forming gigantic steps. Meg's lead had greatly hastened their pace. Rather than waiting for her, they often had to hurry to keep up. After a quick snack of raisins, Meg finally spoke again, "You know, it is strange. We have been together for a full day, slept together, and discussed everything, yet neither of you have said anything about my husband. I know that you both must have had some dislikes concerning what he was doing. Just what did you think of John? And don't either of you lie to me."

Dane spoke first, "We liked your husband, Meg. He was not a close friend, but then that was to his credit. Leaders and top corporate men are not suppose to associate that closely with the troops." He had decided to lie anyway.

"Ev, he just lied to me again. What was it about John that alienated the two of you so? You know that he was not in on any of your so-called conspiracies. Why did you not take your fears to him?"

"Meg, let me think for a bit on this one. As a man he was a pure quality. But I think that your question is not what we thought of him as a man, but as a corporate being. Correct? All right, I will try to tell you......uh, in thirty minutes when we rest again. Let's put another mile or two under our belts."

Meg nodded at Lacey's response, stood and walked off down the trail. They soon walked by another lake just like the Lear's grave and similar to the lake with the shelter. They climbed a hill at the far end of the lake opposite to a cliff with a waterfall from the lake above where they had spent the night. Tall evergreens towered above them. The trees' dark brown and grey gnarled bark gave a perfect background to the green ferns and grapelike bushes with dark green foliage. Looking down on the lake as they climbed, they could see the water stirred by a slight wind that now whispered back toward the lake and the mountains from the valley below. The dense forest was starting to awaken. They could hear the morning calls of various birds that announced their passing.

Mountains evolve through countless subtle differences during a morning, thought Dane. He now had more time to notice the changes. The energetic leader of their small troop was now starting to noticeably falter. The last hill was no easy climb, it had taken a full sixty to seventy minutes, a disappointment to all who had earlier thought their walk would be straight down to a road. Still, the path was now wider and easier. It looked much used and on a Saturday morning, they should encounter some fellow hikers although probably none of student age. School started early in August in the Rockies and the West remembered Dane. Perhaps they would see no one on the way out.

At the top of the hill, they viewed a brown downward switchbacking path into the forest below. Meg begged a rest, although Lacey wished to go on. Looking back at this third lake, it sat like a jewel in a dark icy green bowl. Looking down and away from it, they could see the path now stretching down and away across the far edge of a canyon caused by the stream leading out of the lake.

Other mountains were now in view. Stretched across some of these were wide brown swaths of clear cutting. Men had visited these hills and had left the scars of logging. With luck, they would run into a similar cutting as they descended this mountainside. Such a cutting, Dane knew, would have graveled roads that carried the logs from the mountains, that these dirt cuttings would eventually lead to paved ones, and that the paved roads would lead to towns with sawmills and safety.

The sun was now touching the top of the hill on which they sat. They could feel its warmth sink into them as they sat on an exposed fallen log. Meg made Ev live up to his promise, "Yes, I believe I made it, though don't rest for me, Gentlemen. Now, Everett, have you thought of a delicate enough way to phrase your thoughts concerning my husband?"

"I won't be delicate, Meg. I can not because much of what I will say will probably someday be said of me. We are what our world asks of us, not heroes, but rather corporate men. We are in many ways much like gangsters."

"John was a gangster?"

"Oh, yes, he was a nice gangster, but nevertheless, he was a gangster. I don't know if it is possible to succeed without being one.

"John Jamison was an accomplished gangster. You see, Meg, U.S. corporations are suffering from an economic robbery in the 1980s that puts to shame any comparison to the thievery existing in the 1930s. They are being run by general management who, although they are working for an organization and supposedly attempting to accomplish business related goals, always, always have their own personal success as their primary goal. Personal internal corporate survival is the primary goal, not the survival of the corporation.

"Rather than be individuals who achieve results through the actions and efforts of their subordinates for the good of the Company, they achieve only those results that have some meaning to their own personal success. Your husband had a long history of success within the Company before he was asked to pay the price of operational management. During all those years, he robbed Arrow, the people he worked with, and the Company he worked for as surely as we are sitting here.

"Let me give you some of the most recognizable characteristics and perhaps you will be able to see something of this view. These men are first noticeable by their smiles and good natures, so shallow that only their superiors are protected from the depth of their despair. These individuals attempt to project a corporate man picture, they are pleasant, agreeable, almost plastic. Their reactions to situations that affect the way in which their superiors view them personally are their greatest signal. They are only truly secure when they are involved in securing or reinforcing their boss's image or opinion. I believe, accomplished 'brown noses' would be their best description.

"Within a corporation, there are better clues. Foremost, there is the boundaried department. A gangster always stakes out his territory and is extremely careful not to allow others either to communicate or cross check over his boundaries. Although paying lip service to the concept of being a team member, this team play is applied only to subjects in others' territories. When it comes to his own, he goes no further than being an agreeable chap at committee meetings.

"There is the hoarding of information. Much of the power of these men comes from the ability to shield information that might be essential in the decision making process. This allows the gangster to make the best decisions, if the situation arises where he is called upon to make such a decision, in front of his peers or to show up those peers."

Meg sat silently staring back at the lake. Dane was also quiet. Ev continued, "There is also the elimination of threats. Gangsters pay careful attention to the abilities of their subordinates. They are quite careful in two areas. The first is that of employment. They very rarely bring on board an individual with proven potential for succeeding them as managers. When this has been inadvertently done, either by mistake or by force of a situation, they go to great pains in ridding their departments of this problem. Subtle pressures, innuendos, slanders, assignments of boring tasks, criticism, and other personality destroying weapons are employed. Then, there is always slowing down the salary growth, there is no finer way to terminate a man than to keep his compensation low so that the marketplace has an easy job of attracting him.

"Meg, there is staffing with incompetents, overstaffing, security checks, buffering of staff from higher levels, smothering the individual's ability for personal experience and hence asset growth, I could go on and on. The point being that your husband fit them all. For years he played this game successfully at Arrow Corporation, it was only during the past months when he was thrown out into the real world, the world of sales and services, not the world of bureaucracy, where he began to pay the price. John was perfect for a corporation, he fit the job, he fit the corporate needs better and better each year. Finally, he was so good at it that he was noticed and promoted to a position that required other skills."

Meg continued to stare out across the hills and the water. Finally she turned to Lacey, "Thank you, Everett. I understand what you are saying, but I think you too tough on John and perhaps yourself. Neither of you invented corporate life. The world presents us with roles to play. I have had tennis, bridge, a club, shopping, a house to clean, and an occasional daughter returning from college. When you have such a niche, you are expected to react in a certain way. The reason for that is that experience shows that only very few approaches will succeed in fulfilling these tasks' demands. We do what we do to survive. From the way you talk, I would suggest that you attempt to find another type of environment in which to live your life. If you see so well, you probably will never be happy. Think of yourself as the man who knows that the end of the world will occur in ten days. Everyone who doesn't know is happy, only you will suffer from such a serious understanding."

She rose from a sitting position and consciously stretched, reaching toward the sky. She then led off down the path. Ev and Dane sat and looked at one another. Dane spoke, "I just hope that we get off this mountain in a hurry. She is not only asserting herself as a natural leader of this small troop, but she will take our personalities apart in the process and put us back together. I think you missed something in your little speech though."

"What is that?"

"All gangsters have wives. You would be dynamite with a lady like that as a wife."

The day and the trail wore on. They had climbed another taxing ridge, this one as high as the original one that towered over the lake in which the Lear had crashed. Midafternoon passed and still the mountainous trail continued to curve downward. Dane had not expected this much of a hike and all were exhausted. He continued to search the sky with ears and eyes for a helicopter searching the area. If anyone was looking for them, they would do it the sure and quick way. Dane had enjoyed the day. Like many campers, he had finally relaxed and begun to walk with the pace of Nature. After a late snack, he found that he had to excuse himself with a yell that he would catch up. Privacy and paper were his present needs, and he had much of the former and none of the latter. He was soon on the trail again. Jogging down the path, he felt light, rested, and surprisingly ready to run.

It was then he heard the shout and scream.

He knew that he had been too lazy, too stupid, too exhausted. What had happened? He broke into a full run.

A half mile at a furious pace caused him to pull up short to catch his breath. Just before he was to come around a turn of clear grey basalt rock, he heard the angry voices.

It was as if he had been shot. Dane jumped off the path and back into the underbrush on the left side of the ridge. He rested, bent down like an animal on his hands and knees.

The voices were still there. Dane picked his spots among the brush stems and began his move around the ridge to his left. He had to find a place where he could listen, if not see, before any chance could be acted upon. He thankfully had heard a scream, not a shot.

Finally when he reached such a spot for observation, it was not the type of place that any potential hero would have picked. The basalt top of the ridge was barren of trees. He had half circled the spot where tall men stood. He now looked up and down the path. His quick glance down the path saw an open escape. He looked the other way. He saw what looked like the same two men that he had met in New York standing over two bodies on the ground, each man carried high powered rifles with scopes. Both rifles were pointed at the ground.

Then he looked to Meg and Ev. They were at the ends of the rifles, both face down on the ground. Lacey's hands were tied behind him. How could they have been so careless? These two had obviously picked their spot of ambush below the basalt top. As the path wove across the open area, Lacey and Meg had been open prey.

Dane viewed the basalt top. It was open on three sides. The fourth was bordered by the forest through which he had circled. Toward the far mountains, it opened into space. He guessed it was the cliff face of another glacier bed, this one facing the northeast. Dane ducked across the path and crawled to his left. Finally, he could look down on the actual residual of a glacier that was piled at an angle of thirty degrees against the cliff. No lake below this cliff, just one of the small northern glacial remnants that dotted the northern mountains. Its northeastern exposure had delayed its melting for centuries. Dane Hughes crawled closer to the edge. Could he approach along the cliff, below their view? They were directly above the glacier's ice, still white with snow. It stretched from the cliff for six hundred yards to a grey creek bed and a small blue lake.

The sheer grey face of the cliff stretched down before him. A foot closer and he would slide over the edge. There was no way to get at the guarding men unless he were to charge across thirty yards, half open forest and half open rock. As perfect as the area had been for an ambush, it was totally imperfect for Dane to attempt any unarmed rescue. He peered through the underbrush. With both of their backs toward him, he might be able to rush them. It was, however, totally improbable that he could cover the thirty yards without detection. He must accomplish it in parts.

He crawled closer to the edge and looked straight down. One always overestimates height from this distance he thought. The drop must be sixty, no, seventy feet to the ice. He again looked at the glacier ice and saw that it was separated from the cliff wall. Periodic warming and cooling of the rock had melted the ice against the cliff wall. A distance of fifteen feet separated the ice from the wall. He peered down into the black void between the ice and the cliff wall. How high was the glacier's ice? Perhaps another seventy feet. There was no way to survive the fall onto what were surely boulders one hundred and forty feet below.

Dane turned his attention to the two men who were looking back up the path which Dane had circled as he worked his way around to the left. How could they have been so careless this afternoon? A paved road and an airport must be close by. The two had landed, scouted the area, plotted the Lear's crash signal, and driven up during the night. It was possible, very possible, if the two were as professional as Dane believed them to be.

Dane Hughes almost wept with frustration. Novels of romance would have any reader believe that such times are when men rise to the top of their courage, when they contemplate and accomplish great feats of skill and daring. From Viet Nam, Dane knew that untrue. Most heroic situations are products of average men doing average deeds on average days. History is then a lie perpetrated upon these deeds, usually after the actors have died. Dane sat huddling against a tree trunk in a fetal position while he tried to listen to the men's words.

"Niggra, you get up and walk over to that cliff's edge."

As both men turned to watch Ev Lacey struggle to his feet, Dane took the chance of covering ten yards walking directly at a tree trunk that separated him from the men.

Ev got up slowly. He stretched and in doing so, tested the rope that tied his wrists together behind his back. Solid knots of some sort of a filament were separated by a one foot length of this rope.

With some effort, he struggled in walking over to the cliff's edge. Both he and Meg had taken vicious blows to the head. Meg still lay unconscious from her second blow, the one given with a rifle butt while she lay on the ground. Lacey stood on the edge and looked down. Twenty feet out and perhaps one hundred feet below, he saw a playground slide. The surface of glacial ice stretched downward away from him. He shook off the crazy idea to jump for the slide, to act like a ski jumper, to risk it all in a futile attempt of escape. Could he cover the void? Meg would be left behind. What would these two do with her? What had they already done to her? His body ached with their blows. Why had they hit her?

A harsh voice barked from behind him, "Sit down, Coon."

Ev sat down on the edge with his legs hanging over in space.

"Turn around and face me, Nigger."

Ev shifted his weight away from the edge and pivoted around on his seat. He battled the nausea and the feeling that he was about to tip over backward.

Dane took a second chance and ducked forward to a second tree. Next to the opening of the path that led down the hillside, he saw his escape route open. Instead, he lie flat on his stomach and crawled forward to a third scrub tree that could barely hide his shape. He was then able to see Meg's face as she lie unconscious. One man's hiking boots showed as he stood with one foot on her back. The second man's shoes came into view, turned, and faced Lacey on the cliff's edge. Dane saw forty five feet, just fifteen totally open yards separating them.

"Do you see this stick Nigger?" The man then threw the wood at Lacey in a violent motion, just missing his head and the resulting knocking of Lacey off the edge of the cliff. "And do you see this? We call this Instant Death. Now I want you to carefully answer some questions for us since your lady friend has decided to pass out on us."

313

Dane struggled to see what the second man had shown Ev Lacey. It was obviously a second stick, probably larger or perhaps it was his rifle. Either would mean the same. Lacey could die soon, Lacey was about to die. Dane shifted his position to see the men's faces. Obviously, if he could see them, they could see him. None were looking down the trail. One was, however, constantly looking around. The other kept his attention on Lacey. The former was obviously looking for Hughes. He peered intently up the trail at times, other times he cocked his head to listen to the sounds of the forest.

"How did you survive?"

"Dane Hughes brought the plane down in a lake."

"In a lake! That lucky shit. He must be a cat, a man with nine lives. Where is he now?"

"He walked out last night. He was in a hurry and told us to follow as we could. The lady was slowing us down. He went for help, I was to walk out slowly."

Ev Lacey watched the second man pick up another short limb of dried wood. He saw the stick fly through the air directly at him. He leaned into the missle quickly as it reached him. The blow hit him directly. He leaned back and barely retained his sitting position. His wind was gone from his lungs. It was as close to making him fall back off the cliff as he could imagine.

"Blacky, you are lying to us. We were at the bottom of the trail last night and did not get much sleep because of it. Dane Hughes did not walk out last night. This is the only path and the trail shows all tracks. No one walked out. Is he hurt? Did you leave him to go for help?"

There was silence. Finally, Ev nodded his head. He prayed that his hesitancy would show the truthfulness of the admission.

"Which lake did you come down in? No forget that question, there is only one large enough and we pinpointed it. Did you stay at the camp site at that lake last night?"

Again the slow nod of the head. This time Lacey added the word, "Yes."

The first man spoke again. "Alright, I believe you, but it doesn't make much difference. We will find him anyway. Here, let me show you how this works. You should thank us for Mr. Instant."

Dane was about to move across half the distance, but he saw one man draw a syringe and the other looked his way. Had he been seen?

When he looked again, he saw that the man had pulled Meg's skirt up over her legs exposing her gartered thighs. In a quick movement, he stabbed her in the upper leg and turned his attention to Ev Lacey who had lept to his feet. Dane Hughes too crouched about to charge the two. Dane fought back the nausea. In his mind, he knew that he was too late.

Ev finally spoke quickly, "You could at least close her eyes. She looks quite dead to me." Lacey had seen the movement of Dane Hughes. Dane had knelt on his knee and appeared to be shining something on his coat. He then took a big bite of it. But there was no apple in his hand. Then Hughes spread his arms obviously signaling something large and pointing at the men. Lacey could not keep his attention on Hughes, his time was up. "If I could charge and kill you both from here, I would do it, but I know I would die and that would be a total waste."

He had seen the distant and exposed Dane Hughes on the downside of the path. Dane was free if he, Lacey could freeze him and take away the option of his trying to act like a hero. Hughes would surely die. Ev Lacey's quick thought was of Dickens and the *Bible*. "The greatest deed a man can do, to give his life for a friend."

"We know hero Coon, we know. Especially, when you might not know, we requested this job. We owe your friend a great deal." The second man was dragging Meg's body to the cliff's edge. In a quick motion, he swung her around like a sack and slid her off the edge. What he did not know, was that Lacey was shaking his head at Dane, telling him not to show himself. Then, in the same motion, he completed three quick actions, all under the unbelieving eyes of the first killer who had his rifle trained on Lacey. Perhaps the man did not believe what he saw.

With the second man close to Lacey and watching the departing body and gartered legs of the woman sail over the cliff, he caught only Lacey's motion. Ev Lacey had nowhere to go. Right, left, or backwards and he was over the cliff into space, forward he was surely to be shot, so he went to the fifth alternative. He went straight up into the air. Tucking his arms under his legs, he brought his hands up in a circular motion below his tucked body barely passing the rope beneath his feet in a clearing motion. With his hands now in front of him, he jumped for the man at the cliff's edge and felt the tug of a rifle's bullet across his back.

315

The surprised killer was unable to protect himself. The lunging Lacey pushed him over the cliff's edge to follow Meg with an unbelieving scream. Then just as the second shot was about to blow Lacey off the mountain top, Lacey leapt out to his death.

Dane had watched unbelievingly. It had taken no more than four seconds and two men had disappeared from view. Dane had picked up a large rock. With all his might, he threw it at the shocked second killer.

He missed. He missed high and wide. The stone hit up the path and brought the killer around to look in that direction. Quickly, the man ran up the path with his rifle pointed in the direction of the sound. As quickly, Dane turned and hurtled down the path.

A hundred strides down into the forest, he ran to the hill's edge to again look at the glacier below him. No sign of any body showed on the ice surface of the glacier. All of them must have slipped into the dark void, falling to their death. Sobbing for air and with grief, Dane knew that all were dead. His friends were gone. Was this the price that they must have paid? One who searched for truth in an organization, one who wished to sacrifice for the success of another. Dane knew that he was alone and that he had no chance unarmed in these woods. He again returned to the path and in a neckbreaking pace and no caution, again began his hurdle down the mountainside He was alone.

Twenty minutes and he was nauseated. He could not stop, although he slowed. He forced his mind to think. What was this all about? Why would Lacey have known too that killers would be waiting for them? What could he have found out or what did Dane or Meg know that was worth all their deaths? Why were these the men after him again?

The trail became steeper. Suddenly, he saw the open area where logging had denuded the hillside. Below the first cut area, he saw the dirt road and the jeep that sat with its radio antenna and open windows. He stumbled down to the vehicle. As he grasped the door which easily opened, he was trying to remember how one crossed the wires to start such a vehicle.

The jeep sat on a gravel embankment. He took a moment to see that the embankment was made up of gravel brought in by the loggers to make their access road. Looking to the slope below the embankment, he could see the road cut into the side of the mountain in snakelike loops as it wound down the incline. He knew that these

316

were called switchbacks and would be a constant grade until the bottom of the hill was reached. Peering down into that distance, he could see a straight stretch of the gravel road leading into a forest on which other side stretched a ribbon of concrete. He had found civilization!

Even better luck, he had found the jeep's keys. Sitting in the ignition were the vehicle's keys! He jumped into the seat and was about to turn the switch. Some sixth sense made him stop.

It was unlike professionals to leave keys in an ignition. Dane quickly got out of the jeep and went to the front of the vehicle. He lie on the ground and crawled on his back to look up past the radiator. Red sticks of dynamite packed back against the engine wall stared at him. He reached up to disconnect the wires and yank down the explosives. Crawling out from beneath the jeep, he stood and heaved the dynamite over the mountainside, only to think twice of the action. It was too late. He watched the dynamite arch away and down into an evergreen tree. A miracle or his lack of understanding of dynamite detonation saw no explosion.

He returned to the ignition and turned the key. The starter turned, but the engine would not fire. Dane tried again, no engine noise sounded. The engine appeared dead. Again, he got out, this time to open the hood. Everything appeared wired as it should. He pried open the distributor cap and cursed. The two had removed the distributor's rotor and taken it with them. There would be no ignition, no engine.

But Dane knew immediately that they had not thought of everything. The turning of the key freed the transmission. He could put the jeep into neutral and in neutral, it would roll. Standing alongside the jeep he heaved against the doorstand. He heaved again. Slowly, the jeep began to roll down the hill. It picked up some speed in the soft gravel. He steered to the hard center of the road and then jumped up into the driver's seat. Not once had he looked back up the trail to see if the second killer was following him. Surely, he had discovered by this time the place where Hughes had circled the basalt top. Surely, he would soon break out into the clear cutting area to see Dane's flight.

The jeep was now moving at 20 mph. If it would not run, it would coast down the mountainside. Dane felt the air through the open window as he approached the first switch curve, a deep curl to the right and a parallel reverse course below him. The brakes were aided by the power of the motor. Without that power, he had to stand hard on them to produce any slowing. He had discovered that too late and then he was through the curve hugging the far left side of the road, barely keeping the vehicle from plunging over the side.

Dane felt totally alive. He pried down on the brake. To stay alive, he would have to cut the jeep's speed. He stepped on the emergency brake. The vehicle jerked, but before he could try it again, he was on the second switchback. Again he was through and again heading in the opposite direction. This time he was on the right and looking down the mountain. A longer straight stretch of road gave him time to breath and count the curves below that awaited him. He saw sixteen.

On the seventh turn, he began to relax. He now had the vehicle fully under control. He had taken the turn at just the right speed. It was now enjoyable. As he began to relax, he thought of Meg Jamison and Ev Lacey. Anger boiled within him. The concussion brought him back to the present.

The road in front of him exploded. He knew what he would hear next. As he ran over the crumbled gravel and dust, he heard the rifle's report from high above him. Subconsciously, he had known it would come and in a way he was surprised by its lateness. The second man did not have to go far up the path until he would have come upon three sets of footprints. If he could count to three, he would have turned and found where Dane had left the trail. There was only one place for him to go after that. There was only one way to get there. The only thing that had saved Dane was his breakneck daring coming down the trail. But nothing could save him now.

Like a duck in a shooting gallery, Dane knew that the killer was resting his rifle on a support above him and trying to gauge his speed to time the bullet's flight. The jeep was moving back and forth across a panoramic screen of scenery. Dane released his hold on the brakes. His speed increased as he sped into the next turn.

The next shot came on the straightstretch. It was too high. Dane knew that it was a most difficult shot, although the distance was not yet that great. Give a hunter a level shot and he will make it. Buy him a beer if he can hit something on a downhill angle. Dane was willing to make that bet. But he was not willing to make any bet of beers if he was going to let the man have unlimited practice shots.

He ducked the jeep in against the hill. It made more of a straight down shot, but no shot came. Finally, it did and it was just right in height. It came just at the entrance to the next switch curve. The killer had led Dane a little too much as he hit the brakes to slow for the curve. The bullet made a very neat hole in the left front side of the hood, two feet in front of Dane. The concussion hurt Dane's ears and shattered the windshield.

Dane knew that even a close shot could kill. The concussion of a close blast of the large caliber, high velocity bullet could be fatal. He slowed the vehicle. This time, the bullet passed close by his head to sail down the mountain. A fifth bullet again hit the hood. Dane knew what was to come next. The man had him sighted in. Dane jammed the jeep in against the mountainside as the road in front of him exploded in a hail of bullets from the rifle which was now set on automatic.

Dane jumped out of the jeep and opened the hood. Reaching in, he pulled out the distributor cap and stuck it in his coat pocket. The man might have the rotor, but this was one combusion engine that would not now fire. Then without looking, Dane did what he knew he had to do. He leapt across the road as the jeep and roadway again exploded in a hail of steel and lead and jumped over the side.

Once when flying in Alaska, Dane had spent a 4th of July in a small town called Seward. Every Independence Day the locals invited other Alaska residents and visitors such as Dane to compete in a race up the side of the town's nearby towering mountain. That was only half the race, an act that took forty or fifty minutes. Dane had done well on that part of the race. The second half was one for which he was not prepared. One had simply to run back down the mountain to the finish line. The winner had done it by seemingly flying down the rock path. It had taken him nine minutes, it had taken Dane twenty. Today, Dane tried to repeat the winner's motions.

The light was now beginning to fade on the side of the mountain. Dane ran and jumped in shadows. His motions were those of random movements. To avoid logs and rocks, he cut and ducked. Several times he fell. The marksman above had no pattern to follow and with each shot and each ten seconds of sighting on the fleeing man, the distance was increasing. Dane knew that he was going to survive the test of ability when the killer put his rifle on automatic again as Dane reached the bottom stretch of road that led into a forest to his left. He only hoped that he would win the test of luck.

Suddenly, he was within the protecting forest. His legs hurt, his side felt as if ribs were cracked. He wanted to stop to catch his breath, to collapse by the side of the road. Only the thought of his friend Ev jumping to his death kept him going. Lacey had chosen his death so that Dane would have a chance like this. He was not going to stop. He ran in the still heat of the late mountain day. Not a breath of wind stirred among the trees. He believed that he would suffocate. Sweat had completely drenched his clothes.

He checked his running. There was no excuse for running up and down. He made himself lean forward and step out. How many times had he cheated himself in his running? To step out was to move, to jump up and down was to waste motion and energy. Run on the outside of your feet, he thought. Move the arms. Arms get tired from running too. Some runners have to break stride because their arms are fatigued. Run, Hughes, run, damn you! Don't quit.

Dane Hughes ran out onto the paved highway as if out into a fog. A pickup truck was coming down the road toward him. Dane waved his arms in desperation. As the truck slowed past him, Dane turned to run to where it was stopping. Half way between him and the pickup, the side of the road exploded. Dane looked up the miles to the top of the logged off area. The killer was still at rest looking at him through a telescopic sight. Dane waved at him. Hopefully he could see the farewell in his scope. It would be after dark before he was off the slope of the mountain. By that time, Dane would be in hiding, hopefully with a bed and a good meal.

Dane knew that he was safe and unharmed as he again stretched his legs after being dropped off by the truck's driver. As he broke into the farm house to steal the cash, handgun and ammunition, his mind burned with hatred. He left an I.O.U., but failed to go back to claim credit on the car he found behind the house. He drove it a mile past an old motel with individual cottages set off among the trees and then walked the tiring walk back, his anger driving him. As his exhaustion overtook him still dressed on the motel cottage's bed, his rage remained in his dreams. Men would die tomorrow! It would be a bloody Sunday!

19

Sunday

It was midmorning and Phillip Arrow watched people in the street far below his office window stream from a church. He again glanced at the Sunday morning headlines. The City's newspaper had long wished to crucify him. This seemingly liberal, but most capitalistic L.A. press, had long ago found the perfect way to sell newspapers. Advertising a slander was the profitable technique. They had had the chance this morning and had lept at it with all presses running. For years Arrow had shunned all publicity. Frustrated, the paper had waited. Today, it had its story.

LaBear had turned himself over to authorities in Canada with various charges leveled against Phillip Arrow related to cocaine smuggling and the use of Union Arrow corporate jets. Various accusations regarding homosexual activities were also noted. Frank Turner's death, which had been discovered late last Friday, and the loss of the Corporate Lear in the Cascades were more than extenuating circumstances. The recent lackluster performance of the Company and the dramatic drop in the stock market's price of Union Arrow stock were also noted. It couldn't have been a better story than if his corporate public relations department had written it. All the Company secrets were there. Secrets and lies, thought Arrow, a powerful combination. He wondered if the Union Arrow Public Relations

Department had written the story. It would be typical of the bitch and her lover to have arranged its use.

Phillip looked at his watch. Massendale had made this appointment two long days ago. Massendale had also insisted on bringing Caroline with him. Phillip only wanted to hear Massendale talk. It was imperative to understand his plans. Under no condition would he have Massendale's corporate people handle any part of defending against this slander. This afternoon he would meet with the best personal damage lawyers in Beverly Hills. Never 'buy cheap' on personal services when you need them was Arrow's personal axiom. Control their use, but never contract inexpensive counsel.

Evil was at work and Arrow felt it. He couldn't believe the rapidity of events. Jamison's death had been so quickly followed by others. The flood gates of Hell had been opened. The autopsy report on Jamison's body had informed him that the officials were sure that it had been a suicide. The autopsy report on Frank Turner's body was not as conclusive. A blow to the back of the head was a possibility. All or someone at Arrow Corporation was a suspect. The Kansas City police had requested the right to examine the Lear's crash site when it was found. There were far too many deaths. They all had to be connected in the eyes of the local law enforcement. Tomorrow his office would be besieged. The press, Canadian and U.S. officials, police.......there would be no end.

Arrow sat wondering about Dane Hughes. Was he the responsible one? Could he explain Dane Hughes' quick escape from the Calgary Airport? What a strange set of circumstances. The Lear crashed while LaBear talked with U.S. and Canadian agents on Canadian soil. The result had been unlimited coverage in the Canadian press which transferred to unlimited freedom to slander in the U.S. sister papers. It was a curious coincidence. Union Arrow had two simultaneous negative public relations campaigns in progress.

Arrow again looked at the slander. It was not worth the effort to read it. All would be proved false in time. There was nothing here that the attorneys could not handle. For once, his lawyers could deal from a position of total truth. No, what should have bothered him this morning was the public reaction to this news and not the news itself.

Union Arrow's common stock was already in the toilet. This news would drive the price even lower. A PE of 4 by the week's end was not unreasonable. Anyone with a half a billion dollars could take a major position in Union Arrow. The unions would most probably achieve total control. The recent purchases of stock and these killings were connected. Arrow wondered why his opponents just did not kill him. But that answer was obvious. Settling his estate would slow up the quick taking of control that anyone might plan. All his people seemed to have the freedom to die. At 67 years of age, he apparently was destined to the fate of facing the jackals alone.

Phillip Arrow knew his world of power and control was crumbling. He had held power for so long and it was slipping through his fingers so quickly. Most important at this time, Arrow knew that his control over the Union Arrow Corporation Board of Directors was historically low and tenuous. He either had a slight majority or no majority at all. If Massendale had any luck, they might ask him to step aside at least for an interim period. He wondered again if either of his trusted friends could be bought. Surely, the count was now 6 to 5 against him. Perhaps it was more. Again the cold thought drifted through his mind. Either of his two sons could be bought. Would Mary Sue ever vote against him? He knew that that answer was "No."

He would have to wait for the Monday meeting and take his medicine. Right now, however, he knew his chances were slight to hope for any escape. The rules of probabilities gave him only a 10 % chance. Nothing more existed. He thought again of the lack of information from his computer system. He had known that it would always be the case, that that system on which he had come to depend would be shut down when he needed it most. If only he had the information on old fashioned paper! And most of all, he knew that he missed the mind that might help best today. Everett Lacey had gone down on the Lear. He was surely among the dead.

He had known only one other time like this, it was when he had been fighting Hitler. It was total war. Lacey had been right. When fighting, one had to know his foe. Had old age made him blind? Was he, like Lacey, among the chosen dead?

And that is exactly what Everett Lacey thought at the moment. He was dead, or as close to dead as was possible for a living human. His jump from the cliff wall was a sailing, soaring free fall toward the glacier. Like a dive, he had bent down for the leap as his body weight shifted over the cliff's edge. He had waited for the extra half second to become as close to perpendicular with the cliff and parallel to the ground as was possible.

The price had been the close passage of a high powered bullet as he had sprung from the cliff wall. The reward had been a ninety degree push away from the wall. Turning in the air he had spread eagled his body leaning toward the cliff. The angle of his body against the passing air had slid his body away from the wall and his tuck, half twist and knee bend had placed him right on the back edge of the glacier with only six inches to spare. Ski jumping was no different other than the flat skis spread the pressure over their surface. It was just his shoes and the slick downward sloping surface that saved him.

The angle of the glacier was a steep 45 degrees where he landed. The ice had piled up against and then separated from the cliff's face. He knew he had made a good landing. Muscles in his lower back collasped first as his feet hit the ice in a ski jump crouch. Next came the crushing explosion of his rear and back crumbling back into the ice as his body picked up speed sailing down the glacier's surface. The angle of the ice and the speed of his body had taken most of the force out of the 60 foot jump. He knew he would have made it without serious damage if it had not been for the undulating ice surface and the large stones rising randomly on the glacier's surface.

Two solid blows by rocks standing in their unmelted frames pummeled him has he sped over and by them. The damage slowed his body speed. As he approached the end of the glacier, he thought of how quickly it had all happened. The world was a satisfying blur as time seemed locked in a vise in this mountain land. Muscle sprains and bruises, all he had to do was ride it out and he was clearly slowing as the surface leveled. A clear cold blue lake showed itself at the end of the glacier. He dug his elbows in to the surface. He was slowing down. He knew he would make it. He knew his body. It felt surprisingly good. He had survived though he would never try such a leap again. It was then that the world dropped out from under him and all was black.

It had been chill and bitter cold and the stars had engulfed him. He had hurt horribly. Lacey had shaken his head and turned to look to the left. He had fallen off the end of the glacier onto a rocky stream bed, half the width of which was dry. On these dry rocks he twisted his body. Every bone felt bruised, if not broken. Where had the day gone, he had thought? The brilliant full moon and bright stars reflecting off the glacier's white surface lighted the countryside like a cloudy day with a black sky. He had looked first at the twelve foot drop from the front of the glacier. It was a miracle that he had survived that fall. How could such a short drop have hurt so much when such a long drop to start the slide had caused so little pain? How long had he lain there unconscious?

He had looked back at the cliff. A deep, very dark cave, a whistling hole of darkness shown where the stream poured out from the center of the glacier to feed the lake below. It was the chill wind coming out of the cave that had finally awakened him. He had to escape its draft.

With all parts of his body aching, he had crawled toward a dark ridge. As he had crawled, he had worked at the knots that bound his wrists. His fingers had been nearly swollen double. Conquering the ridge's top, he had felt the fresh blood streaming from his head and right arm. The pain had been undiminishing. He collasped in the hill's lee, safe from the cursed, chill wind, feeling the blood pulsing through his aching hands.

The hot sun had finally awakened him again.

Ev Lacey felt his leg with his left hand. His right arm hung useless as he sat up. Shafts of pain shot through his body. The world first showed itself as a double image and then as a single. Quickly, he decided to stand. If his body was unable, if it would fail him, he must know now. There had to be a reason for his nausea.

Shafts, brilliant lances of pain, spread up through his frame. His left knee was damaged. Below it, he felt a swollen ankle. His right eye was swollen and damaged. He could only feel around it. No mirror would show him the extent of that damage. His right arm was useless. Most of all, Lacey felt the pain. Nausea filled him as his hunger and fatigue blended with sharp pain when he moved and a dull ache when he rested.

He tried to walk. Ten steps and then twenty, then forty with a stick to assist his left side. He knew that he could make it. Forty more steps later, he found the Boy Scout campsite by the glacier lake. A four foot wide trail led to civilization. He knew that he was going to survive. As he looked at the lake, he could picture the boys swimming in the cold ice water. He wondered if they knew that males could become sterile when exposed to enough cold. The male testes hang outside of the body because of temperature control and nothing more. How many boy scouts were ruined for the future, he thought? He knew he was going crazy with pain.

Lacey sat down to shut his mind from the hunger and pain. Soon, he would try to drink. Each step was important. Each step put him closer to survival. Lacey fought the fog that surrounded his mind. He was safe. What of the others? Dane had hopefully fled down the hill. Perhaps he had survived. What of Meg?

Lacey shook his head to clear the fuzziness. Could Meg still be alive? He knew not. He had seen the injection and the open eyes. He had seen her thrown into the dark void between rock and ice. Yet, he did not conclusively know that she was dead.

He believed in his shattered state that she might be alive. If he did not know that she was dead, there was no other alternative, no grey or shade of color. One is either alive or dead. He was alive, wasn't he?

His mind whirled. Had he not heard of people put in cold storage where their body functions slow down? Could she still be alive against the back wall of the glacier? What lie at the bottom of that void? Could something have cushioned her fall?

Laborious minutes later, Ev Lacey stood at the stream's exit from the center of the glacier. A cave housed the rapids which now were but 1/10th the size of the earlier torrents that had carved the stream's passage. The cave was essentially empty. He could walk along the stream. Would it lead all the way back into the glacier to the open area behind? He looked up over the top of the glacier back toward the cliff. To one side, he saw the sunlight reflecting from the waterfall of the stream pouring down the side of the cliff. In the silence of the mountains, he could hear the water's roar. The stream fell into the void and next appeared beside his feet. Surely that stream's water had carved this tunnel under the glacier. He knew that he could not leave without trying it.

Ev Lacey took his first step into the cave's mouth. The chill wind of the cold sinking to the lower pressure of the hotter air at the cave's mouth cut through his clothes. He hobbled on into the cave and the empty blackness.

Never as a young boy had Everett been afraid of the dark. He was now.

He had estimated that the glacier was a 1/2 mile long, yet he knew that the mountain air magnified and lied. His steps were short, yet he had taken 3,240 small, perhaps one foot long steps, and he had seen no lights. Now the cave's ceiling was at four feet and the stream almost filled the full width of the cave. Soon he would be forced to crawl. Sickles of ice hung from the cave's roof. Points of glass like ice cut into him as he walked along feeling the air and the walls with his hands at each step. Blind, he walked mainly by listening to the rush of the water of the stream as it coursed its way beside and beneath his feet.

Lacey knew he was losing his sense of direction and consciousness. The darkness, the loss of blood, the painful injuries, the collapsing walls, the cold, the rushing water through which he now crawled and walked were sapping his strength and will. He knew his body would soon be in shock. To die here, would be to die alone, never to be found.

Ahead he faced only unknown darkness. Behind, he might still escape.

Ev Lacey crawled onward. He wanted to cry. He was now so afraid of the dark. Now he remembered. Alone at age two or three, he had been very much afraid.......so afraid. The walls were closing in on him. Then he hit it square on in the chest. It was a sharp razor edge of ice. He could feel the blood. Oh God, he must be bleeding buckets!

Dane Hughes crawled out of bed. The room was dark, but a shaft of light through the curtains told him that morning had arrived some time ago. He fought back his hunger. The cottage bed had been far too soft, but then the price of $28 told of the small village's ability to keep pace with progress. His room was really a small hut, one of many placed among the trees. It must have been built in the 1930s. Still, it served its purpose. He tried to remember how he had arrived. His mind was in a fog.

What would he do? He had paid with the stolen cash and had used a phony name. Perhaps it was fate that his wallet had gone down with the Lear.

Could someone find him? He was near the crash site and noticeable in appearance. Surely, he could be found if enough effort had been expended.

He thought back on the previous afternoon and evening. After hitching a ride and being left at a fork in the road, he had robbed a house and borrowed an ancient Chevrolet. That beautiful 1953 two tone blue and white auto had brought him to this small town. Left in an open garage, Dane hoped that the car would not be soon found. He had walked the mile and one half back to the motel.

He reached for the .38 caliber revolver he had stolen from the farmhouse. Western farms he knew were all alike. They were small arsenals of weapons. Every western farm contained at least a half dozen rifles thanks to the Bill of Rights. The Russians should be well prepared he thought, any invasion would face the greatest guerilla war of all time. To win the farmland of America, they would have to burn it. No wonder the Civil War had been such a disaster!

He spun the cylinder. All chambers were filled, he had no use for the safety margin of a hammer resting on an empty chamber. Damn, these .38s! He wished it was a .45. Korea had shown that eight .38 slugs would not stop a hopped up enemy. Hundreds of GI's had purchased their own .45's in Nam. Damn, he wished it were a .45!

He then reached for the phone. It would be inadvisable to use his name to seek credit for plane fare and he was short of cash. Sunday morning, he thought, would she be at her apartment? The ringing telephone said that the answer was "No." He knew where she was. He called the office.

"Caroline, it is Dane."

"Dane! Oh, my God! Dane, we thought you were dead."

"Almost, maybe, I need some help. Can you give it to me?"

"Anything, Darling, anything. Oh, so much has happened! They said you were dead. I just knew you weren't. Where are you?"

"I need you to send me a ticket. You pay for it under your name. Put me on a flight from Seattle, that's right, Seattle. United or Western flies that route. I like Western, they are my type of people. Please make the reservation for D. Hugs, that's 'H. U. G. S.' and we will call to confirm the misunderstanding at the ticket booth. I will get by with the misspelling. Make sure you have my home address right and plan some story to confirm my identification. Make the ticket open for any of the next three days. I don't know how long it will take me to get to SeaTac."

"Yes, yes, I will do it in the next 15 minutes and use my credit card. Give me your number if I have problems. That's right, alright, Room 28, I have it. What is the area code? Now listen, I am going to hang up and we will talk again when you reach Seattle."

Caroline almost shouted her concern. "If you don't fly down today, please call me from wherever your are tonight. I will meet you at LAX when you come in."

The phone slammed down with a tone that echoed in his ear. She had hung up on him. Dane, most of all, wanted to talk with her. He stood and stretched and then moved toward the bathroom. He stopped at the small door. Turning back to the bed, he picked up the revolver and then checked the lock and the chain on the door. All were in place. He knew that from now on, he could never be too careful.

Walking through the bathroom door, he closed and then locked it. He looked at the small window over the bathtub. It was a glazed glass through which one could not see. It was closed. Running the water, he soaked in the tub. The feeling of being in a locked jail cell all but overwhelmed him. There was no escape other than the door, the window was far too small above him. He was cornered. He could just not relax. Oh, how he ached!

The pain in his legs began to disappear as he increased the heat of the water. Finally, he drained the tub and stood to wash out his mouth and then wash down his hair under the shower nozzle. He quickly turned off the hot water to place his body awash in cold water. The chill all but buckled him over. Quickly, he turned off the faucet.

If he had not turned the water off just then, he would not have heard the crack of the two foot pliers like wire cutters as they snapped through the motel door's lock chain. Dane lept from the tub and looked under the door, the dark room with its drapes still pulled momentarily lightened then darkened again. If his ears and senses were correct, he was not alone in the room.

He then heard the door latch click shut. Dane quickly reached for the bathtub's water faucet. He turned on the water and then switched on the shower. In only half a step, he crossed the room and sat wet and dripping on the top of the toilet. His feet were on the toilet seat as he faced the door. The .38 was in his hand. He silently patted himself dry while he waited. Whoever it was had but three choices: crash down the door, shoot through the wall, or wait until he came out. Dane heard the choice as water was reaching the top of the bathtub. He had failed to fully open the drain. A clank, not a click, of metal signaled the readying of a weapon of some type.

The silence was echoing loudly in Dane's ears. The suspense would kill him first. He raised his handgun to shoot through the closed door should he get a fix on the direction of any shots.

The bathroom suddenly filled with dust as a machine gun ripped a path from left to right across the width of the room. With Dane's legs quickly lifted out in front of him, he felt the porcelain toilet disintegrate beneath him. The row of metal bullets had been aimed bathtub high and streamed across the room cutting the bathtub to shreds.

Bruised and cut on his thighs from the porcelain and barely able to breath from the dust of the exploded drywall, Dane curled amidst the water from the destroyed bathtub and waited for the next blast.

It came quickly. This time the bullets were at a height of four feet, all above his head. Unharmed, Dane waited. Quick thoughts ran through his mind. How could they have found him? Could Caroline's phone have been bugged? Could Caroline have told someone? It had been just twenty minutes, thirty at the most. It was unlikely, but not impossible with modern communications for Caroline to have told someone and then had them tell someone waiting in the town. Twenty minutes though? No, it was highly improbable. These were Mary Sue Massendale's killers. If he lived, she would be hunted down. Come on, he thought, you have to see if I am dead. Knock the door down!

Although he was waiting, the violent crash came as a surprise. Dane had to consciously force his actions. Amidst the mist and dust, Dane calmly jerked the charging man's body to a halt with three well spaced shots. There would be no mercy.

Suddenly, the man's body was lifted and hurled toward Dane. In the misty half second that it took the four slugs to enter Dane Hughes' body, he knew that two men had entered the room. Surely, a backup man had been in place. The killer had a new partner. Dane knew he had assumed that Lacey had killed his only partner. Dane knew that professionals never, never worked alone. He had called for a replacement. Dane knew that he had just not thought it through.

Dane Hughes tried to squeeze off a shot or two but his body would not obey his thoughts. Slipping into lasting unconsciousness, he had wished himself a little bit quicker, a little bit stronger, a great deal smarter. Darkness settled on Dane Hughes. There was total black darkness.

Ev Lacey fought the total darkness. It was a cold, numbing horror. Crawling through the rocks and darkness, he detected a touch of grey ahead. Forcing his bleeding body to advance a few more yards, he saw the opening. His mind was past feeling the cold. Unheedful of the cave opening, he crawled the extra fifteen feet all the way to the cliff's wall. Standing and turning, he leaned against the killer wall. He had made it. Wet, bruised, cold, and exhausted, he had done it!

Coming in from his right was the stream, now smaller in size than a half mile below. Ev knew that he could not stop. He had to move to his left. To stop was to die. Meg had dropped to his left. He must not stop now.

Everett Lacey stood tall as he hobbled along. None had ever walked the ground that he now tread. No one would ever again until the ice had melted. In the darkened greyness, he struggled over ground that was hallowed in his mind. Four billion people on this earth. In a billion years, only he would walk this ground. Suddenly, he stumbled over a body.

It was the body of Meg Jamison.

The body was cold. It was not really Meg. It just once held the spirit of Meg Jamison. It held a part of him in her and her in him. He walked on. The body of the killer lay on the rocks. There was no wallet. The rifle was damaged.

Everett Lacey returned to again stand above Meg Jamison. He pulled her a few feet, straightened her skirt and placed her body next to the ice wall of the glacier. He began to cover her body with rocks. Would others ever return to take her too back to her homeland of the Maple Leaf? Canada, the fair and good land. Canada, the future of America. He began slowly. It was a chant of this land that was forever to be his and hers,

"The Lord is your Shepherd, you shall not want,
    Dearest Meg,
He shall allow you to lie in green pastures,
He shall lead you beside still waters,
He shall restoreth your soul.
He shall lead you in paths of righteousness for His
    Name sake.
Even though you now lie in the valley of the shadow of
    death,
You shall fear no evil
    for though art with Him,
His rod and his staff, they shall comfort you.
He has prepared a table before you in the presence
    of our enemies,
Your head shall be anointed with oil,
    your cup is overflowing,
Surely goodness and mercy shall follow you,
    and you shall dwell in the House of the Lord forever.
Good by dearest Meg."

Lacey stumbled to the cave entrance. He had seen a flat log wedged in the broken rocks next to the curve of the stream bed as it entered the cave. He pushed it loose. With no strength to crawl down the stream bed and with the cold surely killing him by inches and seconds, he lay stomach forward on the log. Pushing off, he propelled the log into the stream to shoot down into the gaping black cavern. There was no turning back, his course was set.

Fifteen hundred miles away, Phillip Arrow looked up after Lawrence Massendale's words. Damn, these upstarts! They had chosen their time and place over his. His was the ride back from the airport after dropping Meg Jamison off the day before yesterday. They had laughed at him and told him to be ready today, now, in this place. Damn, how did he ever get in such a spot? He had to play by their rules at a time and place of their choosing. It appeared to be all downhill. Arrow had discovered nothing. Massendale was still talking. Was the course set? Could he do nothing about it?

"Phillip, you have to realize that you are on a slide that won't stop descending until you get off and sit on the sidelines for awhile."

It had been a long and heated exchange. Under normal circumstances, Arrow would have kicked the two of them out of his office an hour ago. With Massendale's verbiage and Caroline O'Brian's sparring and most of all, with Arrow's desire to bleed them dry of information, he was extending the discussion until they decided to leave.

Phillip Arrow was confused. It appeared that Massendale was trying a simple corporate takeover with the present Board. He had not once jumped to offer the suggestion that he might control the Company through newly acquired stock ownership. Arrow doubted if he were ever that subtle, yet he harbored the new feeling that Massey might have a carnivorous spirit. Could his grandsons have such a trait? He hoped so. Arrow decided that he would have to turn his attention to Caroline.

He looked at her proper business dress and her chin held high. He wondered if she had ever played poker. It told him that she had just drawn three aces to match a pair of kings.

"Caroline, surely you can talk some sense into this man. Doesn't he recognize that he is talking to the Company's largest stockholder? Even if he should get the Board to support him tomorrow, he faces a Spring challenge from me after the slate is clear of this slander."

"Phillip, that may be so but we don't believe that you are realistic.

You are over 65 years of age. It is time for a young man to take over, someone with fresh new ideas. I think you should look upon this as an opportunity to retire, something that would be most difficult to do in normal times, but most understandable now."

Wrong answer, thought Arrow. He obviously underestimated her subtleness. If these two did not know that someone had just purchased 30% of Union Arrow's stock, they would be more scared than he when they found out. Could they be trying to take over a Board of Directors that was just about due for extinction?

Arrow looked out his office's window. He thought their lack of knowledge doubtful. Their timing was too good, too perfect. Damn them! Why didn't they break?

"Come on Massey, I think we are just wasting our time." Caroline was picking up her briefcase to put away the meeting's agenda that she had developed.

"Yes, my Dear, I believe we are. Phillip, I believe you know that I have controlled certain members of the Board who will meet here at 10:00 AM tomorrow. As Secretary and acting Board Vice Chairman, I have talked with every Board member of the eleven including your children. I believe that I have six solid votes to your five. Tomorrow at this time, you will be terminated and I will be the new Chairman and Chief Executive Officer."

"We believe that you should seriously consider resigning," added Caroline.

Phillip Arrow shook his head in the negative. Their statements would draw no further comment from him. How long would it take them to sense that he was through talking?

Without another word, Arrow watched them get up and walk through the door of his office. Odd, he thought, how badly Caroline carried her success. Her look and body posture during the conquest were an unbearable affront. Perhaps it was because females did not compete in team sports in school. They did not know how to handle victory. For her arrogance, he would die in trying to drive her and her lover into the ground.

He sighed. His options were so limited. He must start with his friends and lawyers. He would wait to talk to his children tonight. He should probably visit each one of his boys personally. He couldn't do it by phone, he would have to see their faces. Neither of his World War II friends would have turned against him. It had to be one of his children.

Arrow turned to the business at hand. He would sketch down the particulars for the lawyers. Strange, how difficult it was for a Company leader to write. Long ago he had learned that one never had time to write, just talk and meet. Now he was forced to put pen to paper. He knew it would be a poor job.

Much later, for the first time in his life, Phillip Arrow felt beaten, crushed, a failure from which one could not, would not bounce back. There would be no further calls, he would walk the beach in the late evening and think of Meg Jamison. A prayer for her and her husband would be in order. Tomorrow, he would take his beating at the Board meeting and spend the rest of the day seeing to the Jamisons' affairs. There would be no conservative controls placed on remunerating their estate, there would be no lawyers ripping off their children.

Phillip Arrow was crushed. Both his boys welcomed his dropping by this evening. He could tell that they were solid. It was his two World War II friends who were unavailable. Far more disconcerting, however, was the fact that Mary Sue was not at home at 10:30 PM when he had dropped by. She was not expected back until Tuesday. Arrow had not thought of that possibility. One did not have to change one's vote, one just had not to vote in his favor. Without Mary Sue, he was through. Oh, Mary Sue, he thought, how could you do this to me? How could you leave me with just 5 votes? Why Mary Sue? Why did I never anticipate such a move? Why Mary Sue? Oh, I love you, Mary Sue. Why do you continue to surprise me?

20

Monday

Everett Lacey had seen the small gas station from the top of a ridge some two miles and fifty minutes before he got there. For hours he had walked mountain paths, dirt and gravel roads, and then paved roads. He had stopped counting the cars that passed by his wave or requesting thumbing for a ride. With the evening hours blending into darkness, he had come to accept the fact that no one would stop for a beaten, dirty Black in this beaten, dirty, black countryside. Everett Lacey had hurt like he had never hurt before. His legs had bothered him the most. Six, eight, ten hours of walking had brought him to a state of exhaustion. He had known that he could not stop. To stop would be to die.

Could his body have absorbed this much punishment? Oh, it was good to be a human alive, alive to taste of success and survival! Alive to smell the trees and see the stars! Pain was eversomuch better than the alternative.

A mile before the gas station he had suddenly seen a gravel road leading from the pavement. After a short, limping struggle up this weeded path, he had found the house. It was vacant. The small open lot in which it stood had echoed of the lack of life. The stillness of the land was frightening. How could anyone live in such quiet? No amount of knocking would waken   those who were not there.

He had tried to turn the knob of the front door. It had been locked. Next he had tried the windows. They too were latched. He had worked his way to the back of the house. A screen over the kitchen window gave way to his prying and a small window cracked open. He had removed several small dishes and vases from the sill and hoisted his body over the bottom edge of the windowsill. Sliding down into the kitchen, he had scraped his front with the nozzle of the high water faucet. The new pain had been almost unbearable. Yet, he knew he could not lie on the floor where he had fallen. He had beaten off his male nausea.

Lacey had struggled to his feet. In doing so, he had reached for the refrigerator door which came open in his struggle. The welcomed light had told him there was both food and electricity. He had reached for the Coors. How long had it been since he had eaten? The search of the kitchen told him that he would have to keep walking. There was no help here.

Walking to the front door, he had looked in the bedroom. Two double beds had beckoned him. He had opened a closet. Pillows and blankets, blankets and pillows - he had fought off their invitation and had thrown all onto a bed. He had known he was about to collapse, yet he also knew that there was no help here. He had to walk on.

Minutes later, he had found himself back on the paved road walking down the hill toward the small, outlying gas station. He had surmised that he had found a road to a skiing area. The small house was a probably a vacation retreat not often visited in the Summer. Lord, he had been tired!

Exhaustion had flooded his body as he approached the station. In the darkness, he had seen that his search was not in vain. A pay telephone stood by the garage wall. Lacey had had one quarter and he had hoped that it was the price of safety. Strange, he had thought, how when it comes to the important things, it is not a great deal of money that is needed - not a great deal, just some. He had deposited the quarter and called the operator for his collect call.

As he waited he had wondered if Dane were safe. If he were, surely he could not yet be back or would not be at his apartment. There was just one number to call. He had prayed that she would be home.

Two minutes of talking and he had given her the address he found on the telephone's side and directions to the small vacation cabin. She had said that she would try to be there either late tomorrow or in the early morning. It had been 10:10 PM when Lacey called. He could remember little of the day. Quick directions followed from the female command mind. He was to leave the front door open. He was to contact no one else. He was to attempt to get some rest. She would try to get the last flight out of LAX.

Just the standing in the telephone booth had been sufficient time to allow Lacey's muscles to stiffen. He would remember every step back to the cabin, the pain, the suffering. Then he had remembered a college coach and the coaching advice that one never remembers pain. Try as one will, the human can remember when they hurt, but they can not remember the essence of the pain. One can not truly remember pain. What was the saying, one remembers only the good times, never the bad? As Lacey crashed onto the bed, he wondered if that coach had ever hurt like this.

He had struggled with his stiff, dirty clothes. He had to shed his body of their filth. Then sleep came painfully. As the waves of exhaustion and nausea passed through him, he had attempted to block out the face of Meg Jamison. Would he look like that in the morning?

Hours passed and the new day began. The dawn had not yet broken over the mountains when the quiet of the valley was broken by the slow hum of a car's engine. Within moments, a green rental car slowly pulled up the driveway and stopped. The car lights were quickly extinquished. Quiet, careful, hesitant footsteps mounted the cabin's front porch. The door was tested. As requested, it had been left unlocked.

Three choices were present to the second occupant of the cabin. An open area indicated living space and there would be couches beyond the corner of the wall. A door led to a bedroom to the left and a ladder like series of steps led to what must be a second sleeping area above in a loft. The stairs were quickly mounted. The loft was empty. Quietly, the person returned to the starting point.

Everett Lacey was found in the bottom floor bedroom. Naked, he had kicked off his light covers. The person standing over him reached down.

One of the blankets lying on the foot of the bed was placed over the bruised and bloody sleeping body of the man. The stocky figure slowly leaned over the unconscious Lacey. Even further went the head to place a gentle kiss on his forehead.

The figure in the darkness walked over to the second bed and spread out a blanket. Quickly undressing in the darkness the now obvious shape of a half naked woman, lay down on the second bed. In seconds, she too, slept the deep sleep of the vanquished.

The sun broke slowly over the western mountains with light already having reached the Los Angeles basis. A tired man had occupied his office since 3:00 AM. Only the security guards had kept him company as he tried to savor what he sensed was the last day of his life as he had known it for decades.

It was the day of reckoning and Phillip Arrow had arrived early at his office to ponder the strategy of the morning. Phillip was still in a state of shock. He could not remember ever being as dismayed. Fifty years in business had supposedly taught him to expect everything. Yet, he had not expected the message from Mary Sue that she would not be at the Board Meeting this morning. He had not expected the announced presence of Aaron Goldstein and John Smedt in a few minutes at a early morning breakfast meeting, a presence requested to answer questions posed to them by the Board's Audit Committee.

Arrow knew that he might be beaten.

Like most disciplined men, however, Arrow knew that losses were inevitable. What disaster had he never learned from and remembered not to repeat? How many successes had taught him nothing? What he most resented was the lack of understanding of who, why, and how all this was happening. It was like looking in the bottom of a murky whirlpool. Who was the real danger? He knew it was time, he had better walk down to the executive cafeteria to the breakfast meeting.

Lawrence Massendale rose from his chair, "Good morning Phillip, here is a seat for you right here."

Phillip Arrow fought back the desire to sit somewhere else at the table. Looking around it, he saw no other chair empty. All Board Members, excluding his two friends and sons, were present along with Smedt and Goldstein. "I thought that this was just to be an Audit Committee meeting? Ms. O'Brian, if I am not mistaken, is not a member of the Board."

"That's correct, Phillip, but I asked her to attend," responded Lawrence Massendale. "We have also asked John and Aaron to attend in light of the actions that I intend to propose this morning, hump, hum, uh......" Massendale had to look down at his notes. He might be set for the meeting, but never, ever would he be able to take Arrow's cold stare.

338

An uncomfortable silence settled over the meeting. Arrow knew that this might be the only time when he could take control. "Well, then let me start by giving a brief report.

"Union Arrow Corporation is basically one of the strongest companies in America. Our resources and earnings potential can not be questioned. This year will be bad and that is a shock to all of you. It is no shock to me. I have had bad years before, losing years in fact. What is adversely affecting Union Arrow at this time, however, are several extraneous factors. Let me take them in order.

"First, we have a seemingly never ending stream of leaks to the press about Union Arrow Corporation's business. These leaks appear to be of a different source than that that we found in the early tender months last Spring. They appear to have just one focus, they are intended to discredit me. Now my lawyers have told me not to comment on the LaBear slanders, but I will say this, all his allegations are untrue.

"Second, we have been besieged with tragedies to our staff. First Richard Smith disappeared, then John Jamison committed suicide, and then Frank Turner. Not leaked to the press has been the fact that the police are fairly sure that Frank's death was not a suicide. I would have to agree. Finally, we have the Lear missing with Mrs. Jamison, a chance passenger, Everett Lacey, and a pilot who I can not imagine flying without a copilot. It appears that that is what occurred however. Any two deaths would be more than a coincidence. Six looks like a war.

"Third, there is the question of what type of war. I am a believer that one can be too sophisticated, too much a believer in the complex. What type of wars have we had? There were the acquisition battles, but those are behind us. Those companies' Generals have all been terminated. Those wars are over. There is the war of profits and we have lost a battle or two, but no one can think that those are anything more than temporary setbacks. Even if we were losing badly, we could call on reserves by selling off a subsidiary here or there.

"No, the only war that I really see is the war of control.

"And that brings me to the final extraneous event. My son-in-law here decides to leave his wife and appears to be the candidate to challenge my control." Turning away from Lawrence Massendale, who appeared not yet able to summon the courage to respond, to look at Caroline O'Brian who had purposely sat at the far end of the table, he asked, "What is Massey up to, Caroline, or better put, what are you up to? I think you know that I am fully aware of your involvement with Lawrence."

Caroline could clearly see that Lawrence had lost control of the meeting from the start. She welcomed Arrow's turning of the floor over to her, no matter what the question. "I think, Mr. Arrow, that we have all thought of those clearly chance and misfortunate coincidences. They, however, pale in terms of importance compared to several realities."

Caroline was sorting out her thoughts. Phillip Arrow had remained a true gentlemen. He had not directly said that she had been having an affair with Massey, he had just said "involvement." Caroline knew that the four new directors' votes were fragile. Sitting here at the table, all were mature enough not to ask questions. They would just sit and observe. The strong would have their votes. Of one thing she could be sure, as representatives of conquered companies they hated Phillip Arrow. She and Massendale would really have to screw up to lose their votes.

"I see three significant topics that the Audit Committee should be aware of. These are operations, finances, and legal issues. Let me first cover the operations and then let John Smedt cover the financial concerns and finally, Aaron Goldstein can address the legal issues.

"Operations are in a shambles. Yes, this year will be a loss in the Rail Division. What I disagree with you over, Phillip, is that this may not just be a one time event. Union Arrow Corporation lacks direction. There is no corporate identity, no corporate culture. Ask any of our employees what they think Union Arrow Corporation is and they will give a confused answer. No wonder the analysts and stock market are confused. We would have a PE of 3 to 4 if our earnings weren't dropping so fast."

"Excuse me, Caroline," interrupted Phillip Arrow, "did you say 'identity' and 'corporate culture'? What has that got to do with our problems? Indeed, what is a 'corporate culture' besides some graduate business school theory?"

"Phillip, I won't argue with you this morning. There are several other problems. John, would you please address your concerns?"

John Smedt had been lost in thought. This was the type of affair that Arlington, Bothell & Hyde counseled their staff to avoid. He was being used again by the broad, but he knew no way out other than to rely on the truth. That, by itself, violated another of the Firm's rules.

"Yes, thank you, Caroline. As you all know, Union Arrow Corporation borrowed over eight billion in cash from a consortium of fourteen New York banks. These banks have informed me that, if you read the fine print, the first ten months of the loan are on a short term basis. Over those months, it had been planned to place that debt in long term positions at rates not to exceed the quoted rate and fee. Union Arrow Corporation pledged to assist in supporting the efforts to secure those placements."

Phillip Arrow interrupted, "That is not quite how I remember the explanation of the consortium's loan."

John Smedt smiled and reached for the floor. From beneath the table he pulled a five inch thick loan document. "I would not think so. Have you read this full loan contract? I never believed that you did. That was for Mr. Massendale and Mr. Goldstein's people to do. What you will find here are several sections that deal with potentially unfavorable situations that might develop.

"Now I know that many consider all this just 'boilerplate.' What this contract contains, in effect, is the experience of what can go wrong in an acquisition as learned from experience by these banks over ninety years in the acquisition business. They clearly have the right to ask that new management take over. It is printed right here on page 237 of the loan document."

"Hold, hold on!" Phillip Arrow was surprised that it would be Smedt who initially brought the issue up. Caroline was, indeed, exceptionally smooth. "You say if I am correct, 'have the right.' That is not the same thing as being able to 'demand' a change."

"That is correct. However, we should look at the reality of the task that you face. These acquisitions do not look anywhere as profitable as they once did. Many in the East, like it or not Phillip, are questioning your judgment. To illustrate this, I have before me a letter to Arlington, Bothell & Hyde signed by every single member of the consortium suggesting that Union Arrow Corporation operate under a more professional management."

"More professional management? You mean a new Chairman and Chief Executive Officer. Do they have any nominations?"

"No, they don't," answered Caroline for the much relieved John Smedt. Perhaps he would forgive her. "But I think that that is a matter for the full Board meeting in eighty minutes time. Before that,

I would like the Committee to hear Mr. Goldstein's concerns."

"Don't you think that the other members of the Board should also hear this?" asked Phillip Arrow.

"Yes, but they chose not to attend the Audit meeting. All said that they thought it appropriate that they just attend that portion of the day to which you had invited them."

It was the first ray of hope that Arrow had seen. His two sons and two friends might be sound. That made it his four plus himself against Massendale and his four stooges. Christ, they just sat there! Not one of them had spoken a word all morning. He nodded to Aaron Goldstein who was smiling at him.

Aaron Goldstein knew that he was going to enjoy the next few minutes. He had been secretly recording the session to replay to the next partners' meeting of Shaffer, Schwab & Meyers. His personal, individually set annual goal was simple. All the Firm's partners had agreed upon it. He was to punish this upstart Westerner for his tapping of the Firm's computer systems. Four other major New York firms had agreed to cooperate with his effort if needed. No one, just no one had the right to secretly review his Firm's activities.

If the U.S. Government was precluded from interfering and messing with New York firms, who did this man, Phillip Arrow, think he was? God?

"Thank you. Phillip, it has come to our attention that someone has compiled a complete record of all planning and actions pertaining to the acquisitions that occurred within Arrow Corporation last Spring. Along with this written record is a set of audio tapes, that although censored to some extent, perhaps even modified, cast a very negative light on your actions.

"We speculate that it may have been either John Jamison or Frank Turner who compiled this record, we may never know. As a legal firm with national standing, we face quite a dilemma. On one hand, we are the counsel for Union Arrow Corporation and all this is privileged information. Yet we face the fact that the allegations have significant SEC implications. We also note the number of deaths and ask whether homicide is involved. Then, of course, there is the problem that we were sent copies of the material. The original is still in the hands of sender who also sent only one request by letter."

"What was that?"

"That Arrow Corporation leave a hundred million in unmarked

cash at some location and time to be later specified."

"Well, let's solve that problem right now," replied Arrow. "There will be no payments of blackmail by Union Arrow Corporation. I suggest that you just make the information public. You all must understand that one can never pay a blackmailer enough. They always come back for more. Now is the time to say 'No'."

"Um, umph," interrupted Lawrence Massendale who finally saw an opening that suggested he could show some legal concern. "There is always the problem of the Corporation, Phillip. We have to keep in mind the fact that with a quarter of a million employees and twice that many stockholders, we have a responsibility to others. This type of disclosure would surely drive our stock price even lower."

"What do you suggest?" Arrow's anger was showing in his face and tone of voice. Did these people really think that one could sweep such allegations under the rug? With the leaks to the press that Union Arrow was experiencing, this revelation was probably already being typeset.

"He suggests," answered Caroline, "that if we had new management at the time of the disclosure, we could say that we are already dealing with this and other problems. We could protect the Corporation. We are sorry, Phillip, but the brunt of this must fall on you. You were the person in charge."

"Thank you, I appreciate your realization of that fact. May I also note that I am still in charge of the Company? We have broken no laws, let's disclose this and start dealing with the other problems at hand."

"I would not recommend such haste, Mr. Arrow," suggested Aaron. "We did break some laws, regulations, Codes, and the like.....perhaps even hundreds of them. It is just not possible today to make a major acquisition without doing so. I know that the public does not appreciate this, but the fact is that the laws in this area are so confusing, so contradictory, that it is impossible not to break the Law. Union Arrow Corporation is at risk under any serious inquiry. So are you, I might add. Please, Sir, recognize the fact that we are talking about both criminal and civil offenses. You could face a jail term."

Phillip Arrow looked down at his cold breakfast. The full Board meeting was just minutes away. Could he survive it? Could he survive such a miserable looking plate? Why was it that he no longer enjoyed eating breakfast? It once had been his most enjoyable meal.

Ev Lacey awoke to the smell of frying bacon. The bedroom window was open and a fresh breeze blew across his body. He hadn't yet moved. Only one of his eyes was open. He knew exactly where he was, or did he? He could actually smell bacon, he could even hear it cooking. Had he ever been so hungry in his life? He could actually feel the need for substance in his body. His whole system was acutely aware of the need for food. Oh, he felt so alive!

A small mountain cabin, fresh air blowing across one's body, the smell of a fresh breakfast. Was this reality, or was this Heaven? Was he dead? Thoughts of the past three days spread through his mind. Like random waves, they washed him back into consciousness.

He placed pressure against his side to roll himself over onto his back. He knew he was alive. No one could hurt this much and be dead. The pain racked his body like sharp knife shafts. He could feel the sweat build on his body as he anticipated the next surge of pain. He had to see who was with him.

Mary Sue Massendale stood looking at the man in front of her. He was struggling to turn over. His moans had brought her in from the other room. She hoped that he wasn't such a baby when she applied the antiseptic that was in her pocket while he ate the breakfast that she now carried for him.

When Everett Lacey had called her, she had first made a list. Next she had called the airlines and found a last, late flight north. The college aged girl who lived next door was summoned to stay with the boys and see that they got off to school. Going to the safe in her bedroom, she withdrew the four thousand dollars of emergency money kept there. She would use only cash, no credit cards. In ten minutes she was packed and had walked out through her back yard to the adjoining back yard of their neighbors. The taxi was waiting in front of her neighbor's house. No one had seen her depart.

Mary Sue felt exhilarated! What a beautiful morning, what beautiful country! She wondered why she and her husband had favored the filth of ancient cities for vacations when the beauty of a far more ancient landscape was available. Probably, she thought, because the silent mountain country makes people look at themselves. There are no distractions. Could she ever stand to really look at Lawrence Massendale? No, here they would have been forced to talk to each other.

She walked around the bed to its other side and set the plate and

344

cup of steaming black coffee down on the bedstand. "Good morning, Mr. Lacey! I knew that you could sleep the morning away, but I thought it best that you have a bite to eat and let me tend to your injuries. You can sleep after that and then we will deal with what to do next. Now let me help you turn over."

It was an hour later after Lacey had eaten, hobbled with aid to the bathroom, and told his story. Mary Sue would not let him yet fade off to sleep. She was sitting looking intently at the fatigued man's face. "That is not all, there is still something else bothering you."

"Mary Sue, if there is, I can't verbalize it. It has to do with something called 'corporate ethics,' business values. None of this should have happened at Arrow Corporation. If people like Frank Turner and others ...."

"Frank Turner is dead," interrupted Mary Sue, "and No, I don't know how it happened. It was the morning you flew out from Kansas City and the police, I am told, suspect either you or Dane Hughes. But don't worry about Frank, I am worried about you! Your absolute presupposition about business is wrong!"

"My 'absolute' what?" Lacey was careful to form the words slowly as his new nurse had begun to carefully shave his three days of beard.

"Yes, your rope of logic that you depend upon to make judgments. You hang by the thread of reality that the Sun will come up in the East, that water is wet, that business is moral or immoral."

"Well, isn't it?"

"No, Everett, it is not! Business, a corporation, is not a physical being, a human, an individual with values, ethics, or morals. You have those, a corporation is only a legal entity."

"Doesn't a legal entity that affects peoples' lives have a responsibility......"

"No, it does not! Now listen, Everett, and listen closely to what my father taught me. A business exists only to produce a product or provide a service at a cost that will assure the longest, largest profit stream and the lowest, most competitive cost to the customer.

"When a corporation turns from that mission to become charitable, community active, provider of social services.....it economically weakens itself. A corporation, by definition, is amoral. It is not, I repeat, a human that can be moral or immoral. Those words, along with 'ethics' and 'values' don't fit a business, a company must be neutral. It must be, as I said, 'amoral'. "

"Mary Sue, do you really believe that?"

"Damn it, Everett! It is not a belief! It is an absolute presupposition! Show me a truly socially conscious corporation and I will show you a dead company to raid or one that is a stagnant monopoly in its industry. Trying to make a corporation into a value driven being drains resources, kills those with the good intentions.

"It is for you and I as human beings to have morals, ethics, and values.......not the task of Union Arrow Corporation."

"Mary Sue, you and your father have one flaw in your thinking.... excuse me, in the air you breath, your absolute presupposition." Lacey knew that he had to be careful in developing this argument. Mary Sue was becoming animated as she talked. The hand gesturing with the razor was not at all reassuring.

"What is that?"

"Corporations do have identities and the people who work for them, just by the nature of the human spirit, mimic those identities and look to the corporate leaders as mentors. I think many corporate boards desire their companies to be moral, ethical, charitable and exhibit these values because it attracts and creates those talents in its human employees. That is, they say that their corporation's identity exists to set a goal of behavior."

"Garbage, Everett, garbage!"

"Maybe so, Mary Sue, but don't you see that that very same human molding and mentoring will occur in the amoral corporation, the one you have just described ?"

"I am sorry. I do not follow."

"It will attract only the amoral man or make those key employees act and then become amoral. People will copy that trait and in recruiting or promoting staff, only hire and reward those types of people, the Frank Turners of the world. Even your father has described Frank to me as a 'barracuda'. If Frank's body is dead, it has only gone to match his spirit. He became amoral or more amoral because of his association with Arrow Corporation."

Mary Sue stood up and walked to the window. Everett Lacey was suddenly very attracted to this mother of four. Her efficiency was as attractive as her figure. He could not blame her for being confused about the responsibility of any business. After all, she had had Phillip Arrow as a father. Finally, she turned and again addressed him.

"You are not thinking straight, Everett. I can understand why your

346

thinking is fuzzy. I don't disagree that a company should hire and promote honest, hard working, ethical people and try to enhance their value systems. Look at my father. He built a business by hiring men like John Jamison. They are.....were, decent, ethical..... but Dad's corporation is amoral. His solution was not to change the nature of the corporate entity or its identity, but to work with the people directly. He does not allow the Company to give to charity, but he gives millions himself. He is a moral man, but his company is amoral."

"My thinking is fuzzy?"

"Let me say it another way. Those Boards that try to enforce their values by monkeying with the Corporate Charter have the correct goal, but they have the incorrect approach."

"I am glad that you are not my employer."

"If I were you, I would be afraid of any other type."

Mary Sue leaned down to pick up the shaving bowl and the razor. "Come on, get up!"

"Oh, why? I am so tired. I hurt so much. I need to sleep....."

"And I need to wash your wounds better than this. I also need to see if any bones are broken and test every muscle in your body. It is a question of where I take you to a doctor, here or back in Los Angeles."

Everett Lacey watched her get up from the bed. Although it hurt, he admitted that he could now turn his head and body. He watched her sweatered, tight fitting jeaned body walk around the bottom of the bed and into the bathroom. Perhaps he would live after all.

Moments later, she returned. "Now get up! I started the water and it is going to overflow that luxurious tub in there if we don't make it back there by the time it fills up."

"Oh, why? I want to sleep."

"Mr. Lacey, you stink! Let me be honest. You smell of grime, puke, sweat, blood, fear and death. Now get your ass up out of that bed!"

Embarrassed, crushed with humiliation, Ev Lacey stumbled across the room toward the door. He cried with the pain of the hurried walk. He screamed with the flash of heat as he stepped into the tiled, large bath area. Not really a tub, it must have taken all the water in the hot water tank of this small cabin. As the flush of pain relieving water washed over his body, he thought of the hot water tank. The owner must have installed an especially large tank.....probably by special order. Eyes shut, the scalding hot water made him feel as if his body were melting.

He opened his eyes. "What are you doing?"

Mary Sue Massendale was slipping out of her jeans. Her sweater was already on the side of the sink. "Someone has to wash you and these are my only dry clothes. Now shut your eyes or shut up. I am doing this for you."

Lacey found that he could not shut his eyes. She had unhooked her bra. The rest of her clothes followed. He looked at her eyes. She had picked up a wash cloth and a bar of soap. He knew the look from long ago, the mother's look of attacking every bit of dirt on a young boy's body. Could he stand it? He closed his eyes and felt one foot touch at the side of his waist and then the other on the other side.

Ev Lacey knew that he was embarrassing himself. He could not open his eyes.

As she lowered to begin washing his face he felt her hand and heard her say, "Well, at least not all your body is broken. That feels like it is just fine. Don't try to move. I will loosen you up a bit while I wash away this blood. I think we have a problem with your eye."

Later, after she had dried him in the water drained tub and almost carried his exhausted body across the room to the bed, he knew that peace and sleep awaited him. Not gently, he was suddenly thrown onto the bed. He looked at her face. Beads of perspiration showed the struggle to carry his heavier frame. They had been talking of his prior week. Without notice of his pain, she asked, "What would you want to do next?"

"The next thing I wish to do is talk to your father. Then, I think we should find someone official to talk to."

"Who? Where would we start? The FBI, state or city police? It seems that we have left dead bodies all over two countries. We still don't know why all this has happened. It appears to me that any disclosure will bring all the focus on the survivors. It is you, my father, and I who will attract the attention. As you so well know, I can't afford any close inspection. I doubt if the acquisitions could afford any close attention, either. Clearly, my father has broken laws in the acquisition. Everyone knows one can not acquire firms without doing so. He will probably have to serve a full jail sentence if it doesn't kill him. We need help, but we can only help ourselves. It is all up to us."

"You are right," replied the half convinced Lacey, "Say I agree to scratch the idea on the officials? I still wish, though, to talk to your father. I think that he may have the answer, he may know without realizing it. And one other thought, though it need not be mentioned. I am missing and presumed dead by everyone but you. I think it best that I keep it that way. I would want only you and your father to know that I have survived."

Mary Sue had risen from the bed. She was placing his washed clothing at his feet. Still slightly damp from an early morning washing at the village laundromat, she knew that it would have to do.

"Well, then let's get started. We can be in Los Angeles by late afternoon."

The suggestion brought the fading Everett Lacey wide awake. "I thought that you said that once we finished talking, once I finished, once you finished in the bath, that I could go back to sleep. I am so tired. You said......"

"When will you ever learn? When an Arrow tells you that when something is done, you can rest, you should forget it! It is the successful management technique of squeezing out the best in a subordinate. What you have done in the past is forgotten. I am only interested in what you do in the future. And that is simple, you can sleep in the car or on the plane. See if you can dress yourself and I will finish cleaning up. And don't complain. We both know that there is nothing important wrong with your body.

Mary Sue looked at the disbelieving Everett Lacey. Perhaps she should should get off that subject altogether for now. "Do you think if I left ten dollars that it would cover our use of this place?"

Everett Lacey was already struggling to sit up. He knew when he was beaten. "Why don't you make it twelve dollars?"

"Fine," answered Mary Sue with a happy smile. She turned and left the room with a contented look of fair play in her face. She had missed Lacey's tone of voice. No wonder these Arrows were rich! Lord, they were cheap!

21

Tuesday

Phillip Arrow walked up the path to Mary Sue Massendale's home. The brick pathway, bordered by red flowers and a green lawn, towered over by high sycamores, wound up through shrubbery that gave the feeling of welcomed peace. He wanted to stop and smell the damp grass, drink in the sight, glory in the silence, but he knew that he could not hesitate. The next sixty years of his grandchildrens and their children's future was hanging on the balance.

What could he say to this daughter he loved? Had she stayed away from the Board meeting because Massendale and his new love were there? Had Mary Sue, the proud Mary Sue, been unable to face them in a vote that was surely to discredit her father? He had been asked and complied with the request to refrain from voting. Did Mary Sue realize that none of her brothers had broken, that his two friends had been true? The vote had been 4 for Phillip Arrow and 5 against. Did she know that her vote was critically important, that he had lost because of her?

What a shock it had been to Lawrence Massendale to have him, Arrow, agree to Massendale's running the Company on an interim basis for three months until the next Board meeting. Phillip Arrow was officially on a sabbatical. Perhaps they were right, it was time to pass the torch.

351

Why not? To all following the Company, it appeared that his hand picked team was dead, disappeared, or terminated. Frank Turner would have had his five years until he was 62, then Jamison his seven years until retirement. By that time, Lacey would have been ready. At least that is what people thought. The reality was that if he had to leave Union Arrow to any one of them, he would have sold it to the highest bidder. Surely, he thought, Exxon or General Motors would have been interested.

He rang the doorbell. The door quickly opened.

"Father, how could you? How could you have made Massey the acting Chief Executive Officer? He can't even organize his life!"

She had been again thinking his thoughts. He gathered her in his arms. "Mary Sue, I love you. Now where are the boys and thank you for letting me drop by like this on such short notice. Where have you been?"

Mary Sue stepped back from her father. She peered intently into this princely man's eyes. Phillip Arrow never wanted to be answered when he asked double and triple questions in one statement. "Father, I think it is time to talk seriously, you and I. We haven't done so since I was in the ninth grade, if you remember."

"I remember it well. You wanted to try out for the freshman basketball team. I gloried in your determination."

"And I thought you horrid. I haven't changed, Father. It is just that I learned not to show it. Now I ask you again, what made you allow Massey to be CEO for an interim period? I know that he had enough votes to make you hurt, but not enough to elect himself if you had suggested someone else. He should have had to abstain on any vote for himself. You could have held him up at 5 to 4 like he did you."

"Honey, it is not the type of job that I would want to see someone I care for take. It will ruin 99.99% of all the men who would take it. He is destined for failure."

"I know that, but I also believe that you would not let that decide the issue. You would want the best person for the job and that just can not be Massey. You have a quarter of a million people working for you, surely there are two hundred thousand who could do a better job."

"True, but I had only one chance to stop their backup plan. Massey would not have abstained from a vote for her. It would have been 5 to

352

5 and that, by our Bylaws, is enough for an interim appointment for the three month period."

"I think I heard you correctly, you said 'her'?"

"Yes."

"Come with me."

Mary Sue walked Phillip Arrow down the hall to the stairs that led up to the master bedroom. As she proceeded him up the stairs, he felt suddenly embarrassed. She looked exceptionally pretty this afternoon and very much alive. A low cut, light dress, stockings, and high heels made her a pretty sight, too pretty. Walking up to her and Massey's bedroom bothered him. He had never reconciled any man sleeping with his little girl. "Where are the boys?" He had stopped half way up the stairs.

"They are staying at friends, they will be home tomorrow after school. Now come on up here, we have to discuss something seriously."

Arrow reached the top of the stairs and looked at the wall to the left. "Mary Sue, this smells so fresh, it's pink, you just had this done."

"Yes, and the master bathroom also. Massey gave me his decision Tuesday and the room was totally redecorated by Friday. Do you like it?"

"Yes, I............" Phillip Arrow had stopped still as he looked to his right. Propped up on a pink pillow, with white and pink covers, framed against a wall of white with small pink roses, sat the discolored dark figure of Everett Lacey.

"Hello, Sir."

"My Goodness, it is you! Everett, it's you! I thought you were quite dead like the rest. Come boy, tell me your story. Mary Sue, tell it to me quickly."

"Sit down Father, right here. Good, now let me get a chair and we will all discuss it. But first, you must tell Everett what you just told me." Mary Sue was looking intently at her father. Perhaps the shock was too much for him. His color was poor. She could not remember him looking this bad.

"Fine, that won't take long. It was a simple affair. I neither had the votes to save myself nor did Massey have the votes to elect himself. His counter plan was to offer the Executive Vice President of the Rail Division as the acting Chairman, that is, Caroline O'Brian. He could

353

assure 5 votes for her and leave me with only 5. The first vote would go against me 5 to 4, the next against Massey 5 to 4. Caroline would have been a compromise. I decided instead that I would go for Massey. He is a known commodity, however, so damaged."

"I am sorry Sir, but I don't think it matters much. You will have a new CEO soon and it won't be one of those mentioned."

"Who?"

"You are looking at your new CEO."

"Lacey, I am shocked at you. I have felt for years that you have the potential, but I don't believe that you are ready. Even you know that you are not ready."

"I was not speaking of myself, Sir."

"Then who, you said........."

"He means me, Father. You know, your daughter Mary Sue Arrow. I will be the new CEO of Arrow Corporation."

"Mary Sue, please, you are a housewife! You even have the name of the company wrong. You are a damn good housewife, but not a corporate manager for a company with 250 thousand people. It is not the same thing as keeping a house clean. You have to manage people, manage organizations. Mary Sue, you don't delegate anything. You clean, cook, and sew everything yourself. Where have you got......oh, I see, you were just kidding me. I am sorry, I am tired...."

"She is not kidding you, Sir. I would also treat her with great respect. She now owns 30% of your stock."

"You.......Mary Sue......you were the one who was/is buying my stock? You are the one with the secret files? You used Massey's computer here at home.....you got your information from Massey .....that mouth? Lacey, I thought you told me, you implied that it was Frank."

Phillip Arrow was hoping that he could convey a picture of disbelief that Mary Sue would accept. Could she really have thought that her borrowing of money from major California banks would be unknown to him? He hoped not. Surely her ego wasn't that large. Surely she must have guessed that it had taken a secondary guarantee from Arrow Corporation itself to establish her trust's massive borrowings.

It was Lacey that Arrow feared. All hung on the balance of Lacey's ignorance or knowledge of estate tax laws. That, after all, was what this was all about. And Lacey was a surprising man. He was still alive.

"Excuse me Sir and you too Mary Sue, let's discuss all that later," answered the surprised Lacey. "If you are going to discuss which one of you is the bigger stock market shark, we can argue that all night. I want to talk of death and destruction. Dane Hughes is missing, unheard from. I saw Meg Jamison die. Mary Sue has told me that Frank Turner is dead, as is John Jamison, as is Richard Smith. It is time to talk of death, not money.

"I am here in this house because for me to venture out, is to die. There is a contract on my head. The question is 'by whom' and 'why.' If we don't answer it, I believe that I will have to disappear forever."

In his characteristic thought gesture of looking through his poised fingers, Phillip Arrow peered out at the earnest, serious face of Everett Lacey. What was his story? He would not ask. When it was told, he would hear it. So Dane Hughes was dead and so was the beautiful Meg Jamison. He wondered who Lacey suspected as being responsible. Who? The choices were now so very limited.

The silence continued. Finally Arrow relented. "Alright, this may take some time, but let's compare notes. I will tell my story first, you second.....and Mary Sue, if you have anything to add, please do so. But first if you don't mind, let me look at your body, Everett."

Arrow stood and reached for the pink sheet. He pulled it down. He had seen the cast on Lacey's right arm and the patch over his eye. The large lump he had seen was a waist cast girdling Lacey's body. The left knee was in a cast as was the left ankle.

"Can you move and what happened? What is damaged?"

"Barely enough to get to the bathroom. As to what's wrong....hairline fractures, pulled ligaments and tendons, torn cartilage, a damaged eye and a compressed vertebrae. Nothing serious enough to prevent an outpatient clinic from handling it or to put me in a hospital. Please cover me up and as you suggested and let's compare notes. Would you start with why you really let Massendale takeover rather than risking the chance that Caroline O'Brian would end up with your position?"

Caroline O'Brian walked into the new Chairman's office. Massey had had Turner's office cleaned out and made ready last night. For his growing nerve, he had not found the courage to evict Phillip Arrow from his office.

Caroline was in a state of shock. She could not believe what had just been delivered to her in a sealed Personnel envelope with the 'Confidential' sticker. She had first wished to vomit, but the thought of this being a practical joke or a mistake clearly existed. She found that she could not read all of the words on the papers. Clearly there must have been a mistake.......a cruel joke.

John Smedt and Aaron Goldstein were sitting in Lawrence Massendale's new office. Caroline thought nothing of interrupting them. "Massey, I need to speak with you."

"Caroline, you are among friends. These two know you, or should I say 'have known you' in the Biblical sense."

Caroline could not believe the cruel slander. "Massey, that is unfair. I have to talk to you....I need to show you what I just received from Personnel."

"Could they be your termination papers? I requested that they be drafted after the Board meeting yesterday. I am shocked that they took this long to be delivered! As I said, Caroline, you are among friends. We have all known you for a long time. I have told John and Aaron that you would be leaving us soon."

"Massey, what is this all about and what about us?"

"Us? Caroline, you are a liability. Look, we have had a little romp in the hay, just like you have had with others. So what? You did it for free. You have no claim on me or the Company."

"Massey! I am talking about me! I am a woman! It took me ten long years to work up through the ranks. If I was a man, I could just go out and find another corporate position. I am a woman! I have nowhere to go!"

"Yes, you do, you can hit the street. You would be good there. You are being hysterical. You can turn around and walk out that door. I would like you to pack your things and be gone by this afternoon. Please see that you have vacated your Kansas City office by the end of the week."

Caroline could not help it, the tears were streaming from her eyes. Smedt and Goldstein were laughing at her. Lawrence Massendale sat tall in his chair, pretending to be Frank Turner. He needed her.....but she knew that that was now false. He once needed her. From here, he could survive by himself. It was she who so desperately needed him.

The room was silent. Caroline wondered at the vividness of the colors of the room, the way in which she could see the blemish on Massey's cheek, even through her tears. She had never seen this clearly before.

"Caroline, don't make a scene. Please, just leave. John and Aaron have much to tell me. I have proposed selling the Rail Divisions as my first act. Arrow Corporation should never have been in that business."

"To whom?"

"Caroline, please, it is none of your business now. But to satisfy any curiosity, these gentlemen have a qualified buyer. In fact, we were once thinking of purchasing their nest. Now damn it! Get the Hell out of my office! Don't make this a bad scene to be reported and laughed about throughout New York. As it is, you are already the talk of the town."

Caroline turned to walk to the door. She was beaten. She had no one to fall back on. This Company was her family, it was her love and life. In a state of shock, she half heard Massendale's parting remark, "Oh, and Caroline, one last thing. We all agreed that your performances both inside and outside the office were not much..... too rigid, no creativity, no imagination, too much pattern, if you know what I mean."

Hours had passed in the house in San Marino. Mary Sue had brought up crisp sandwiches during a pause in which the two men were pledged not to continue talking about the past week's happenings. Later, she brought up a tray of cold drinks made to order.

"Here, Everett, have this. We will wait until after Father leaves for your pain pill."

Phillip Arrow was startled, "What, you have not given him any pain relief?"

"Father, you know that I don't believe in all the medicine Americans take these days. They make themselves sick. Moreover, I wanted him to be alert for your story. I think we have known who the culprit has been all along."

"It has to be just one of two people, Lawrence Massendale or Caroline O'Brian. I find it difficult to believe Massey could tie his shoes. That leaves the young lady." Would his daughter still take his lead, wondered Arrow?

"Father, that is what I said from the start."

"Both of you are still guessing. Neither of your guesses have any connection to the facts involved." Lacey softly noted his disagreement.

"She almost had herself elected President and CEO of my Company this morning. That is enough for me. Oh, it was clever. She had it all set so that neither Massey nor I would win," answered Arrow.

Mary Sue could not restrain herself, "I still don't know why you ever let yourself get in a spot where it was a choice between Massey and the Devil."

Phillip Arrow shook his head, "You young ladies are tough, very tough. Everett, you are right. We have no facts, it is all speculation."

"We do have some facts, Dad. Such as she was the one whom Dane told that Everett had discovered who had been the guilty party. All he told Hughes was that it was a female. Correct? Everett was referring to to me. Caroline, being the only other female, had to think that Everett had caught onto her act. Second, she is the one who has obviously coached and maneuvered Massey into both his infidelity and treason. Third, there is something, there has been something strange with her travel. Massey once told me that she will disappear for periods of time around the Washington D.C. area."

Arrow interrupted, "Next you will tell me she works for a foreign power. You are using facts that Massey has given you. I don't see Ev agreeing with you. Let's be honest Mary Sue, you have been hurt by Caroline's ability to attract your husband."

Mary Sue blushed but refused to rise to her father's challenge. "No Dad. She doesn't work for anyone, she just works with her maiden aunt's brother, her only living relative. Think of why you did all this. To my knowledge, you did it because a union pension fund manager had such power that he could demand that you pay up for partial and total withdrawals. In effect, his two funds had rights to two thirds of your assets."

"No, it was 30% of the total assets and then 30% of the remainder. It works out to 51% of Arrow Corporation's assets. With the purchase of the railroads with their huge unfunded liabilities, I believed that I would be safe. Congress has responsibility for the Railroad Retirement Fund, which is even more underfunded. They would never let such a claim arise that would destroy a future chance of paying off the debt. By creating greater liabilities, I had hoped to find a harbor of safety."

"Father, it was not so safe. You only lost your Company."

"Mary Sue," Lacey had decided to break into the conversation, "you have been keeping something secret from me. How can you be so sure that she is his niece. Have you found any proof?"

"It is all there in front of you if you care to look at the totality of the evidence. Check the man's trust fund for his children and relatives. One of them looks like a niece with a similar name."

Arrow looked worried. "Mary Sue, she came to work for me based

358

on her talent. It has taken her over ten years to work up through the ranks. You are suggesting that she was a 'mole,' a spy planted in my Company from the start. Now keep in mind that I agree with you. The cause of all these problems is Caroline. She is a murderous bitch that we will probably have to deal with on our own, but I find your idea of a reason for her perfidy to be reaching a bit."

"Why not? If governments plant spies in other countries, why wouldn't competitors recruit young MBAs to infiltrate their enemies? Say you give me a budget of $400,000. I could hire twenty MBAs and have them interview ten targets. Some of them would be hired. Over time, some of them would rise to positions of prominence."

"Well, its imaginative although the Mafia has been doing it for years. Why do you think I put up with......."

"Not as imaginative as having a niece or a daughter that you plant in the same manner. It would be far better. You could turn a hired hand, it would be far more difficult to coopt a blood relation. Keep in mind what the future of a union official is. It is not the type of position that can be passed on to one's children. To do that, one has to own equity." Mary Sue had cut her father short.

"You are suggesting that Caroline is a blood relative and put in place so that this man's family could take over Union Arrow Corporation. I still find that difficult to believe."

"Perhaps so, but I am sure that it is Caroline!"

"Mary Sue, my daughter, so am I. I just can't follow your conclusions as to the reason for her actions," replied Arrow. All was still going as planned. Where was Massendale? Was he always to be late for every important meeting?

Everett Lacey interrupted. If left to themselves they would soon convince themselves of the wrong answer. "Good, then you are both wrong together. I hope that you were listening to yourself, Mary Sue, during the past ten minutes. This could hurt a bit." Lacey had decided that it was time they heard the truth. Why did he have the idea that Phillip Arrow already knew what he was about to say?

A loud roar interrupted Lacey. All their heartbeats jumped and eyes turned toward the end of the bedroom. Lawrence Massendale stood red faced in his blue three piece suit with his eyes looking at only the fully covered Everett Lacey.

"What is this? What is this? It didn't take you very long, did it? What are you doing with a Black in my bedroom.......what are you doing in my bed?"

Mary Sue had stood and slowly crossed her arms in front of herself. "It is not your bed, Lawrence. You have signed it away. Even if that were not true, you will note that he is on my side."

"Look at you!" Massendale had turned his attention to his wife. He approached several steps as he looked her up from bottom to top. "The last time you wore stockings and heels in this home during the day was back when........."

Everett Lacey knew that if the confrontation continued, Massendale would have the upper hand. Moreover, there was no reason to wait.

"Ladies and Gentlemen," he whispered, "may I introduce to you the real mole, recruited as a law student at USC, and committed to his Corporation to its rotten core? Before you stands an Oriole!"

There was silence in the room. Massendale had taken a step backward. Both Mary Sue and her father picked up on the body language that said that everything that Lacey had stated was truth.

"I suppose that I should be more explicit," added Lacey. "What stands before you is the man who hired killers, destroyed lives, and perhaps even took a life himself. If he didn't kill Richard Smith, who did?" Lacey glanced quickly to see Phillip Arrow's reaction.

Massendale authoritatively answered. "What the Hell are you talking about? Listen, Blackie, if you think you are going to make me overlook the fact that you are sleeping with my wife...."

"I don't believe that she is your wife any longer," responded Phillip Arrow. "At least that is what your lawyer tells me." Arrow could not believe Massendale's sudden nerve. Surely Mary Sue..........

Everett Lacey turned to look at Mary Sue. She had slowly walked back to a chair and sat down. She was crying. She would no longer take part in this conversation. Her thoughts were turned inward. She, like her father, had seen her husband's admission of cheating in his response. In this moment of truth, she knew that he was indeed a planted spy. He had married her and used his position for power. And all this time she had so appreciated his lack of interest in her wealth! He had not married her for money.....he had coveted power.

"Let me be clear with my accusation, Mr. Massendale," continued Lacey. "You were hired in college to act as a corporate undercover agent and had a surprising string of luck. You married the Boss's daughter. The Orioles set up the union leader, he was just a pawn. The Orioles had the opportunity to enjoy a diversion with the niece.

That is why it was so difficult to find a cause. Caroline O'Brian wasn't using you. You were using her.

"But the motive for the crime is obvious. While the Orioles are eating up the East, we were to take care of the West. I imagine that your first act as Chairman would be to recommend that Union Arrow divest themselves of the rail lines."

"That is correct, Ev," replied Phillip Arrow. "I was told this morning that Smedt and Goldstein are already working on it. From a business standpoint, it does make good sense. There is no reason why all the non railroad subsidiaries should have to reflect a railroad's PE. What would make it an even better idea, would be to change it into a simple spinoff leaving all the subsidiaries with unfunded liabilities in the debt ridden railroad company. But that is not what you have in mind, is it Massey? You are just selling rail lines."

"Well, then, we already know the buyer. That is correct, isn't it Massey," interjected Lacey. He wanted to get Massendale talking again. These Arrows always had to dominate the conversation.

Lawrence Massendale looked at the three with a smile. "Try to do something about it I will drag you all down into the muck with me. But you are all wrong about one thing. I did not kill Richard Smith. Phillip, Mary Sue.........I think you know who did."

With those words, he turned and walked toward the door to the bedroom. Mary Sue could not let him escape, "How could you?" she screamed.

At the door, Massendale stopped and turned. "How could I what?"

"How could you work for another master, another employer than my father? How could you turn your back on me? How could you be disloyal?"

Lawrence Massendale appeared to be another man. His tenseness was gone. "Why Mary Sue, it was not hard. Business is only a game. I have always been loyal to my first employer. I have never cheated him. As for you and me.......If you cared for me one tenth as much as you do your computer, I would still be your husband.

"Your first question is the tough one. It is one that a religious and moral man has to answer constantly in his business life."

Massendale seemed to stare at Ev Lacey. "Strange, isn't it? All those who worked for only one master perished. It is the one truth that I have learned about modern corporate life ...... Give your all to one worldly master and he will, at some time, ask for or take your life.

It is people like us, Lacey, who balance our work and interests who live the best lives. These single minded Arrows will never understand."

Lawrence Massendale turned and left the room. All that was left were three silent people. Soft sobs were heard from one, but the other two were lost deep in thought.

Lacey finally turned to Phillip Arrow and asked a one word question, "Smith?"

"Ev, I have told you before, don't give Richard Smith a second thought. He has come and gone. I have had all his records destroyed, including those related to Henry's phone. You can forget about Smith."

Phillip Arrow smiled at the flashes of light in the young Lacey's eyes. Lacey definitely had good thought patterns even if he had not yet calculated the impossibility of the Arrows keeping significant stock control should estate taxes ever be levied. Perhaps he would leave him beaten, but with a gem of wisdom by which he could rebuild a life in the corporate world.

"Now hear me well Everett. I told you once before and I will tell you again, 'the people is grass'. There is a time to sew, nuture, weed, and mow. There is never a slack time in an organization. The people is grass, Everett. The people is grass.

"Oh, and by the way. I have reconsidered about that Board position. I think that what your career needs is to be free and clear of Union Arrow Corporation for awhile. Please consider any employment and consulting arrangements severed as of tonight."

A thousand plus miles away as night descended, Dane Hughes woke to unbearable pain. Voices were mumbled in a room that receded and moved before his eyes. First the room's color of drab green swept over him and then the smell. He was alive. Someone must have found him in the bathroom. Surely enough noise had been made.

A huge, tall body approached him. He could make out the doctor's face. The voice said, "He is coming around. He had better be glad of the paramedic services that exist today, there is no boundary on good health care. Can you hear me young man?"

Dane could mumble an, "Um hum."

"Good, then, you were brought in with no identification. We have one question that we must ask you before I take you in for another bout of surgery."

"Um hum."

"Do you have medical insurance?"

Dane mumbled an "Um hum." As he drifted off into unconsciousness, he wondered whether the man had understood the affirmative. What would be the difference in his fate under either answer? Dane knew for sure now that he was south of the Canadian border. The Canadian Government guaranteed the health of its citizens regardless of their ability to pay.

Dane felt he was drowning. He made himself rise from his sleep to lift his hand. He had found that he could not talk. Had he been shot in the throat? He motioned with his hand. He had to make them bring him a telephone He could at least dial her number. Please have her there!

Ev Lacey could hear the rustling sounds of whatever she was wearing. It was dark and the promised pain pills had not yet been received. It had been dark before Phillip Arrow left. He had confirmed Lacey's thoughts and Massendale's only partly spoken admission. The Oriole President had told him, Phillip Arrow had said.

As Arrow left, he had muttered something about "cabbage patches" and grandchildren who would rule the world. For a man who had lost a company, seen good men and women's lives destroyed, and watched the destruction of his grandchildren's home, he had appeared to be in the best of spirits.

Lacey's solution had come from an apple. Dane Hughes had indicated on the mountainside that the two killers were those he had seen in the Big Apple. Lacey knew that they had first been hired by the Oriole President, it only followed that they were still in his employ. If Caroline were employed by the union manager, Massey was the only one left to be employed by the Orioles. Caroline must have told Massendale of Dane's conversation.

Even at that, it had been a guess. His confronting Massendale had unsettled the man. The correct accusation of a connection to the Orioles had been a shock. There was obviously no discoverable connection between the two. From all his work, Everett had proved that to himself. No one should have tied the two together. Yet, there was always the chance that someone would get lucky and guess the connection. No wonder, the man had always been so nervous! He had built an entire life on a closely guarded lie.

And then, of course, there was Mary Sue. Massey had been confronted in front of her with his greatest infidelity. She had been used, bore his sons, all for business purposes. He had not married her for money, he had married her for power. Rich young girls always guard themselves against the former, never the latter.

Lacey had watched Phillip Arrow while Mary Sue cried. He had seen Arrow smile and barely picked up his comment.....something to do with having great hope for the generations. If anything, Phillip Arrow had left happy. Lacey had heard him whistling as he walked to his car.

Had everything worked out to Arrow's satisfaction? Was this the way in which he had decided to retire from business...with his daughter and son-in-law at each other's throats for the next forty years? Had not it been Arrow who kept talking of the best motivator being hate?

If that was so, suddenly thought Lacey, then did Arrow have this all planned from the start?

A cold sweat broke out on Lacey's body. If it was so, then his guess that disclosed Massendale was the wrong conclusion. It wasn't the Orioles and Massendale who had hired the killers this time. He had thrown the challenge at Massey for all the wrong reasons.

His body moved as Mary Sue sat at the bottom of the bed. She pulled the sheet from his body. In the darkness, Lacey could see her body's outline through the thin fabric that she was wearing.

"Are you awake?"

"Um."

"I never knew him, did I?"

"Most married people never do know their spouses."

Lacey felt her body shifting onto the bed beside him, the gentle shifting of her weight next to his. She brushed him with her lips and then he felt her cheek. Perhaps this was necessary, perhaps just his presence consoled her. Slowly, she shifted some more, he felt the softness of her throat.

At least she had quit talking. If there was one thing that he wanted her to do, it was to quit discussing the mergers and the future of her stock holdings. These Arrows were all alike, never satisfied, always talking business, never content with what one's done for them lately, always wanting more.

Her body's weight resting against his side hurt him. He felt Mary Sue Arrow quiver. Yes, he believed it was the first time in two days that she had quit talking business. He wondered if she had any plans for him after tonight.

364

Epilogue

Four Years Later
September 22, 1989

Caroline O'Brian sat in her rain drenched stationwagon reading the newspaper. Arrow Corporation, shorn of its trucking, transportation and rail lines in a "spinoff" of those entities in 1986, was again the darling of the stock market. With a PE of 28 and record earnings, its performance was again worthy of notice.

Mary Sue Arrow, the daughter of the founder, Phillip Arrow, had taken full control of the Company in 1986. In a carefully orchestrated series of steps using an Employee Stock Ownership Plan, stock trades, and prudent purchasing of Arrow Corporation stock, the Company was slowly removing publicly traded common shares from the stock market.

Stockholders were beginning to hear rumors of a SEC filing for a tender by the Arrow family for all remaining shares held outside the family. No longer would the Company need to report earnings, share data with the Government, or hold stockholder meetings. Arrow Corporation, like the Bechtels, Basses, and Mars, was to become a hidden empire.

Caroline thought back to the division in 1986 of the larger Union Arrow Corporation into two new companies, each with its own board

365

of directors, common stock, and separate legal identities. The Arrows had gathered their favorite companies into a major subsidiary corporation, Arrow Corporation, and then assigned the rail lines, other transportation companies, and several debt laden companies to a second major subsidiary, Union Transportation Corporation.

New shares in the latter subsidiary had then been issued and distributed   to all present stockholders, one new company share for each share originally held in Union Arrow Corporation. To allow stockholders to own additional shares in this larger transportation company, the Arrows had offered to trade any new shares that they held within the family for the original shares of the remaining Union Arrow Corporation, now renamed Arrow Corporation.

Many stockholders had taken the family up on the offer. With the press' criticism of the family, the criminal investigations then in progress, and the civil complaints filed against the Arrows, many institutional holders had decided to concentrate their interests in the asset rich and professionally managed Union Transportation Corporation. Now in retrospect three years later, these investors were not at all pleased. Whereas tremendous favorable reaction had been received for the unique spinoff of those corporate entities in late 1986, there had been little questioning of the Arrows' motivations. Many were now doing so. It appeared that the Arrow family had rid itself of hidden debt not originally shown on the balance sheets. Arrow Corporation was, by far, the more viable company.

Nor were stockholders pleased with the newly created company, Union Transportation Corporation, of which the Arrows still owned 10%. After a prolonged and heated internal battle for control in late 1986, the stockholders had approved - over the Arrow family objections - Lawrence Massendale as Chairman of the Board and CEO. Mary Sue Arrow held similar titles for the resurrected Arrow Corporation. The two individuals were now obviously competing against one another with Mary Sue easily outperforming her former husband who had turned into a total "work addict." The "inside word" on Wall Street was that Lawrence Massendale was struggling with massive liabilities and was doing as well as could be expected for any human being. His hate for the Arrows was well publicized. If anyone was going to succeed with the Union Transportation Corporation, the consensus was that it was probably going to be the "driven" Massendale.

Caroline's eyes noted the name of a New York investment banking firm mentioned in the article. Both new corporations continued to use Smedts and Goldstein's firms. Caroline knew why. A corporation's personnel was constantly changing. "Who on the executive or middle management staff of either corporation had been there when Caroline was part of management?" It was the service firms that brought stability to the world of business.

Caroline O'Brian put down the copy of the *Journal*. It was the only touch of her past world that she allowed herself. She had followed Phillip Arrow's abortion of the single U.S. rail monopoly. Phillip Arrow, in going into semiretirement, had spent all his time in 1986 and 1987 in Washington D.C. assuring that Massendale's proposed combination with the Orioles did not occur. There was talk, she understood, of Phillip Arrow's now becoming Secretary of Commerce because of this good work in keeping the economy free from monopoly power.

Caroline looked out the window of the automobile. It was raining. Oh, how it was raining! Her thoughts drifted back over the years.

Ev Lacey had seemingly disappeared. Like Caroline, there was no place for him in the new corporations. Like Dane, he continued to receive disability payments from Arrow Corporation. His computer detective agency had been closed down and he had purchased a gas station under an assumed name. From all reports, he was a failure at managing it. If not for his occasional contact with her husband, Caroline would have thought that he, like she, had become divorced from the corporate world. As it was, she knew that he had, as Dane described, an "Omega fixation."

There they were! Caroline watched the nursery school aide run the two tots toward her car. She felt her stomach. The doctor said that it would again be twins. That would make her Uncle especially proud. "What sort of world would they grow up in?" she wondered. This rainy and union dominated Northwest that her husband had vowed never to leave, or would corporations control this poor land then too? Amid her happy youngsters' greetings, she started the car. She could not be late in picking Dane up after his full day of teaching. She still prided herself on being punctual.

367

www.ingramcontent.com/pod-product-compliance
Lightning Source LLC
Chambersburg PA
CBHW021548210326
41599CB00010B/354